PRINCE EUGEN OF SAVOY

Prince Eugen of Savoy

Nicholas Henderson

FREDERICK A. PRAEGER, *Publishers*
NEW YORK • WASHINGTON

BOOKS THAT MATTER

Published in the United States of America in 1965
by Frederick A. Praeger, Inc., Publishers
111 Fourth Avenue, New York 3, N.Y.

© 1964 by Nicholas Henderson

Library of Congress Catalog Card Number: 65-12157

Printed in the United States of America

A tribute to his
military genius.

CONTENTS

ILLUSTRATIONS

MAPS

PREFACE

'THE CIVILIAN who attempts to write a military history is of necessity guilty of an act of presumption,' wrote Sir John Fortescue in his Preface to his *History of the British Army*. This biography of a military leader should begin with a similar admission. I have not, however, tried to enter into technical details of strategy or tactics which would have been out of place in a general life. Moreover, for the overall military background, I have fortunately been able to rely on much expert help from Mr David Chandler and Dr C. J. Duffy of the Department of Military History, the Royal Military Academy, Sandhurst; I am much indebted to them. I am deeply grateful as well to Professor John Bromley of the University of Southampton for the advice he has given me on the history of the period, and for the amount of time and trouble he has taken with my manuscript. I wish also to thank Dr Ragnhild Hatton of the London School of Economics, who has been characteristically generous in devoting many hours to detailed examination of the subject and expansive encouragement of the author. More astringent, though scarcely less valuable, have been the corrections and disciplines I have received from Mr John Stoye of Magdalen College, Oxford. Mr Julian Bullard of All Souls College, Oxford, has rendered invaluable support by combing through the whole manuscript and suggesting many improvements. Stylistically I have relied on many suggestions made by my mother.

For the sections on Eugen as a patron of the arts I am much indebted to Mr Gerald Burdon. This aspect of the Prince's life has not, I think, hitherto received the attention it deserves, even from Austrian and German historians. If the present work breaks new ground on this subject it is largely due to the researches which Mr

Burdon has carried out on my behalf. He has helped, too, in the selection of illustrations for the book which have been confined exclusively to reproductions of eighteenth-century works for which much pursuit has been required. The photographs of the engravings by Salomon Kleiner are reproduced with the kind permission of the Trustees of the Sir John Soane Museum. I am also obliged personally to Hofrat Dr Hans Pauer, the Director of the Bildarchiv der Österreichischen Nationalbibliothek, to the Director of the Rijksmuseum, Amsterdam, the Trustees of the British Museum and to the Curator of the Victoria and Albert Museum for authority to reproduce the engravings in their collections. I am also grateful to Mr Anthony Hobson for friendly promptings about Eugen's library, and to Mr Denys Sutton and Mr Benedict Nicolson who have rendered invaluable support on the artistic side of Eugen's life.

I owe thanks for different services to various friends, including Mrs Betty Alexander, Mr Russell Burlingham, Mr Roy Jenkins, the Earl of Longford and Mr F. W. Deakin. I must also acknowledge my debt to Mr A. J. P. Taylor, who has been a strong, not to say disturbing, influence throughout my life on anything to do with European history. Finally, I must say how grateful I am to my wife and daughter for acquiescing in the considerable demands which Prince Eugen has made upon my time.

INTRODUCTION

NAPOLEON BUONAPARTE ranked Prince Eugen of Savoy among the seven greatest commanders of history.[1] Frederick the Great acknowledged him as his main teacher, describing him as the 'Atlas' of the Habsburg Monarchy, and as the 'real Emperor'.[2] Voltaire paid a single-edged tribute to him saying that 'he shook the greatness of Louix XIV and the Ottoman power; he ruled the Empire and during all his victories and his ministry he scorned alike the temptations of pomp and wealth'.[3] In Austria his reputation has always been unrivalled since he first became the undisputed hero-in-chief of the Habsburg Monarchy at the turn of the seventeenth and eighteenth centuries. Although opinions vary as to his character, there is no dispute about the three outstanding achievements of his life. He saved the Empire from conquest by Louis XIV. He broke the last westward thrust of Ottoman power, liberating central Europe after a century and a half of Turkish occupation. And he was one of the greatest patrons of the arts the world has ever seen. Vienna today would be unthinkable without him: his presence remains there in the palaces he built and in his great collections. It is commemorated in the enormous equestrian statue in the centre of the city inscribed on one side, 'To the glorious conqueror of Austria's enemies', and on the other, 'To the wise counsellor of three Emperors'.

If Eugen's public achievements stand out unmistakably, there is less precision about the outlines of his private life. Here, on the

---

[1] The other six were Alexander the Great, Hannibal, Caesar, Gustavus Adolphus, Turenne and Frederick the Great.

[2] Frédéric II, *Histoire de Mon Temps*, 1850, p. 12.

[3] F. Voltaire, *Le Siècle de Louis XIV*, Garnier Frères, 1878, p. 348.

contrary, there is both uncertainty and mystery. Eugen left behind him no personal papers or memoirs; at any rate none that have survived—surprising in a man so unreserved and literate. He never married, and there is nothing personal from the hand of anyone who knew him well. We have therefore been left very much in the dark about his inner thoughts and feelings. We have also inevitably been subjected to much rumour, speculation and even forgery. 'There can be few figures in history,' wrote Eugen's official biographer, Alfred Arneth, 'about whom greater errors have been spread, with whose character more mischief has been made, and in whose name more wretched fabrications have been invented.'

Yet despite this tempting combination of distinction in his public life and obscurity surrounding his personal affairs, Eugen has remained strikingly neglected by British writers. No serious foreign work on him has ever been translated into English. No full-scale biography has ever been published in the English language. He occupies a vague and unimportant place in our historical lore. He is nothing like so well-known in Britain as is the Duke of Marlborough on the European continent. His fleeting imprint upon conventional English text books is of a dashing soldier, a hero indeed, but decidedly a secondary character, a sort of military Man Friday to the Duke. The truth is that he was far from being a subordinate figure. There is no doubt that Marlborough was the military and diplomatic leader of the Grand Alliance against Louis XIV in the decade 1702–1711, and there is no doubt about his brilliant achievements in these years; but his was not a solitary responsibility or single-handed command. The two men were indispensable to each other. Blenheim, Oudenarde and Malplaquet are household names of triumph in British history, inseparably associated with the name of Marlborough. Yet in reality the part played by British soldiers in these battles was far from decisive;[1] and the Duke's share in them was by and large no greater than Eugen's. Not that they were rivals. Their collaboration was constant and selfless. Utterly dissimilar in personality and temperament though they were, the two men combined so exquisitely that they were described as 'like two bodies with but a single soul'. On one occasion, at the zenith of their association, a medal was struck likening them to Castor and Pollux. In his biography of Marlborough, though the Duke is naturally his hero,

[1] Though Britain made a great contribution in mercenaries and hard cash, native British troops only amounted to about a fifth of the Allied total at the battle of Blenheim, an eighth at Oudenarde, and a seventh at Malplaquet.

Sir Winston Churchill has not overlooked or belittled Eugen. He recognizes their partnership as a 'glorious brotherhood in arms ... of which the history of war furnishes no equal example'; and he does full justice to the magnanimity between them, writing that, 'only with Lee and Jackson have we a similar self-effacement among warriors of genius'.[1] But Sir Winston's treatment is exceptional amongst British historians of the campaigns against Louis XIV, which indeed are often described simply as The Marlborough Wars.

Britain's history and Eugen's life are closely, and at one moment—from England's point of view—shamefully, entwined. There can be few more perfidious episodes in modern times than the way English Ministers carried on separate peace negotiations with Louis XIV behind the backs of their Allies, and then deserted them on the battlefield in 1712. Eugen probably suffered the full effects of this betrayal more directly than any other man. Yet he remained unembittered, and continued all his life to advocate close Anglo-Austrian relations. Britain's greatness as a commercial and Imperial nation springs directly from the defeat of Louis XIV, which established her as a force on the continent, as mistress of the seas and as a thrustful colonial power. But remarkably little heed has been paid to the contribution made to the development by Eugen through his partnership with Marlborough.

This book seeks to make good this neglect: to show Eugen's part in the history of Britain and of Europe at the end of the seventeenth and the beginning of the eighteenth century—and, against this background, to give a portrait of his remarkable life and personality.

[1] Winston S. Churchill, *Marlborough, His Life and Times,* two-volume edition published 1947, I, p. 773 *et seq.*

CHAPTER I

THE FOREGROUND

PRINCE EUGEN was born in the Hôtel Soissons in Paris on October 18, 1663. He was the fifth and youngest son. Three sisters were born after him.

He entered a world glittering in the rising sun of Louis XIV. The King had not yet launched his military bid for world dominion which was to last on and off for half a century, and to be frustrated as much by Eugen as by any other man. By 1663 Cardinal Mazarin had been dead for two years and the King was now absolute ruler of France. But, for the moment, he was content to see his Controller-General of Finance, Colbert, striving to restore the national economy after the drain of the Thirty Years and Spanish Wars, and to let Le Tellier, the Secretary for War, and his son, Louvois, refashion the army,[1] whilst he limited himself to diplomatic triumphs, creating all the while a new setting of magnificence at Versailles. It was the time and place for parties, both there and at the Hôtel Soissons—vast extravagant parties where dancing, masquerades and fireworks succeeded each other hectically in a ferment of scandal and intrigue, to be followed the next day by quarrels, duels and sometimes banishment. Hosts of courtiers, dressed in blue cassocks, revolved subserviently around the King, but women dominated his orbit, and the brightest of all at this time was Cardinal Mazarin's niece and Eugen's mother, Olympia.

She was one of the advance guard of three nieces whom Mazarin brought to Paris in 1647 from their modest home in Rome to further

[1] They made it the best army in Europe, unbeatable until Eugen and Marlborough showed the way.

his, and to a lesser extent their, ambitions. The Cardinal had power. Anne of Austria, the Queen Regent, was reputedly his mistress— some say his wife—and he was virtual sovereign of France. But it was rootless power; the usurped authority of an Italian immigrant, requiring family entrenchments. For years he had affected to enjoy his lack of domestic ties, saying, with a debonair wave of the hand in the direction of the beautiful statues he had brought from Rome, that they were the only relations he wanted to have in France. But time had made him less jauntily detached. He conceived the idea of bringing his sisters' children to Paris, where he intended to marry them off to the noblest families of France—an ambition eventually to be fulfilled beyond his worldliest dreams.[1] The Cardinal began by assuming an attitude of indifference towards his nieces, but no one was taken in, and all watched to see his astute pawn play, the Marshal Nicolas de Villeroi observing: 'See those little girls who are now not rich; they will soon have fine châteaux, good incomes, splendid jewels, beautiful silver services, and perhaps great dignities.'[2]

At the very outset the Italian girls met with coolness from society. Mazarin, the creature and heir of Richelieu, was not loved by the nobility. Corrupt, immoral, avaricious and autocratic, the son of a bankrupt hat-maker from Sicily, he was snubbed by the aristocracy, who resented his insidious charm. Nevertheless, the Mazarin trio, as the nieces were called, were immediately given the entrée to the Queen Regent's residence, the Palais Royal, where they were brought up with the young King (who was Olympia's age) and with his brother Philip. The Queen treated them just as she did the royal children. But, alas, this routine, so easy and auspicious, was soon to be rudely interrupted by Mazarin's enemies. At last the nobility could bear his power and avarice no longer. Ridicule, their favourite weapon hitherto, had proved ineffective. They must act. So they joined forces with the over-taxed bourgeoisie and the Paris mob to compel him to flee the country with his family. However, by 1653, the Second Fronde, as the uprising

---

[1] Cardinal Mazarin had two sisters living in Rome: the eldest was married to Comte Martinozzi and had two daughters; the other was married to Signor Mancini and had three sons and five daughters. The elder Martinozzi daughter married the Prince de Corti; the younger, the Duke de Modena. The eldest Mancini daughter married the Duke de Mercoeur. The second, Olympia (Prince Eugen's mother), married the Comte de Soissons; the third married the Prince Colonna; the fourth became the Duchess de Mazarin; the fifth the Duchess de Bouillon.

[2] *Mémoires de Madame de Motteville*, ed. M. F. Riaux, 1886, p. 371. Marshal Nicolas de Villeroi was the father of François de Villeroi, later Eugen's opponent in the Spanish Succession War.

was called, had been overcome, and the Cardinal was able to return to France with all his nieces except Laura—Olympia's elder sister—who had meanwhile married abroad.

With their flamboyant high spirits they quickly captured the centre of the royal stage. Whether at St Germain, Compiègne or Fontaine-bleau, they were the life-givers, the organizers of entertainment, the constant attenders at all balls and intimate parties. Soon Olympia was to be seen always at the young King's side. Influence may have placed her there in the first instance, but now she had no one to thank but herself. She and the King were for ever dancing together, acting together and laughing together. She was the dominant one, developing and forming his tastes and interests, yet feminine enough to appear to be interested in doing the things which best pleased him—at this early age, amateur theatricals. Where Richelieu had spent thousands on staging tragedies, Mazarin lavished tens of thousands on ballets and operas, bringing companies and décor from Italy. It was his idea of opium for the nobility. The young King became an addict. With Olympia giving encouragement, he participated whenever he could. In a performance of the ballet, 'The Marriage of Peleus and Thetis', the most extravagant production yet staged at court, he played no less than five parts—Apollo, Mars, a Dryad, a Fury and a Courtier.

In 1654, the second of the nieces married, and this encouraged much speculation about Olympia's intentions towards the King. Of course, they were still both absurdly young—only fifteen; but it was considered a marriageable age, and the blue-stocking Christina, ex-Queen of Sweden, then living in France, who had made much impression on the King, spoke to him as man to man, strongly advising him, in her irresponsible way, to marry Olympia and be damned. At one moment Louis was obviously dithering. He had lost his heart to her in the head-over-heels fashion of first love. But his eye soon wandered and Olympia's emotional hold over him became spasmodic. It was only after many sulks and tantrums that she came to face reality and to accept the fact that she would have to abandon any hope of a royal marriage. She was helped on her way to this decision by Mazarin, some say at the bidding of the stars which he was accustomed to consult on public issues. More probably he was moved by the hard calculation that Olympia's future at court would be securer as trusted friend than as upstart wife of an inconstant king. Rank and position must be secured for her by a suitable marriage. Fortunately a patient suitor was at hand, Eugen Maurice, Prince of Savoy-Carignan, later to become Count of Soissons, a title he inherited from his maternal grandfather. Olympia graciously accepted him and they were married on February 21, 1657. According to Madame de Motteville, a close observer of the royal household, 'the King saw this marriage without regret or grief'.[1]

The Count of Soissons was a brave, uncomplicated soldier, with few interests outside his profession, except hunting, for which he had a passion. By all accounts he was a most considerate husband to Olympia, disappearing at frequent intervals and giving her ample time and freedom to be unfaithful and to manoeuvre for position behind the throne. They had scarcely been married a year when he went off to join his regiment; and two years later the King sent him to London to the Coronation of Charles II, where he had the highly responsible task of securing Charles' sister, Henrietta, as bride for Louis XIV's brother Philip, Duke of Orleans. The Count had a remarkable elder brother, Emanuel Philibert. Deaf and dumb from birth, he triumphed marvellously over his handicaps to become a writer of great force. Of all Prince Eugen's relations, this uncle was probably the one he most admired.

Meanwhile Olympia had been making good use of her liberty and climbing irons. Louis had married three years after her, but neither this nor her regular child-bearing interfered with her relationship with the King, which, indeed, now became stabler and more purposeful than it had ever been before. Officially, she held the post of Superintendent of the Queen's Household. Unofficially, she was recognized as the first Lady of the court and impresario of the King's pleasures. She was exactly where she wanted to be. If nobody called her beautiful, everyone avowed her charm, the product of physical vitality rather than any brilliance of taste or mind—indeed, so low was her intellectual repute that the pamphleteers of the day called her 'La Bécasse de Soissons'. Her face was long and pointed; her eyes small, but lively—traits inherited by Prince Eugen. Madame de Motteville, in her observations on the royal circle, singled out Olympia's plumpness, her complexion, the agreeable coincidence of dimples and a long face, and her beautiful arms and hands as her outstanding features, though it was 'her gracefulness and splendid clothes which gave brilliance to her only moderate looks'.[2] She was always extravagantly dressed, and contrived a most elaborate ambiance, holding court in a setting of miniature dogs and tropical birds. 'Nothing equalled the luxury which

---

[1] *Mémoires de Madame de Motteville*, op. cit., p. 82.
[2] Ibid., op. cit., p. 51.

encompassed her,' Saint-Simon has written, 'and the King refused to leave her side before or after his marriage.'[1] Added to the other attractions, she employed a genius of a chef who was accustomed to preparing fabulous dishes for the King and the thirty-odd other regular guests at the Hôtel Soissons. Amongst his répertoire was an olive salad in which the olives derived their flavour from being stuffed one by one into quails, then the quails were stuffed into partridges, the partridges into pigeons, the pigeons into chickens, the chickens into sucking pigs, and finally, the sucking pigs into calves, which were then basted on the spit until each olive had soaked up enough varied juices to permit it to be set before the King.

The Hôtel Soissons, converted from a nunnery into a palace by Catherine de Medici, had come down to the present Count through a Bourbon ancestor. It now proffered a web of enticements including statuary, pavilions, artificial water—and a horoscope chamber, with glass retorts and human skeletons, where Olympia indulged her strong appetite for astrology and magic. The château and gardens soon became the centre of the King's enjoyment world, 'and it was there that he acquired that air of politeness and gallantry which he was to retain all his life without any loss of royal dignity'.[2] To Olympia's salon flocked all the other men and women who counted for anything in Paris until it became 'the centre of gallantry, intrigue and ambition of the whole court'.[3]

Olympia was strikingly unfaithful even in that unfaithful circle. She was also strongly possessive. It was really this combination of promiscuity and rapaciousness that was her undoing. Then, as ever in society, a woman might succeed in holding the hearts of many men at once, provided she was without passion, giving herself completely to none and making no emotional demands on any one of them. But Olympia was made of much more spontaneous, combustible and predatory stuff. She wanted to dominate the King. She did not mind his lovers—she had plenty of her own. But they must only dwell in the suburbs of his mind; she alone could hold the centre. Alas, Louis was as promiscuous as she was. Already before he was married, he had fallen in love with her younger and cleverer sister, Marie. With his penchant for blue-stockings, he had probably felt more deeply about her than he had ever done about Olympia. But Olympia had the

[1] *Mémoires du Duc de Saint-Simon*, publié par M. M. Chéruel et Ad Regnier Fils, 1904, VI, p. 184.
[2] *Mémoires du Duc de Saint-Simon*, op. cit., xii, p. 3.
[3] Ibid.

ultimate triumph of being sent by Mazarin to distract the King in the lonely days after he had been made to renounce Marie for interests of state, and to accompany him on the long journey to the Spanish frontier for his marriage to the Infanta. Then there was Madame de la Vallière, the King's first *maîtresse-en-titre*, for whom Olympia developed an implacable envy. About the time Prince Eugen was born, Olympia took part in an elaborate plot against her. Precariously based, after the fashion of the day, on forged correspondence, it was eventually unmasked amid scenes of unsurpassed scandal. The conspirators quarrelled and betrayed each other publicly. Olympia and Henrietta, Duchess of Orleans, who had been close friends in gossip and conspiracy for some time, indulged in a high-pitched quarrel in the presence of the King at a performance of a ballet in the Palais Royal. It was the end of their friendship. It also marked the beginning of Louis' disillusionment with Olympia. His eyes had suddenly been opened, and, with Mazarin now dead, he took the plunge of banishing her to the country.

But the rustication was brief. She was soon forgiven and allowed to return to court, her appetite for power now whetted by a thirst for revenge. She immediately resumed the old life: her parties became if anything more extravagant, the gambling wilder than ever, and the King was once again caught up in her toils. That she was among the privileged few invited to accompany the King to Chambord the following autumn was taken by everyone as a mark of complete reconciliation. Inevitably her reinstatement was eased by Henrietta's premature death which occurred immediately after she had negotiated the Treaty of Dover in 1670—a responsibility, it may be noted, which demonstrated the powerful position that women then held in public life.

However, the Count of Soissons' sudden death, through illness on active service in 1673, completely undermined her position. Like many a profligate hostess, she only realized the true value of her marital status when deprived of it. She was forced to give up her post in the Queen's Household. The King came to feel himself not quite so involuntarily bound to her. She picked many quarrels and, to plummet to the abyss, she managed to fall out with the King's new mistress, the Marquise de Montespan. Needing some desperate stroke to restore her position and recapture the King, she resorted to her pet devices of astrology and black magic, and in this way came into contact with the notorious Catherine Deshayes. It was a fatal relationship. Before long La Voisin, as her new acquaintance was called, was accused of trading in poisons, and Olympia found herself involved in the infamous 'affaire des poisons'. Needless to say, Madame de Sévigné kept her daughter posted of the details of the scandal which furnished the sole topic of chatter in Paris at the time : 'Madame la Comtesse de Soissons', she wrote on January 31, 1680, 'asked if she could win back for her a lover who had deserted her; this lover being a great prince; and it is maintained that she said that if he did not return to her he would rue it.'[1] Olympia's innocence once doubted, she came to be suspected of having poisoned her husband—whose early death had certainly been mysterious and had occasioned much speculation—as well as of having plotted to kill Louis XIV. The King thereupon ordered her to leave the country or to be sent to the Bastille and committed for trial. It is a riddle of history how far these suspicions against her were well-founded; Saint-Simon arguing that they were, Liselotte, Duchess of Orleans (who had married the Duke after Henrietta's death), that they were not. Whatever the truth, however, Olympia was afraid, probably with good reason, that the wrath of her enemies, particularly Louvois, the powerful Minister of War, and de Montespan, would preclude a fair trial. So she decided to flee. On a cold January night in 1680, not many hours after receiving the King's orders, but not omitting to pack her hoards of gold and jewellery and to provide grey jerkins for the lackeys and coachmen, and eight horses for the coach, she set out for the frontier. She was accompanied by the Marquise d'Alluye, a companion in frivolity and scandal, with whom she was playing basset at the time of the King's summons—which was indeed served upon them both. According to Saint-Simon, the Marquise was a gossip who had nothing malicious about her but who loved intrigue and gambling beyond anything else and who devoted a long life of eighty years exclusively to pleasure, enjoying every night and day of it without a moment of anxiety or restraint.

Olympia was never to return to France. With the charges against her and the enemies she had made, she would surely have been executed had she stayed and stood her trial. La Voisin and a number of accomplices were found guilty after a fourteen-month ordeal, and burnt at the stake.

Writing many years later about the strong feelings Eugen was known to entertain against Louis XIV on account of his mother's exile, Liselotte, Duchess of Orleans, said that the Prince was quite wrong to nourish such a grievance:

[1] *Lettres de Madame de Sévigné*, ed. L. J. N. Monmerqué, 1862, VI, p. 231.

'Few people know what real clemency the King showed in advising the Countess of Soissons to flee abroad. Whether she was innocent—as I have always believed she was—or guilty, it is certain that had she remained in France, Madame de Montespan and Louvois would have found witnesses ready to swear that she had poisoned her husband which would have cost her her head.'[1]

Olympia's children were abandoned to the care of their grandmother, Mary of Bourbon, Princess of Carignan. There was little money available for them, since Olympia had left nothing behind; but to Eugen, the youngest son, who was sixteen years old at the time, the emotional loss was probably greater than the material. According to Liselotte, Duchess of Orleans, Olympia had 'neglected him and let him run around like a street-urchin',[2] but whatever the shortcomings of her tangible attentions, there is no doubt that she showered love upon him and that strong feelings ran between them. It is not to be wondered at, therefore, that the severance of their relationship came as a great shock to Eugen at so formative an age. Besides the suddenness of the parting, the scandalous manner of Olympia's going can have been nothing less than traumatic in its effect upon him. During three whole days before she fled, Louvois staged demonstrations against her outside the Hôtel Soissons, using a hired caste of street-criers and trumpeters. Then, in the lonely and forsaken aftermath of her departure, Eugen must have been made more miserable than ever by tales of the Minister's unrequited passion for revenge still directed against her: how he reputedly arranged for mobs to insult her en route, for all shelter to be denied her, and finally, when she had at last found refuge in Brussels, for a hideous dance of cats, all tied together in a prancing chorus line, to be there to greet her as she emerged from church on Sunday morning. We can be sure that the news of all this persecution only had the effect of intensifying the boy's immediate sense of loyalty to his mother. But as time went by, and the impact of her personality began to fade, Eugen's feelings towards Olympia ceased to be quite so simple; despite the separation he still loved her deeply, and he remained dominated by her emotionally, but a hesitation started to unfold, a doubt, a resistance it may be—not towards her personally, but against her extravagance, against her selfish and disordered way of life and, even more sharply, against the whole dissolute atmosphere of the Hôtel Soissons. This complexity,

[1] *Correspondance de Madame*, ed. Ernest Jaeglé, 1890, II, p. 50.
[2] Armédée Renée, *Les nièces de Mazarin*, 1857, p. 225.

however, came slowly. It was not the reaction from a lightning vision, but appears to have been the belated exposure of some strong vein in his character, hitherto concealed below the surface. What is significant and surprising in the development of Eugen's personality is the unexpectedness of this change, the absence of the slightest streak of puritanism, the lack of evident will-power in him, when he was a small boy. According to the first-hand evidence of the inveterate scribbler, Liselotte, Eugen was 'nothing but a very debauched boy who seemed to promise no good'[1]—an opinion requiring just the smallest pinch of salt because Liselotte was writing many years later, just after the Imperial forces under Prince Eugen had severely mauled the armies of her beloved Louis, which no doubt exercised a toxic effect on her judgment. Even allowing for this prejudice, however, there can be no doubt of the existence of shadows in Eugen's early boyhood. He belonged to a small, effeminate set that included such unabashed perverts as the young Abbé de Choisy, who was invariably dressed as a girl, except when he wore the lavish ear-rings and make-up of a mature woman. Eugen himself is also said by the Duchess of Orleans to have 'played the part of a woman amongst the young people', to have been much laughed at and been jeeringly called 'Madame l'ancienne' by his contemporaries. But it is impossible to be categorical about how much he participated personally in the worst of the clique's orgies.

From the age of ten he was brought up for the church. It was the King's decision, based on his poor opinion of the Prince's physique and bearing. He was tonsured and wore a soutane, and Louis called him, not without mockery, 'the little Abbé'. Certainly Eugen was unimpressive to look upon. This is how the Duchess of Orleans described him as a boy:

'He was never good-looking or distinguished in appearance. It is true that his eyes are not ugly, but his nose ruins his face; he has two large teeth which are visible all the time. He is always dirty and has lanky hair which he never curls.'[2]

On another occasion the Duchess admitted his intelligence and gave faint praise again to his eyes, but said flatly 'that he was small and ugly

---

[1] E. Bodemann, *Aus den Briefen der Herzogin Elisabeth Charlotte von Orléans an die Kurfürstin Sophie von Hannover*, 1891, II, p. 248.
[2] *Correspondance Complète de Madame, Duchesse d'Orleans*, ed. G. Brunet, 1886, p. 324.

in appearance, with an upturned nose, extended nostrils, and an upper lip so narrow as to prevent him ever shutting his mouth'.[1]

For an understanding of the evolution of Eugen's character it is singularly unfortunate that we have nothing at all in retrospect from his own hand relating to the time of his mother's departure and his early years. This is, as we have seen, a time of extraordinary transition. From being a weak, feckless hanger-on of a dissolute set, the youngest son of a dominating profligate mother and the despised Bible-clerk of the King, he suddenly becomes a man of purpose and authority. The ways of his coterie and of the Hôtel Soissons are renounced, and he begins to develop a severe self-discipline which is to stay with him the rest of his life. We do not know the exact moment of the change; nor the occasion. All we are certain of is that when still a boy he starts to strengthen his body by riding and gymnastics, both thoroughly and vehemently performed. And he comes to the inner decision, which he keeps to himself for some time, that he is not going to enter the church but is going to become a soldier, come hell or high water from the King. He begins to delight in the history of war and in the day-to-day accounts, which ricocheted around the court, of Louis' military adventures in Germany, Holland and the Spanish Nether-lands. His favourite reading is Curtius' life of Alexander the Great. He applies himself steadfastly to the study of mathematics under the tuition of the brilliant Joseph Saveur. And then, when at last he is physically and mentally prepared, he sallies forth on his own. He leaves his grandmother's house, takes humble lodgings in Paris and begins to look about him for ways of securing admission to the army. It is February 1683. His mother has been gone three years. He is nineteen years old.

He was fortunate to have among his friends Prince Louis Armand Conti, a nephew of the Great Condé and son-in-law of Louis XIV, having married the King's daughter by Madame de la Vallière. Eugen persuaded Conti to present him to the King so that he could ask him personally to be allowed to join the army. Ever since Olympia's disgrace, Louis had shown no compassion for her abandoned children. At first his attitude had been one of indifference, except to fall in love— seemingly a reflex action towards any beautiful member of the family— with Urania de la Cropte, the wife of Eugen's eldest brother, described by Saint-Simon as 'radiant as the glorious morn'. Urania, however, did not respond, and this turned Louis' indifference vis-à-vis the Soissons into resentment. He therefore received the young Eugen with

[1] *Correspondance de Madame*, op. cit., II, p. 22.

plenty of ill-will. To the boy's petition, he returned a flat 'no'. It was as a priest that he had always thought of him, and a priest he must remain. So peremptory and final was the fashion of his refusal that Eugen decided then and there to leave the country as soon as he could and to seek service in some foreign army. Later he is said to have sworn never to return to France except with a sword in his hand[1]—an oath as fateful eventually for France as Hannibal's had been for the Romans. Revenge against Louis XIV became the unspent passion of his life. Louis XIV was asked some time afterwards why he had refused Eugen's plea. 'The request was modest,' he replied, 'but the applicant not. Nobody ever ventured to stare me in the face so insolently, like an angry sparrow-hawk.' Nor did any of the satellites around the sun speak up in Eugen's favour. 'Do you think that with his departure I have suffered a severe loss?' Louis asked his courtiers when he heard of the young Prince's flight. They assured him that the Abbé of Savoy would always be feeble-minded, '*un homme incapable de tout*'. But they were judging him, as Voltaire has pointed out, 'by certain excesses of youth, by which men should never be judged'.[2]

One of Eugen's brothers, Louis Julius, had entered the Imperial service the previous year, had been warmly welcomed, and, with the help of his cousin, the Margrave Louis of Baden, had been given command of a regiment of dragoons. But he was killed almost immediately on active service against the Turks at Petronell in 1683. When Eugen received news of his brother's death he decided to flee to Austria, drawn there by the twin hopes of avenging Louis Julius' death and of taking over command of his regiment. Eugen persuaded Prince Conti to go with him and they set out eastwards from Paris on the night of July 26, 1683, disguised as women and armed with enormous swords. When he heard of the escape, the King was furious—on account not so much of Eugen as of Conti. How could he tolerate his son-in-law, the nephew of the Great Condé, going over to the camp of the Habsburgs? He ordered the French frontier to be closed, mobilized his diplomatic missions and sent a special envoy after them. They were apprehended in Frankfurt and such were the threats and pressure put upon Conti that he was induced to return. Eugen, however, continued across the Rubicon on his way to Austria. He was alone. He had no money. But he could not go back. Conti bade him farewell with a generous gift of gold and a valuable ring. In the

[1] E. Mauvillon, *Histoire du Prince François Eugène de Savoye*, 1741, I, p. 164.
[2] F. Voltaire, op. cit., p. 348.

middle of August Eugen reached Passau, where he found the Emperor, Leopold I, who had fled there to escape the Turkish army rapidly approaching Vienna. The Prince's ascetic ways and appearance, so little to the taste of the French Court, appealed to Leopold who, like Eugen, had been brought up and trained for the church. Moreover, there were urgent reasons of State which moved the Emperor to hail Eugen's arrival. In the east the Turkish threat to Vienna had become acute, whilst in the west Louis, who had just gobbled up Strasburg, showed an appetite for further portions of Germany. In this predicament it was not surprising that Leopold warmly welcomed the new recruit. The boy was frail, unimposing and not Austrian, but he was a refugee from Louis XIV and he was eager to fight and in search of a cause.

There were no disqualifications of race, religion or language to service under the Habsburg Monarchy which constituted a truly international society, perhaps the first and only one, so far, of the modern world. Many of the Emperor's leading soldiers came from abroad.[1] Their only loyalty was to the Crown or dynasty.[2] They paid no homage to our modern notion of patriotism. But this was not unique to the Habsburgs. It was the same throughout Europe in the century after the Treaty of Westphalia. War was not the pursuit of churches, as it had been, or of nations, as it was to become, but of kings; and kings were prepared to look anywhere for support, irrespective of national or religious frontiers—Bourbons, Stuarts and Hanoverians no less than Habsburgs. 'It was an epoch of divided loyalties,' Sir Winston Churchill has written, 'of criss-cross ties, of secret reserves and much dissembling.' It was also an era when war, though frequent and gory, was nevertheless limited—kings and their contingents fought each other, not whole nations.

Although he was completely non-Austrian, Eugen did have Habsburg blood. Thomas Francis, his grandfather, the founder of the Carignan line of the House of Savoy, was the son of the Infanta Catherine (a daughter of Philip II of Spain) and the great-grandson of the Emperor Charles V. But what was of more immediate interest to the Emperor was that Eugen was a second cousin of the Duke of

[1] E.g. Charles of Lorraine, Louis of Baden and Montecuccoli. In the seventeenth century the Italians provided most of the sappers of the Imperial army, though in the last decade engineers also came from England and Holland. Italian was the service language of the Habsburg navy.

[2] The famous story of the last Holy Roman Emperor illustrates this nicely. Francis was told that someone was a good patriot, on which he asked: 'Yes, but is he a patriot for me?'

Savoy, and Leopold was eager to seize any opportunities that might occur for winning the Duke to his side against the likely possibility of war with France.

Eugen's request to be accepted into the Imperial army is a vivid landmark at this first turning-point of his career. It lays bare his deepest springs and impulses:

'I confess frankly to have reached this decision only after having tried to follow my ancestor's example of serving my country and the Bourbon Court with all my heart, and only after having in vain sought service many times under the French Crown. But my mother's fate prevented me having a career in the French Army although nothing could ever be proved against her or me. I assure you, most merciful Emperor, of my constant loyalty, and that I will devote all my strength, all my courage, and if need be, my last drop of blood, to the service of your Imperial Majesty, and to the welfare and development of your great House.'[1]

This may not be the crowing of the cock, but it is daybreak, the end of all the dark frustrations of his miscast boyhood, his mother's fate and Louis' rebuff; the dawn of a new loyalty and a new cause, not the ministry of God or King, but secular service, service to the House of Habsburg, where the individual, so limited and unimportant, could be sacrificed and exalted in impersonal and all-embracing activity. There is no crusade about it. No mission. Unselfishness is pursued, for no higher purpose than personal fulfilment.

[1] Original in Latin in the Fürstenberg archives in Prague: German translation in Friedrich Engel-Jánosi, *Die Anfänge des Prinzen Eugen*, Historische Blätter, 1921-22, I, p. 447.

CHAPTER II

THE TURKISH CHALLENGE[1]

ALREADY BEFORE he was twenty-one Eugen's career collided with the vast, primitive force of the Turkish army which had been seething westwards for a century and a half. It was an experience unlike anything he had seen before: the Saracen dress, the furs, the puggarees, the panaches of herons' plumes, the scimitars and pistolled waist sashes and the sheer number of marauding Ottoman soldiers.

The Ottoman Turks, Mongolian in race and Mohammedan in religion, had stormed out of Asia at the beginning of the fourteenth century and had succeeded in the course of the next two centuries in shattering the small kingdoms of south-east Europe, which had been formed on the ruins of the East Roman Empire, and in humbling the Venetian Empire. At the time of Eugen's arrival in Vienna they were at the zenith of their territorial power in Europe.[2] For over a century and a half since their victory on the field of Mohács in 1526, the Turks had been in occupation of most of Hungary. Throughout this time the frontier of control had swayed backwards and forwards, but the Turks had kept up a constant pressure westwards, threatening the Habsburgs. Threatening, yet also stimulating. 'Austria's strength,' so a modern writer, Gordon Shepherd, has expressed it, 'seems to resemble that of a railway buffer. The harder it is rammed, the more it resists: but once remove the frontal pressure and the whole mechanism

[1] See map at the end of the book for Eugen's campaigns against the Ottoman Turks.

[2] The Ottoman Empire in Europe at this time stretched from the middle course of the Dniester, south-east to include Moldavia and Wallachia, Transylvania, most of Hungary, Rumelia (which comprised present-day Bulgaria, Thessaly, most of Yugoslavia and Albania), Bosnia and Greece.

swings loosely in its well-oiled socket.'[1] Ever since their triumph at Mohács, the Turks had given the multi-national, loose-jointed Monarchy a badly-needed *raison d'être* as the last bulwark of Christendom against Moslem expansion. As Holy Roman Emperors the Habsburg Monarchs were 'the elected representatives of Christ' amongst temporal rulers. They rarely let anyone forget it. It had only been fear of the Turks after Mohács that had induced Bohemia and Hungary to acquiesce in a Habsburg as King, while it was only the recurring Ottoman peril thereafter that ensured to the Habsburgs their successive elections as Emperors, since their hereditary dominions enabled them, alone of the German rulers, to make an effective resistance to the Turks. Though it was an ill-assorted combination of Cavour, Bismarck and President Wilson, coupled with the ambitions of the nobility and intellectuals of the constituent nationalities, that finally shattered the Habsburg Monarchy, it was the removal of all eastern pressure consequent upon the dissolution of Ottoman power in the twentieth century that ultimately paved the way for dismemberment by undermining Austria's historic mission.[2]

However, even at the height of their response to the Moslem challenge the Danubian Monarchy had not been uniformly welcomed by the western world as the standard-bearers of Christendom. The Emperor's authority was often questioned in his own hereditary lands, but nowhere so bitterly as in Hungary. The Habsburgs had made precious little effort to liberate occupied Hungary, and the Magyar nobility had come to dread the idea of domination by Vienna just as much as by the Porte. They had often collaborated with the infidel, just as Russian patriots of the early middle ages, such as Alexander Nevski, had temporized with the Mongol invaders from Asia, in preference to submission to the West. Austrian-occupied Hungary was mainly Protestant, and the Jesuits, who came to wield great power in Vienna under the Emperor Leopold, worked incessantly to try to bring it into the Roman fold, never cherishing any illusion that this *Gleichschaltung* could be achieved by peaceful means. In 1671, not many years before Eugen's arrival on the scene, Magyar resentment against Vienna had boiled up into open revolt, which was only quelled by the most savage measures of repression. All the leaders of the Magyar conspiracy were slaughtered except for Tökölyi. Finally, to aggravate

---

[1] Gordon Brook-Shepherd, *The Austrian Odyssey*, 1957, p. 22.
[2] The term Habsburg Monarchy is used here and elsewhere in this book to refer to the Austrian or Danubian branch of the family. See Appendix A for further discussion of the terms Habsburg Monarchy and Holy Roman Empire.

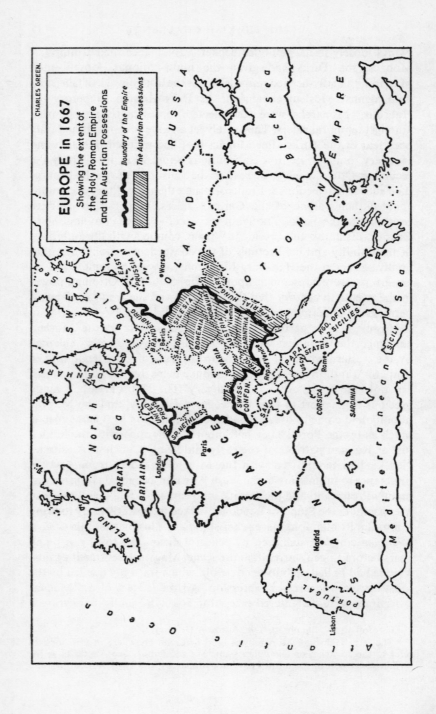

CHARLES GREEN.

EUROPE in 1667
Showing the extent of
the Holy Roman Empire
and the Austrian Possessions

Boundary of the Empire
The Austrian Possessions

the Emperor's chronic malaise in the east, French kings from the time of Francis I had formed the habit, to which Louis XIV became an addict, of conspiring with the Sultan in order to weaken the Habsburg Monarchy, the interests of Christianity notwithstanding.

By the late summer of 1683, when Eugen first offered his services to the Emperor, the Ottoman threat to Vienna was graver than it had ever been before. The Hungarians under Tökölyi had made common cause with the Porte. Rumours of the devastation and extravagance perpetrated by the advancing Turkish forces had been percolating west since the Sultan, Mahommed IV, and the Grand Vizier, Kara Mustapha, had set out from Adrianople at the opening of the year's campaign. The beginning of each Turkish campaign was signified to the world at large by a peculiar ritual. On a pole crowned by a golden ball horse-tails were hoisted. These were the badges of rank of the Ottoman hierarchy: thus an ordinary bey had the right to unfurl one horse-tail, an ordinary vizier three, and the Grand Vizier five. But there were more sinister portents than horse-tails that the Turks were on the move westwards. The particular lavishness of Ottoman prodigality had declared itself in the form of a monstrous hunt arranged for the Sultan: 30,000 beaters had been employed and the whole countryside between Gallipoli and Philipopoli was despoiled to provide for their upkeep. Such were the deprivations that the number of human dead exceeded the game killed. The Sultan, we are assured, bore these losses with equanimity and even enthusiasm. On seeing the corpses he said: 'No doubt these people would have come to curse me; well they have received their punishment in advance.'[1]

The Sultan's and the Grand Vizier's camps, sumptuous even by Ottoman standards, dazzled the eyes of the subject Balkan populations and even of the Turkish troops as they moved west jubilantly in that spring of 1683. On no previous campaign had the harem been so brilliant or so numerous. It required a hundred carriages to transport it. The saddles and harnesses of the horses were covered with velvet. The Sultan's coach was made of silver. The luxury of the Grand Vizier's retinue was said to have been unsurpassed since the time of Darius and Xerxes.

In this, as in most other campaigns, it was not long before the Grand Vizier took command of the Ottoman army. Since he and his successors are to be pitted against Eugen so often in the next few years, it may be useful to observe the extraordinary powers of the office and the

[1] J. De Hammer, *Histoire de L'Empire Ottoman*, traduit de l'Allemand par J. J. Heller, 1838, XII, pp. 79–80.

no less extraordinary restraints upon it. Appointed by the Sultan, the Grand Vizier was virtually in control of the whole military and civil machine of the Ottoman government. He had enormous opportunities for corruption and patronage. He was assisted in his public duties by a corps of scholars not unlike the mandarins of China, who bore the collective name of 'Men of the Pen'. But there were heavy pressures upon him. His power was always being challenged by a strange mixture of authorities: firstly, the Moslem church, which interfered in both military and civil administration; secondly, the Ulema, a body which regarded itself as the keeper of the public conscience with special responsibilities in education and public law, and which carried much weight in the imperial council (Divan); and thirdly, the Chief of the Black Eunuchs, who appears to have controlled the women of the Sultan's Household (Serail) as well as the eunuchs, and, with noticeable impartiality, to have welded these two forces into a remarkably sharp instrument of intrigue. Moreover, as if these constrictions were not enough, the Grand Vizier was always under threat of a mutiny by the infantry *corps d'élite* of janissaries. Such was the office of Grand Vizier, a post held by a rapid succession of men, powerful and ambitious all of them, but totally dissimilar in every other respect from Prince Eugen, their nearest opposite number in the Habsburg Empire for so many years.

The Ottoman army was composed of locally enrolled auxiliaries known as Seratkuli, 'Slaves of the Frontier', who may have numbered at this time about 100,000 infantry and 50,000 horsemen. The regular formations consisted of about 50,000 janissaries, and the standing cavalry, spáhis, who amounted to about 15,000. Like the armies of Europe, the Ottoman forces made use of foreign military engineers, English, Dutch and Italian. A troop of craftsmen from Constantinople followed the army lest any necessity or comfort should be wanted. Finally, bringing up the rear, were a straggling mob of gypsies and panders and a contingent of clowns and jugglers with the responsibility for sustaining morale—a task in which they received no little help from the special corps of poet janissaries trained from youth in bawdy songs. This was the motley throng, numbering altogether over 200,000, which pitched camp outside Vienna in July 1683 under command of Kara Mustapha.

The Grand Vizier, Kara Mustapha, bequeathed to posterity a number of beautiful mosques and fountains—in Constantinople, Adrianople and Belgrade—but his place in history is assured less by these than by the enormity of his appetites, his cruelty and his débâcle

1. Prince Eugen: engraving after a picture by Kupetzky

2. Eugen's mother,
   Olympia Mancini

3. The Hotel de Soissons in Paris, Eugen's birthplace

Prosp. de l'Hotel de Soissons.

at Vienna. His harem consisted of 1,500 concubines. He had seven hundred black eunuchs to guard them. The number of his servants, horses and dogs ran into thousands.

His enemies nicknamed him 'the scourge of humanity', and his behaviour before Vienna showed that he had every intention of living up to it. He gave his army free rein to loot and burn. They set fire to Perchtoldsdorf. The villagers took refuge in the church whence they negotiated terms of release. The agreed ransom was duly paid over and the inhabitants crept out of their hiding place led by a young girl bearing a crown and flag. Scarcely had the procession emerged than the Turks fell upon it and massacred some four thousand innocent villagers. During the course of their two months' stay in the heart of central Europe the Ottoman troops ravaged the entire countryside between the Danube and the Enns, meeting with resistance only from the fortified monasteries of Melk, Lilienfeld, and Klosterneuberg. This was the nature of the Turkish incubus which had been oppressing the Habsburg Monarchy intermittently for a century and a half and which it became Eugen's life-purpose to dispel for ever.

On offering his services, Eugen was admitted to the army and sent directly to battle under the immediate command of his cousin, the Margrave Louis of Baden, and under the supreme command of the imperturbable Duke of Lorraine, the Emperor's brother-in-law. The Imperial army had the urgent task of relieving Vienna where a garrison of only about ten thousand was surrounded by a Turkish force twenty times the size. Their chances of prolonging resistance seemed hopeless. They were ill-supplied. The morale of the Viennese was abysmal. The Emperor had fled with his whole court. Sickness and despair ruled the city. An appeal for help sent in code through the Ottoman lines fell into the Grand Vizier's hands. He returned it by arrow over the city's ramparts after adding the following characteristically encouraging postscript: 'If the people of Vienna continue to doubt the Grand Vizier's clemency they will very soon experience the direct impact of his divine wrath.'[1] Despite urgent entreaties from the Duke of Lorraine for help, the succours promised by Poland, Bavaria, Saxony, Swabia and Franconia seemed slow in arriving. It must have looked to the Viennese that summer, as it has appeared evident to posterity ever since, that the Turks could have taken the city without great difficulty. But Kara Mustapha preferred to wait, believing that it would eventually fall into his hands without a full-scale attack. He

[1] J. De Hammer, op. cit., XII, p. 106.

wanted to avoid having to give his men the promise of wholesale loot without which they could not have been galvanized to attack. He coveted the entire booty for himself. His greed saved the Empire.

By the late summer a sizeable Imperial force under the Duke of Lorraine had been assembled with support duly provided by the various German states, and this, together with a powerful Polish army under the dashing King Sobieski,[1] was poised ready for the relief of Vienna. As the first rays of the sun appeared on Sunday morning, September 12, Mass was celebrated in the open air at Leopoldsberg on a hastily improvised altar. King Sobieski addressed his officers saying that victory beneath the walls of Vienna would save not only the town but all humanity. Meanwhile, Eugen was taking his orders from the Margrave of Baden alongside thirty-two other princes. It was to be his first taste of sustained fighting.

By nightfall Vienna, besieged for sixty days, was saved and the Ottoman troops were routed. It was a climacteric in the history of western Christendom comparable in significance to the Battle of Tours.[2] It was not only the Sultan who had been turned back; the failure at Vienna had been a rebuff to his supporter Louis XIV, who had set much store by the Ottoman intentions to emasculate the Habsburg Monarchy.

In Eugen's own life it was also an important landmark. During the long day of battle he had fought his way from the Kahlenberg overlooking the city to the Burgtor of Vienna. He had often been dangerously exposed. Not only had he experienced the fluctuations and ordeals of prolonged fighting, but he had seen the Turks at first-hand and been able to assess their strengths and weaknesses.

He had also had his first sight of the extravagant impedimenta carried by the Ottoman army and the incentive this provided to his own men as loot. In the suburbs of Vienna he saw the soldiers help themselves to the hoards of money and jewels abandoned by the Ottoman forces, while the townspeople seized the colossal treasure of animals and stores: 20,000 buffaloes, bullocks, camels and mules; 10,000 sheep; 100,000 quarters of corn; whole storehouses of flour,

---

[1] The king was moved by a happy combination of self-interest and higher duty: to pay off a family debt of his wife's against Louis XIV, who was aiding the Turks; to secure for his son the hand in marriage of the Emperor's daughter; and, not least, to serve the cause of Christendom.

[2] Turkey's nickname, 'the sick man of Europe', probably originates, not with the Czar Nicholas I, as often suggested, but with the Ottoman defeat at Vienna commemorated in the German song written in 1683 with the sublime title, *Der Turk ist krank*.

sugar, oil and coffee.[1] The Ottomans also abandoned much of their arms and all their standards except that of Mohammed which bore the words, *There is no God but God*. There is nothing from Eugen's hand to show what the impact on him personally was of the fabulous booty captured from the Grand Vizier, but we have a vivid account of it given by King Sobieski in a letter written to his wife on the evening after the battle: '. . . I find it quite impossible to convey to you the exquisite luxury of the Vizier's tents: there are baths, small gardens, fountains, rabbits and even a parrot.'[2] But he managed to overcome his difficulty enough to describe to her the shining lamps and chandeliers, the carpets worked in silver and gold, the diamonds, rubies, sapphires and pearls, and 'the most beautiful sable furs in the world', all of which had fallen into his hands after Kara Mustapha's flight. There were also two macabre *trouvailles*: the bodies of a beloved ostrich and of a favourite wife, both of whom had been decapitated by the Grand Vizier rather than that they should become the living property of the Christian dogs! It was not long before Kara Mustapha had some of his own medicine. He was strangled in Belgrade on Christmas day of the same year.

So distinguished had been Eugen's part in the Vienna battle that the Duke of Lorraine congratulated him personally on his bravery, and presented him with a pair of golden spurs. At the conclusion of the campaign the Emperor sent for him and promised him the first regimental command to fall vacant. That winter, when still only twenty, this promise was fulfilled and he was nominated Colonel of the Regiment of Dragoons of Kufstein.[3] Alas, he had no money, and such commands, though eventually remunerative,[4] involved a heavy initial outlay which he could not afford. Penury looked like forming an immediate and fatal stumbling-block to his career. However, he had a stroke of luck: his cousin, Victor Amadeus, Duke of Savoy, agreed to advance him some money and with this and the

---

[1] It was from the immense booty of Turkish coffee seized at this time that the Viennese acquired their taste for that drink and started the first of their inimitable coffee houses.

[2] J. de Hammer, op. cit., XII, pp. 117–8.

[3] Infantry regiments contained from 2,000–2,500 men, cavalry regiments 500–1,000. In his reforms of 1711 Eugen reduced the number of battalions in a regiment from four to three. A battalion contained five companies, each with 140 men. Dragoons were expected to fight on foot or on horseback and were armed with a carbine.

[4] The perquisites of a Colonel of a regiment were said to equal those of a Margrave; an Austrian General was said to have the profits of an Italian Duke.

proceeds of the sale of the ring Conti had given him, he was able to take up the appointment.

Military campaigns in those days were mercifully short. They usually started late in the spring well after the snows had melted and the mud hardened. In Eugen's second year with the colours the Imperial forces were exceptionally slow off the mark, although the chance which presented itself for the first time for years of hustling the Turks out of their strong positions in Hungary should have dictated speed. The Holy League had been formed in March 1684 between Leopold, King Sobieski of Poland, and Venice to prosecute what amounted to a crusade against the Porte; and in consequence, the Turks found themselves at war on two other fronts apart from Hungary: in the Adriatic and in the Polish Ukraine. However, not till well on into June 1684 was the Duke of Lorraine ready to advance towards Ofen (the modern Buda) which had been in Turkish hands since 1541 and was now their military headquarters. During the ensuing brief spasm of fighting Eugen distinguished himself at the head of his regiment by first fending off a resolute Turkish attack at St Endre and then helping to shatter a relief force sent by the Sultan to try to get through to the Ofen garrison. But the Turks, always tenacious behind walls, were still in command of the city when winter put an end to the fighting for 1684.

Defeats were inflicted on the Turks the following year at Neuhäusel and Gran prior to the renewal of the attack on Ofen. Again Eugen covered himself with glory. The Margrave of Baden was so impressed by his valour that he asked permission to present him personally to the Emperor. Taking him by the hand, the Margrave said to Leopold: 'Sir, this young Savoyard whom I have the honour to present to Your Imperial Majesty will in due course emulate all those whom the world regards as great generals.'[1]

Such was the glory of the Turkish war echoing through the capitals of western Europe, and such the desire to follow Eugen's example, that many foreign princes were eager to serve against the Turks: the Princes of Commercy and Vaudemont, both from Lorraine; the young Turenne, a cousin of Eugen's; Conti's brother; and the Marquis Fitzjames, a natural son of King James II and afterwards Duke of Berwick—all hurried to serve the Imperial cause. Lord Cutts, later to be nicknamed the Salamander, was appointed Adjutant-General to the Duke of Lorraine and distinguished himself at the taking of Buda in 1686; a Neapolitan, Count Anthonio Carafa, was given

[1] E. Mauvillon, op. cit., I, p. 43.

command of the Imperial army in Hungary, with the task, to which he addressed himself gleefully, of smashing the remnants of the Hungarian Protestant revolt against the Jesuit-ridden Austrian court.

At the end of 1685, when still only twenty-two, Eugen was made a Major-General. In the campaign of 1686, which led to the taking of Buda on September 2, he had his horse shot from beneath him and was twice wounded. The fall of Buda, bravely defended by Abdi Pasha for seventy-eight days, meant the loss to the Turks of their chief centre in occupied Hungary. With the season over, Eugen repaired to Venice for the carnival. This was in accordance with the practice amongst Imperial officers in those days, but the journey itself was the limit of Eugen's compliance with custom. The Republic went to lavish lengths to entertain and honour the heroes from the front. Sumptuous balls were given and the Venetian beauties threw themselves at the officers' feet. A contemporary historian has written that at Venice voluptuousness reigned supreme more than anywhere else in the world, particularly at carnival time.[1] But Eugen was unmoved. His official biographer, Von Arneth, has ascribed his reserve towards women, noticeable now for the first time and later to earn him the sobriquet of 'Mars Without Venus', as being due to his great 'self-control'—a diagnosis less revealing of the subject than of the strabismic, mid-Victorian author.[2] Whatever the cause, there is no doubt that Eugen was vastly more interested in inspecting the famous Venice arsenal, in seeing cannons being cast and ships launched, and in watching a specially staged mock sea battle, than in receiving the attentions of his splendid hostesses.

In the succeeding campaign he commanded a Cavalry Brigade which fell like an avalanche upon the Turks, contributing materially to their defeat at Mohács in 1687. Eugen was one of the first to penetrate into the enemy's camp, where he set up the Imperial Eagle and carried off the Crescent. As a reward, he was chosen to convey to the Emperor the news of the victory. Leopold gave him a portrait miniature set in diamonds, and later in the year promoted him to Field-Marshal-Lieutenant, a rank corresponding in the British Army to that of Lieutenant-General. As a result of the Mohács victory, the Archduke Joseph received the crown of St Stephen at Buda on December 9, 1887. Among those taking part in the charge at Mohács was the Frenchman, Villars, with whom Eugen's life was to become inextricably involved. 'He has a lot of courage,' Villars wrote of him

---

[1] E. Mauvillon, op. cit., V, p. 57.
[2] A. Arneth, *Prinz Eugen von Savoyen*, 1858, I, p. 26.

now, 'more common sense than inspiration, plenty of application aimed at making him a good officer, which he is well capable of becoming. . . .'[1] This patronising tone was abandoned on further acquaintance. Eugen's success was beginning to become widely known. The King of Spain saw fit to bestow the Order of the Golden Fleece upon him. His cousin, Victor Amadeus, Duke of Savoy, provided him with the money he needed for the golden chain of the Spanish Order. He was now proud to proclaim kinship, and succeeded in persuading the Pope to confer on him the revenues of two rich abbeys in Piedmont.

Meanwhile, we should note that on their southern front the Turks had lost the Morea and Athens to Venice in 1687; and that the Parthenon, in use as a powder magazine, was largely destroyed by a Venetian bomb in that year.

In 1688, the Elector Max Emmanuel of Bavaria succeeded the Duke of Lorraine as Supreme Commander of the Imperial armies. His instructions were to take Belgrade, which had been in Turkish hands for 166 years, having surrendered to Suliman the Magnificent in 1522. It was the key to the Turkish position on the Lower Danube and much prized by them as the frontier fortress against the Infidel. Eugen took part in the ensuing battle which led to the capture of Belgrade on September 6, 1688. During the action he received a sabre cut which penetrated his helmet. It was a severe wound, but he managed to repay the blow, laying the Turk who gave it to him dead at his feet.

As has already been emphasized, Eugen had a poor natural physique, which had only been fortified and made fit for service by drawing upon his considerable reserves of nervous energy. Thanks to all the stresses and deprivations of the eastern front, he had for some time been suffering from chest trouble and had had to resort to a special milk diet. Now, with a serious wound as well, he became dangerously ill—so much so that the Duke of Savoy sent his private physician to Vienna to attend him. Only after many months of fever did he recover.

From convalescence he was able to look back on six years of hectic activity—activity which had provided an essential, and pleasurable, compensation for the stagnation of his boyhood. It had been a testing and dangerous time as well. He had proved to himself, not that he was without nerves in danger or unaware of the imminence of death, but that he was elated by them and that, by a happy contagion,

---

[1] Louis Hector, Duc de Villars, *D'Après Sa Correspondance Inédite*, 1892 II, p. 4.

those around him were somehow elated too. Most necessary of all, these years of Turkish war had meant success. He had deeply ventured and greatly won. He had rocketed to the upper stratum of command. But in doing so he had been able to watch and learn from others. He had witnessed the harmonious collaboration between the bravura of Sobieski and the moderato of Lorraine, but he had also seen the difficulties inherent in a conglomerate army of many different states under independent, headstrong rulers such as the Elector Max Emanuel of Bavaria and the Margrave Louis of Baden. He had observed how the Ottoman soldiers, whose swords had for so long wreaked panic and destruction in the West, could be checked by trained musketeers, fearlessly led. Highly disciplined soldiers firing in line could master individual swordsmen, however expert or numerous. Diplomatically he had perceived the interdependence of the Porte and Versailles. Whatever the religious differences between them they would always be tempted to conspire together to smash the Monarchy which must therefore be ever vigilant on both fronts. Nor did Eugen yet entertain any feeling of disillusionment towards the Emperor and his court. For him these represented chosen and not innate authority; against which there was no cause to react; and, having seen little of them as yet at first-hand, he had no reason to abate his initial enthusiasm.

But was he entirely satisfied with his new life? Was there any lurking conflict of loyalty, or had the catharsis been complete?

We have seen the shadow thrown by his mother over his material prospects; she had also cast a mantle over his personal life which was still to curtail his freedom. By now Olympia had settled down in Brussels, a small court sibilating around her, and many an admirer ready to break a lance on her behalf. Eugen kept in touch with her by correspondence all through the Turkish campaigns,[1] and he visited her once in Brussels. Even if his continued unresponsiveness towards women, that 'self-control' which had been first manifested in Venice, had no deep psychological significance and was little more than natural reaction against the voluptuousness of his early background at the Hôtel Soissons, there is no doubt that his mother still exercised a powerful influence over him, and that this emotional pull promoted an inner tussle of loyalty. It was her purpose during all these years to seduce him away from Austria and persuade him to join the Spanish service. For if he were to do so there would be a good chance, she thought, of his being posted near her in the Spanish Netherlands. The

[1] No letters survive.

Spanish Court were accessory to this plan and the Spanish Ambassador in Vienna, the Marquis of Borgomero, had for long used all his skill in an effort to suborn Eugen. Frequently, we may be sure, did the Ambassador remind Eugen how the blood of Charles V and Philip II flowed in his veins. One winter, in between Turkish campaigns, Olympia persuaded him to accompany her on a brief visit to Madrid. With characteristic vitality she mobilized the Spanish Court to implement her scheme for bringing over her son to the Spanish service. King Charles II was induced to bestow on Eugen the rank of a Grandee of the First Class and to promise him financial support. Olympia even intrigued in an effort to marry him off to a Spanish heiress. Eugen, who in the meantime had received the Order of the Golden Fleece from the King of Spain, went so far as to seek the Duke of Savoy's permission some time later to found a new Spanish branch of the House of Savoy. But by then the laws of gravity which invariably governed Olympia's path had had time to operate and she had fallen heavily from favour with the Spanish Court. The Queen, Marie Louise, a niece of Louis XIV's, had died suddenly in mysterious circumstances suggesting the possibility of poisoning. Saint-Simon charges Olympia with having assassinated her. He implies that she was an accomplice of the Vienna Court:

'The weather was hot. Milk is hard to come by in Madrid, and the Queen wanted it. The Countess of Soissons, who had found more and more opportunity to be alone with her, promised to bring some, iced. It is said that it was prepared at the house of the Emperor's Ambassador in Madrid, Count Mannsfeld. The Countess of Soissons took it to the Queen, who swallowed it and died shortly afterwards, just like her mother.

'The Countess of Soissons did not even wait to see what happened. Having seen the milk swallowed she returned home where her luggage was ready. She immediately fled to Germany, not daring to go to Flanders any more than to remain in Spain.

'As soon as the Queen was taken ill it was realized what she had swallowed, and from whom she received it. The King sent for the Countess but she was not to be found. He sent search parties out for her everywhere, but she had made good her escape. She lived in Germany for some time, always in obscurity. Mannsfeld was recalled to Vienna where he was given the highest post at court, President of the Imperial War Council.'[1]

[1] *Mémoires du Duc de Saint-Simon*, op. cit., VI, pp. 185–6.

But no charge was ever preferred against the Countess and there is no corroboration for Saint-Simon's intriguing story, which may be less the outcome of serious research than of his wish to round off his portrait of Olympia as the poisoner *par excellence* of the age. Nevertheless, it is a fact that for one reason or another, whether excessive gambling, witchcraft or intrigue, Olympia had to leave Madrid in a hurry under duress. This was the end of Eugen's Spanish marriage project and it was the last occasion that he contemplated a step which might have been incompatible with service to the Austrian Habsburgs. It had only been an idea with which he toyed at the bidding of his importunate mother.

We may be sure that in the physical struggle for recovery from his grave condition, which he waged throughout the winter of 1688–9, his mind was at rest, satisfied that in the tolerant, ecumenical service of the Habsburgs he had found fulfilment.

CHAPTER III

WAR AGAINST LOUIS XIV
AND FIRST STEPS IN PATRONAGE

HIS ENERGIES were soon to be needed again, this time in the West
against Louis XIV. The English were preoccupied with their bloodless
revolution—smug-sounding to foreigners, glorious to themselves—
so much so that they gave the impression of being aloof from what
Macaulay characterizes as 'continental affairs'; whilst the Emperor,
having taken Belgrade, had failed to seize the excellent chance which
it offered of making peace with the Turks. It was not with anxiety
that for the past five years Louis XIV had been witnessing the successful efforts of his hereditary rival, the Emperor, to strengthen his
position in the East at the expense of the Turks. The work of his two
great Ministers, Louvois and Colbert, in reforming the army, recreat-
ing the navy and restoring the national economy, had not been carried
out in order that the Habsburgs should be allowed to encircle France.
So he resolved to strike quickly to prevent the consolidation of
Habsburg power in Germany. Using the occasion of a dispute about
who should wear the electoral hat of Cologne, he sent French troops
across the Rhine in the autumn of 1688. They proceeded to devastate
Heidelberg, Mannheim, Speyer and Worms, and more than a
thousand other towns and villages in Germany, in a campaign of such
unforgettable savagery as to leave behind memories of hatred against
the invader comparable to the noxious heritage bequeathed by the
Germans in France two centuries later. More self-righteously, but no
more wisely, Louis coupled this attack on Germany with an attempt
to assert his belief in the Divine Right of Kings by forcibly restoring
James II to the English throne. This produced a primordial and
xenophobic explosion in England against 'the most Christian

Turk, the most Christian ravager of Christendom', as the English vilipended him. The Grand Alliance of the Empire, England and Holland was thereupon called into being to resist Louis.

A letter to the Duke of Savoy indicates what folly Eugen saw in the Emperor's decision not to make peace with the Turks, and to contemplate war on two fronts. 'Most people believe,' he wrote, 'that we want to continue the two wars, although anyone with any sense who has the public good at heart is furious about it and knows that it is only monks who uphold this point of view.'[1] In addition to an understandable backhander at the Church, which was providing the Emperor with priestly advisers, we have here for the first time that reference to the public good which is to appear so often in Eugen's language, and that note of acerbity which seems to have been constitional in him.

Like most of the ministers and military advisers in Vienna, Eugen believed that the Emperor should make peace with the Turks so as to be able to concentrate his forces against the French. This was the advice which William III, the organizing brain of the Grand Alliance, also urged upon him. But Leopold's reluctance to abandon his ambitions in the East are understandable. Never can the pull between Habsburg interests in the East and West have been more difficult to resolve. For at this moment the opportunities down the Danube for further gains of territory, appealing at all times to the predatory instincts of the House of Habsburg, must have seemed almost irresistible. After the fall of Belgrade and the deposition of the Sultan Mohammed IV, the Ottoman Empire was in disarray. There was rebellion in Bulgaria, stirred up by the Catholic Church, unrest in Serbia, instigated by the adventurer George Brancović, and pressure in the Bánat and all along the river Sava, from Habsburg forces. The East appeared to lie open to the Emperor and, indeed, expansion there at the expense of the Turks seemed called for as a matter, not merely of spoliation, but of Christian duty. It was a question, therefore of finding fresh allies in the West against Louis XIV so that this double task could be carried out. The Duke of Savoy would have to be won over to active support. He ruled both Savoy and Piedmont, territories so strategically placed that their ruler 'could not', in Eugen's words, afford to be honourable'—not that Duke Victor Amadeus II put himself to much expense in the effort; on the contrary, he showed himself consistently ready to sell the Alpine passes, of which he was guardian, to the highest bidder. Eugen was accordingly sent to Turin

[1] Eugen to the Duke of Savoy, 28.11.1688, A. Arneth, op. cit., I, p. 451.

on his first diplomatic mission. He succeeded. The Duke agreed in July 1690 to support the Emperor. In the meantime Spain had been attacked by the French and had joined the allied side. The Grand Alliance was beginning to resemble its name.

After serving against the French on the Rhine and being severely wounded in the capture of Mainz in September 1689, Eugen was sent the following year with five thousand Imperial troops to North Italy. He was to help the Duke of Savoy and ten thousand Spaniards recruited from the Spanish Duchies in Italy. From now until 1697 he took part in the yearly campaigns against the French in Italy.

He thought little of the Spanish troops serving on the allied side. Their lack of thrust symbolized the decline in Spanish power, and Eugen said so in trenchant fashion:

> 'Nothing that I have ever heard of the Spaniards can compare with what I personally have now seen of them. I realize more clearly every day that their one aim is to do nothing. They see difficulties in every proposal and I doubt if there is a place in all Piedmont which they could be sure of holding.'[1]

Later, in another despatch to Vienna, he wrote:

> 'If these people were to display as much ability and zeal for the public good as they show skill and cunning in serving their own purpose, which is complete inactivity, our affairs would be in a very different state to what they now are.'[2]

The age in which Eugen lived saw a rapid wizening in the Spanish power. In the year of his birth, Madrid had been compelled to recognize the independence of Portugal. He himself was first to witness and later to contribute to the process of disintegration.

At the outset of the war, the northern sea powers were not able to show much more resilience than Spain. On June 30, 1690, the allied fleet was ignominiously defeated off Beachy Head, largely as a result of bad leadership. The same defeatism paralysed the polyglot, divided command in Italy at the outset of the campaign. The French were allowed to go about their looting and devastation of Piedmont almost unhindered. Eugen describes one occasion, however, when they were checked. One day his forces fell upon a small detachment of French soldiers returning laden with booty taken from the town of Rivoli. They overwhelmed them; and such was their vengeful wrath

[1] Eugen to Graf Tarini, 30.9.1690, A. Arneth, op. cit., I, p. 452.
[2] Eugen to Graf Tarini, 13.11.1690, A. Arneth, op. cit., I, p. 452.

that, in Eugen's impenitent words, '*nos gens ont fait à la turque coupant des testes et ne donnant point de quartier*'[1]—a barbarous tit-for-tat which he apparently condoned.

However, the chances of effecting such successful, if cruel, reprisals were rare, for in the multifarious allied army in Italy there was not that ruthless will or capacity for revenge which might have prevented the French army from laying waste the whole of Piedmont. In his first winter in command of the Austrian troops Eugen was to experience the discomfort attendant upon having quarters amidst a disaffected community. The Duke of Montferrat, in whose territory Eugen's army was wintering, had taken the French side and had incited his subjects to do their worst to Eugen and his troops. 'Never have I seen such treacherous scoundrels as in this country,' Eugen reported to Vienna in mid-January 1691, 'you hear of nothing but poison and assassination. I receive reports daily that I am to be poisoned, and that I am to be taken dead or alive . . . But this does not trouble me and my only aim is to make them rue that they ever needlessly attacked the Emperor's troops.'[2]

Already in 1691, we find Eugen complaining bitterly of the inadequacy of the Imperial forces in Italy and we see him making the first of his many journeys to Vienna in quest of reinforcements: 'The Emperor should either have no army in Italy, or a sufficiently strong one; and the forces there must either be completely withdrawn or abundantly strengthened.'[3] This was a cry he was to make innumerable times in the following decades. On this, the first occasion, he was successful, and after his special pleading in person in Vienna further forces and supplies were promised. He was fortunate in Vienna in finding strong support from the Imperial Vice-Chancellor, Graf Leopold William von Königsegg, and from the Court Chancellor, Graf Theodor Heinrich Strattmann, both of whom stood high in the Emperor's estimation. Arneth gives a clue to the prevailing ethics of the time when he writes solemnly of Strattmann that 'he was heartily opposed to the view which was widely held then, and which attained universal acceptance in the first half of the eighteenth century, that the best politician is he who succeeds most completely in outwitting and deceiving his opponent'.[4] Strattmann indeed was an unfashionably honourable man.

[1] Eugen to Graf Tarini, 30.9.1690, A. Arneth, op. cit., I, p. 452.
[2] Eugen to Graf Tarini, 10.1.1691, A. Arneth, op. cit., I, p. 453.
[3] Eugen to Graf Tarini, 31.1 and 3.3.1691, A. Arneth, op. cit., I, p. 453.
[4] A. Arneth, op. cit., I, p. 55.

Thanks to reinforcements, the allied army in Italy was now more numerous than the French. But this did not suffice to make them victorious, largely, in Eugen's view, because of the lack of the right offensive spirit amongst the officers. Eugen did not make himself popular with his brother officers by his continual criticisms of their inactivity and by his no less frequent exhortations to attack. 'The enemy would long ago have been beaten,' he wrote to Vienna, 'if everyone had done his duty. They can say what they like of me and I will take no notice, because it would be wrong if the service of the Emperor and the common cause were to suffer through looking after one's private interests.'[1]

Obviously, the easy-going officers in the allied army in North Italy found this sharp-tongued, restless renegade Frenchman a thorn in the flesh. Not only did he have sweeping ideas about strategy, but he questioned most of the basic traditions and tactics upon which battles were conducted. To begin with he did not sympathize with the current practice of postponing the start of the campaigning season until well into the middle of the year. More fundamental, he was quite unresigned to the punctilio and caution of siege-warfare. If Eugen was a rebel in any aspect of his life it was in his resistance to the prevailing military convention that war was a formalized, almost static, exercise directed largely to the defence or capture of fortresses. Vauban, the presiding French genius of siege-warfare, had never in fact intended that his fortresses should be looked upon as ends in themselves; he had seen them as shelters for troops and magazines for arms in preparation for attack.[2] But the original purpose had become distorted and the objectives of warfare as seen by contemporary generals, irrespective of nationality, until the arrival on the scene of Charles XII, Marlborough, Villars and Eugen, appeared to consist, not so much of destroying the enemy's army as of capturing the strong points defending his territory. The assault and defence of a fortress were conducted according to an elaborate ritual which provided for the surrender of a garrison at the precise moment when honour could be salved without annihilation. Already in North Italy at this early stage of his career, Eugen showed his determination to break with the static tradition

[1] Eugen to Graf Tarini, 2.8.1691, A. Arneth, op. cit., I, p. 455.

[2] In the defence of a fortress Vauban attached great importance to the use of enfilading fire, defence in depth with the help of outworks and ravelins, and sorties, often at night, from specially constructed sally-ports. For the capture of a fortress he developed a science based on lines of 'contravallation', which were trenches for offence against the fortress and lines of 'circumvallation' intended to protect the besieging army from investment by relieving forces.

of siege-warfare. The key to success, he believed, lay in movement.

Deeply convinced of the correctness of his views Eugen could not refrain from castigating those who opposed them, including those at the top. The Elector Maximilian Emanuel, in command of five thousand Bavarians, was, he realized and pointed out, no longer the same force as the liberator of Belgrade and Buda; whilst Count Carafa, the Italian general in command of twelve thousand Imperial reinforcements, was *hors concours* in incompetence. 'I don't believe,' Eugen wrote of him, 'that there could be anyone who is less of a soldier and who understands less of war.'[1] To Eugen, Carafa's cruel oppression of the civilian population in Italy was as evil and counter-productive as similar behaviour had already proved itself to be in Hungary before his own eyes. So strongly did he now feel about Carafa's incompetence that he said he would no longer serve under him, adding that he would even prefer to leave the Imperial service; or if he was to continue in it, he would insist on being transferred to the German front.

This attitude was generally regarded in Vienna as the sign, not of uncompromising integrity, but of upstart arrogance. However, his immediate superiors handled the situation astutely: Eugen was sent off to spend the winter with his mother in Brussels; and the next year Carafa was replaced by another Italian, Count Caprara, with the Duke of Savoy in supreme command.

Allied prospects now began to look distinctly more favourable since the French had had to withdraw troops from Italy. The English and Dutch fleets inflicted a decisive defeat on the French Admiral, Tourville, in May 1692. To Eugen there appeared to be an excellent opportunity of launching an attack on France through Savoy. 'Nothing stands in the way of our marching to Grenoble,'[2] he declared. But in the Supreme Command the old lethargy triumphed over enterprise, and the season ended with nothing accomplished. Caprara, though a relative of Montecuccoli, had inherited none of his military verve. Off Eugen went to Vienna once again. He was determined to put to the Emperor personally his ideas on how the war in Italy should be fought. Only with difficulty did he succeed in penetrating to Leopold across the stagnant moat of envious courtiers encircling him. But once there, he triumphed. The Emperor was impressed by Eugen; he was so impressed by his person, by his palpable disinterestedness and his passion for the Imperial cause that he promoted

[1] Eugen to Graf Tarini, 29.9 and 6.10.1691, A. Arneth, op. cit., I, p. 455.
[2] A. Arneth, op. cit., I, p. 74.

him Field-Marshal.[1] However, he does not appear to have had the same faith in his strategic ideas. The following campaign, with Eugen serving under Caprara, again started belatedly and was conducted with the old faint-heartedness. In 1694, however, Eugen's chance seemed to have come. Caprara was moved to Hungary, and he was made Supreme Allied Commander in Italy. However, the Duke of Savoy, increasingly doubtful of the Empire's ability to turn the French out of Italy, had initiated secret talks with the French aimed at extricating himself and his stricken country from the war. While the negotiations were being carried on, the Duke, naturally, did not wish to sever his lifeline with the Emperor. Nor did he want to incur further losses, so, in order to forestall an allied offensive yet show himself willing, he suggested the holding of a Council of War. Such tergiversations on the Duke's part succeeded in stultifying operations in this and the following year. We can imagine Eugen's scathing comments, and it was probably these to which Frederick the Great referred when he wrote: 'Prince Eugen used to say that whenever a general is disinclined to undertake anything his best course is to call a Council of War; this is very true because experience shows that in such a council the majority are in favour of a negative policy.'[2]

The Emperor remained for long optimistic that the Duke of Savoy would be prevented from going finally over to the enemy and that something would be saved from the wreck of the allied effort in Italy. Eugen was the lodestar of all his hopes. Leopold relied on his 'great prudence and known ability'.[3] But Eugen realized that no dependence could be placed on his cousin. The disposition of the Duke's troops told more of his real intentions than all his professions of zeal for the common cause. In 1696, the Duke finally took his army over and became Commander-in-Chief on the French side, a shift of allegiance sweeping even by Savoy standards. The Imperial position was rendered hopeless, and the Emperor, who, throughout all these years, had seen fit to keep a large part of his army involved in the East against the Turks, agreed to an armistice in Italy. Meanwhile, however, the French desire for peace had reached craving point. The war had been a severe strain on the French economy. In 1695 Louis had levied a new tax,

[1] Eugen was not yet thirty. There were over twenty Field-Marshals in the Imperial service at the time. By a coincidence the French commander, Catinat, was made a Field-Marshal at about the same time as Eugen, after as many years' service as Eugen had years of age—testimony as much to the poor relative quality of the Imperial officers as to Eugen's abilities.

[2] Friedrich der Grosse, *Militärische Schriften*, Berlin, 1882, p. 89.

[3] Emperor Leopold to Eugen, 10.5.1696, A. Arneth, op. cit., I, p. 457.

the capitation, but this had only produced about half the expected revenue. The King had for some time realized that he would ultimately have to pay the price of peace, the recognition of William III, with whom indeed his agents had been secretly in touch since 1693.[1] In the early summer of 1697 he offered terms upon which the Allies agreed to negotiate. Peace was thereupon signed in the Dutch village of Ryswick in September 1697, despite the procrastination of Spain which, in William III's opinion, had contributed nothing to the common cause but rodomontades, and of the Emperor, who wanted the war in the Netherlands to continue at others' expense, and who in the end signed a month later than the rest. The first big war of modern times, referred to, with equal inadequacy, sometimes as King William's war, sometimes as the war of the League of Augsburg, was at an end.

Although France had had the best of the fighting, she came out of the war smaller than she had entered it. They had retired to the left bank of the Rhine, returned Lorraine to the Duke, recognized William III as King of England, and renounced all attempts to restore James II to his throne—this last a considerable blow to Louis XIV's pride.

This relatively successful outcome was due less to the military proficiency of the Allies than to their skilled diplomacy, of which William III was the past master. The value of such diplomacy, the way William had kept the Alliance together despite its centrifugal tendencies and initial defects, probably formed for Eugen the most useful lesson of these years, if we exclude what he must have learned on how not to conduct a military campaign. Leopold, mesmerized by the mirage of a *Te Deum* in Saint Sophia, had never seemed to put his heart into the war against France, and this dispiritedness had pervaded his armies in the West.

Eugen had already seen how the Habsburg eagle could soar serenely above the little birds and suffer them to sing their varied songs, encouraging and indeed exploiting them for its own purposes; but now he had also been able to see how its claws were of common clay—earthbound talons which at moments held the Monarchy in hopeless bondage. On closer acquaintance, Leopold had proved himself much less endearing than initially. He was no soldier, of course—it was in panic-stricken flight from the Turks besieging Vienna that Eugen had first met him. As a statesman he was governed by a most impassive

[1] Mark A. Thomson, *Louis XIV and William III*, 1689–1697, The English Historical Review, 1961, p. 37.

phlegm, such as was indistinguishable at times from inertia. The only public issue which appeared to move him was that of Hungary, where he was accustomed on occasion to swing from lethargy to violence in one frenzied oscillation. His working day was spent in signing orders drawn up by his ministers, in writing to his many relations, and in giving audiences—fustian affairs conducted according to the strictest etiquette and marked by numerous obeisances. He dressed in Spanish fashion, with red stockings and shoes, the great collar of the Golden Fleece around his neck; a frail, elfish figure, surmounted by a huge flowing wig, weak on his legs, his speech impeded by the thick Habsburg lip which drooped so low as to leave his eye-teeth constantly exposed. Compared with his contemporary sovereigns, Louis XIV and Charles II, Leopold was a paragon of pious virtue, but as Dr Vehse, the historian of the court, expressed it, his qualities were those whose distinction lay in the absence of their opposite vices.[1] His piety was such that each morning he heard three masses in succession. It also meant, though, that he was the slave of the priesthood. The Jesuits who surrounded him—there were said to be 250 in Vienna alone—were not far from being the ultimate rulers of Austria. Recognizing the generosity of their patron, they endowed the Emperor with the name 'Leopoldus Magnus', an honour they extended to no other emperor except Carolus Magnus. True, the nobility filled the main offices at court and in the council and army. But from the time of the downfall of Prince Lobkowitz (1670) until the era of Prince Kaunitz, the leading figure in Central European politics from 1750 to 1792, not one of them was able to attain a position of supreme authority. During all these years the only men who stood out from the bickering crowd at court were the two foreigners, Montecuccoli and Eugen. Those of the aristocracy—and they were not many—who participated in public life, did so from a desire, not so much to share as to dispute the burden of power. As a rule, however, the nobles showed little zest for public affairs—certainly much less than their compeers in England and Prussia. Wickham Steed tells a story to illustrate the extent to which shooting seemed to be the chief object of aristocratic life. Count Czernin on the point of death was heard by his faithful servant to mutter, 'And when the Lord enquires of me, "What hast thou done with thy life?" I must answer, "Oh! Lord. I have shot hares, shot hares, shot hares." It is really very little.'[2] As a *vis inertiae*, however,

---

[1] Dr E. Vehse, *Memoirs of the Court, Aristocracy and Diplomacy of Austria*, trs. Franz Demmler, 1856, II, p. 4.

[2] Henry Wickham Steed, *The Hapsburg Monarchy*, 1913, p. 133.

Wickham Steed admits that the influence of the aristocracy was great.

Did Eugen's apparent disillusionment over Habsburg rule have any effect on his allegiance to the Monarchy? It has often been said that at this time of frustration Louis XIV made great efforts to win Eugen back, offering him secretly the baton of a Marshal of France, the governorship of Champagne, and a pension. Though the detail in this story makes it sound plausible, no foundation for it exists in fact, and there is a lot of circumstantial evidence to the contrary. Had Louis XIV really hoped to secure his return, he would surely not have behaved so badly to Eugen's eldest brother, the Duc de Soissons. We have already seen how Louis had attempted, without success, to seduce Soissons' wife.[1] A few years later, at the time when Eugen was winning renown in the Imperial army in Italy, Louis dismissed Soissons from the French army, refused to let him acquire any position commensurate with his rank, and then, after the Duke had gone abroad in search of a career, had cut him off from the pension and income that were his due.

When, in 1696, Eugen's cousin, the Duke of Savoy, broke with the Emperor and went over to the French side, rumours of Eugen's hesitation were rife. He found himself obliged to publish a denial. 'What is absolutely certain and what I will let all Europe know,' he declared, 'is that neither my blood nor the interest of my House will outbalance for an instant my honour and my duty.'[2] The rumour was best refuted by the consistent efforts he had so visibly been making to drive his roots even deeper into Austria. Already in 1693 he had possessed himself of a house in the Himmelpfortgasse in the centre of Vienna; though he did not have the money to pay for it immediately. Then a few years later, when still unable to afford it, we find him commissioning the young Styrian architect, Fischer von Erlach, to build a magnificent palace on the same site, enlarged by the acquisition of additional properties on either side. Eugen's bold decision when still young and penurious to build a Stadtpalais or Winter Palace, as it came to be called, shows how his love of splendid and beautiful things, afterwards to become his most fruitful passion, was something innate in him and not merely the outward flourish of a rich man. Not that he lacked a streak of panache. He loved symbols—symbols of strength, courage and beauty—and was unabashed enough to place reliefs of Hercules and Antaeus and of Aeneas and Anchises, either side of the main entrance to the Stadtpalais, and inside to have heavily

[1] See p. 10.
[2] Max Braubach, *Geschichte und Abenteuer*, 1950, p. 32.

burdened Atlantes lumbering up the great staircase, the ceiling of which was painted with the legends of Apollo.

But the building of the Winter Palace did not quench Eugen's rapidly-growing thirst for possessions. In the last decade of the seventeenth century and the first of the eighteenth, it became the fashion amongst the important families to construct enormous palaces round Vienna beyond the glaçis which had to be kept clear for defence. There were two hundred by 1720. It was the hour of Ictinus and Phe¡dias. Eugen fell a victim to this *Bauwurm*,[1] which was to transform the face of Vienna. In 1693, he began acquiring land on a slight eminence to the south-east of the town where he later built the Belvedere Palace and garden. Magnificently overlooking the town, with a view of the Vienna woods beyond, the Belvedere was Eugen's first aesthetic coup. He had come to Austria, not to destroy but to fulfil, and the Belvedere, as much as any of his military triumphs, helped to gratify at once both his yearning to belong and his passion to succeed.[2]

---

[1] The following are the principal palaces (with dates of first planning or commencement of work) built from 1683–1700: Dietrichstein-Lobkowitz town palace (1685–7); Theresianum (reconstruction in 1687–90); Liechtenstein garden palace (1689); Mollard-Clarg town palace (*c.* 1690); Harrach town palace (*c.* 1690); Schönbrunn garden palace (1692 or 1693); Liechtenstein town palace (1694); Eugen's garden palace (1693); Eugen's town palace (1694); Mansfeld-Fondi (now Schwarzenberg) garden palace (1697); Caprara town palace (1698 or earlier); Batthyany-Schönborn town palace (1698). For the dates see B. Grimschitz, *Wiener Barockpaläste*, 1947.

[2] See Chapter XIX on Eugen as patron of the arts.

CHAPTER IV

1697–1701: ZENTA AND
AN INTERLUDE OF PEACE

WHILST THE war against Louis XIV had been proceeding in desultory fashion, the Turks had experienced one of those convulsions of activity which punctuated their protracted demise. From his own complex mixture of territorial greed and Christian duty, the Emperor Leopold had refused to make peace with them in the high-tide of the Habsburg advance eastwards which followed immediately after the capture of Belgrade in September 1688. The Ottoman forces, under the inspiring leadership of the Grand Vizier, Mustafa Pasha—named Fazil, the Virtuous—had recaptured much of the land they had lost to the Empire in the previous decade, and had even retaken Belgrade. True, the Russians, who had joined the Holy League a decade earlier, won their first victory against the Turks in 1697 and succeeded in taking Azov from them. But the Ottomans were meanwhile full of lively plans for advancing west into Europe. The new Sultan, Mustapha II, was to take command for the ambitious 1697 campaign later that same year.

There was much discussion about who should be appointed to command the Imperial armies. Caprara was clearly not up to it. Eugen had already won a considerable reputation in Italy as a thrustful commander, but he was only thirty-three and the Emperor considered him too young. However, the President of the Imperial War Council, Graf Ernst Rüdiger Starhemberg,[1] was strongly in favour of appointing him. 'I do not know anyone,' he told the Emperor, 'who

---

[1] Ernst Rüdiger Starhemberg, 1638–1701; he distinguished himself at the siege of Vienna, 1683, and became one of the most eminent officers in the Austrian Army.

has more understanding, experience, industry and zeal for the Emperor's service, who has a more generous and unselfish disposition, or who holds the love of the soldiers in a higher degree than the Prince.'[1] Typically, Leopold at first temporized, making the Elector of Saxony the Supreme Commander, with Eugen in an indeterminate position alongside him. But the Elector was suddenly made King of Poland and therefore had to renounce his command and leave Hungary, with the result that the Emperor was finally induced to agree to Eugen's appointment, though only on the condition that he 'should act with extreme caution and . . . forego all risks and avoid engaging the enemy unless he has overwhelming strength and is practically certain of being completely victorious'.[2] With this helpful directive Eugen was ordered in mid-1697 to proceed to the front as Supreme Commander. The situation was critical since, with the help of French money, the Turkish Army had been rendered much more efficient, and the Sultan was known to have every intention of reconquering Hungary. This was Eugen's first truly independent command. No longer was he to be thwarted by the excessive caution of Carafa or Caprara, or by the deviations of Victor Amadeus. The army which he took over at Esseg was in deplorable condition: pay was in arrears, clothing in rags, munitions and supplies wasting. But he quickly set about making improvements and sought to restore confidence. On being informed that the forces numbered 31,142, he said: 'Thank you for the information. I am the 31,143rd, and we will soon be more.'[3] The self-assured staccato of his tone sent a wave of hope through all ranks. As soon as he had started pulling his forces together, he wrote to the Emperor: 'Let the enemy but allow me a few days in which to assemble Your Majesty's soldiers and then, with God's help, I will confound his purpose.'[4] The indulgence was granted and in a matter of weeks he had refashioned the army.

In the second week of September 1697, Eugen learnt from a prisoner whom he threatened with death should he refuse to speak, that the Sultan had thrown a bridge of sixty ships across the river Theiss at Zenta in order to take his army eastwards into Transylvania. By the afternoon of September 11 a good part of the Turkish cavalry

---

[1] Report by Graf Starhemberg to the Emperor, 15.3.1697, A. Arneth, op. cit., I, p. 96.

[2] Instruction to Eugen from the Imperial War Council, 5.7.1697, A. Arneth, *Das Leben des Kaiserlichen Feldmarshalls Guido von Starhemberg*, 1853, pp. 187–8.

[3] Egon Caesar Conte Corti, *Der Edle Ritter*, 1941, p. 36.

[4] *Feldzüge des Prinzen Eugen von Savoyen, herausgeben von der Abteilung für Kriegsgeschichte des k.k. Kriegsarchivs Wien*, 1876–92, I Ser., II, p. 132.

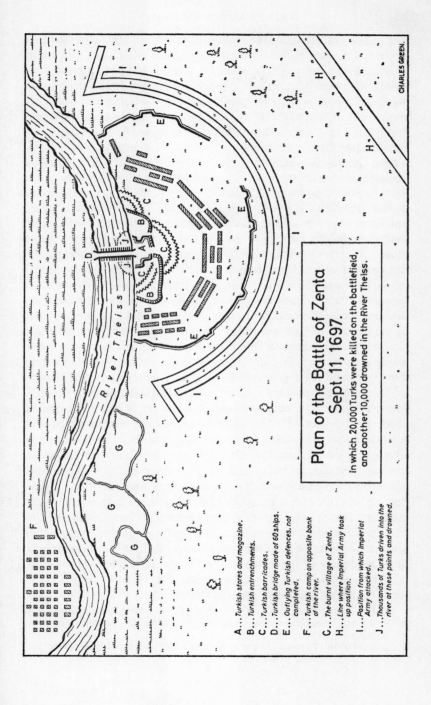

Plan of the Battle of Zenta
Sept. 11, 1697.

In which 20,000 Turks were killed on the battlefield, and another 10,000 drowned in the River Theiss.

A ... Turkish stores and magazine.
B ... Turkish entrenchments.
C ... Turkish barricades.
D ... Turkish bridge made of 60 ships.
E ... Outlying Turkish defences, not completed.
F ... Turkish camp on opposite bank of the river.
G ... The burnt village of Zenta.
H ... Line where Imperial Army took up position.
I ... Position from which Imperial Army attacked.
J ... Thousands of Turks driven into the river at these points and drowned.

CHARLES GREEN.

had already crossed, but the remainder and all the infantry were still on the right bank of the river, on the western, or Eugen's side, and it would obviously take many hours for them all to be got across. They were entrenched in a semi-circle round the bridge. Eugen, now within striking distance of the river, saw his chance. His forces were still some distance from Zenta, and there were only a few hours of daylight left; but if the Turks were left unharassed they would be able to take the whole army over under cover of dark and proceed into Transylvania. On the other hand, with the enemy divided in two, and most of their cavalry, without which the janissaries would not fight, on the further side of the water, if he could but drive his army on and attack before nightfall . . .! Although his men had already done a forced march of over ten hours that day, Eugen gave the order to advance and then galloped ahead to see the scene at first hand. He spotted how, just above the bridge on the near side of the river, the water was shallow with a sandbank leading up to dry land. There were two hours of daylight left by the time his army had reached battle position before the semi-circle of Turkish defences. He ordered one wing of his army under Guido Starhemberg[1] to deliver a left hook to the enemy and to reach the sandbank, from which they should be able to penetrate the Turkish camp from the river side. This stratagem took the Turks completely by surprise and was carried out to perfection. Meanwhile, the centre and right wing under Prince Commercy and Graf Siegbert Heister respectively were ordered to attack. Eugen placed himself in the centre so as to be able to gallop wherever he was most needed. The janissaries, assaulted on all sides and confined within a small space, cast their firearms aside and started thrashing about with the sword. But nothing could stop the squeeze of the Imperial pincers. Defence turned to retreat, retreat to rout, rout to slaughter. Some of the janissaries tried to flee across the bridge where they were cut off by Eugen's left. Others rushed headlong into the river and were drowned in such numbers that in the words of Eugen's report, his 'men could stand on the dead Turkish bodies as if on an island'.[2] Eugen's forces gave no quarter so that few prisoners were taken. 'A frightful bloodbath' is how he described the battlefield, adding that his soldiers were 'so worked up that they showed no mercy, even though many Turkish officers and bashibazouks promised them money if they would spare

[1] Guido Starhemberg, 1657–1737. Cousin of Ernst Rüdiger Starhemberg (see p. 39), he was probably the ablest Austrian officer of his day. For his relationship with Eugen see Chapter IX, p. 128.
[2] Report to the Emperor on the operations September 9–15, 1697, *Feldzüge*, 1 Ser., II, Suppl.—Heft, p. 52.

them'.[1] The Turkish army was annihilated: altogether 20,000 were killed, and more than another 10,000 were drowned. Less than 1,000 reached the safety of the further bank of the river Theiss. The Sultan himself had fled. The Grand Vizier and four other Viziers, the Governors of Anatolia and Bosnia, and numerous high functionaries and officials were killed—some by their own disenchanted troops, for many of the janissaries mutinied in the midst of the fight. The battle only ended at nightfall, 'as if,' in Eugen's account to the Emperor, 'the sun had been unwilling to go down before it had witnessed the full triumph of your Imperial Majesty's glorious arms'.[2] Eugen's losses were only three hundred killed and two hundred wounded. The next day, the fourteenth anniversary of Eugen's first encounter with the Turks beneath the walls of Vienna, the Imperial army crossed the Theiss and took over the Ottoman camp. The captured booty included 9,000 wagons, 60,000 camels, 1,500 head of cattle, 700 horses, as well as quantities of money and arms. Eugen also took possession of the Great Seal which the Grand Vizier had worn round his neck as a symbol of his absolute authority and which had never before fallen into enemy hands.

The battle of Zenta revealed Eugen's tactical skill, his capacity for sudden and bold decision, and his ability to inspire his men to exertions far beyond their normal powers of endurance. In terms of history it marked a turning-point in the rise and fall of Turkish power. According to the leading historian of the Ottoman Empire, 'the battle of Zenta sealed victory on the side of the Austrian Empire . . . and marked irrevocably the decline of the Ottoman Empire'.[3] There is no doubt that, though they made several come-backs later, the Turks were on the decline in Europe from Zenta on. But the question for us is how far this was due to Eugen himself or to what extent Zenta and his other victories against the Turks were really caused by a decline in Ottoman fighting power.

It must be recognized that serious flaws had become apparent in the Ottoman army and that they had been shown to be not invincible even before Eugen took command against them. The janissaries were less disciplined than formerly and there was always a possibility that they might flee in panic or mutiny. According to a contemporary historian of the Ottoman army, there was a well-known saying that 'the janissaries were renowned for their good eyes and limbs, the

[1] Report to the Emperor on the operations September 9–15, 1697, *Feldzüge*, 1 Ser., II, Suppl.—Heft, p. 52.

[2] *Feldzüge*, loc. cit.

[3] J. De Hammer, op. cit., XII, p. 425.

former to keep an eye on the unreliable cavalry who were prone to take flight, the latter to enable them to follow'.[1] The organization and training of the Turkish army were out of date and this was not remedied until the renegade Comte de Bonneval[2] instigated reforms in the 1730s. Finally, the Turks were much slower than the West in introducing new techniques, a handicap which became more serious against Eugen in the later battles of the eighteenth century. Thus they were behindhand in equipping their musketeers with flintlocks in place of the old matchlocks. The firing mechanism of the flintlock was much quicker, simpler and more reliable than the matchlock. The powder was ignited by a flint making a spark instead of by a smouldering match which was frequently extinguished before it could do its work at the touch-hole. The rate of fire was almost doubled and could easily reach two rounds a minute. Even when the janissaries had been equipped with the flintlock, most of the auxiliaries continued to rely on the old weapons: sabres, javelins, bows and arrows and lances. In artillery, their attempts to make progress by firing small cannons from the backs of camels were merely comical—except to the camels.

But allowing for these shortcomings the Ottoman army was still a very formidable enemy in Eugen's day. It was awe-inspiring, firstly, by reason of sheer size. It was the biggest army in Europe. The tendency of the janissaries to mutiny was in a way a reflection of their sense of power, of their independence; it was the other side of the coin to their *esprit de corps*. It did not make them any less frightening to a foreign foe. Indeed, their fanatical devotion to their twin gods of religion and loot continued to make them almost irresistible in the heat of battle, provided their tails were up. There was another incentive which operated throughout the Ottoman army. To about every three hundred men the authorities appointed one executioner to inflict summary punishment; it can readily be imagined what an encouragement his presence on the battlefield must have afforded. The Ottoman forces were skilful and resilient in defence of the fortresses upon which so much of their power in eastern Europe had depended for so long. They were also most economical in their victualling.[3] But the élan

[1] Le Comte de Marsigli, *L'Etat Militaire De L'Empire Ottoman*, 1732, II, p. 197.
[2] See Chapter XVIII.
[3] The Tartars were the most handily fed of all the nationalities represented in the Ottoman army. The only provisions carried by their soldiery were cheeses made of mares' milk. As soon as they were made, these cheeses were buried in the ground and kept there for six months, until they had become as hard as stone. When required for use the Tartars scraped a little into a pan of water, stirred it with their finger, and then swallowed it. They had no other nourishment.

of their massed rushes was probably their most unique and frightening tactic. It needed Eugen's cool brain and sharp eye to resist these multitudinous Turkish onslaughts: to preserve battle order in the mad scurry of fighting, and to inspire the Imperial forces with calm confidence both to resist the enemy's charge, and then, when the mercury of battle had changed, to go over to a firm and disciplined counter-attack. Some measure of the difference he personally made can be gauged from the disastrous results which occurred when the Imperial forces confronted the Turks soon after his death.

There is one other general comment to which the battle of Zenta gives rise. Most historians have accepted and disseminated the view that warfare at the end of the seventeenth and beginning of the eighteenth century had become less barbaric and more dignified than ever before: casualties were fewer in proportion to participants, looting was more restrained, and prisoners and civilians were to some extent protected by the observance of certain rules of war. All this may have been valid for western Europe,[1] though as will be shown later there were plenty of exceptions even in the War of the Spanish Succession, which is often singled out for its comparative decorousness.[2] But it was decidedly not true about the Turkish wars where no holds were barred and where the suffering inflicted on soldiers and civilians, both directly and indirectly, was prodigious.

By the time the Turks had been defeated at Zenta it was too late in the year for Austria to hope to recapture Belgrade. Eugen, therefore, decided to take a raiding force south into Bosnia. He marched seven thousand men over enormous mountains and through dense forest and deep gorges. They mopped up various castles en route. The Christian inhabitants welcomed them, but the Turks all withdrew to Sarajevo, at that time one of the richest trading centres of eastern Europe, a sprawling city with over a hundred magnificent mosques. When Eugen arrived there at the end of October 1697, he sent two soldiers forward into the city, carrying terms of surrender. The Turks fired on them, killing one. This so incensed Eugen that he ordered the city to be plundered and then burnt to the ground. Mention has already been made of one atrocity to which Eugen was party; and this further procedure marks him out as not above the code of cruelty of his age; though doubtless expediency required such behaviour if he was not to suffer the disfavour of his own none-too-civilized troops.

[1] See M. S. Anderson, *Europe in the Eighteenth Century*, 1961, p. 131.
[2] M. Bernard, *The Growth of Laws and Usages of War*, Oxford Essays, 1856, pp. 103, 112.

That was the end of the campaign for the year. Back in Vienna in the winter of 1697–8, Eugen was given a tumultuous welcome as the greatest of all victors over the Turks. The Emperor bestowed on him a richly jewelled sword and a property in Hungary. A medal was struck in his honour—the first of many—commemorating his triumph at Zenta. But the applause was not unanimous. He had made many enemies in Vienna. The gusto, audacity and drive which carried him headlong forward in the open sea of battle were ensnaring qualities at home, catching him up inextricably in the meshes of intrigue and envy at the Imperial court. He never sought to temper his criticism or mask his advice. He had none of the Duke of Marlborough's art of insinuation. He was quite incapable of suggesting rather than stating, of implanting furtively his own idea in another's mind. He never realized that

> *Men must be taught as if you taught them not,*
> *And things unknown proposed as things forgot.*

His colours were black and white, not shaded, and, to confound the prophets and infuriate the foe, they nearly always won. It was this success, of course, that caused the greatest consternation at court. How could this upstart foreigner achieve such glory? Were the military victories against the terrible Turk really due to him? Some suggested that the glory of Zenta was due to a miracle, others to the delusion of the Turks, or to anything except the courage and dexterity of the Imperial Commander-in-Chief. There was even a story carefully disseminated then, and much recounted later, that the Emperor had sent Eugen orders before Zenta not to give battle under any circumstances, with the result that when he ultimately came in triumph to Vienna, he was received most frigidly by Leopold, and even put under arrest prior to being court-martialled for disobedience. It was only because of the enthusiasm of the multitude for Eugen, so the story runs, that the Emperor thought better of it and refrained from proceeding with the trial. Although this story is spurious, the fact that it was widely spread abroad and believed reveals the atmosphere of intrigue and false witness, the monumental pettiness and back-biting at the Imperial court. Moreover, there was this much substance in the rumour, that the secret Imperial War Council, when it took note of the outcome of the battle of Zenta, apparently declared Eugen's conduct to have been a matter for praise rather than reproach —a tacit admission that there had been talk of the latter, for otherwise why mention it? But such tales undoubtedly originated more in the minds of their would-be believers, Eugen's jealous rivals, than with Leopold who had, after all, shown his true feelings by the bestowal of the spangled sword and the Hungarian estate.

That Eugen was still in Imperial favour is also illustrated by a detail from the contemporary life of the court. In the summer of 1698 Peter the Great paid a ceremonial visit to Vienna. The highlight of the hospitality offered him was a fancy-dress party given in the Favorita Palace, which was transformed for the purpose into a tavern. This kind of entertainment, in which the master and mistress of the house installed themselves behind a buffet and acted the part of mine host and hostess, was much in vogue in Vienna at the time. On this occasion the Emperor impersonated the wirt or landlord, and the Empress the landlady of the inn. Eugen was cast in the honoured rôle of waiter to the Imperial tavern-keeper.

Zenta had put an end to the immediate Turkish threat to Christendom. The Peace of Ryswick concluded between the Allies and Louis XIV, shortly after Zenta, enabled some of the Imperial troops to be released for service in the East. Leopold wanted to continue the fight and retake Belgrade. But the old paralysis of penury once again halted the Monarchy and there was neither the means nor the will to renew hostilities in the following season. The Imperial troops were, as usual, badly fed and supplied, and with no immediate prospect of glory or loot ahead of them, their morale sank to the point of mutiny. The Ottoman soldiers, too, were heartily fed up with fighting, particularly after the reverses suffered against Eugen. There was, in fact, a common antipathy to war, and in this mood, with England, and to a lesser extent Holland, acting as intermediaries, peace talks were opened between Turkey, Austria, Venice, Poland and Russia at the little town of Carlowitz on the Danube, opposite to Peterwardein. It was a dramatic occasion. Here for the first time in history the Turks were prepared to sit down and negotiate with a consortium of European powers; and it was the first occasion in which they accepted the mediation of European states. Eugen played no part in the long negotiations which were notable for the consummate tact displayed by the English intermediary, William Paget, in preventing the Russian representative—a worthy exponent of the contemporary manners of his country—from irrevocably offending the subtle and sophisticated Turkish representative, the Greek Alexander Mavrocordato. Peace was ultimately signed at Carlowitz on January 26, 1699; it was the first favourable peace treaty ever to be wrung from the Turks by Christian powers.

By this peace the Porte was made to renounce various tributes hitherto levied on the Monarchy and Venice. More important, the Emperor recovered possession of Transylvania and most of Hungary. Venice acquired the Morea and Dalmatia. Thus the seal was set upon the achievements of sixteen years of war. The flood-tide of the Ottoman advance had at last been turned back. Not only had the immediate menace to Vienna been extirpated, but the Empire's centre of gravity had been shifted eastwards out of Germany; and, for the time being, the French had to abandon their favourite game of ruffing the Empire through the Ottoman Alliance. Austria had, however, given one hostage to fortune in the Peace of Carlowitz. She had failed to carry Russia with her in the need to make peace. The Treaty rankled long with Tsar Peter, who had wanted the Holy League to continue the war in the East.

Eugen was glad of the chance afforded by peace to cultivate his newly-acquired taste in architecture. The land in Hungary given him by the Emperor, which lay between the Danube and the Drave, yielded him a good income. He was suddenly a man of means. He paid off all his old debts in France, and bought Ráckeve estate on the island of Czepel on the Danube just below Budapest. Here he commissioned the architect, Johann Lucas von Hildebrandt, to build him a palace.[1] If, henceforth, Eugen was to devote to this side of his life almost as much enthusiasm as to soldiering, there was to be nothing mutually exclusive about them. Like Marlborough, he carried his building schemes about in his head even when at war, and frequently dealt with correspondence about them at the front. Thus we find him in North Italy in April 1702 receiving a letter from Hildebrandt written in Italian asking whether the wall in the Belvedere garden should be put up *a traverso o non*.[2] His palaces and the gardens were studded with allegorical reminders of battle: helmet-crested putti, warriors and weapons in stone and stucco, reliefs of Venus bestowing arms upon Aeneas, and Turkish soldiers duly fettered in stone.

War was not the sole theme of decoration. In the Belvedere,[3] his bedroom ceiling, painted by Martin Altomontes, depicted the legend

[1] Letters from Johann Lucas von Hildebrandt in S. Davari, *Vienna Jahrbuch*, 1895, XVI. There was one in Italian to Eugen discussing two alternative designs, assuming a considerable technical knowledge on the part of the Prince. See B. Grimschitz, *Johann Lucas von Hildebrandt*, 1959, pp. 51–55, see also Chapter XIX for account of Schloss Ráckeve.

[2] B. Grimschitz, op. cit., p. 92.

[3] For fuller account of the Belvedere see Chapter XIX.

of Selene and Endymion, though this did not betoken, still less induce, a mood of uncelibate ease. He seems to have been as far removed as ever from domesticity. But the absence of any private papers and, still more, the tantalizing discretion of his friends, make it largely a matter of guesswork to reconstruct the inner content of his being—his *lebensgefühl*—at this stage of his life around the turn of the century. Since the abortive Spanish match, his name had appeared amongst the suitors of a German Princess, Franziska von Sachsen-Lauenburg, and in 1690 they were even to be found staying under the same roof in Bohemia. But the affair did not prosper. 'On the one side there seemed to be a lack of *empressement* and on the other an equal absence of inclination,' was the comment of an observer. The occasion is only worth recording because it seems to have been his last effort, albeit half-hearted, at marriage.

He had not seen his mother for some time, and showed no inclination to do so. The vacuum in his emotional life left by her evanescence was increasingly filled by his growing passion for beautiful things coupled with a kind of collective, but none the less personal and deep-felt, almost sentimental, paternalism for the soldiers serving under him, though there is no record of any individual with whom he was particularly involved at this stage.

Meanwhile his links with his brothers and sisters, and with France, were becoming remorselessly weaker. Of his four brothers, only one, Louis Thomas, was still alive. His fourth brother, Emanuel, had died aged fourteen in 1676; his third, Louis Julius, as already mentioned,[1] had died on active service in 1683; and his second brother, Philippe, exiled after an adventurous life as priest, soldier, and Venetian sea-captain, wandered about Europe, became involved in England in a duel over his aunt, and in an affair with the Duchess of Portsmouth, and eventually died of smallpox in 1693. The one survivor, Louis Thomas, the Duc de Soissons, after being ostracized by Louis XIV, and having gone from country to country in search of a career, turned up a mendicant on Eugen's doorstep in Vienna in March 1699. 'Here he is,' reported the French Ambassador, the Duc de Villars, 'at a court in which his younger brother is held in the greatest esteem, and has built himself a splendid palace, whilst he himself, through no fault but his own, has fallen on evil times and does not even know where to lay his head.'[2] A few days after his arrival in Vienna, Louis Thomas called on Villars, confessed the desperate plight

[1] See Chapter I, p. 11.
[2] *Mémoires du Maréchal de Villars*, 1884, I, p. 221.

he was in, due to Louis XIV's displeasure, and offered to expiate his errors in a French prison. But the French King, to whom the Ambassador referred the plea, refused to have him back in France on any terms. However, with Eugen's help, he joined the Imperial army at the outset of the War of the Spanish Succession only to be killed a few weeks later, on August 24, 1702, in action against the French. His wife, the beautiful Urania, for whom Louis XIV had had such an infatuation,[1] betook herself to a nunnery in Turin, only to suffer the fate of all her family, banishment—for tactless talk—following which she moved to France where she lived in complete retirement, and died there in 1717. She had a daughter[2] and three sons. Eugen fastened upon them his ambitions for posterity. Like Marlborough, he had a strong dynastic sense. Although childless, he cherished the hope of bequeathing to a member of his family and hence to history both his name and the undivided inheritance of his elaborately amassed property—yet all in vain, as we shall see.

Of Eugen's three sisters, all born after him, the youngest had died in childhood, and the other two, Marie Jeanne-Baptiste and Louise Philiberte, known respectively as Mademoiselle de Soissons and Mademoiselle de Carignan, led untidy and unhappy lives. After their mother Olympia's flight they had been left, like Eugen, to the neglectful care of their aunt and grandmother. They were presented at court. Before long their inherited instincts ran them into trouble of truly Olympian proportions. Banned from court circles for their dissolute behaviour, they turned the Hôtel Soissons into a gambling den and bawdy house, so notorious as to call forth a closing order from the authorities. Neither sister was beautiful, but the elder, Mademoiselle de Soissons, had large beautiful eyes and, though lame, had inherited some of her mother's talent for hot pursuit. She was alleged at one time to be producing a bastard child a year without being able to specify the fathers of many of them. It is hardly necessary to add that in due course she became the object of a duel and was expelled from France. She joined her mother in Brussels. Olympia thought so little of her that she tried to shut her up in a nunnery. However the 'unworthiest of all creatures' (as she described her daughter) escaped, and, at a time when her brother was having honours showered upon him in Vienna for his victory at Zenta, she eloped to Geneva with a renegade priest with whom she lived unhappily until her premature death in 1705. Of the other sister, Mademoiselle de Carignan, there is little

[1] See Chapter I, p. 10.
[2] Princess Anna Victoria, who became Eugen's heir, see Chapter XXI, p. 290.

4. A new piece of Turkish artillery which was to prove purely comical in its effect

5. Letter in Eugen's hand

6. Eugen's signature in a mixture of languages

information after her early salacious years in Paris; but it is known that she left France, lived for a time in a convent in Savoy, and died in 1722.

At the turn of the century, then, we see Eugen, in mid-career and nearing his fortieth birthday, vouchsafed a breathing-space, between the defeat of the Turks at Zenta and the outbreak of the War of the Spanish Succession, in which to pursue his new-found interests. He is already a most distinguished soldier with such a reputation that Peter the Great, having studied in person the art of shipbuilding at Amsterdam and Deptford, is anxious to seek him out in Vienna and learn at first hand something of the science of war. For though, unlike Peter, no manifold innovator eager to experiment with new industrial techniques, he is nevertheless modern in his approach to fighting, and in his interests in philosophy and the ideas of the Newtonian age. Compared with the obscurantists and alchemists of the Imperial court, he is a herald of the Enlightenment, and nowhere more so than in his dealings with the ordinary soldiers and in his attitude towards the peasants and the soil itself of the newly-won lands in Hungary. He is most anxious to establish himself as a good landlord, and by careful husbandry, to restore to the earth some of the wealth filched from it during the Ottoman occupation. By now a wealthy man with a strongly developed sense of acquisition and taste, the possessor of a new country, new allegiance and new property, he is nevertheless without family ties, without personal commitments, his considerable emotional feelings sublimated, his attentions fastened upon the ideas of war and beauty personified in his soldiers and his palaces.

CHAPTER V

THE WAR OF THE SPANISH
SUCCESSION: THE EMPIRE ALONE

FOR MANY years before the death on November 1, 1700, of the childless, feeble King Charles II of Spain the problem of who was to succeed to his inheritance had tormented the rulers of Europe. For many years, too, the whole Spanish State had been as moribund as its King: the treasury bare, the army demoralized, the fleet rotten, the entire authority inert save for the ubiquitous Inquisition and the elaborate court ceremonial. Yet the territories of the Spanish Empire were still enormous, exceeding those of Rome when Rome was at the zenith of its power.[1] The very size of the inheritance may, of course, explain why Europe's statesmen took such pains to try to arrange an ordered disposal in advance and why they failed so abysmally. In retrospect there seems to be something clownlike rather than statesmanlike about their elaborately unsuccessful efforts: first, their exultant recognition of the obvious, then their solemn collaboration in constructing successive contrivances each of which collapsed ignominiously.

There were three candidates for the Spanish crown: the French claimant, Philip, Duke of Anjou; the Austrian claimant, the Archduke Charles; and the Bavarian claimant, the Electoral Prince Joseph Ferdinand of Bavaria.[2] Neither France nor Austria could tolerate the

[1] The European possessions included Milan, Naples, Sicily, Sardinia and the Balearic Islands, as well as the Spanish Netherlands and Spain itself; the overseas possessions were vaster still, comprising the Philippines, the Canaries, Cuba, Mexico, Florida, Panama, and the great continent of South America, except for the Guianas and Brazil.

[2] The Duke of Anjou was the grandson of Louis XIV and Maria Teresa; the latter was Charles II's elder sister. Upon marriage, she had renounced all claim

The Spanish Succession   THE THREE CLAIMANTS: 1698—1700

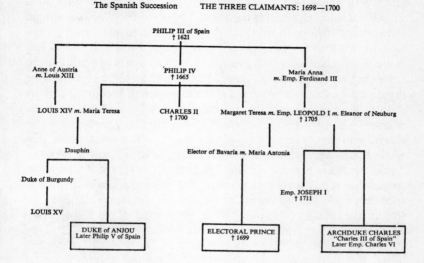

idea of the massive aggrandisement of the territory or influence of the other. England and the Dutch Republic were not prepared to see the commerce of the Spanish Indies and Americas monopolized by France[1]; nor, for time-honoured strategic reasons, could they suffer French domination of the Spanish Netherlands; besides which, both states, being Protestant, deplored the prospect of a union of two Catholic powers.

Louis was in a mood for compromise, the Emperor not. Unknown to Leopold, therefore, the French opened negotiations with the English and Dutch for a partition of the Spanish inheritance. In the Partition Treaty signed by the three powers in the autumn of 1698, it was agreed that the Spanish crown and bulk of the Spanish Empire should go, as a reward for weakness, to the least powerful candidate,

to the Spanish inheritance provided that her dowry was fully paid, a condition that had never been fulfilled. The Archduke Charles was the second son of the Emperor Leopold I of Austria, who was a first cousin of Charles II, both being the grandchildren of King Philip III of Spain. The Electoral Prince was the grandson of the Emperor Leopold I by his first marriage to Charles II's younger sister Margaret Teresa.

[1] For some time the Spaniards had been letting English and Dutch ships conduct trade under Spanish colours between Cadiz and the Latin-American colonies.

the Electoral Prince of Bavaria; the other claimants being compensated with slices of Spanish territory, the Maritime powers with valuable trading rights. But the sudden death of the Electoral Prince in February 1699 stultified this solution—which would anyway have been repellent to Leopold since it gave France Italian territory. The horse-trading had to start all over again, with now only two candidates.

By the Second Partition Treaty of March 1700, signed by the same three powers, Louis XIV agreed that the Austrian Archduke Charles should become King of Spain, the Spanish Netherlands and the overseas colonies, though on the condition that they would never be united with the Austrian dominions, and on the understanding that all the Spanish possessions in Italy would go to the French candidate.[1] Again Vienna expostulated. The signature of the Treaty of Carlowitz, concluding the Austro-Turkish war, had given the Emperor greater confidence. He saw no reason at all why his son should be made to forfeit the Italian territories, the most coveted of all the Spanish possessions. His intransigence has been treated with contempt by British historians. 'It was characteristic of Leopold,' so a modern writer had judged it, 'that his obstinacy was not accompanied by activity: though his refusal to accept the treaty was senseless, unless he was prepared to fight for what he wanted, he did nothing to strengthen his forces, and for this omission his chronic irresolution was even more responsible than his chronic penury.'[2] But there is a little more to be said for the Emperor's attitude than that. He had a purpose in dawdling. He believed that, given time, Charles II's German wife would induce the King to leave the whole inheritance to the Austrian candidate. It was a hope, albeit an ill-based one. For in placing such confidence in Anna of Neuburg, the Emperor was forgetting the enormous influence of the French on the Spanish court. True, the Spanish grandees had no objection in theory to the Austrian solution; their only concern was the fulfilment of their proud wish that the inheritance should pass undivided; but they believed, as a matter of practice and geography, that the French could and would enforce their claim more surely than Vienna. Meanwhile, the French took advantage of Leopold's delay to play upon the pride and anxiety of the Spanish court so successfully that Charles II, now more than half out of his mind and at long last on his death-bed, was inveigled into signing a will which made the Duke of Anjou his sole and universal

[1] France was to give Milan to the Duke of Lorraine, in exchange for Lorraine.
[2] M. A. Thomson, *Louis XIV and the Origins of the War of the Spanish Succession*, Transactions of the Royal Historical Society, 1954, IV, p. 111.

heir. A fortnight later, on November 1, 1700, Charles died. This put
Louis in a quandary. He could either accept the will and repudiate the
Partition Treaty, which would, of course, gravely displease the other
signatories of the Treaty, as well as the Emperor, or he could accept
the Treaty and repudiate the will, which would also infuriate Leopold
and antagonize the Spaniards. It must have looked to him as though,
whichever choice he made, he would be bound to have war with the
Emperor. The balance of advantage seemed to lie in favour of the
will, which Louis, after some heart-searching, decided to accept. At
Versailles, in the presence of the Spanish Ambassador, he proclaimed
his grandson, the Duke of Anjou, King of Spain. These were his
fateful words: 'His birth called him to this crown. The Spanish nation
has wished it and has demanded it of me: it was the command of
heaven; I have granted it with joy.' Then turning to his grandson he
said: 'Be a good Spaniard, that is now your first duty, but remember
that you are born a Frenchman to bring about the union of the two
nations; that is the way to ensure both their happiness and the peace
of Europe.'[1]

But despite this terrifying revelation that henceforth France and
Spain might be one, the English Tories, who had a majority in Parliament, were unperturbed. Their fitness to judge the national interest
had been pellucidly demonstrated only a few years earlier by their
proposal to disenfranchise all the Huguenot refugees in England and
to exclude from office all men of foreign birth. Now, having reduced
the army to seven thousand men in the wake of the Treaty of
Ryswick, the Tories were disposed to swallow Louis' glib assurance
that his grandson would never become king of France as well as of
Spain, and they seemed ready to throw over the Partition Treaty—
which had been negotiated by the hated William without reference
either to his ministers or to Parliament— and to accept the Spanish
will. England, therefore, joined the Dutch in recognizing the Duke
of Anjou as King Philip V of Spain. Spain herself had already done so.

The Emperor was desperate. He had been left in the lurch by his
allies of the Nine Years' War. The iniquitous Louis had got his way
once more. Even Leopold's son-in-law, the Elector of Bavaria, who
was also Governor of the Spanish Netherlands, veered to the French
side, as did the Elector of Cologne; besides which, the Duke of
Savoy was showing tiresome and unnatural loyalty to the wrong side.[2]

[1] *Mémories du Duc de Saint-Simon*, op. cit., II, pp. 397–8.
[2] The Duke of Savoy's territories, comprising Savoy and Piedmont, were of
great strategic importance. Lying athwart the Alpine passes, their control decided

His younger daughter had married the Duke of Anjou; his elder, the Duke's brother Burgundy, heir-presumptive to the throne of France. In comparison, the Austrian dominions could offer nothing so tempting. However, Leopold was spurred on to bold activity by Prince Eugen, who perceived both the dangers and the opportunities. There was a grave risk of the consolidation of the Bourbon hold upon Italy—upon Milan, Naples and Sicily. But looked at more adventurously, these territories might also be an alluring prize for Austria. They were indeed the only part of the Spanish inheritance which the Emperor stood a chance of securing unaided. Besides, their acquisition could eventually lead to Habsburg mastery of the whole Italian peninsula. From this moment then, in the interests of both prudence and glory, and at Eugen's prompting, Italy became the cynosure of Imperial ambitions. The Emperor maintained that Milan, an Imperial fief, had in any case reverted to the Holy Roman Empire upon Charles II's death.[1] Without allies and with the country's finances in a characteristically parlous condition he could scarcely contemplate a full-scale war with France, but he believed that he could rightfully occupy Milan without involving himself directly in war with Louis XIV who would, even if he chose to resist, be acting merely as an agent of Philip of Spain.

After a meeting of the Imperial War Council, Leopold gave orders for the Habsburg army to enter the Duchy. However, there was much delay in mustering the troops and, before they were ready, the Duke of Savoy opened the Alpine passes to the French. In February 1701, Louis sent French forces to strengthen the Spanish garrisons in Milan, and to occupy the famous fortresses of the 'Quadrilateral': Verona and Legnago on the Adige, Peschiera and Mantua on the Mincio—control of which ensured strategic mastery of Italy. The Duke of Mantua admitted a French garrison which allowed the French Commander, Marshal Catinat, to assume control of the Po valley. Without any declaration of war both sides were poised to strike the first blow in the struggle for the Spanish Succession.

Eugen was in command of the 30,000 Habsburg troops. Serving under him were Graf Guido Starhemberg, the French-born, expatriate Prince Commercy, and General Börner, who had risen from the ranks

whether Austrian armies could invade southern France, or French forces could be deployed into northern Italy and hence threaten the Austrian dominions from the south. As already shown, Victor Amadeus' defection to the French side in 1696 had been instrumental in shifting the balance of opportunity against the Empire and in bringing about the Peace of Ryswick.

[1] O. Klopp, Der Fall des Hauses Stuart, 1875–88, IX, pp. 245–6.

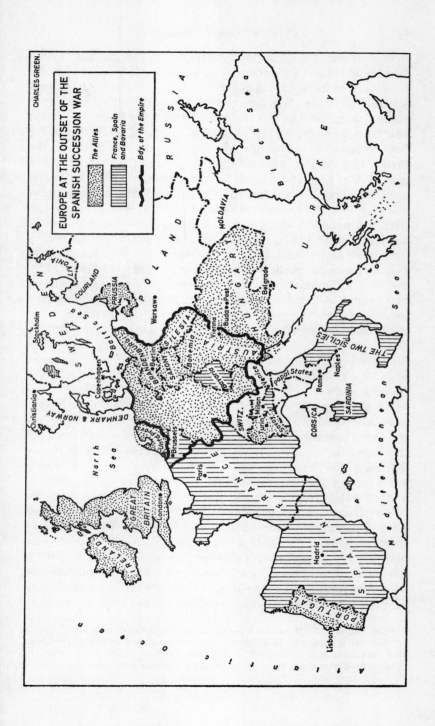

CHARLES GREEN.

EUROPE AT THE OUTSET OF THE
SPANISH SUCCESSION WAR

The Allies

France, Spain
and Bavaria

Bdy. of the Empire

to become one of the foremost artillerymen of Europe. 'Let us only start marching and we will soon find allies,' he declared ebulliently. But his first problem was not one of allies but of geography: how to get his army, which had been assembled at Rovereto in the South Tyrol, down through the Alps into the Italian plain, when the French army, 10,000 more numerous, were blocking the gorge of the Adige leading from Rovereto to Verona, the only apparent way into Italy.[1] To the French Commander, Marshal Catinat, sitting at the mouth of the pass, it must have seemed as if he had effectively bottled up Eugen in the mountains. According to local legend neither cart nor horse had ever been able to reach the plain by any other route, so savage were the mountains either side. But Eugen knew the local legend too and realized the cover that it offered. Simulating preparations for a frontal attack on Catinat, he decided to take his army over the mountain tops eastwards and to make for Vicenza. On May 26, 1701, this Hannibalian march began. Fifteen pairs of oxen were yoked to each cannon. Altogether 6,000 horse and 16,000 men clambered their way with their artillery over Monte Baldo into Italy. In the course of the journey Eugen left his name linked eternally with the region: a mountain spring from which he drank is called to this day the Fontana del Principe Eugenio. So effective was the deception that, as late as May 30, Catinat was issuing warnings of an attack from the north down the Adige.

No sooner had his army debouched into the plain than Eugen, nonchalantly violating Venetian neutrality, caught the enemy on the wrong foot twice again. At first Catinat was encouraged to think that he would strike west for Milan; so he manned all the fortresses defending the river crossings.[2] Instead Eugen began to march south giving the impression that he was heading for Ferrara and ultimately Naples. His aim was to force Catinat to spread his troops thinly over a wide front and then to attack him at the weakest point. Catinat again complied. He stretched his army in small detachments on a line of over sixty miles. Eugen then turned suddenly west and pounced upon Catinat's extreme right at Carpi. He inflicted a jab sufficient to shake Catinat's nerve and make him withdraw his whole line westward over the Mincio. Eugen had his horse shot under him and suffered a slight bullet wound, but this did not deter him from

[1] See map at end of book for Eugen's campaigns in North Italy.
[2] Strategy in these wars of the seventeenth and eighteenth centuries in northern Italy was dominated by the need to seize and hold the rivers which flowed in parallel lines across the country—gridirons of defence and communication.

hurrying on immediately, this time northwards, thereby boxing the compass. As Colonel Malleson has put it in his military biography of Eugen, the Prince 'was one of those real generals who hold that a victory not followed up is a victory thrown away'.[1] Catinat, who was now joined by the Duke of Savoy, fled back over the Oglio, bent only on defending Milan. The failure of the French army to withstand the advance of the much smaller Imperial army under the contemptible 'petit Abbé' evoked strident indignation at Versailles. As Louis XIV himself admitted, he was now experiencing the pains of a self-inflicted blow. 'I sent you to Italy,' he wrote to Catinat, 'to fight a young and inexperienced Prince; he has flouted all the precepts of warfare. But you appear to be mesmerized, and let him do as he pleases.'[2]

Catinat was thereupon supplanted as supreme commander by Marshal François de Villeroi, a childhood friend of the King's, who was later to show a particularly suppliant knee before Madame de Maintenon at the French court. Saint-Simon has described him scathingly as, 'a man formed expressly to preside at a ball, to act as judge at a carousel, and if he had the voice, to sing at the opera the rôles of kings and heroes: very well suited to lead the fashions—but for nothing else.'[3] Like all sycophants, Villeroi was a terror to those under him; and like many bullies, which modern opinion has judged him to have been, he was no soldier. He was certainly very inferior to Catinat and his appointment, therefore, represented a gain for Eugen. The enemy forces, which included Spaniards and Savoyards as well as French, were strengthened until they numbered 50,000 men, against Eugen's 32,000. Villeroi joined his army on August 22. He was under orders to attack, and boasted that it would be an easy matter to drive Eugen clean out of Italy. By the end of August he had succeeded in taking his army east over the Oglio. Eugen, foreseeing the enemy's intention to attack at any price, had been content to dig himself in at the fortress at Chiari—a step dismissed by Villeroi in a message to the King as a 'proof of weakness'. On September 1 Villeroi attacked. Eugen had by now acquired a good deal of experience of the French army. He knew the fury of their initial attacks and how, if once checked, they seldom struck again with the same momentum. He gave his troops orders to lie flat on their chests behind their entrenchments and hold their fire until the French were right upon them. It worked to perfection. The French suffered a

---

[1] G. B. Malleson, *Prince Eugen of Savoy*, 1888, p. 69.
[2] Louis XIV to Catinat, 10.8.1701, *Feldzüge*, 1, Serg., III, p. 239.
[3] *Mémoires du Duc de Saint-Simon*, op. cit., XI, p. 219.

blood-bath, losing two thousand men and two hundred officers, against thirty-six dead and eighty-one wounded on the Imperial side, Villeroi was so disheartened that he abandoned all hope of renewing the attack, and in November, after continued harassment by Eugen's excellent cavalry, lead by Pálfly, Vaubonne and Colomba, withdrew over the Oglio. Eugen occupied most of the Duchy of Mantua before going into winter quarters. To Sir Winston Churchill, the audacity and success of the series of manœuvres and combats in which Eugen had been engaged since May suggest Napoleon's campaigns on the same battlegrounds a century later.[1]

To his contemporaries the effect was no less startling. The wavering states of Italy were encouraged to throw in their lot with the Empire; the Princess of Mirandola, with Eugen's help, was emboldened to expel the French forces from her territory; and the Duke of Modena opened the important fortress of Brescello to Imperial troops. But the influence was much more widespread. The English Government hoped that it would move the French to make concessions and avoid a general war. They had been badly shaken earlier in the year by the French occupation of the Spanish fortresses in the Low Countries. Louis had subsequently seized the Dutch barrier guaranteed by international treaty. All the fortifications so laboriously won by the Grand Alliance of a decade earlier as a bastion against further French expansion had fallen into Louis' hands without a shot being fired. Since then Louis, in defiance of the assurance he had solemnly given only a few months previously, formally recognized his grandson's right of succession to the French throne, thereby heralding the long-feared union of the two Empires. In July, King William and Marlborough had started negotiations at The Hague with the representatives of the Empire, Holland and all the other powers interested in the disposal of the Spanish Empire and fearful of further French aggrandisement. Most of the diplomatic work was left to Marlborough, who quickly won the confidence of the most influential official of the Dutch Republic, the calm, serene and determined Grand Pensionary, Heinsius.[2] Even now the Tories at home were still reluctant to break what they regarded as their special and pacific relationship with Louis. They commissioned Marlborough to enter into secret discussions with the French and Spanish representatives in a last-

[1] Winston S. Churchill, op. cit., I, p. 469.
[2] The Dutch Republic was a Federation of seven states, referred to as the United Provinces. Although power in theory was divided between the seven, in practice it was the leader, the Grand Pensionary of Holland, the richest of the provinces, who had the decisive say in foreign affairs.

minute attempt to save the peace, at the same time as he was negotiating a military alliance against the French. Weightier than any arguments available to him in this ticklish, not to say perfidious transaction, was the reception he expected French forces to continue to encounter at the hands of Eugen in Italy. '. . . we are here in very great expectation of the success that may be in Italy, being persuaded that the French will be reasonable, or otherwise, according to what shall happen there . . .' he wrote to London on August 12, 1701.[1]

But Louis showed no sign of reason despite the fiasco of Chiari. On the contrary he extorted from Spain the *asiento*, or right of importing negro slaves into Spanish America, a serious blow to British and Dutch commercial interests. On September 7 the Treaty of the Grand Alliance was signed pledging England, the Dutch Republic, and the Empire to impose their terms on France by force if peaceful means failed. The terms were moderate: tacit acquiescence in Philip V continuing to keep the Spanish throne and American possessions, provided the crowns of Spain and France were never united; the assignment to the Austrian Archduke of the Spanish possessions in the Netherlands (subject to certain security guarantees for the Dutch), Italy and the Mediterranean; no French participation in Spanish colonial trade which the English and Dutch were to monopolize. Thus, central to the Alliance was the clear intention to divide the Spanish inheritance. Agreement was also reached between the three powers on the number of soldiers to be put into the field against France if it should come to general war: the Empire promised 82,000, the Dutch 100,000, and the English 40,000 (of whom 18,000 were to be British, the remainder foreigners in English pay). It is difficult to exaggerate the importance of England's new-found power which, exerted in the form of money rather than men, was highly flexible and could be thrown in at will to pay for munitions, mercenaries or transports, or to provide loans to foreign governments. This financial ascendancy gave London a weight in the counsels of Europe which was out of all proportion to her actual military contribution to the war. The lack of the *nervus rei gerendae* had a correspondingly weakening effect on Austrian policy throughout.

The practice of hiring men was not limited to the allied side. The French entered the war with over 80,000 mercenaries—Irish, German, Italian, Walloon and, most numerous of all, Swiss. It was the custom for the hirer to pay compensation for mercenaries killed. We know from an agreement between England and Prussia concluded in 1709

[1] Winston S. Churchill, op. cit., I, p. 472.

that the rate for a dead man was twenty taler, for a dead horse, forty taler.[1]

If Eugen's successes in Italy were insufficient to make Louis accept the allied stipulations, the impact both of them and of the subsidies offered by England and Holland was instrumental in dispelling the doubts of many neutral countries and persuading them to rally to the allied side. During the winter 1701–2 several German states agreed to hire out their forces to the Grand Alliance, the most important being Hanover, the Palatinate, Münster, Hesse-Cassel and Baden. The prospect of succeeding to the English crown fortified the Elector George of Hanover in his decision. The Elector of Brandenburg committed himself further than the other German princes. He undertook to enter the field with ten thousand men, exacting as his pound of flesh his recognition as 'King in Prussia' by the Emperor. Unfortunately, two German states, Bavaria and Cologne, were to come down on the French side, and this was to add greatly to Eugen's strategic difficulties. Finally, the Danes guaranteed six thousand men to the Emperor in north Italy. But not even Louis' final insult to England upon the death of James II in September 1701, when he proclaimed the latter's son the rightful heir to the English crown—a flagrant breach of the Treaty of Ryswick—was enough to goad England into war. The forces of the Empire, led by Eugen, were to stand alone in the field against Louis for a whole year before the Allies finally took up arms beside them in May 1702.

[1] See footnote on p. 78 for conversion table. See also Max Braubach, *Die Bedeutung der Subsidien für die Politik im Spanischen Erbfolgekriege*, 1923, for general discussion of the subject.

CHAPTER VI

EUGEN'S CAMPAIGN
IN NORTH ITALY

EUGEN DID not much believe in the customary practice of allowing the battlefield to lie fallow during the winter. Lack of green fodder and the condition of the roads normally confined the campaigning season to the summer months, but with attention to supply he believed this could be extended. Apart from not wanting to let Villeroi become too comfortable in Italy, he was eager throughout the winter of 1701-2 to hearten his non-belligerent allies. But first he must do something about his supply position which had been jeopardized in an unexpected way. Pope Clement XI, whose reign had only started in 1700, had directed the allegiance of the Holy See firmly to the Bourbon side, and was commanding his flock to deny the Allies foodstuffs. Eugen was suffering from an appalling shortage of grain, ammunition and, worst of all, money. There was nothing unusual in this, except the degree, and he issued the time-honoured supplication to Vienna for more supplies of everything—to be answered by the usual silence.

The frustration only made some violent activity all the more necessary. He therefore conceived the idea of capturing Cremona, a strongly fortified city on the river Po some fifty miles south-east of Milan where Villeroi had his headquarters. The summit of its bell-tower commanded an unrivalled view of the Po as it coursed through the broad plain of Lombardy. To besiege the place or to deliver an all-out attack upon it was out of the question in mid-winter with an inferior force. More jesuitical means were required. For some months Prince Commercy, one of the many distinguished French officers fighting on the Emperor's side, had been in touch with a priest in Cremona and had discovered that a disused and unguarded canal,

scarcely two feet wide, led from outside the town through the walls
and fortifications, and connected with the priest's cellar in the centre.
Eugen decided to use this canal to infiltrate a body of men into the
heart of the city and then to deliver a surprise assault simultaneously
from within and without. On the last night of January 1702, the
four thousand troops selected for the raid moved forward to Cremona in drenching rain. By early the following morning the canal
party were inside the walls ready to spring unseen upon the French
guards and then to throw the city gates open to the supporting Imperial forces outside. At first the intricate plan went well: the French
guards were taken by surprise and butchered, and the portals of the
town thrown open. The Imperial cavalry stormed in at full gallop,
the infantry close behind them. Villeroi was still in bed at 7 a.m.
when he was awakened by the sound of musketry. At that moment
his servant rushed in screaming: 'The Germans are in the town.'
Villeroi sprang out of bed, ordered his horse, and began scrambling
into his clothes. Still only half dressed he mounted and tried to ride
away, but he was surrounded by Imperial soldiers who immediately
started quarrelling amongst themselves as to who should have the
honour of taking him prisoner. Villeroi looked like being torn to
death between them when an officer in red uniform intervened; an
Irishman, Captain MacDonnel, serving with the Imperial army.
Villeroi offered him the bribe of ten thousand pistoles and a regiment
in the French army if he would let him go, but MacDonnel was not
to be tempted—only a few hours later he was himself taken prisoner.

So far a miracle. But then a series of misfortunes—not least the
weather—coupled with the valour and resilience of the French forces
began to turn the day against Eugen. He had still not taken the citadel.
The French, unexpectedly reinforced, started to counter-attack, and
threatened to exterminate the Austrians, who after ten hours' fighting
were now running out of ammunition. At 5 p.m. Eugen decided to
withdraw. He took many prisoners with him, including Villeroi,[1] and
his casualties were only about half those of the French—six hundred
men. But on the whole the coup was less successful than he had hoped.
Not only did the city remain in enemy hands, but Villeroi was replaced
by a much abler commander, Marshal Vendôme, who had already
won renown in Spain. The French celebrated their double deliverance

[1] Villeroi was treated with the customary chivalry shown towards captured
officers in those days; he was sent to live, completely free, in a castle, first at
Innsbruck then at Graz; after nine months he was allowed to return to France
from where he sent Eugen 50,000 livres ransom money which Eugen immediately
returned.

with the following song, said to have been on everyone's lips:

> *Français, rendez grâce à Bellone.*
> *Votre bonheur est sans égal:*
> *Vous avez conservé Crémone*
> *Et perdu votre général.*[1]

However, in the field, the raid had left the French forces decidedly jumpy, and they cautiously withdrew from their exposed strongholds on the Oglio to a more secure position west of the river Adda, thereby relieving Eugen of the threat to his supply lines north to the Tyrol. Moreover, Cremona, which could well have served as a model for some of the daring raids of the Second World War (such as the kidnapping of the German General Kreipe by a British party in Crete), had a galvanizing effect on contemporary England—then, as ever, inclined to derive more stimulus from near, than from complete, military success. John Evelyn wrote in his diary a few days after the adventure: 'The surprise of Cremona . . . was the greate discourse of this weeke.'[2] A drinking song suddenly became popular in England, ending with the lines:

> *Drink, drink, drink we then*
> *A flowing glass to Prince Eugen.*[3]

A combination of Louis' poison and Eugen's medicine had begun to work on the English Government by the spring of 1702, and on May 15 England joined Holland and the Empire in formally declaring war on the French. The architect of the Grand Alliance, William III, had died two months earlier at the age of fifty-two, worn out by his exertions, yet in Voltaire's words, 'showing no other anxiety than for the troubled state of Europe'. With his death the leadership of the Maritime Powers passed from the Dutch Republic to England, and Marlborough was accepted as Commander-in-Chief of the Dutch and British armies when they were acting together against France. But this did not give Marlborough complete authority. The Dutch insisted that he was always accompanied during campaigns by Field Deputies, representing the States General, who had the power of veto. When the time came for the Maritime Powers to join the Austrians,

[1] F. Voltaire, op. cit., p. 352.
[2] *The Diary of John Evelyn*, ed. E. S. de Beer, 1955, V, p. 488.
[3] G. M. Trevelyan, *England under Queen Anne*, I, p. 152.

the principle of supreme command was left unsettled in theory, though in practice there was acceptance of Marlborough as military leader of the Grand Alliance, with the Austrian forces remaining independent, a relationship only made workable by the personal collaboration between Eugen and the Duke.

At sea England and Holland were superior to France in sheer size of fleets, but this advantage had lost much of its value since the previous war. Spain was now fighting with, instead of against, France, with the result that the most important harbours of the Mediterranean and its approaches—Naples, Port Mahon, Barcelona, Gibraltar, and Cadiz—were denied to the Allies. Uppermost in Marlborough's mind at the outset of the war was the need to wrest from the French the control of the Mediterranean, now an enemy lake. Moreover, the coasts of South America and the Indies were all hostile. Portugal was still neutral.

The change which had taken place in the strength of the two sides since the Treaty of Ryswick less than five years before was just as heavily unfavourable to the Allies on land as at sea: the Dutch barrier, now mostly in French hands, instead of being the rampart of Holland, had become what Sir Winston Churchill calls the 'sally-port' of France; Cologne was hostile; most uncomfortable of all, the Elector of Bavaria, whose forces were reckoned at 45,000, was on the point of making an alliance with Louis, thus presaging the emergence of a hostile enclave in the heart of the Empire, the entry of French troops into the Danube valley and the severance of the allied lines of communication. Centrally placed and organized, Louis' army was much more manageable than the peripheral and precariously connected Allies with their many independent commands and divergent interests.[1] It was only thanks to the mastery which Marlborough managed to assume from mid-1702 onwards over the management of the war in the Netherlands and on the Rhine, to the dominance which Eugen came to exercise over Imperial strategy, and to the harmonious collaboration between the two of them, that these handicaps of dispersion were surmounted.

However, at the outset of the war there was no allied cohesion, and

[1] The armed forces of France at the beginning of the eighteenth century have been said to have equalled in number those of the Roman Empire at its height, i.e. 450,000 men. This establishment surpassed anything which had been seen in the interval. The total population of France in 1700 has been estimated at about 19 million, compared with 7½ million in the Austrian lands of the Habsburgs, 6 million in Spain, 7½ million in England, Scotland and Ireland, and 2½ million in Holland. The total population of the Empire may have been about 20 million. See G. N. Clark, *The Seventeenth Century*, 1947.

Louis was free to attack a divided foe piecemeal. He sent a strong army to the Lower Rhine, hoping thereby to deepen the consternation in Holland following King William's death, and to confirm the scepticism of the English Tories as to the expediency of England's engaging in full-scale war on the Continent. He also ordered Vendôme to take the offensive in Italy with a greatly strengthened army. Vendôme was a first cousin of Eugen's and a boyhood companion. The royal blood of France flowed in his veins, for his grandfather was a natural son of Henri IV. Voltaire has given a vivid account of his qualities, contrasting them with Eugen's. 'He was not thought to ponder upon his plans so deeply as Prince Eugene, or to understand so well the art of maintaining an army. He paid too little attention to details, and allowed military discipline to fall into neglect, too much of his time being taken up with eating and sleeping; ... but in the day of action he redeemed all by a presence of mind and a power of judgment which danger only served to make keener, and such days of action he was always seeking; from all accounts he was adjudged less fitted to carry on a defensive war than Prince Eugene, but quite as capable of taking the offensive. ... Vendôme was victorious on every occasion that he was not directly engaged with Prince Eugene; but as soon as the latter was at the head of his troops France ceased to hold the advantage.'[1] In their unselfconscious magnetism, their personal recklessness and disinterestedness, as in their lack of false pomp and ceremony, the two commanders had much in common.

As so often, Eugen was faced now and throughout the ensuing year with war on two fronts: the enemy in the field and the government in Vienna; and the strength of the former was scarcely more frightening than the feebleness of the latter—feebleness, unless it was a question of prevarication, when the old Emperor Leopold and the newly-elected President of the Imperial War Council, Graf Mannsfeld, formed an impressive and united front.[2] However, it must be admitted that to the commander in the field their very weakness had one great consolation: it meant that in the detailed conduct of battles he was given a free hand by the Imperial War Council. In this respect Eugen and the other Imperial Commanders had much less to grumble about than their French opposite numbers, who were always kept on a very short rein by Versailles. No, it was sins of omission rather than com-

[1] F. Voltaire, op. cit., pp. 352–353.
[2] There were two other principal organs of government apart from the Imperial War Council: the Council of State or Secret Conference (*Geheimkonferenz*) responsible for political and judicial matters; and the Treasury (*Hofkammer*), in charge of finance and trade.

mission by Vienna of which Eugen had so justifiably to complain.
Mannsfeld was hopelessly incompetent and Eugen decided to give
vent to his feelings in a characteristically uninhibited letter to one of
the Emperor's advisers: 'Unless someone with experience and energy
is soon put in charge of the war, the army will be wiped out and the
Emperor faced with the likely loss of crown, sceptre, lands and
people.'[1] It was not surprising that just when Vendôme was preparing
to attack in Italy, Vienna decided to step up their pressure on Eugen
to release men for another theatre. They wanted 10,000 of his troops
to support an uprising in Naples against the Duke of Anjou,[2] now
Philip V of Spain, who had been recognized as King and whom
Vienna wished to unseat; yet he only had 28,000 men against
Vendôme's 80,000, and even these were shamefully provided for.
Since the beginning of the winter he had been making ceaseless appeals
to Vienna for reinforcements and supplies 'to end the misery of his
brave but tattered soldiers whose condition tears the heart'. But these
continued to be ignored or merely to arouse criticism. His personal
triumph in Italy since the start of the war there a year before, coupled
with his frank criticisms of the activities of the High Command in
Vienna, were earning for him a harvest of envy and resentment at
home such as he had gleaned for himself after his victory at Zenta.
Foremost amongst his ill-wishers at Vienna was the Empress Eleonora.
At one time the shower of such laurels became so overbearing that he
could refrain no longer from unburdening himself to someone. He
chose the Emperor's confessor, the Jesuit, Engelbert Bischoff.

'I would be more disturbed,' he wrote to him in March 1702, 'by the
ceaseless stream of abuse that comes to me from Vienna if I did not
know that nowadays criticism is universal and that so far as it is
directed at me it comes from people who like to puff themselves up
with brave words, but who have not the smallest understanding or experience of war. I am accused of all manner of evil. My manner of
conducting war is ridiculed as being Croatian. . . . I am provided with
neither money nor supplies . . . If I were a traitor and wished to
jeopardize the possessions we have gained, then assuredly I would
advise the despatch of a detachment to Naples, leaving me with an
army of 18,000 men to confront an enemy of 80,000, much better
trained. Throughout the winter I have been appealing ceaselessly
for more help, never saying one word beyond the truth and acting

[1] A. Arneth, op. cit., I, p. 171.
[2] There was something repetitive about Eugen's problems, as shown by the
renewal of this demand for troops for Naples in 1707.

only as a faithful subject of the Emperor in accordance with my oath, conscience and duty.'[1]

After questioning again the motives of his critics, he asks Father Bischoff to place his petition before the Emperor with the humble request that in the absence of greater support from Vienna, His Majesty should be so gracious as to relieve him of his difficult command and give him some other employment. The result of this approach was the same: no help, no answer. He waited a little, and then renewed the appeal. He also repeated the threat of resignation. But repetition was useless with this most single-barrelled of all weapons and nobody took any notice. Heavily outnumbered by Vendôme, Eugen was at least thankful that the French had abstained from attacking him in the early spring.

'Had the enemy begun operations in March,' he wrote to Vienna, 'as they should and could have done, I do not know what would have happened, how I would have resisted, or whom I could have turned to for assistance. As I have already said, it was a stroke of luck that the enemy gave us such a breathing space.'[2]

As the correspondence between Louis XIV and Vendôme shows, it was not mere luck that forestalled an attack; it was also petrifying fear. Louis XIV was inhibited from ordering an offensive, and Vendôme from taking the initiative on his own through sheer terror of Eugen.

However, the French could not be expected to remain paralysed much longer. Eugen therefore decided to make a fresh approach to Vienna for reinforcements. He had already come to the conclusion that long-range bombardment was useless. So he hit upon the idea of sending a personal representative, Graf Johann Pálffy, to the Emperor. Pálffy belonged to one of the few Hungarian aristocratic families which had remained consistently loyal to the Emperor through all the vicissitudes of the past century. He could, therefore, be sure of a welcome at the court and his special mission was to try to persuade the Emperor to send his son Joseph to the Italian front. Eugen knew that with such a hostage he would no longer be denied supplies. But unfortunately Joseph considered that his proper place was with the Imperial army in Germany rather than Italy, and in this he was backed up by Eugen's enemy, the dominating Empress Eleonora. Nothing therefore came of the ruse, and Pálffy's interviews

---

[1] Letter to Pater Bischoff, Luzzara 18.3.1702, *Feldzüge*, 1 Ser., IV, Suppl. Nr. 21, p. 72.

[2] *Feldzüge*, I, Ser., IV Suppl. Nr. 21, p. 113.

in Vienna did not augur well for any improvement. In his report on his visit Pálffy described how the Emperor had asked tenderly after Eugen's health: 'Was it true that Your Highness had turned quite grey and had begun to look so ill? To which I countered by asking how he could expect anything else when your letters received no reply, let alone money or deliveries.'[1] The Emperor appears to have had some sort of premonition. While Pálffy was in Vienna, Eugen was in truth taken very ill. So bad was he that for a time there were fears for his life. However, he recovered quickly under the spur of a serious French advance. For meanwhile, at the beginning of May, Vendôme had launched his offensive, and had surged forward to recapture Mantua. Left with a choice of evacuating Italy altogether or seeing his communications with Austria severed, Eugen chose the latter, determined to stay on the bastion formed by the confluence of the Mincio and the Po. What after all was the good of supply lines from Vienna? But he was disturbed by the élan of the French troops under Vendôme and he feared that unless something drastic was done he would be driven out. The obvious cure, he decided, was to try to remove Vendôme as he had done Villeroi.

He discovered that Vendôme was living in a solitary house in Rivalta near where the river Mincio flows into the Upper Mantuan lake. He knew already of his sloth which often kept him in bed through most of the day as well as night, regardless of danger. . . . *la table et le sommeil lui dérobaient trop de temps*, as Voltaire put it.[2] Under cover of dark he planned to send a party by ship to overwhelm the guards, take Vendôme prisoner and bring him back over the water. Accordingly, on the night of June 10–11, the Marquis of Davia set out with two hundred men in twelve boats. He went ashore with a few soldiers at a landing stage near the Marshal's quarters, leaving the remainder of his men behind in the boats. Boldly he called out to the sentries that he was transporting wounded French soldiers from Mantua. His intention was to get right up close and despatch them in silence without alerting Vendôme's household. All went nefariously well until one of Davia's soldiers lost his head and resorted to his carbine instead of the sword. This, in turn, scared the stay-behind party in the boats who thereupon started firing. The guards were immediately aroused, Vendôme himself was able to slip away, and Davia had no alternative but to retreat empty-handed. Eugen's reaction to the failure of the raid is revealing of his character. He did

[1] June 1702, A. Arneth, op. cit., I, p. 173.
[2] F. Voltaire, op. cit., p. 209.

not content himself with a tolerant shrug of the shoulders. Rash though he often was in the midst of battle, he was calculating rather than romantic before and after. When Davia returned, therefore, Eugen had all the officers and men who had taken part in the expedition arrested and tried. Those found guilty of failure of duty were severely punished 'as an example'.

There is another story of Eugen's attitude to punishment which comes from the later years of the war in Flanders but which is worth relating here, in defiance of the dead hand of chronology. One of his soldiers was condemned to be hanged for marauding. The man happened to be a favourite with his officers who interceded with Eugen in an effort to save his life. Their request was refused, so they then applied to Marlborough. The Duke took the matter up with Eugen, who was adamant. 'If your Grace,' Eugen said to Marlborough, 'has not executed more men than I have done, I will consent to the pardon of this fellow.' Enquiries were made and the numbers turned highly in favour of Eugen; on which he said to the Duke: 'There, My Lord, you see the benefit of example. You pardon many, and therefore have to execute many; I never pardon one, therefore few dare to offend, and of course but few suffer.'

But he was doing an injustice to his own flexibility. During the Italian campaign, the shortage of supplies and money was at times so acute that he was obliged to look the other way while his soldiers looted, realizing, as he did, that looting was the only method of survival—and discretion the better part of discipline. 'Things have reached such a pass,' he wrote to the Emperor on one occasion, 'that the troops are not afraid to say quite openly that they can't live without money or bread and that they must therefore keep themselves alive by pillaging. I try to maintain discipline but I must at times turn a blind eye to what is going on if I am to avoid a general revolt.'[1]

Galvanized by his shock at Rivalta, Vendôme had pulled himself together and was now clearly maturing some extremely dangerous attack. At the beginning of July the Prince was once again writing in a despatch to Vienna that in the absence of more men and money nothing but a miracle could save the army in Italy; and he did not believe in miracles. On the last day of the same month he wrote to the court secretary, von Palm:[2] 'If ill-luck prevails and everything is lost, I at least will not be to blame. . . .' He added: 'If everything goes well it will be thanks exclusively to the help of the Almighty.' Then, reading

[1] Oct. 9, 1705. A. Arneth, op. cit., I, p. 334.
[2] Borgoforte, 31.7.1702. *Feldzüge*, 1 Ser., IV, Suppl. Nr. 77, p. 197.

the letter through again, he paused at the word 'exclusively' and struck it out. At any rate he had not been dehumanized by trial.

The priority given by the enemy command to the Italian front at this time was shown by the arrival in Vendôme's camp of King Philip V of Spain. Fired by this encouragement, Vendôme attacked savagely and inflicted heavy casualties on an Imperial detachment as it lay near the Crostolo. When, at 11 o'clock at night, Eugen first heard of this disaster, he mounted his horse at once, reached the shattered troops an hour before daybreak, and proceeded forthwith to make the necessary dispositions to check the rout. Then, fearing that his forces were to be squeezed to death by the rapidly encircling superior enemy, he decided to end the 'extremity' in which he said he found himself and to strike out against one of the enemy's detachments. On August 15, 1702, the two armies met at Luzzara, south of the Po. It was a bloody and indecisive battle for which Te Deums were sung both in Paris and Vienna. Early on in the day, Eugen's bosom friend and compatriot Prince Commercy was killed. Eugen, driven by grief and anger, fought with even more than wonted frenzy. There was something of the Homeric hero about his ideas of friendship, and when night fell and the tumult was over, he was unable to restrain his tears as he stood beside Commercy's body on the battlefield.

The battle of Luzzara had been enough to chasten Vendôme and to prevent him trying an all-out assault on Eugen again that year. Marlborough wrote to Eugen from Flanders to congratulate him on his campaign. Eugen replied from his camp near Luzzara. This is the first extant exchange of correspondence between them and the letters are therefore worth reproducing in full. The texts are as follows—in translation, the originals having been written in French.

In camp at Asch,
September 4, 1702.

Sir,

For a long time I have wanted to do myself the honour of writing to Your Highness; but the hope of being able to send you some good news from here consistently restrained me. However, the victory which Your Highness has just won over the enemy gives me now an excellent opportunity which I cannot miss of congratulating you upon it as I indeed do from the bottom of my heart. It is a successor to the great actions in which Your Highness has participated since arriving in Italy, and which have been so valuable to the common cause. We feel the same sense of relief and deliverance as Your Highness in view of the superiority in numbers of the enemy. Your Highness's part in this encounter cannot be adequately praised, but I beg you to believe that amongst all your admirers there is none more happy or more full of respect for your Highness than I am,

Sir, etc.,

Marlborough[1]

To which Eugen replied:

From camp near Luzzara,

October 3, 1702.

My Lord,

I feel the more deeply honoured by Your Excellency's letter of yesterday assuring me that you interest yourself in the affairs of this country since I have long desired to become acquainted with a man who fills with such dignity the command of an army only accustomed to obey one of the greatest kings in the world. I do not doubt that the campaign will end in your quarter as fortunately as it has begun; as for the affairs of this country the superiority of the enemy prevents advantage being taken of the recent action: it is to be hoped that the situation will change and this army will soon be placed in a state to act offensively. I await with impatience news from the land where you are, being interested in glory above all men.

From your Excellency's

very humble and obedient servant,

Eugene de Savoye[2]

Marlborough was so moved by this letter that he wrote again, on October 31, from his camp near Liège. It was the end of the campaign and he was about to leave for England. But he could not depart, he explained, without assuring Eugen that he could rely on him 'as a friend who admired and honoured him as much as it was humanly possible to do and who would always be proud to show marks of this esteem'.[3]

In England the response to Eugen's action at Luzzara was

---

[1] *The Letters and Dispatches of John Churchill, First Duke of Marlborough from 1702–1712.* Edited by General The Right Hon. Sir George Murray, 1845, I, p. 30.

[2] Winston S. Churchill, op. cit., I, p. 603.

[3] Murray's Dispatches, op. cit., I, p. 52.

dithyrambic. 'It can truthfully be said,' Grat Johan Wenzel Wratislaw, the Austrian representative in London, reported to Vienna, 'that
the English revere and love the Prince like one of their own heroes.
What has been happening on the Upper Rhine or Flanders, the
activities of their own Fleet—about which there is indeed much to
say—all these things are looked upon with relative indifference. The
eyes and ears of the English are concentrated upon Prince Eugen.'[1]

Though reports soon started to come in from the French, claiming
Luzzara as a victory for them, the people of London were not to be
deterred from rhapsodizing. The Queen hurried in from Windsor
immediately after hearing the news and ordered a salvo of guns to be
fired from the Tower, while the crowds made ready to respond to her
wishes that huge fires and illuminations should be lit to mark Eugen's
triumph.

'I can say without exaggeration,' the Austrian Minister in London
wrote the same day, 'that in English eyes no Alexander the Great, no
Julius Caesar, can compare with Prince Eugen. You cannot believe
their enthusiasm.'[2]

In this mood of ecstasy over the Prince it is not surprising that the
Queen and her ministers hotly opposed the idea put to them only a
few weeks after Luzzara by Wratislaw that Eugen should be super-
seded in Italy by the Elector of Bavaria. Max Emanuel, though
already in secret negotiations with Paris to take up arms against the
Emperor, had contrived to make overtures to Leopold, offering to
declare war upon Louis if he got better terms from him than from the
French, including more money and the promise of the command of
all the Imperial armies in Italy. The innocent Emperor was fooled
into taking this approach seriously and was contemplating relegating
Eugen to take charge of an expedition to Naples. He proceeded to
ask the Maritime Powers if they could provide the necessary subsidies
and accept the change of command. But the English jibbed at the
removal of Eugen. The Secretary of State showed Wratislaw a letter
in the Queen's own hand saying: 'I am prepared to enter into a Treaty
with Bavaria. But I will never agree to the displacement of Prince
Eugen. Tell the Imperial Minister that if my help is wanted Prince
Eugen must be left in his command.'[3] The English Government in any
case were against the idea of the Naples expedition, and had reversed
William III's earlier half-promise of a supporting fleet. But their

---

[1] O. Klopp, op. cit., X, p. 185.
[2] Ibid.
[3] Ibid., p. 134.

reaction was, in the event, unnecessary for Eugen's salvation. Unknown to the parties in London, the Elector had declared war on the Emperor just at the very moment when Wratislaw was asking Her Majesty's Government to agree to Eugen's demotion.

When both sides went into winter quarters in November, Eugen could at least be content that with a small army, and despite all his difficulties, he was still in possession of the Po and Mincio. But of the morale and condition of his men he could not be anything but alarmed. There were frequent desertions. The spirit of the army was fast deteriorating. Not surprising, he realized, when the men were consistently unpaid, unclothed and ill-armed—conditions, as he informed Vienna yet again, 'beyond description and which nobody could believe unless they had seen them with their own eyes'.[1] This letter had been preceded by the inevitable entreaty and fruitless threat of resignation. But the litany met with the same old lack of response from Vienna, where there was apparently insufficient money now even to pay for a courier—a measure of the financial state of the Habsburg Monarchy at what is often considered to be one of the high points of its history. Eugen decided that he must seek authority to proceed to Vienna to describe the situation in person to the Emperor. 'We are at the end of November,' he wrote in despair, 'and the troops have not yet received their pay for the previous winter, let alone the summer. Meanwhile the men are having to go naked.'[2] In a private letter he said that if his request to go to Vienna, which had he not visited for two years, was refused, he would not hesitate to lay down the command of men who could no longer deserve the name of army. But this time he got an answer and made off home straightaway, leaving Graf Guido Starhemberg in command.

Writing of Marlborough's return to London after the frustrations of the 1703 campaign which caused him to vow he would never exercise command again, Sir Winston Churchill has said: 'Since the days of Job no man's patience has been more tried than Marlborough's in 1703.' Eugen may not have exceeded this record of endurance the previous year, but he certainly set a hard pace, and it must have been even more of a strain on him than on the less nervous, more buckram-skinned Marlborough, who was after all sustained throughout, not so much by Sarah—particularly wayward and difficult that year—as by his own unwavering love for her.

[1] Eugen to Palm, 16.10.1702, A. Arneth, op. cit., I, p. 185.
[2] Eugen to the Emperor, 21.11.1702, *Militärische Correspondenz*, ed. F. Heller 1848, I, p. 505.

CHAPTER VII

PRESIDENT OF THE
IMPERIAL WAR COUNCIL

EUGEN FOUND chaos and old night reigning in Vienna. Age had left the Emperor, now sixty-four, less constant in good causes, more obstinate in bad, and far more dependent than ever on his incompetent and far from disinterested advisers. There is lively first-hand evidence in the memoirs of the famous French Marshal, the Duc de Villars, of Leopold's increasing reliance on his ministers. Villars was the French representative in Vienna during the three years prior to the outbreak of war. He always thought that if he had been given a free hand by Louis XIV he could have reached a settlement with the Emperor for the partition of the Spanish inheritance, which would have satisfied France and averted war. But Louis and his Minister, Torcy, were too suspicious of Vienna's intentions to give him the necessary authority. Villars' memoirs describe how he said good-bye to Prince Eugen before leaving Vienna after relations had been broken off. The two soldiers conversed long and amicably together. The courtiers in attendance, astonished that there should be such bonhomie between two men who were about to fight each other, asked how it could be so. 'Gentlemen,' Villars replied, 'I rely absolutely on Prince Eugen's goodwill; and I am convinced that he wishes me all good fortune, as I for my part wish him all the luck he deserves, provided, of course, that it does not conflict with the King's interests. But do you wish me to say where Eugen's real enemies are to be found? I will tell you. They are at Vienna, and mine are at Versailles.'[1] It was the familiar cross-frontier cry for military solidarity in the face of civilian meddling. Sixteen years later Villars recalled this remark when writing to

[1] *Mémoires du Maréchal de Villars*, op. cit., I, p. 349.

Eugen to congratulate him on his capture of Belgrade and to warn him of his enemies at court.[1] The freemasonry of old soldiers never dies.[2]

Army commanders as a tribe are not given to suffering long in silence from the slings and arrows of their civilian chieftains, but Eugen especially, with his highly-strung temperament, needed an outlet for his frustration, and found it by the pen if there was no opportunity by the sword. It was an essential part of his character. There is no doubt too, in extenuation of his outbursts, that compared with his contemporaries, the French commanders, or the much-tried Marlborough, or even with the tortured generals of today, Eugen did have a great deal to endure from his superiors in these early years of the War of the Spanish Succession. Now, back in Vienna, he let off steam to Graf Guido Starhemberg, whom he had left in command of the army in Italy. 'If the people who run this country,' he wrote in French, 'are not traitors, then assuredly they are the biggest asses I have ever seen in my life. Addressing them is like speaking to a brick wall.' As for Leopold, 'he promises everything, issues peremptory orders . . . but nothing happens'.[3]

The Emperor was all too aware of his own shortcomings. 'Oh Thou, My Father in Heaven,' he would cry out repeatedly, 'how I hate having to make decisions.' He had, in fact, been privy to a momentous decision which the Imperial War Council had taken at the beginning of 1703. Distressed at the plight of the Imperial armies both in South Germany and Italy, the Council had agreed upon a plan for abandoning the campaign in Italy and transferring troops from there to the German front. Eugen objected strongly. *'Je n'ai jamais rien vu de si sot en ma vie,'* he wrote to Graf Guido Starhemberg.[4] It was not only that all the Italian States would thereby be encouraged to throw in their lot with France, but Austria would be giving up her one field of diplomatic activity that was independent of the Sea Powers. His arguments won the day and the Italian front was reprieved. But, of course, the resentment against him in the Council welled up, and his

[1] A. Arneth, op. cit., III, p. 517.

[2] It may not be out of place to record a recent story which illustrates the eternal strength of the Marshals' International. Pétain met Goering after the fall of France and was asked afterwards how they had got on. *'Entre Maréchaux on s'entend toujours,'* he replied.

[3] Letters to Guido von Starhemberg, 7.2 and 30.5.1703, *Feldzüge*, I Ser., V, Suppl. Nr. 21, pp. 6 and 72.

[4] 7.11.1703, Eberhard Ritter, *Politik und Kriegführung; Ihre Beherrschung Durch Prinz Eugen 1704*, 1934, pp. 16–17.

enemies now concentrated on getting him off out of the way to the front as soon as possible. Meanwhile Eugen had been coming to some very definite conclusions in his own mind about the higher conduct of the war. No amount of appeals from the front or representations in person, so he decided, would secure the necessary support for the army so long as the present leadership continued in office in Vienna. Indeed, if he was to have any chance of saving the Empire from rout, he must himself assume one of the main positions of authority.

Catastrophe came to his aid. The Monarchy was on the point of complete financial breakdown. The Emperor's revenue was estimated to be less than one fifth of Louis XIV's revenue (which had risen with the war to about 187 million livres);[1] but according to the Venetian Ambassador the amount actually provided at this time was considerably less than this. For much of its revenue the Treasury had to depend upon subventions voted yearly by the Diets of the different provinces (though in Hungary this occurred only every three or four years). Owing to the depredations of war, many of the Diets began to vote smaller and smaller sums. Vienna's only other resources were indirect taxation, lotteries, and loans from abroad.[2] But the gap widened. To make things worse, the watchdogs of the nation's finances, the members of the Treasury, *Hofkammer*, were, many of them, undistinguished for vigilance or honesty. This insufficient and undependable control began inevitably to produce a spastic condition in the state's finances, and this was aggravated by the sudden bankruptcy in the summer of 1703 of the Emperor's banker and army contractor, Samuel Oppenheimer; a blow which was, in the Imperial Treasurer's words, 'heavier than any the French had been able to inflict'—and one which, incidentally, threw into relief the advantage England had obtained by the foundation, only nine years before, of the Bank of England.

In this febrile atmosphere Leopold was at last persuaded to change the leadership of his Government, largely, it is believed, as a result of the efforts of his confessor, Father Bischoff. At the end of June 1703 Mannsfeld was kicked upstairs to honourable oblivion and Eugen took his place as President of the Imperial War Council,

---

[1] The conversion rate was roughly as follows:
    1 pound sterling = 4 Crowns = 4 Reichstaler = 10½ Dutch guilders (florins) = 8 Rhine Gulden (florins) = 12 livres.
[2] It has been estimated that the Imperial Government borrowed from England 1·75 million Reichstaler, and from the Netherlands 2·95 million Reichstaler in the years 1701–1713. See Max Braubach, op. cit., p. 41.

Hofkriegsrath. The Prince was still only thirty-nine years old. Graf Gundacker Starhemberg,[1] his ally in the struggle against the old guard in the Government, relieved Graf Salaburg as President of the *Hofkammer.*

This is an important milestone in Eugen's life. Hitherto his career has been confined to soldiering in the field. He has made a great reputation for himself there. He has shown personal bravery and the qualities of military leadership. But he has been tactician rather than strategist. Now, with his appointment to the Presidency of the Imperial War Council, a new era begins: he becomes, in theory at any rate, the supreme controller under the Emperor of all military affairs.

The *Hofkriegsrath* was responsible for the general direction of the war (though it never dictated policy to commanders in the field) and for all questions of organization and appointments. But its power was subject to an important restriction: it did not control supply and finance. These were the responsibility, at headquarters, of the *General-Kriegs-Kommissariats-Amt* and the *Hofkammer* and, in the field, of a separate *General-Proviant-Amt* which stocked the magazines. Not till several years later, when his power had become greater throughout the Imperial machinery of government, did Eugen succeed in establishing some measure of influence over these powerful institutions.

Though not by nature a reformer Eugen perceived that sweeping changes were necessary in the military organization of the Monarchy as a matter not of dogma, but of expediency.[2] The most urgent was to establish the principle of promotion and honours according to service rather than influence or intrigue. He was up against strong vested interests. Many senior officers made a great deal of money by the sale of commissions, and they let it be known that any curtailment of this privilege would be regarded as downright robbery. It therefore required courage and determination on Eugen's part to induce the Emperor, as he succeeded in doing soon after becoming President of the Imperial War Council, to issue a decree forbidding this practice. Not unexpectedly the abolition of the sale of commissions, a measure which was regarded by many at the time as dangerously revolutionary and which, incidentally, was not matched by a comparable reform

[1] Gundacker Thomas Starhemberg, Hofkammerpräsident stepbrother of Ernst Rüdiger Starhemberg, c.f. p. 39.

[2] For general account of Eugen's views on military organization, see Eugen v. Frauenholz, *Prinz Eugen und die Kaiserliche Armee*, Münchener Historische Abhandlungen, 1932.

in England until the second half of the nineteenth century, inevitably brought down on Eugen's head the wrath and misrepresentation of many of his most influential contemporaries. But he was resilient enough to insist that the decree was not merely passed but implemented meticulously no matter the unpopularity. This led to much unpleasantness. There was also at least one embarrassing incident: one of the most senior and respected generals in the Imperial service, the Cavalry-General Sigmund Joachim Trauttmansdorff, who had fought with distinction in a long series of battles, defied the decree and sold a commission. When he heard of this, Eugen, despite the deference shown to the General at the Imperial court, insisted on removing him from active service. In his view the higher the rank of the offender the more certain must be the punishment.

It was more difficult to ensure promotion by merit. Obviously this could not be achieved by mere reliance on a law. But he was determined to enforce a change: he would resign rather than tolerate the deterioration of the war machine under his Presidency owing to the continuation of the old system of privileged promotion. He told the Emperor this in writing, and from then on he was always able to rely, at any rate nominally, on Imperial support in this respect, though in practice this was never anything but grudging, whether under Leopold I, Joseph I or Charles VI.[1]

Instead of all appointments being the responsibility of regiments, he tried to get them approved by the Imperial War Council. This was in keeping with his general aim of enhancing the authority of the Council, a step resisted by many senior officers. In 1705 Eugen abolished the separate Imperial War Council which had met hitherto in Graz with responsibility for the South. This obviously helped to centralize power in the hands of the *Hofkriegsrath* in Vienna.

One example taken from a later phase of his life shows how strict Eugen was in the application of his principles. Field-Marshal Graf Siegbert Heister wanted his younger son to succeed his elder son in the command of his regiment after the latter had been killed in battle at Belgrade. Every argument of humanity cried out in favour of the old man whose services had deserved well of the Monarchy. On personal grounds Eugen was most sympathetic to the application, but he felt bound to reject it. The regiment had gone downhill under the elder brother, and the younger one did not have the qualities

---

[1] The three Emperors under whom Eugen served reigned as follows: (a) Leopold I, 1658–1705, and his sons; (b) Joseph I, 1705–1711; (c) Charles VI, 1711–1740.

necessary to pull it up again. He decided that personal feelings must be sublimated to the public interest.

Tribute to Eugen's success in eradicating the 'old-boy' basis of promotion was paid years later in a report sent by St Saphorin, the British representative in Vienna, to London in 1727:

'The army gets its best officers from the well-educated petite-noblesse and petite bourgeoisie who know well that it is only by their personal merit that they can secure advancement and who for that reason apply themselves to the service with the utmost zeal.'[1]

Eugen had very definite ideas on discipline and leadership. 'The private soldier should not be exposed heedlessly to too great exertions, and unkindness should only be used on the rare occasions where kindness fails.'[2] To his subordinates he was invariably courteous, venting his feelings only on his superiors. He inveighed strongly against any tendency by his officers to try to win the respect of their men by brusqueness, a substitute, he thought, for real authority.

As commander-in-chief of the Habsburg forces Eugen also introduced important changes in tactics. He had a good eye for country and liked to exploit this wherever possible in a war of rapid movement. He made unprecedented use of light cavalry or hussars, for raids, foraging and reconnaissance. He greatly increased the effectiveness of the cavalry in general, making it the supreme instrument of the Imperial army. With considerable ingenuity he issued 'galloper' guns to the infantry. He also saw the great potentiality of the Frontier Forces, *Militärgrenze*, particularly the Croatians, as a new and inspired element in the Imperial army. Another innovation was in the realm of supply. Hitherto it had always been assumed that the army could not venture more than five days' march away from its main magazine. Eugen instituted a system of forward supply depots which became an integral part of his mobile strategy.

He was careful to see that the unfit and crippled were only used on garrison duties. Hitherto they had been forced willy-nilly into the fighting line. He was strongly opposed to the general practice of using anyone, including tramps and crooks, in the army. He regarded this as the surest guarantee of desertion, as well as being in conflict with the idea which he tried to inculcate, that it was an honour to

[1] A. Arneth, op. cit., III, p. 525.
[2] Eugen to General Graf Traun, 26.5.1728, A. Arneth, op. cit., III, p. 527.

serve the Emperor even in the lowest ranks. He deplored the lack of technical training and skill which impaired both artillery and engineers. It took time to remedy this, and in 1710 he still had to admit to the Emperor that there was not a single engineer in the Imperial service capable of building a proper fortress—some handicap in an age of siege warfare against an enemy trained by Vauban. Only in 1717 did Eugen succeed in founding a school of engineers.

There is also one administrative reform for which military historians at least must always be grateful to Eugen: his foundation in 1711 of the *Kriegsarchiv*. In the setting up of this war library, which has made possible the systematic study of Austrian military history from that time, his two loves, of books and war, were happily combined.

Finally, realizing that the sharp decline which had occurred in army discipline was due mainly to the failure to pay the soldiers what was due to them, he decided that the Treasury's revenue must be increased, and that the only way to do this was by taxing the clergy and aristocracy. Only after much obstruction did he eventually succeed in implementing these measures which did, however, secure him the loyalty of the younger officers, however much they scandalized the old guard.[1]

Exasperated on one occasion by the resistance to all reform on the part of the reactionaries in the Imperial War Council, Eugen wrote to the Margrave Louis of Baden in November 1703: 'Everybody thinks that there must be treachery; but I do not give them the credit for that. I am convinced that it is sheer ignorance, idleness, malice and avarice. . . . The Emperor is quite aware of it but lacks the will to inflict punishment.'[2]

In his very first week of office as President of the Imperial War Council Eugen was invigorated by a military crisis after his own heart. The Elector of Bavaria, Max Emanuel, sent a Bavarian-French army into the Tyrol; his plan being to link up with Vendôme's army in Italy, attach the Tyrol to his dominions, and then to make a combined assault upon Vienna. Eugen sent three thousand men to the Tyrol to attack the enemy in the rear after they had moved well forward and were storming the Brenner Pass. The mountain peasantry of the Tyrol, loyal to the Habsburgs and led by Martin Sterzinger, rose in arms against the invader. Max Emanuel had no alternative but to evacuate Innsbruck and withdraw his forces to Munich. But the good effect of this was offset by a defeat which the Imperial army

[1] Eberhard Ritter, op. cit., p. 23.
[2] Ibid., 9.11.1703.

suffered at Höchstädt on September 20 at the hands of Marshal Villars.

There were other turns of fortune that year, though they owed little to the Empire's exertions. Portugal, which, at the outset of the war had been France's ally, and a year later had declared her neutrality, had by May 1703, as a result of the skill and persistence of the successive English envoys to Lisbon, John Methuen and his son Paul, agreed to change her policy once again and to join the Grand Alliance. This tergiversation reflected a real dilemma : Portugal would be hard pressed to avoid becoming a vassal of Louis XIV if French influence became paramount in the Peninsula; and, if they tried to curry favour in advance by joining France in war, the English fleet could take its revenge by sinking theirs and throttling all communication with America; but if they declared war on the allied side, the danger was that there seemed to be no way of safeguarding their frontier against a Franco-Spanish invasion. However, England, who badly needed the Lisbon harbour and who saw the economic opportunities that offered, was prepared to make proposals which eventually brought Portugal into the Alliance. The treaty which the Allies in due course signed with Lisbon carried far-reaching consequences for the conduct of the war against Louis XIV. The English and Dutch were hereby committed to sending armies to the Peninsula. They and the Emperor were pledged to proclaim and install the Archduke Charles as King Charles III of Spain and to oust Philip V. This amounted to a very considerable extension of the original aims of the Alliance. Having accepted Philip V as King in the original treaty of the Grand Alliance (see Chapter 5), they were now bound to use force to eject him. The cry, 'No peace without Spain' (for Charles), was to become an albatross round the necks of the Alliance and to prolong the war for several years. It was a heavy price for the Allies to pay in order that England should have the use of Lisbon and be able to reap the economic benefits flowing from the work of the Methuen family![1] Moreover, the Emperor was more interested at the moment in Italy than in Spain and hesitated long before finally agreeing that the Archduke Charles should set out, as he eventually

[1] According to a recent article the practical effects of the treaty can in any case easily be over-estimated. Port-wine was still a development of the future, and even without a treaty England would have gone on importing Portuguese wine because of wartime interruptions of trade with France and Spain. Without a treaty, too, English woollen cloth would probably have continued to enter Portugal. See A. D. Francis, *John Methuen and the Anglo-Portuguese Treaties of 1703*, The Historical Journal, 1960, pp. 103–124.

did in September 1703, on the hazardous enterprise of the Peninsular War.

There was a better change: the Duke of Savoy had intimated a wish to shift allegiance once again and was engaged in secret talks with the Emperor's representative in Turin. But he was always difficult to trap and the negotiations dragged on uncertainly. Eugen was dubious of the Duke's intentions to come over at this juncture; disillusion about his cousin, sown by the defection of the previous war, had been ripened into belly-hot distrust by family differences over an inheritance. On October 18, 1703, he was writing to Guido Starhemberg: 'If Savoy signs the Treaty with Vienna it will be thanks to the French and will be one of the miracles of the House of Austria.'[1] England was doing everything possible to lure the Duke over: showing the flag off the Italian coast, and giving an earnest of their intention to provide financial aid; and it was thanks to the British representative in Turin, Richard Hill, that matters were brought to a head. As a result of an amazing piece of imprudence on Hill's part, the French got wind of the secret talks between Turin and Vienna. Vendôme thereupon peremptorily arrested a number of Piedmontese generals, disarmed the Duke's guards and insisted on the surrender of several fortresses. The Duke was outraged, and without more ado threw himself into the arms of the Allies. On November 8, he signed up with the Empire, a blow as injurious to the French as Bavaria's desertion had been to the Allies. Sir Winston Churchill has described Hill's indiscretion which led directly to this beneficial result as 'an astonishing breakdown in English diplomacy', but then he has never been one to perceive Machiavellian brilliance behind every apparent peccadillo of the Foreign Office.

'It is certain our new ally has no manner of bowels or other principles and cares for nothing on God's earth but his own dear self,'[2] wrote the British representative in Vienna, Stepney. He was faithfully echoing local reactions to the Duke of Savoy's decision. Yet he may also have been guilty of overlooking the Duke's concern, not so much for his own dear self, as for the interests of his country.

Meanwhile in Hungary, revolt against the Monarchy had broken out and spread like a prairie fire. For long it had been smouldering only just beneath the surface. Austrian rule, which had been established over most of Hungary only in the last fifteen years, had proved itself in many ways more exacting than Turkish occupation. Large

---

[1] *Feldzüge*, 1 Ser., IV, Suppl. Nr. 5, p. 134.
[2] Winston S. Churchill, op. cit., I, p. 644.

parts of the Imperial army had been quartered there, living off the country. Heavy taxes had been imposed on the magnates and peasantry and many lands had been confiscated. Nor had personal liberty been left any more inviolate than private property. Protestants had been persecuted, and all persons distinguished for wealth or independence had been arraigned. On Leopold's instructions, Hungarian representatives had been deliberately excluded from the Carlowitz Peace Conference, notwithstanding the discussion of their interests. The most unforgettable of all Vienna's instruments of horror had been a tribunal, known as the Bloody Assize of Eperies, set up in the wake of the Duke of Lorraine's victories against the Turks in 1687. General Carafa, who was proud to call himself 'Attila, the scourge of the Hungarians', had been in charge of this drum-head, summoning before it all those suspected of disaffection and meeting out the most savage forms of torture. Thanks to his reign of terror, the Emperor had been able to rattle a hastily-convoked Diet into recognizing the hereditary right of the Habsburgs, in the male line, to the Hungarian Crown. He had also cudgelled them into renouncing the ancient right of resistance, the privilege of insurrection against the Monarch if he infringed their rights, which had been granted to the Hungarian nobility by the Golden Bull of 1222. This historic prerogative had enabled the nobility to take up arms against the King without incurring the penalty of treason. Its loss was a grave blow. But this did not break the independence of the Hungarians. On the contrary, the spirit of resistance grew with extortion. And this was not limited to the nobility. By the early years of the seventeenth century there was widespread peasant revolt. A mood of desperation burst forth amongst all classes and amongst all races—Magyars, Slovaks and Ruthenes—throughout the country. And in this mood they revolted. Rather anything than this; rather fly to ills they knew not of than have to bear those ills they had— the reaction of most brave peoples confronted with oppression— better rebellion with all its sacrifices and uncertainties than survival in constraint. So in the spring of 1703, the Hungarians, untrained and ill-equipped, but armed with their traditional national fortitude, launched their insurrection against the new authority, bringing down upon their own heads eight years of war and a toll of physical damage and suffering greater than all that had been endured during the century-and-a-half of Turkish occupation.

Their leader was Prince Francis Rákóczi, one of the wealthiest landowners in the country. After a sheltered youth in a Jesuit academy he was spurred into activity by Count Miklós Bercsényi, formerly a loyal servant of the Emperor and indeed his civilian Commissioner in North Hungary, and now a fanatical resister. Bercsényi was described by an Austrian contemporary as 'the new Hungarian Cromwell'. It was not long before nearly all the nobility rallied to their side, including the great landowner, Count Alexander Károlyi, who at the outbreak of the revolt had been in command of one of the Imperial garrisons. The size of the dissident army quickly snow-balled to 70,000 men. Against this the Emperor could only amass about 12,000. The Hungarians had chosen their moment well, spring-ing their revolt just at the time when Leopold was forced to withdraw troops for the war in the West.

In this favourable situation, and with the promise of French subsidies and military instructors, Rákóczi was able within a few months to drive the Austrians almost clean out of the country. All that the retreating troops could do by way of response was to leave behind a desert of burnt and devastated villages.

It is a great moment in Hungarian history. During the short gap of a few months Hungary seems to hold the destiny of Europe in its hands. The fate of the Habsburg Monarchy; the outcome of the War of the Spanish Succession; and even the balance of power in Europe —they all appear for an instant to hang upon the result of Rákóczi's rebellion.

The Emperor ordered Eugen to go himself to Pressburg just over the Hungarian border and organize the resistance of his few remaining bedraggled troops. Eugen was delighted. He hated desk work, saying he would rather be employed in a galley than as President of the Imperial War Council.[1] Writing earlier, in June 1703, to Guido Starhemberg, he confessed how deeply ashamed he felt to be in Vienna, when fighting was going on elsewhere.

It has often been said that Eugen favoured a policy of leniency, of negotiation with the Hungarian insurgents rather than suppression by force. But however much he was opposed in theory to the infringe-ment of human liberty, he qualified this whenever it was a question of rebellion against his cause, the Habsburg Monarchy; and he believed that the Hungarian uprising could only be overcome by superior strength. In this he differed from the Emperor who per-sonally believed that it would be best to try to come to terms with Rákóczi. Eugen knew Rákóczi; they had lived in the same street in Vienna; and he was convinced that the protestations of peace which

[1] *Feldzüge*, 1 Ser., V, Suppl. Nr. 5, p. 148.

he had been making were meant merely to lull Vienna into a false sense of security; moreover, Rákóczi was, he believed, entirely under the influence of the uncompromising Bercsényi. Anyway there had always been one glaring point of injustice in the Hungarian attitude, and this was so unreasonable as to warrant, in many Austrian minds, an equally immoderate treatment in return; the two sides coming together upon the lowest common denominator of behaviour. The Golden Bull of 1222, the renunciation of which the Hungarians soon sought to set aside, went very much further than the English Magna Carta, which pre-dated it by seven years. It exempted the Hungarian nobility from all taxation. But not only did the nobility thus refuse to contribute to the defence of their country. Even more unacceptable to Eugen and the other Imperial leaders was their claim that freedom from the stationing of Imperial troops on Hungarian soil was one of the liberties in defence of which the Golden Bull permitted legalized rebellion. Their attitude might be courageous; it might be acceptable in the circle of Hungarian history. But to someone like Eugen, pre-occupied almost exclusively with the defence of Habsburg interests, it was tantamount to treason—it was a posture that might jeopardize the safety of the whole Monarchy.

Eugen found the army in Hungary in the same state of neglect as that in Italy. 'Your Majesty,' he reported to Leopold, 'has neither an adequately equipped army in Hungary, nor the means available to make it so.'[1] Such was his pessimism about the situation that he had the Hungarian crown moved from Pressburg to Vienna. He even recommended acceptance of the King of Poland's offer of troops under Prince Lubomirski, although he knew the only interest the Polish King had was in finding somewhere for his forces to live free of charge off the land. The Emperor was sympathetic enough to Eugen's appeals, but he had nothing to send, nothing but the horses from the Imperial Riding School, which were despatched in a gesture of austerity. A number of wealthy families also made offers of horses, but, as Eugen impatiently observed, their generosity did not extend to the supply of the necessary saddles. From day to day things deteriorated in Hungary; and as the winter of 1703–4 deepened, the danger grew of the Danube freezing over, and of the rebels being able to cross the river without difficulty and dislodge the Imperial forces from their last foothold in the country.

To add to the Emperor's discomfort, the Maritime Powers were most unfriendly towards his efforts to suppress the Hungarian revolt.

[1] A. Arneth, op. cit., I, p. 222.

They had sympathy for the insurgents as Protestants. They complained that Leopold was neglecting the real war against the common enemy, asking for subsidies and devoting all his resources to the destruction of his own people, boldly struggling to be free. Sublimely disregarding the Irish beam in their own eye, the English were most attentive to the Hungarian mote in the Austrian, and none more so than the English ambassador, George Stepney, a faithful representative of the prevailing 'Republicanism for Others' of his government. Such tender solicitude for the oppressed of other countries is a mark of Great Powers. Strong though they recognized the emotional forces in favour of the Hungarian rebels to be, the Austrians considered that from the standpoint of expediency—from the practical angle of winning the war against the French—the English attitude was completely suicidal. As Vienna knew from intercepted correspondence, there was no question of the Hungarian rebels seeking a limited and untreasonable objective: Rákóczi was in collusion with the King of France and the Elector of Bavaria, and the three of them were plotting a combined assault against the very continuance of Habsburg power—encouraged very much by England's seemingly romantic support for the Hungarian insurgents.

What a heavy fall for the Habsburg Monarchy had been the year 1703, after the glory of the opening campaigns of the war and Eugen's triumphs in Italy! Already in May Marlborough had been writing: 'You see how little the Empire dose [sic] for themselves.' As so often, Eugen would not have disagreed with him. Since his return from the Italian front the previous winter, Eugen had had plenty of first-hand experiences of the rottenness of the Habsburg system as an instrument of waging war. Though he now had power he nourished no illusions about being able to put everything right in a matter of months. On October 3 he sent a progress report to Guido Starhemberg in Italy:

> 'You cannot possibly believe or imagine what confusion prevails here in the Government . . . I am certain that had I not been present myself, and seen everything with my own eyes, nobody would possibly accept my account. For, if the whole Monarchy had been in the direst straits, and fifty thousand gulden or less were required to save it from utter destruction, even so it would be impossible to obtain that sum.'[1]

At the beginning of January 1704, the Elector of Bavaria once
[1] *Feldzüge*, I Ser., V., Suppl. Nr. 5, p. 126.

again launched an attack against Austria. With Rákóczi maintaining pressure from Hungary, Vienna seemed to be simultaneously at the mercy of East and West. Panic spread within the hastily-constructed city ramparts.

'Everything here is quite desperate,' the Dutch Minister reported to The Hague in mid-January; 'the Monarchy is on its last legs and will go down in a general military collapse unless there is some miraculous intervention of the Almighty. . . . It looks as though the enemy will soon be at the gates of Vienna—advancing from both sides. There is absolutely nothing to stop them. There is no money. There are no troops. Nothing for the defence of the town. And we will soon be without bread. I fear that a general uprising is likely because you cannot imagine with what unrestrained venom people speak of the Emperor, of the Government, and of the clergy—yes, most bitterly of all of the Jesuits, who will certainly be the first victims of their rage.'[1]

The Minister goes on to refer to the rumours, which were circulating through the city, relating to the court's plans for evacuation, possibly to Klagenfurt in Carinthia. But he says that he 'cannot see where the Emperor can go in safety because there is absolutely no place that can be defended'.

The Emperor feebly implored Eugen to give him all the advice and help he could to help him out of the crisis; but Eugen retorted acidly that in such a predicament his advice and help could be of no avail. The only things that would help would be more men and money. He decided to rub this home in writing:

'I hope Your Majesty will not be unmerciful if I give free play to my pen, for otherwise I could not answer to God. The situation seems to me to be graver than it has been at any time in Habsburg history. Extreme perils require extreme measures. There are many wealthy families in Your Majesty's lands who have not yet made much sacrifice and who could be called upon to do so; and I cannot in all conscience say that I think the clergy should be exempt from this. Our fight is recognized the world over as a struggle for the right, the good—for what God himself has given the world. Moreover, the preservation of your spiritual, like your temporal, subjects turns on the outcome; so that everyone is bound by duty as well as by oath to give all the help he can. . . . The state of your

[1] Hamel Bruynincz to Anton Heinsius, Vienna, 16.1.1704, Eberhard Ritter, op. cit., p. 181.

Army is well known to Your Majesty. Most of the soldiers have not a rag to their backs, and no money. The officers are as poor as beggars. Many are nearly dying of hunger; and if they fall ill there is no one to nurse them. None of the fortresses has any reserves, nor supplies for more than a few days. There is not a magazine anywhere. No one is paid and the distress is universal: officers and men are alike despondent so that on all sides nothing is heard but complaints and lamentation.'[1]

Two days later he wrote again to the Emperor in the same vein: 'I implore Your Majesty, in heaven's name, to take immediate and far-reaching decisions; and what is more to stick by them and see that they are carried out. The Most High will perhaps extend greater mercy, and Your Majesty and all Your Majesty's hard-pressed lands and kingdoms will once more find salvation—to which cause I will devote all my strength.'[2]

To the Emperor's son, Joseph, he sent copies of all these appeals, accompanying them with yet further entreaties and the announcement of his return to Vienna: 'The proverb says that God helps him who helps himself. It is all too painfully clear what will happen if the war is pursued merely on paper and by argument. Your Majesty will forgive me if I go too far, but the time has come when my conscience will let me keep silent no longer. Between tomorrow and the next day, I hope to appear in person so as to do my utmost to check the worst disaster.'[3] Of the three Emperors whom Eugen served, Leopold I, Joseph I and Charles VI, it was probably with Joseph that he had the easiest relationship. There is a famous saying attributed to Eugen, which, whether apocryphal or not, sums up his attitude to his three chiefs. 'Leopold was my father, Joseph my friend, and Charles my master.' Already by December 1703, Joseph was becoming exceedingly influential as heir to the Imperial crown, and Eugen was on the closest of terms with him.

Eugen's decision in January 1704 to leave the front in Hungary and make for the capital was due to his fear that the situation in the West was even more dangerous than in Hungary. The Elector of Bavaria, who had been joined by a powerful French army, had occupied Passau in the second week of January, and was now threatening an imminent advance on Prague and Vienna.

[1] Eugen to the Emperor, 12.1.1704, A. Arneth, op. cit., I, p. 231.
[2] Eugen to the Emperor, 14.1.1704, Ibid.
[3] Eugen to Joseph, 14.1.1704, Ibid., p. 232.

CHAPTER VIII

BLENHEIM

FOR THE next eight years 1704–11 the allied war against Louis XIV was dominated by the combined genius of Marlborough and Eugen. The campaign of 1704, culminating in the Battle of Blenheim on August 13, was the start of their partnership. The two men had been in intermittent correspondence before but they had never met until the middle of that year.

About the importance of Blenheim in the history of Europe there has never been any dispute. 'It was one of those battles,' Ranke has written, 'which determine the relation of powers to one another, and the fate of nations dependent thereupon, for many years to come.'[1] However, two intriguing questions hang eternally over the Blenheim campaign: firstly, who was primarily responsible for securing the acceptance of the plan for a link-up between the British and Imperial armies on the Danube; and secondly, who most deserves credit for the successful outcome?[2]

As already shown, since the beginning of 1703 there had been a serious danger that Austria would be knocked clean out of the war. On one front she faced the Hungarian insurrection, on the other the threat of a Bavarian-French march upon Vienna. The city was

[1] L. von Ranke, *A History of England* (English translation), 1875, V, p. 320.
[2] For detailed discussion of these two questions the following are recommended among a mass of authorities: Winston S. Churchill, *Marlborough, His Life and Times*, op. cit.; G. M. Trevelyan, *England under Queen Anne, Blenheim, 1931*; Onno Klopp, *Der Fall des Hauses Stuart*, op. cit., and Eberhard Ritter, *Politik und Kriegführung, ihre Beherrschung durch Prinz Eugen 1704*, op. cit. A good modern account by David Chandler has been published in *History Today*, Dec. 1962 and Jan. 1963.

practically defenceless, and the Austrian armies were far away in Italy and Germany. This danger—the gravest the Alliance was ever to confront in the war—had been postponed, not exorcized, by the events of 1703. Yet the military weight of the Alliance was still not deployed to meet it. The bulk of allied power remained in the north—on the Dutch frontier and lower Rhine, whence indeed the French traditionally most feared attack. But for two years Marlborough had been thwarted by the Dutch from undertaking the all-out battle he believed necessary. The Spanish Netherlands were still in French hands. Hoping to profit by this inflexibility the French and Bavarians had shifted their threat southwards along the Danube to the heart of the Empire.

As early as February 1703 Count Wratislaw, the Emperor's representative in London, had spoken to Marlborough about the need to send troops to the Danube; and in October of the same year he discussed the idea again both with the Duke and with the Grand Pensionary Heinsius,[1] emphasizing that it was in the south, in Bavaria, that the decisive campaign would have to be fought the following year. Wratislaw had been in Vienna in the summer of 1703 when Eugen had first been made President of the Imperial War Council, and it must be supposed, though there is no supporting documentation for it, that they talked over the future strategy of the war, and that much of the expertise and confidence which Wratislaw displayed on the subject in the coming months derived from these discussions.

Wratislaw was a most charming and persistent man. Born in 1669, he was only thirty-one when he first became Imperial representative at the Court of St James's, where he quickly won renown for his wit, his geniality, and his enormous size.[2] He probably more than any other man is responsible for pushing through the idea of a combined operation against the Bavarians and French in the heart of Europe. His tireless advocacy of this project in London and the Hague throughout the winter of 1703–4 proved charismatic in its influence upon events.

Here, however, we are beguiled by a historical mystery. Archdeacon Coxe, who had free run of the Blenheim archives when writing his life of Marlborough at the beginning of the last century,

[1] See footnote on p. 60.
[2] Graf Johann Wenzel Wratislaw, 1669–1712, the outstanding Austrian diplomat of the time, combining firmness of purpose with gaiety of manner. His independence of mind was exemplified in 1712 when he, alone of the Austrian Cabinet, opposed the continuation of the war for the sake of Spain. A few months later he died of fatty degeneration.

states that the Blenheim campaign was secretly arranged in correspondence between the Duke and Eugen. The idea has been accepted and repeated by subsequent historians. Now it can easily be imagined that, as they turned their thoughts to the forthcoming year, the two commanders must each have realized independently that the allied army in the Netherlands would be wasting its time if it remained there trammelled by the Dutch, and that unless some additional help was given to the Empire in the south there would be no hope of stopping the eastward march of the Franco-Bavarian army. But there is no documentary evidence to support the idea that Marlborough and Eugen corresponded together about this, let alone that they reached agreement upon a plan. Among recent historians to examine the subject, Sir Winston Churchill, after thorough immersion in the Blenheim archives, has emerged with the un-Archimedean declaration that he has found nothing. Sir George Trevelyan has followed up another clue: a letter referred to in a life of Eugen published in Venice in 1738, purporting to be from the Prince to Marlborough asking him to come to recover Bavaria. But, as Sir George points out, this does not help us very much: the letter is in Italian in *oratio obliqua*. not in inverted commas, and with no date. How then do we account for the Archdeacon's assertion, made indeed upon two separate occasions, that there had been a secret interchange between the Duke and the Prince?[1] It has much puzzled later writers. One possibility, of course, is that Coxe saw the documents, but that they have subsequently been mislaid or stolen. But this is unlikely since, so far as is known, no other important originals are missing, and why should these particular papers alone have been misappropriated? A much more probable hypothesis is that the Archdeacon unaccountably departed in this instance from the normal standards of scholarship—an explanation supported by the fact that Coxe gives no dates for the alleged correspondence, though these would have been highly relevant to his thesis.

It was easy, of course, for both Marlborough and Eugen to realize in theory the need for a bold stroke delivered in a joint campaign; but it was quite another thing to see how this could be brought about in practice. How could Marlborough extricate himself in the north and disengage an independent army from the toils of the Dutch, who clung to them for protection but would not let them risk a major fight? How was an army with all its artillery and impedimenta of war going

[1] William Coxe, *Memoirs of the Duke of Marlborough*, 1905 edition, I, pp. 148 and 153.

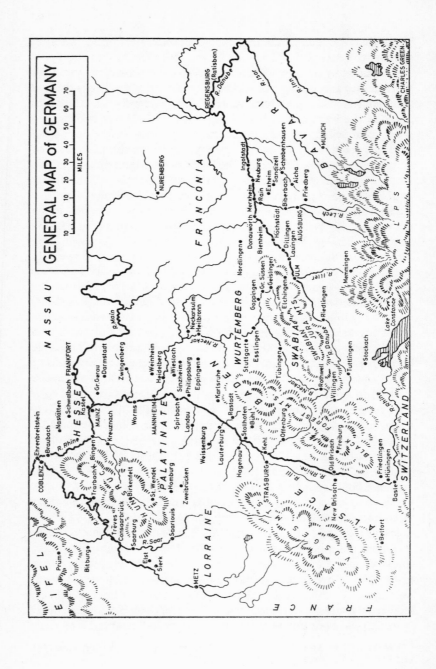

GENERAL MAP of GERMANY

MILES
10 0 10 20 30 40 50 60 70

NASSAU

EIFEL

COBLENZ
Ehrenbreitstein
Braubach
Nastätten
R. Rhine
HESSE
Schwalbach FRANKFORT
Kostel
MAINZ
Bingen
Kreuznach
Worms

R. Main
Gr. Gerau
Darmstadt
Zwingenberg
Weinheim
Heidelberg
Wiesloch
MANNHEIM
Sinzheim
Philippsburg
Eppingen
Neckarsulm
Heilbron
R. Neckar
Nördlingen

FRANCONIA

REGENSBURG
(Ratisbon)
R. Danube

BAVARIA

R. Isar

MUNICH

ALPS
R. Lech

Ingolstadt
Neuburg
Rain
Exheim
Sandizell
Schrobenhausen
Aicha
Friedberg

Donauwörth Mertheim
Blenheim
Höchstädt
Dittingen AUGSBURG
Lauingen
R. Iller

ULM
Memmingen

NUREMBERG

Karlsruhe
Rastadt
Stollhofen
Bühl
Offenburg
Kehl
STRASBURG
Hagenau
Lauterburg
Weissemburg
Landau
Spirbach

WURTEMBERG
Stuttgart
Esslingen
Göppingen
Gr. Süssen
Geislingen
Elchingen
Tübingen
Rothwell
Villingen
R. Danube
Riedlingen

SWABIAN MTS
SWABIA

Lake
Constance

BLACK FOREST MTS
Freiburg
Old Brisach
New Brisach
Friedlingen
Hüningen
Basle

SWITZERLAND

PALATINATE
Homburg
Zweibrücken
Saarlouis
St. Wendel
Birkenfeld
R. Saar
Treves
Consaarbrück
Saarburg
Eist
Sierk
METZ

LORRAINE

Bitburg
Prüm
R. Saar

ALSACE
VOSGES MTS
Belfort
Stockach
Tuttlingen

FRANCE

CHARLES GREEN

to be led over several hundred miles, much of it rough country, to the heart of Germany?

At the end of January 1704, Marlborough confided to Wratislaw his 'intention to induce the States-General to decide upon a siege of Landau or a diversion to the Moselle'. He hoped to lead an army of forty-five battalions and sixty squadrons, and if he succeeded in taking Landau, he 'would help the Margrave of Baden with as many troops as possible to enable them to overthrow the Elector of Bavaria'.[1] By this time, then, the Duke's ideas, which Wratislaw was expressly authorized to communicate to the Emperor, to Eugen, and to the Margrave of Baden, did include the possibility of some action on the Danube, though all that he was prepared to divulge to the Dutch Government at this stage was the possibility of a Moselle operation.

In Vienna discussions took place in January and February on the forthcoming campaign. Eugen was present, as was the Margrave of Baden. The Margrave favoured attacks at Landau and on the Moselle, and the defence on the Danube. He spoke specifically against a combined operation—probably because he was not prepared to see anyone else in supreme command. Eugen's views were the complete opposite. He favoured standing on the defensive on the Moselle and at Landau, whilst waging war against Bavaria on the Danube and carrying this through to success *à quel prix que ce soit*.[2] A combined operation was essential if Austria was ever to regain her freedom of movement. This is important evidence showing how early Eugen had decided that a joint Danube action must be the primary objective of the forthcoming campaign. Eugen confided these views to the Dutch Minister, saying that they were unofficial.

Discussion on these conflicting ideas was still in progress in Vienna when a report was received from the Hague showing how adamant the Dutch were against any adventurous military operations. It was therefore decided in Vienna to promote only the idea of a Moselle operation, and Leopold sent a message to Marlborough to this effect on February 13. The depressing report from Holland apparently also caused Eugen personally to pull in his horns; in a talk with the British Minister in Vienna, Whitworth, on February 11, he made no mention of Marlborough's coming to the Danube. Marlborough also seems to have lost heart at this time. He would envisage

---

[1] O. Klopp, op. cit., xi, pp. 91–92.
[2] Eberhard Ritter, op. cit., pp. 53–63.

nothing beyond the Moselle. Just before sailing home from Holland on February 22, he wrote to Sarah:

'For this campaign I see so very ill a prospect that I am extremely out of heart. But God's will be done; and I must be for this year very uneasy, for in all the other campaigns I had an opinion of being able to do something for the common cause; but in this I have no other hopes than that some lucky accident may enable me to do good.'[1]

While Marlborough and Eugen thus appeared to go backwards in February, Wratislaw continued to thrust ahead. Throughout March he was importuning Marlborough to come to the Danube. And he was in correspondence direct with Eugen. On April 1 he reported to the Emperor that he would never leave the Duke's side until he had persuaded him, and through him the States-General, to come to the aid of the distressed German fatherland. Marlborough, though sympathetic, refused to be pinned down, so Wratislaw in order to try to obtain a binding commitment from the British Government addressed a memorandum to Queen Anne. This memorandum, dated April 2, is the basic document for the Blenheim campaign. It referred to the fact that there were still several plans under discussion for allied operations that summer. A decision would only be reached after Marlborough's return to The Hague. Her Majesty was therefore requested 'to instruct Marlborough to concert with the States-General the provision of effective help to the Emperor, or at least to ensure that the troops which Her Majesty maintained on the Continent would be used to protect Germany from a complete collapse'.[2]

It is important to bear in mind that Wratislaw drafted this memorandum in agreement with Marlborough and the First Lord of the Treasury, Sidney Godolphin. We can conclude, therefore, that they were as eager as he to see England committed to the Danube venture. They probably thought it expedient from the point of view of British and Dutch opinion for the Emperor's pressure to be on record so that none should think it was merely the Duke's bright idea to take the army to the Danube. They were indeed much exercised about the likely Dutch reaction. They thought there was a serious danger of their leaving the Alliance and making a separate peace. However,

[1] Winston S. Churchill, op. cit., I, p. 716.
[2] O. Klopp, XI, op. cit., p. 100.

Wratislaw convinced them that the most urgent threat was that the Empire might be eliminated from the war unless more help was forthcoming.

On April 4 Wratislaw received an answer to his memorandum which met his needs. It stated that Marlborough had been instructed to agree with the States-General upon the necessary measures for the urgent support of the Emperor.

When Marlborough returned to Holland in the third week of April, accompanied by Wratislaw, his mind was made up on the necessity for marching to the Danube. Relying on shock tactics with the States-General, he told them that if need be he was prepared to march to the Moselle alone. Those were the Queen's orders. He said nothing of any more ambitious plan farther south. The Dutch, duly shaken, acquiesced in a combined Moselle operation. To the Emperor he explained his real plan for going to the Danube and said how essential it was that Eugen should be allowed to join him, a plea which Wratislaw reinforced saying that from his point of view it 'was absolutely necessary to have a supporter of his zeal and experience'.[1] The Emperor agreed to release Eugen, but very reluctantly:

'From this decision on my part there should readily be deduced the eagerness with which I take part in this matter, and how greatly I hope for a happy issue, inasmuch as in the present state of affairs I am sending away from myself and my supreme war council a person whom I value so highly.'[2]

While all these palavers had been going on in the allied capitals, the French had decided to stand on the defensive in the Low Countries and attack in south Germany—as most allied experts had predicted. A French-Bavarian army of forty-thousand men under the Elector and Marshal Marsin (who, happily for the Allies, had just replaced the much more competent Villars) was holding the upper Danube from Ulm to below the Austrian frontier. Menacingly poised though it was to advance down the Danube to Vienna, this army neverthe-less needed reinforcements before it could strike, and the difficulty of this was that lying between it and the nearest French force, under Marshal Tallard in Alsace, were Imperial troops under the command of the Margrave of Baden blocking the passes through the Black Forest. There were more Imperial troops in Franconia and Swabia,

[1] O. Klopp, op. cit., XI, p. 110.
[2] Ibid.

so that the Elector and Marsin were virtually cut off from their main source of support. However, Tallard was instructed to try to pass reinforcements through the Black Forest towards them—which he succeeded in doing to the number of about ten thousand in May despite the efforts of the Margrave of Baden to stop him.

There was much criticism of the Margrave for this failure. The Emperor himself was indignant and spoke to Eugen about it before the Prince set out from Vienna at the end of May for the Imperial Headquarters near Ulm. The Margrave was senior in rank to Eugen and insisted on remaining Commander-in-Chief of the Emperor's forces in Germany. But Leopold gave Eugen instructions to report on his superior officer, and eventually, if the widespread rumours of the Margrave's disloyalty and incompetence proved well-founded he was to supplant him. It would have been an easy opening for naked ambition. But Eugen could not forget that the Margrave, besides being a relation, had been his first Commander and military teacher, and early on had given him a leg up the ladder of promotion. His disinterestedness was summed up in the letter he wrote to the Duke of Savoy immediately before setting out from Vienna: 'Clearly everyone must do the utmost in his power. Success depends on harmonious collaboration, on everyone's thinking of nothing but the common good.'[1] Even a few weeks later when distrust of the Margrave was rife he refused to join the chorus, explaining to the Emperor: 'It is only too well known that calumnies are never more actively propagated than when the victim is in trouble. I have closely observed the behaviour of the Margrave and seen absolutely nothing which would give grounds for suspicion.'[2]

Since May 19, Marlborough had begun to march the allied army south; a march which has earned Sir Winston Churchill's highest hyperbole, the annals of the British Army containing, according to him, 'no more heroic episode'. As it rolled south, Marlborough's army snowballed; Danes, Dutch and troops from the Empire gathering to join it.[3] The enemy and much of allied Europe were held in suspense wondering where Marlborough would strike. At first it

---

[1] May 24, 1704, A. Arneth, op. cit., I, p. 242.

[2] July 4, 1704, Eugen to the Emperor, A. Arneth, op. cit., I, p. 244.

[3] There is considerable discrepancy in the figures given by historians for the size of Marlborough's army at the start of its march south. Coxe gives about 50,000 men; Trevelyan 40,000; von Noorden 25,000; Churchill 19,000. Klopp, usually so lavish with detail, fails to give any figure at all. The number of native British troops which set out is variously computed between about 13,000–16,000, not more than 9,000 of whom were present at the battle of Blenheim.

looked as though he was going to attack on the Moselle; then, as he crossed the Rhine eastwards at Coblenz and continued on south following the course of the Rhine, he seemed to be meditating a campaign against Alsace. It was only by the end of the first week in June, when he suddenly struck away from the Rhine at Wiesloch, that it became apparent to all, friend and foe alike, that the Danube was his aim.

Marlborough was now afraid that as he marched south-east to Bavaria, the French would answer with an attack on the upper Rhine, where the Imperial forces remained interposed between France and Bavaria. He therefore asked Wratislaw, whom he had brought with him on the march, to go ahead to the Imperial Headquarters to urge the rapid reinforcement of the Rhine army. He was most anxious that it should be the Margrave who would take command there so that he could have Eugen with him for the big struggle on the Danube. This was due partly to his respect for the Prince's fighting qualities but also to his wish to avoid the embarrassment of sharing command with someone of the Margrave's higher rank. Marlborough told Wratislaw therefore that 'a general of great experience and vigilance' would be needed on the Rhine; and as between the Margrave and Eugen he would be very glad if the former, 'being the most experienced', could take command there. But the Margrave was just as handy at compliments as Marlborough. He did not at all want the difficult, lack-lustre Rhine command. Accordingly he neatly deflected Marlborough's pass, saying to Wratislaw in Eugen's presence: 'Try to persuade the Prince to take the command. For in the army he is the only man who could be entrusted with a command so responsible and subject to so many risks.'[1] Ever anxious to prove himself, Eugen readily concurred saying: 'The Emperor has sent me into the Empire to serve under the command of his Lieutenant-General, and as I have never made difficulties about going wherever duty called me, I am quite ready to carry out the order of the Lieutenant-General.'[2]

But though this was settled, a meeting of the three commanders was necessary to co-ordinate plans. Eugen and Wratislaw tried to persuade the Margrave to go with them to Marlborough's head-quarters, but he demurred. This made them think that he might be wanting to respond privately to the peace-feelers which he had received from the Elector of Bavaria. Such a move would not, in

[1] O. Klopp, op. cit., XI, p. 128.
[2] Ibid.

fact, have been all that treacherous since neither Marlborough nor Eugen excluded the possibility of reaching a settlement by negotiation with the Elector, and Marlborough had even sought special powers from London for the purpose. Moreover, to negotiate secretly with the other side was not necessarily thought incompatible in those days with loyalty to your own.

Eugen and Wratislaw thereupon proceeded alone together to Marlborough's camp, which they reached on the evening of June 10. At Mundelsheim, half-way between the Danube and the Rhine and close by the river Neckar, Eugen and Marlborough met for the first time. With characteristic humour, Joseph Addison, in his twenty-three page poem on 'The Campaign', in which Eugen's name only appears twice in passing, describes their initial encounter thus.

> At length the Fame of England's Heroe drew
> Eugenio to the glorious interview.[1]

The Duke accorded Eugen the highest military honours and gave him a magnificent banquet. This was followed by a long conference. 'At once,' so Sir Winston has inimitably summed up their first encounter, 'began that glorious brotherhood in arms which neither victory nor misfortune could disturb, before which jealousy and misunderstanding were powerless, and of which the history of war furnishes no equal example. The two men took to one another from the outset. They both thought and spoke about war in the same way, measured the vast forces at work by the same standards, and above all alike looked to a great battle with its awful risks as the means by which their problems would be solved.'[2]

Though the numbers of men they commanded were far less than those engaged in any great campaign of modern times, their responsibilities were in a way much greater than their successors' today. In the brief headlong clash of eighteenth-century battle there was no time for instructions from home. But it was not merely that. Armies then were much more irreplaceable than they are nowadays. As Clausewitz has described it:

'If an army was completely destroyed it was impossible to make another: and behind the army there was nothing. This called for

[1] Joseph Addison, *The Campaign, A Poem to His Grace the Duke of Marlborough*, 1705, p. 6.
[2] Winston S. Churchill, op. cit., I, p. 773.

great prudence. Only when some decisive advantage was likely to be gained, could the risk be undertaken. It was in the creation of such chances that the art of the commander lay.'[1]

Eugen and Marlborough both carried massive burdens extending well beyond the immediate campaign: Eugen was not only in command in the field but also Head of the Imperial War Council and answerable for the war on other fronts; Marlborough, besides being Commander-in-Chief of the English and Dutch armies, was virtual Prime Minister as well. But the very extent of their responsibilities also had its advantages. It meant that they both saw the particular problems of the campaign against a wide background; it gave them an invaluable breadth of vision.

The following day Eugen accompanied Marlborough on a review of the English cavalry at Gross Heppach. He was astonished to find them in such perfect trim after so arduous a march. 'My Lord,' he said to Marlborough, 'I never saw better horses, better clothes, finer belts and accoutrements; but money which you don't want in England, will buy clothes and fine horses, but it can't buy that lively air I see in every one of these troopers' faces.' To which Marlborough replied: 'Sir, that must be attributed to their heartiness for the public cause and the particular pleasure and satisfaction they have in seeing your Highness.'[2] The next three days were spent in the frankest discussions. Eugen afterwards reported to the Emperor on 'the incomparable ability' of the Duke, and of his indefatigable zeal for the common cause and the Emperor's interests. He wrote in the same lyrical terms to the Duke of Savoy. A few weeks later he drew the following 'true picture of Marlborough: here is a man of high quality, courageous, extremely well-disposed, and with a keen desire to achieve something; with all these qualities he understands thoroughly that one cannot become a general in a day, and he is diffident about himself.'[3]

Of Eugen, Marlborough wrote to Sarah that he 'has in his conversation a great deal of my Lord Shrewsbury, with the advantage of seeming franker. He has been very free with me, in giving me the character of the Prince of Baden, by which I find I must be much more on my guard than if I was to act with Prince Eugene. . . .'[4] This

---

[1] General Karl von Clausewitz, *On War* (English translation), 1908, VIII, p. 97.

[2] The journal of Francis Hare, Marlborough's Chaplain, quoted in Winston S. Churchill, op. cit., I, p. 775.

[3] Undated letter to the Duke of Savoy, *Feldzüge*, I Ser., VI, Suppl., p. 131. O. Klopp, op. cit., XI, p. 167.

[4] W. Coxe, op. cit., I, p. 166.

reference to Shrewsbury is at first sight surprising. Shrewsbury was so untenacious of opinion and office that he was said to shift ministerial posts as easily as he changed his clothes. Nevertheless, he had infinite charm of manner and was known to all as the King of Hearts. Marlborough had a great affection for Shrewsbury and the comparison reveals the personal conquest Eugen had already made of him.

The Margrave finally joined their councils at Gross Heppach on June 14. The tree beneath which they had their first talks stood for decades and became a much visited historical landmark. Of the triumvirate, Eugen was the least in years—he was forty—but far the greatest in military renown. Nevertheless, he made no complaint about being cast in the least glittering part of the three. To avoid wounding the Margrave's vanity he agreed that the daily orders to the allied forces should be signed alternately by the Margrave and the Duke, as though they held joint command. The military task which he had accepted earlier, under the impulse of the Margrave's flattery, involved the guarding of the Lines of Stollhofen[1] and the holding of the French Marshals, Villeroi and Tallard, on the other side of the Rhine to prevent them going to the help of the French-Bavarian army on the Danube. For this duty he had a mixed force of soldiers from Prussia, Denmark and the Palatinate, making a total of 30,000 to confront a French army of 60,000. He was under no illusions about the problems ahead. 'I realize very clearly,' he wrote on June 14 to Guido Starhemberg, 'that I am placing myself in a serious impegno . . . yet I have not in the present circumstances been able to decline this dangerous command.'[2]

As Eugen went to the Rhine, Marlborough led his army on to the Danube to join up with the Margrave's forces. Adding to the difficulties of crossing the Swabian Jura, the rain fell incessantly for ten days. But there was a good side to this for Marlborough, who realized that continual rains would help to immobilize the superior French force opposite Eugen on the Rhine. 'As they do us hurt here,' he wrote to Sarah, 'they do good to the Prince Eugene on the Rhine, so that we must take the bad with the good.'[3]

Eugen soon reciprocated this unselfish thought in deed. On July 1, Marshal Tallard, having broken away with 26,000 men from the rest

[1] The Lines of Stollhofen stretched for twenty miles between the Rhine, just below the Kehl bridgehead, and the Black Forest. They might be described as an early Maginot line in reverse.

[2] *Feldzüge*, VI, Suppt., p. 55.

[3] Winston S. Churchill, op. cit., I, p. 790.

of the French army, crossed the Rhine at Strasburg and started marching through the Black Forest to join the French-Bavarian army, under the Elector of Bavaria and Marshal Marsin, on the upper Danube. This presented a dilemma for Eugen. If the Allied army on the Danube was not now to be outnumbered he must either try to cut Tallard off before he could get there or hasten to reinforce Marlborough. But the danger was that if he withdrew from the Rhine, Villeroi might also break away and march south to link up with the French-Bavarian army. However, that risk had to be run if there was to be any chance of winning the big stake on the Danube. Marlborough never doubted Eugen's judgment in this dilemma. On July 16, he wrote to Godolphin, 'I depend very much on the vigilance of Prince Eugene.' His confidence was superbly rewarded. Leaving 12,000 men behind on the Lines of Stollhofen, Eugen marched off after Tallard with a force two-thirds the size of the Frenchman's. His plan was to try to catch and attack him before he could get too far. But Tallard was equally determined to avoid an engagement and to reach the Danube unscathed. He succeeded so well in this that Eugen had no alternative but to make for Marlborough with all speed. First, though, it would be worth while to exercise some sleight of hand in an effort to tie Villeroi down for as long as possible at Strasburg. Before proceeding to the Danube, therefore, he began marching north so as to give the impression that he was returning to his old watch on the Rhine. By the use of spies and deserters he ensured that Villeroi was kept fully informed of his progress in this direction. Then, suddenly, he about-turned and hurried off south to throw his decisive weight into the scales in Bavaria, whilst Villeroi remained on tenterhooks on the Rhine. Without these masterly tactics, closely co-ordinated at all times between the Prince and the Duke, the Allies would not have had the necessary relative strength on the Danube indispensable for ultimate victory there.

What had Marlborough been doing all this time? He had first won the battle of the Schellenberg and secured a bridgehead over the Danube at Donauwörth. Following this, he had been systematically and barbarously devastating the towns and countryside of Bavaria in an effort to force the Elector out of his fortresses to fight a battle before Tallard could come to his aid, or, if that failed, at least to deny the land to the enemy. Eugen had serious misgivings both about the relations between Marlborough and the Margrave, and about the expediency of the Bavarian destruction. 'Up to now everything has gone well enough between them,' he wrote to the Duke of Savoy, 'but

I fear greatly that this will not last. And to tell the truth since the Donauwörth action I cannot admire their performances. They have been counting upon the Elector coming to terms . . . they have amused themselves with the siege of Rain and burning a few villages instead of, according to my ideas, which I have put before them plainly enough, marching straight upon the enemy . . . to put things plainly . . . I do not like this slowness on our side; the enemy will have time to form magazines of food and forage, and all our operations will become the harder.'[1]

To the Emperor he expressed his fear that delay might ruin everything. 'If only we act in time,' he wrote on July 1, 'the Elector will be unable to save himself. . . . I am afraid that if we waste this opportunity the English and Dutch will start to think of marching back.'[2]

These outbursts are typical of Eugen. It was a weakness of his that he always had to give vent to his feelings when the pressure became intense, though it did not mean any relaxation of his grip. He knew perfectly well, on this occasion, that so long as the Elector of Bavaria continued to lurk in his fortresses, Marlborough could not, in the absence of siege-artillery, attack him effectively. He also realized that the Duke was determined with heart and soul to do everything he possibly could to disrupt the enemy. Marlborough was so deeply committed that he had no alternative. 'If he has to go home without having achieved his objective,' Eugen wrote to the Duke of Savoy, 'he will certainly be ruined.'[3] This was no exaggeration. The Tories of the Blue Water School, who distrusted any continental commitment of British troops, were loud in protective indignation over:

> *The illustrious youths, that left their native shore*
> *To march where Britons never marched before* . . .[4]

Sir Edward Seymour, the fractious old spokesman of the hunting-squires, boasted that if Marlborough failed: 'We will break him up as the hounds do a hare.'

At times the strain was too much even for Marlborough. In mid-July he confessed to Sarah that his blood was so heated he had had a violent headache for the previous three days. This was the depressed condition in which Marlborough, like Eugen, was often to be found before some tremendous triumph; and in these moments it was always

[1] Undated letter to the Duke of Savoy, *Feldzüge*, I Ser., VI, Supp., p. 131, O. Klopp, op. cit., XI, pp. 164–6.
[2] O. Klopp, op. cit., XI, p. 166.
[3] O. Klopp, op. cit., XI, p. 166.
[4] J. Addison, op. cit., p. 8.

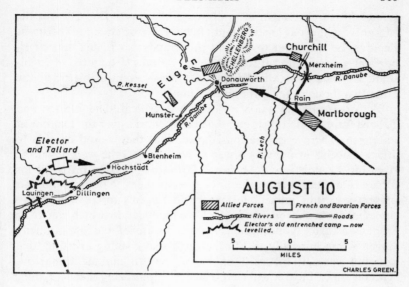

a relief to both men to be able to turn their thoughts from war to the private problems of home, to the ideas and plans, never far below the surface of their minds, for altering and enlarging their buildings and collections. In the midst of the present campaign Marlborough wrote to Sarah asking for a drawing of a stable for their home at Holywell House, which with its rambling garden, well-stocked fish-pond and accumulation of treasures remained, even after the much more magnificent Palace of Blenheim had been constructed, the repository of his most cherished thoughts and trophies from abroad. Likewise, throughout this tense year, Eugen drew comfort from the castle which was building in his mind's eye: a vision of steps and terraces, lawns and fountains; and serried ranks, not of soldiers, but of statuary forming up peacefully in the Belvedere between the long lines of clipped hedges and espaliers—an oft-recurring topiarian dream.

When Eugen reached Bavaria at the beginning of August, he was impatient for immediate action. Tallard was joining up with the Elector and Marsin; and he feared it might not be long before Villeroi would summon up courage and start marching to the Danube. His impatience was increased by the bad news he received of allied defeats in Italy and the successes of the rebels in Hungary. The enemy must be engaged in battle soon or the Empire would fall apart and the

Grand Monarch remain in undisputed sway over Europe. But the Margrave demurred to an all-out attack. Like the slight, unmeritable Lepidus, he was meet to be sent on errands; so Eugen and Marlborough packed him off to besiege the Danube stronghold of Ingolstadt. He took away with him 15,000 men—a reasonable price, the other two thought, for getting rid of him.

By August 10 the allied position was critical. The Elector and Tallard were passing their combined army north over the Danube at Lauingen. There was a serious danger that they would be able to attack Eugen's army, which was at Münster a little way down the river on the north bank, before Marlborough could bring all his forces from Rain across the river to join them. Not only did this present a serious immediate menace to Eugen's forces, but it also threatened Marlborough's lines of communication which ran from Donauwörth to Nördlingen. Intensely aware of the predicament, Eugen wrote hurriedly to Marlborough that evening insisting 'that you put yourself forthwith in movement to join me tomorrow, without which I fear it will be too late'.[1] Emphasizing that everything depended upon speed, he proposed that they should link up between Münster and Donauwörth. Marlborough complied immediately. Some of his cavalry had already gone to join Eugen. With the rest of his army he now made straight for Eugen's camp which he reached the next day. On August 12 the two commanders rode out to direct their telescopes upon the masses of the enemy taking up position behind the river Nebel. There and then they resolved upon a full-scale battle the following dawn—upon an attack, which, according to the records, very few of the senior officers in the allied army would have ventured against so big an enemy in so strong a position, and of which, certainly, no one in the French-Bavarian camp had the slightest suspicion as they went untroubled to their rest that evening.

Marlborough spent some of the night in prayer. He also visited Eugen, whom he found writing letters. At 3 a.m. on August 13, the allied army started moving forward from their camp at Münster, a force of about 52,000 men. The enemy numbered about 56,000. Their position was strong. They held a front four miles wide, shielded from the enemy by the river Nebel and its marshes, with the right flank secure upon the Danube, the left resting in wooded hills. When the autumn mists hanging over the valley had dispersed, revealing to the French the whole might of the allied army advancing towards them

[1] Winston S. Churchill, op. cit., I, p. 837.

from the north-east, their officers believed that Marlborough and
Eugen must have decided to make a bolt for Nördlingen and that in
desperation they were manoeuvring across their front to get away
before daybreak. It did not occur to them that the two experienced
commanders would be so foolhardy as to try to attack the Grand
Army, superior in number and position. Even as late as 7 a.m.,
Marshal Tallard was confident enough to write a message to the King
informing him of the enemy's withdrawal.

The plan agreed between the two allied commanders was that
Eugen should advance upon the enemy's left—under the Elector
and Marsin—which stretched from the hills to Oberglau, whilst
Marlborough struck at Tallard between Oberglau and the river. The
natural weakness of the enemy's section between Oberglau and
Blenheim was increased by the bad relations between their commanders, which meant that the French and Bavarian armies were practically
separate and invited attack at the feeble hinge. Though Marlborough
was the senior in command, no question of relative rank or authority
appears to have arisen between them, so close was their understanding. Eugen had under him 13 battalions and 74 squadrons, a total of
about 16,000 men.[1] Marlborough's command comprised 53 battalions
and 86 squadrons, a total of about 36,000 men. Eugen had against him
on his part of the front 29 battalions and 67 squadrons, or about
23,000; Marlborough was facing 49 battalions and 68 squadrons, a
total of about 33,000. Though Marlborough was confronting the
flower of the French infantry sheltering in the hastily barricaded
village of Blenheim, it will be seen from the above figures that he just
outnumbered the enemy's battalions, whereas in cavalry he had a
superiority of four to three. Eugen, however, had to contend with a
much longer march, more difficult country, and the ablest of the
enemy commanders, the Elector. For these tasks he was outnumbered
in infantry by over two to one, which was scarcely compensated for
by his small superiority in cavalry.

In his Journal, Marlborough's Chaplain, Francis Hare, who was
present at the time, gives an account of the interview which Eugen
had after the battle with many of the French generals: 'Prince Eugen
much commended the conduct of the Elector of Bavaria, as well as
the behaviour of his troops, and frankly told how often and how
bravely he had been repulsed by them. When he spoke of his own

---

[1] A battalion contained about 500 infantry, a squadron about 120 cavalry.
At the beginning of a campaign they might have numbered 700 and 150
respectively.

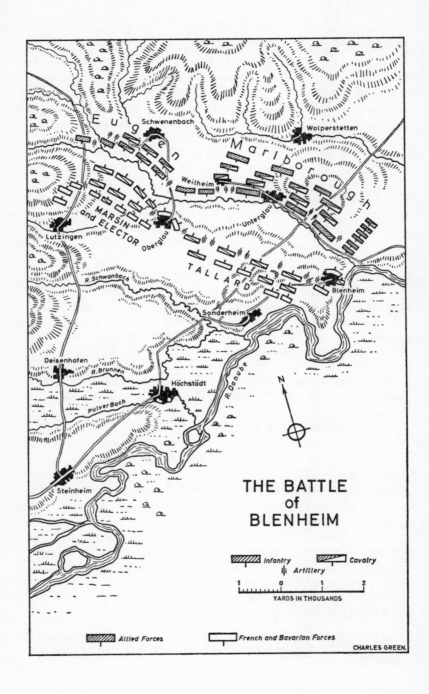

THE BATTLE
of
BLENHEIM

Infantry   Cavalry
Artillery

1   0   2
YARDS IN THOUSANDS

Allied Forces   French and Bavarian Forces

CHARLES GREEN.

troops, he said, "I have not a squadron or battalion which did not charge four times at least".'[1]

At the most perilous moment of the whole battle when Lord Cutts, known as the Salamander, had still not been able to penetrate the palisades and musket-fire defending Blenheim village, the French counter-attacked in the centre around Oberglau—nine battalions of them, with the Irish Brigade, known as the Wild Geese, yelling in the van. They threatened to divide the allied army in two and sever Eugen irremediably from Marlborough. Eugen unhesitatingly responded to an urgent personal message from the Duke for the loan of an Imperial Brigade. He was himself in a most critical position at the time, but he immediately gave orders for the Brigade to join Marlborough. This held the situation until the moment, an hour or two later and already well on into the afternoon, when Marlborough, who had made many sacrifices for the sake of bettering his overall strategic position, was able to deliver the decisive blow. Over the two-mile stretch between Oberglau and Blenheim, across a field of stubble unbroken by ditch or hedge, the most decisive cavalry action of the century took place. Interlining Marlborough's cavalry were strong bands of infantry, armed, not as formerly with pikes, but with the new invention, the ring bayonet.

The final charge was made about 5 o'clock. Marlborough drew his sword, ordered the trumpets to sound and the cavalry to advance. They were under instructions to gather speed as they approached the enemy. The impact was overwhelming. The French were routed. Resistance in the centre was at an end. It was not long before the French troops in Blenheim were hemmed in and disposed of. Many, including Tallard, were taken prisoner. A large number were drowned as they rode headlong into the Danube. At the other end of the front the Elector and Marsin decided they could make no headway against Eugen and that the only course was to retreat rapidly. They had had an ignominious day against the smaller forces of Eugen, and they had not even been able to give help to other hard-pressed parts of the front.

Two small incidents occurred during the battle which typified the two allied commanders in action. At one time, Marlborough caught one of his generals retiring with a force of cavalry in disorder. 'Mr —, you are under a mistake,' he cried out to him with elaborate punctilio; 'the enemy lies that way: you have nothing to do but to face him and the day is your own.' On which the general about-turned and re-entered

[1] W. Coxe, op. cit., I, p. 211.

the fray. Much later in the long hours of fighting, it cannot have been before 6 o'clock, Eugen was infuriated at what he regarded as the lack of thrust of his cavalry. It was their third attack of the afternoon, but he expected the same courage as in the first. In a spasm of temper he is said to have shot two fugitives from the fighting, and then to have abandoned to others the command of his beloved cavalry, and taken personal control of the infantry. He went forward recklessly to the most exposed of his troops. He was just about to be fired upon at point-blank range by a Bavarian dragoon when one of his own men transfixed the soldier with his sword.

Of the personal bravery of the two commanders in the battle we have the testimony of the Prussian liaison officer at Headquarters who wrote: 'Eugen and Marlborough exposed their persons repeatedly. Eugen went so far that it is almost a miracle that he escaped with his life.'[1]

Afterwards, when the Emperor received the news of the battle, he wrote to Eugen to congratulate and thank him for his part in the victory. 'But he could not conceal,' he added, 'that his pleasure had been tinged with fear for the danger in which Eugen had put himself. He must implore him therefore to take more care of his safety in future since he must realize how dependent on him are the Imperial House and the whole alliance.'[2] His gratitude was expressed perhaps less egotistically and certainly more concretely in his designation of Eugen's Vienna Stadtpalais as a 'privileged palace', free for ever from all taxes and civic impositions. So that other householders did not have to bear the burden of this exemption, Leopold handed over to the municipality an equivalent sum from his own income. His reward to Marlborough became a controversial issue, not altogether creditable to him, even less so to the recipient. When Marlborough had been marching to the Danube in June, the Emperor had offered to make him a prince of the Holy Roman Empire, to give him a principality, and allow him the right to vote in the Diet of the Reich. Marlborough, never one to scorn property or rank, had been eager to accept. But for one reason or another, including his own inclination to wait until the French had been roundly beaten, the matter was delayed until a week after the battle of Blenheim, when the Duke himself approached Wratislaw and asked him to write to Leopold to jog his gracious memory. Meanwhile the rout of the French had reduced the Emperor's sense of dependence upon his

[1] *Feldzüge*, I, Ser. Bd. VI, p. 521.
[2] A. Arneth, op. cit., I, p. 274.

allies and had increased his inhibitions over finding a suitable territory. 'To the most illustrious Prince of Us, and the Holy Roman Empire, John Duke of Marlborough,' he wrote in Latin on August 28.[1] He accorded him the title of Prince for his part in the victories 'which no ages can parallel', and promised to use his endeavour to procure a place and vote in the Diet; but of the gift of the principality there was no mention. Marlborough was indignant and made no bones about it: he must have, not just the title, but the Imperial fief and the seat in the Diet as well. Wratislaw put much pressure upon the Emperor, appealing not so much to his personal feelings as to the interests of state which would suffer if this man 'indispensable to Your Majesty for many years to come' were offended. It was only after the lapse of many months, a change of Emperor, and a visit by Marlborough to Vienna that the matter was finally cleared up. The estate of Mindelheim, fifteen miles square, which had been taken from the Elector of Bavaria after his desertion to the French, was eventually bestowed upon Marlborough with due ceremony. Yet, like the ending of a cautionary tale about avarice, the outcome of this story was humiliating for Marlborough. The Treaty of Utrecht restored Mindleheim to the Elector; and all that the Churchill family were left to enjoy was the empty title of prince, for which the first Duke had had to pay an exorbitant installation fee.

Even more ironical is it that Southey should have hit upon Blenheim for his famous poem designed to expose the insignificance of all war. Few battles in history can have had a more decisive influence upon events. Unfortunately for the victors, the opportunity was not taken to follow it up and put an early end to the war. But the real measure of Blenheim is to be gauged by imagining what would have happened if there had been no battle or if Louis XIV had won. How much longer would the Habsburg Monarchy have survived? Or an independent Dutch Republic? Would religious liberty have been able to endure? When would Britain have begun to emerge as a great power? By such a negative yardstick it is impossible to deny the momentousness of Blenheim. The battle is immortal, in Sir Winston Churchill's judgment, not because of the extreme severity of the fighting but because 'it changed the political axis of the world'. The allied casualties had been high, 12,000; but the French and Bavarians had suffered 30,000 in killed, wounded and prisoners. Their real defeat, however, was a moral and political one. Louis XIV and his reputedly invincible army had not only been defeated, they had been humbled. As Eugen's

[1] W. Coxe, I. p. 222.

biographer, Arneth, has expressed it, 'the nimbus enveloping the French army had been dispersed forever'. And now shining above it was a new power, England, whose strength of arms and system of government were from Blenheim onwards to become a decisive influence in the affairs of Europe and the New World; so far did the pendulum of power swing between dawn and dusk on August 13, 1704, on that four-mile front on the Danube.

This metamorphic effect of the battle upon English history may help to explain why Blenheim is so often regarded in England as primarily a British event, dominated by British soldiers and British generalship. It is true that England—like the Dutch Republic—had a major role as paymaster; between them they may have 'hired' as many as 32,000 out of the total 52,000 allied troops who participated. It is also indubitable that the quality of the British soldiers was supreme. Nevertheless, of the total number of allied soldiers who took part in the battle less than a fifth were British; and the proportion of British casualties to the whole was about the same.[1]

Surprising though it may be, it is also a fact that more Dutch soldiers fought at Blenheim than British—something which should be kept in mind in view of the readiness of posterity to malign the Netherlands' attitude to the war.

Britain's historical chauvinism about the battle may, of course, have been encouraged by the building of the colossal palace of Blenheim near Woodstock as a reward to Marlborough from a grateful government. The avenue of trees in the park was laid out to correspond to the order of battle at Blenheim, which has needless to say encouraged many a visitor to ask to be shown the exact spot where the fighting took place. Even the construction of the palace, like the battle itself, may have owed more to Austria than the British have acknowledged. Fischer Von Erlach, the Styrian architect who designed Eugen's winter palace in Vienna,[2] and Wratislaw, the Imperial representative, renowned for his love of grand buildings, were both living in London at the time Vanbrugh was working on his plans, in the baroque style, for Blenheim Palace.[3] It is not impossible that they had some influence upon him.

But there is no doubt that Addison's glittering figure of Marlborough, riding 'on the whirlwind' and 'directing the storm' has

---

[1] Total allied casualties: 4,500 killed (including 670 British) and 7,500 wounded (including 1,500 British).

[2] cf. Chapter IV and XIX.

[3] See Victor L. Tapié, *The Age of Grandeur* (English translation), 1960, p. 184.

contributed to Britain's proprietary feelings about the field of Blenheim, where, according to the poet.

> *fam'd Eugenio bore away,*
> *Only the Second Honours of the Day.*[1]

Certainly there is no gainsaying the Duke's great part, but it is a travesty of history to disregard or belittle Eugen's. Victory on that August day owed as much, in fact, to Eugen as to Marlborough and the same may fairly be said of their contributions to the conception and preparation of the campaign which made the battle possible.

Looking back it is impossible not to be struck by the complete absence of any sense of rivalry between the two commanders themselves. They never bickered about the laurels; they never criticized each other. Only once did Marlborough descend from this high standard of magnanimity and that was in private to Sarah just after the battle. To Harley he wrote on August 14, 'I cannot say too much in praise of the Prince's good conduct'.[2] But to the Duchess he confided the same day: '. . . the army of M de Tallard, which was what I fought with, is quite ruined; that of the Elector of Bavaria, and the Marshal de Marsin, which Eugene fought against, I am afraid has not had much loss, for I can't find that he has many prisoners . . . I can't end my letter without being so vain as to tell my dearest soul that within the living memory of man there has been no victory so great as this; and as I am sure you love me entirely well, you will be infinitely pleased with what has been done, upon my account as well as the great benefit the public will have. For had the success of Prince Eugene been equal to his merit, we should in that day's action have made an end of the war.'[3] Even allowing for the fact that this was a private letter to his wife, it does not show Marlborough in a particularly happy or impartial light. In contrast, Eugen was always unstinted in his praise of Marlborough at Blenheim and outspoken in his admiration for what the Duke and his brave troops had done for the Grand Alliance as a whole.

On the European continent the battle of Blenheim, or Höchstädt, as it is called, is generally regarded as Eugen's triumph, just as much as Marlborough's. The Dutch commemorated the selfless collaboration by striking a medal likening them to Castor and Pollux. The official Habsburg history of the battle, written in the last century,

[1] J. Addison, op. cit., p. 17.
[2] *Murray's Dispatches*, op. cit., I, pp. 391–2.
[3] W. Coxe, op. cit., I, pp. 213–4.

says that 'the secret of their harmony resided in the fact that the two men resembled each other in their good and not in their bad qualities'.[1] So far the Austrian analysis is calm and impersonal, but then comes an outburst: 'Prince Eugen hated to push himself forward, whereas the Duke of Marlborough loved public recognition. So when the task was accomplished Eugen withdrew again into the background and let others do the talking.' Here speaks the voice of the Imperial subconscious letting off decades of pent-up envy against Marlborough.

Sir Winston Churchill is extremely fair in his summing-up of the rôle of the two commanders. He does not think it necessary to ignore, still less denigrate, Eugen in order to extol Marlborough. He pays tribute to 'the glory of Prince Eugene, whose fire and spirit had extorted the wonderful exertions of his troops; who after contending all day against very heavy odds held the initiative and the offensive to the end; and who, moreover, in the midst of local disaster had not hesitated to answer Marlborough's call for the Cuirassier brigade'.[2] Above all he recognizes that the whole impulse and vigour of the allied campaign depended upon the two men working indivisibly together.[3] This is indeed the only conclusion history can fairly draw about the part of the two commanders in the campaign and battle of Blenheim: that the course of destiny was altered, not by either of them alone, but by their exquisitely united genius.

[1] *Feldzüge*, I Ser., VI, p. 529.
[2] Winston S. Churchill, op. cit., I, p. 865.
[3] In his *History of the Second World War*, Sir Winston Churchill refers to Blenheim in the account of his visit to Moscow, in August 1942, when he stayed in State Villa Number 7, a few miles out of the city: 'Late the next morning I awoke in my luxurious quarters. It was Thursday, August 13—to me always "Blenheim Day".'

On the same day General Montgomery took over command of the 8th Army in North Africa. A week later Sir Winston Churchill was staying with him in the Western Desert, on his way back from Moscow. The General asked him to write something in his personal diary. This is what he wrote: 'May the anniversary of Blenheim which marks the opening of the new Command bring to the Commander-in-Chief of the Eighth Army and his troops the fame and fortune they will surely deserve.'

From numerous passages in Sir Winston Churchill's *History* it is evident that the parallels of the War of the Spanish Succession were frequent springs to thought and action during his conduct of the struggle against Hitler.

7. Medal with the heads of Eugen and Marlborough struck to commemorate Malplaquet, 1709

8. Eugen and Marlborough at the battle of Blenheim, 1704; engraving after a contemporary picture by van Huchtenburgh

9. Portrait of Eugen by Kneller: engraving after the lost portrait
painted in London in 1712

CHAPTER IX

TURN OF THE TIDE IN ITALY;
THE BATTLE OF TURIN, 1706

NO SOONER was the Habsburg hull caulked in one place than it sprang a leak elsewhere. All chance of Eugen and Marlborough taking advantage of Blenheim to carry out their dream of a combined advance upon Paris the following spring was dispelled by the worsening situation in Hungary and Italy which required Eugen's immediate presence in Vienna.

'I and others long for you to be here,' wrote Graf Niklas Pálffy, one of the Emperor's loyalist Hungarian supporters, from Vienna on October 25, 1704, 'especially as the Hungarians secretly have great love and trust in you, a fact which could be put to most useful account.'[1]

Peace negotiations between the Emperor and the rebels had been dragging on fruitlessly throughout 1704, interrupted by occasional Hungarian reversions to force when the Monarchy's weakness in the East became too temptingly apparent. The rebels had captured one Imperial general, Georg Adam von Riczan, an event which Leopold reported personally to Eugen in a letter written in Italian in his own hand; and they had attacked Vienna, choosing the Emperor's birthday for the injury, and then adding to it the insult of a raid on Leopold's private menagerie in which they killed his two favourite hunting-leopards given him by the Sultan. Such information, reported characteristically with equal emphasis on the important and the unimportant, had been reaching Eugen in Germany all through the summer as he had tried to apply his mind to the Blenheim campaign.

The Hungarian 'thorn', as Marlborough described it, continued to

[1] A. Arneth, op. cit., I, p. 473.

fester after Eugen's return to Vienna at the end of the year. Twenty thousand Imperial troops were still tied down there. Particularly irritating to him, as to the Emperor, was the high-flown attitude of the English Government who thrust themselves forward as mediators, insisting that concessions be made to the Hungarian rebels for the sake of an early peace.

The British representative in Vienna, Stepney, and the Dutch representative, Bruynincx, told the Emperor that an armistice in Hungary would be regarded as a friendly return for the help given at Höchstädt. In the peace talks which took place at Schemnitz in October-November 1704, Stepney and Bruynincx participated, but, despite their intervention, nothing was achieved—except the exacerbation of relations between Vienna and the Sea Powers. Stepney was convinced that the negotiations could have succeeded had Austria put its heart into them and appointed a suitable representative. He and his Dutch colleague appear to have convinced themselves of two basically incompatible propositions: that the Hungarian rebels were in earnest in seeking peace, and that the Empire was not militarily capable of subduing them by force.

Rákóczy was much weaker than the English and Dutch believed and his relations with Louis XIV closer. The French, of course, were extremely active in their efforts to dissuade him from coming to terms, and they were rewarded with an assurance brought by one of Rákóczy's officers that nothing of the sort was contemplated at Schemnitz. Looking back on it all with the hindsight of centuries we may acknowledge the British and Dutch desire to induce the Monarchy to make peace in Hungary for the sake of the bigger war against Louis XIV—an interest they frankly admitted. But we must also recognize that they failed abysmally to take account of the strong and natural feelings which internal rebellion aroused in Austria at this time of national peril; and they also appear to have ignored the existence and consequences of the close link which joined the rebels and the French. The net result of their efforts was in fact to make peace less, not more, likely since the Austrians were thereby rendered more obdurate than ever, and the rebels more confident. Eugen felt particularly bitter towards the British representative, Stepney, whom —with justice—he believed to be unfairly prejudiced in favour of the Hungarian insurgents. The Prince and Wratislaw wrote to Marlborough asking him to secure Stepney's withdrawal. This was eventually done, the Earl of Sunderland, Marlborough's son-in-law, taking his post, but not before full-scale hostilities between the Imperial forces and the rebels had been resumed.[1]

The situation in Italy was even more menacing to the Empire and to the Allies. The combined forces of Guido Starhemberg and the Duke of Savoy had been unable to halt the French under Vendôme, and by the autumn of 1704 Turin was the only place of importance in Savoy not in French hands—and it was dangerously threatened. Added to their endemic state of destitution, the Imperial forces were suffering from an even more than habitual malaise in the higher reaches of the command. Eugen appointed the brilliant Vaudemont to take over one of the army corps, but he died of fever almost immediately. He was replaced by Graf Leopold Herberstein, who admitted soon after assuming the command that he did not think himself tough enough for the post. This detail is worth recording for its sequel. Eugen, far from losing all patience with Herberstein for his self-confessed weakness, recognized in him rare qualities of honesty and loyalty, and appointed him Vice-President of the Imperial War Council.

Eugen was hesitant to ask anyone to become supreme commander in Italy at such an inauspicious moment. He decided that he must take it on himself. There was no false modesty in his make-up, and he said quite frankly that if he 'failed to take over the command there and then he might never have another chance of doing so'.[2] He found things even worse in Italy than he had expected. In a report to the Emperor from Rovereto dated April 26, 1705, he wrote:

'I should be pressing on with all speed, but with starving and half-naked soldiers, and without money, tents, bread, transport, or artillery, this is quite impossible. Wherever I turn I hear nothing but complaints, and see nothing but want and misery.

'If you send a detachment of say 100 soldiers on a march of not more than half-an-hour you can be sure that 50 will drop out from sheer exhaustion. The troops are so starved that they are more like shadows than men. Up till now they have been patient in the hope that I would bring substantial relief. But as I have been provided

[1] Sir Winston Churchill, who has never sought to save the Empire to which he belongs by aiding in the liquidation of another, believes that the state of indignation in Vienna over the attitude of the Sea Powers can readily be judged by imagining what the feelings would have been in Britain had the French proposed to send a mission to mediate between Great Britain and Irish Home Rulers in 1917.

[2] *Feldzüge*, VII, Suppl. pp. 94, 104.

with very little I fear that my arrival will merely lead to despair. Desertions have already increased—to a rate of nearly 50 a day.'[1]

But, to the Allies in Turin, Eugen's return to Italy meant a lot. Hitherto they had been planning flight but now, so the British Minister, Mr Richard Hill, reported to London on June 24, 'We sleep quiet in Turin, in full assurance that Prince Eugene is making all the haste he can to do something for our deliverance. We have that Prince's word which nobody can suspect.'[2]

His name exercised the same magical effect on Versailles. Though in a strong position to attack, with superiority in numbers and supplies, the French suddenly seemed paralysed with fear, and the King tried frantically to prevent Eugen from taking the offensive. Louis no longer sought to throw the Austrians out of the country, but merely to prevent Eugen linking up with the Duke of Savoy and relieving Turin. Vendôme, however, was not to be reined in. To prevent Eugen crossing the river Adda he attacked him at Cassano in mid-August. It was an indecisive and bloody battle—far bloodier even than Luzzara three years before. Eugen suffered heavy casualties and failed to pass the Adda, but he achieved something of a personal triumph, as Hill reported to Stepney:

'The French have indeed the advantage of the places, the posts, and the rivers ... besides the infinite supplies of money, artillery and ammunition, and recruits, which come constantly from France; all of which are supplied very sparingly to P. Eugene. We see nothing to balance all those advantages, but the merit, the conduct, and valour of P. Eugene, of which we have the greatest idea that you can imagine.'[3]

Eugen's shortages of men, forage and equipment were now more acute than ever. 'It is a miracle,' he wrote to the Emperor after Cassano, 'that the army still hangs together in view of our dire needs.'[4] But his spirit was quite unbroken. He was eager to move on quickly and relieve Turin, and when that proved impossible owing to the lack of troops and supplies, he strongly resisted the pressure put upon him by some of his German generals to retire into winter quarters at

---

[1] *Feldzüge*, VII, Suppl. p. 102.
[2] *The Diplomatic Correspondence of the Rt. Hon. Richard Hill*, 1845, II, p. 560.
[3] 2.9.1705, Hill, op. cit., II, p. 612.
[4] *Feldzüge*, VII, Suppl. p. 372.

Ferrara. In doing so he gave an illuminating exposé of his objectives in Italy.

'We are carrying out here in Italy,' he wrote, 'not a war of conquest nor of establishing winter quarters, but a war of diversion. This diversion already involves a heavy expenditure for the French in men and money. They have to keep 80,000 men in Italy . . . whereas the Allies only have 40,000 there. In order to preserve this favourable situation, which prevents the French from achieving superiority in Flanders, Germany and Spain, it is essential to hold places in Italy throughout the winter which will cause the French constant uncertainty.'[1]

Eventually, however, the misery in his army compelled Eugen to withdraw to Venice, for whose neutrality he had little respect. 'I would rather hear their complaints,' he told the Emperor, 'than see my army disintegrate.' There was indeed a plunge in morale as winter 1705–6 froze about the Imperial troops. Conditions were as black as in 1702 and once again looting had to be condoned to prevent a general mutiny. At the end of October Eugen had reported to Joseph, who had become Emperor following his father's death on May 5, 1705:

'Everyone from the highest to the lowest is desperate. The soldiers just laugh at threats and resist punishment with force. I have to choose between the extremes of leniency and severity.'

With that Pilate touch which is beginning to creep into his messages he added:

'The army belongs not to me but to Your Majesty. It is the Monarchy's last means of support. Lose it and the consequences are easy to foresee. In the eyes of God, of Your Majesty and of the entire world I will not be to blame if everything suddenly goes to ruins as may well happen any day.'[2]

The core of Eugen's strength, the eight thousand Prussian soldiers whom Marlborough had winkled out of Bavaria the previous year, had been sadly reduced in number. The French had meanwhile grown

[1] O. Klopp, op. cit., XI, p. 455.
[2] Frauenholz, op. cit., p. 8.

stronger. Starhemberg, in command at Turin, was on very bad terms with the Duke of Savoy. The Republic of Venice and many small Italian Principalities were threatening to enter the war on the French side. The total collapse of the Allies in Italy seemed only to await the opening of the 1706 campaign. Eugen, sensing his own impotence, asked Starhemberg, on transfer to the Hungarian front, to take a personal message to the new Emperor. He tried the old squeeze-play of threatening resignation unless more support was provided. He also introduced a new and none-too-glorious note. 'My goods, my blood, my life—all these Your Majesty, am I humbly prepared to sacrifice, but not my honour and reputation.'[1] He had reached the degree of exasperation and the stage of life when he had begun to talk more about personal honour than about the public interest. Marlborough was in much the same mood. He was hurt by the lack of gratitude and attention from home; and he minded particularly the barbs of the Tories who expected a victory a day while railing unceasingly against the expenses of the continental war and the unreliability of Britain's allies. Marlborough had one sensitive spot, Sir Winston Churchill has admitted: 'In the armour of leather and steel by which in public affairs he was encased there was a chink into which a bodkin could be plunged. He sought not only glory but appreciation.' He certainly had little coming to him at this time from England—disillusioned over the 1705 campaign in the Low Countries, where allied progress had been thwarted mainly through the obstructiveness of the Dutch. However, Eugen was full of understanding and advice and conveyed them to Marlborough in a letter dated September 13:

'. . . It is extremely cruel that opinions so weak and discordant should have obstructed the progress of your operations, when you had every reason to expect a glorious result. I speak to you as a sincere friend. You will never be able to perform anything considerable with your army unless you are absolute, and I trust your Highness will use your utmost efforts to gain that power in future. I am not less desirous than yourself to be once more united with you in command.'[2]

The idea of joining together with Eugen again the following spring of 1706 had also been coursing through Marlborough's brain. He was more worried over Eugen's problems in Italy than his own in the

[1] Dec. 5, 1705, O. Klopp, op. cit., XI, p. 458.
[2] W. Coxe, op. cit., I, p. 322.

north. He realized the Emperor's dire need of money and reinforcements for the Italian army. 'It seems to me high time to think seriously
about this war in Italy,' he wrote to Wratislaw on October 5, 'a war
which employs so great a number of enemy troops, who would fall
upon our backs everywhere if we were driven out of it.'[1] Wratislaw,
strongly backed by the Emperor and Eugen, implored Marlborough
to come to Vienna. Marlborough agreed, and after a voyage down the
Danube, which he described as tedious, arrived there on November 12.
He had expected to meet his friend and colleague in the Austrian
capital; but the front in Italy was too precarious at that moment for
Eugen to be able to leave it. However, the Prince made sure that
Marlborough did not remain in ignorance of his views by sending
him a typically direct letter:

'I am delighted that you have undertaken a journey to Vienna,
however inconvenient at this season. . . . The chief point is to settle,
that none should proceed according to their own whim, but to
resolve which army shall act offensively, and which continue on the
defensive. These remarks relate to the Empire and the Netherlands;
as to this country, the measures which your Highness has adopted
with the King of Prussia, and those which you will take in your
journey, with the elector palatine, are highly advantageous.

'The first object is money, so necessary to carry on the war with
vigour and effect. You will, my lord duke, judge on your arrival at
Vienna, from your own experience, that a sovereign who is troubled
with an intestine war, and has large armies to maintain, cannot
supply all without extreme difficulty. The loan, therefore, is of the
greatest consequence . . . my army is ruined, the horses worn out
with past fatigues, no sure footing in the country, and the enemy
reassembling their forces in my front. Besides, the Venetians
threaten to declare against us, if we do not quit their territory;
the princes of Italy join in this declaration, and are inclined to
form a league for their common defence. The remedy is difficult,
but must be found. If Barcelona is taken, surely the fleet, with a
corps of troops for disembarkation, may support the duke of
Savoy, draw contributions from Genoa and Tuscany, and keep
Italy in check, while the ministers of England and Holland strongly
remonstrate with Venice, for the other princes of Italy are not
worthy of a moment's consideration. At the same time, succours
of men and money should be prepared for this army, so that it be

[1] *Murray's Dispatches*, op. cit., II, p. 293.

enabled to take the field, at the latest, towards the end of March; for which purpose the magazines should be established, the recruits and horses for remounting the cavalry at hand and the fleet ready to co-operate in the spring, either on the coast of Spain, or to invade Naples, which is without troops. I am much concerned that I cannot have the honour of joining your Highness in Vienna.'[1]

Upon arriving in Vienna, Marlborough was immediately immobilized with gout. Most of the conferences therefore had to take place around his bed—a field-bed set up in Sunderland's house at the Duke's special request rather than in the palace prepared for him by the Emperor. Highly successful they were from the Empire's standpoint. Pain made Marlborough neither crotchety nor cautious. He engaged his private fortune with the bankers of Vienna to obtain a hundred thousand crowns for the Austrian Government to enable them to pay outstanding wages. And in the name of the Sea Powers, he promised another loan of £250,000 for Eugen's army, though only on the condition that the money did not pass through the rapacious hands of the Imperial court. On the touchy subject of Hungary everything also went gratifyingly well for the Monarchy. Marlborough and Sunderland were persuaded that the insurgents and not the Austrian Government were to blame for the continuation of the intestine conflict. Even the embarrassing personal issue of Marlborough's principality was resolved. When the time arrived for the Duke to leave his field-bed and Vienna, he took with him the Emperor's assurance that the state of Mindelheim would be carved for him out of conquered Bavaria. He promised to hurry to Berlin to secure increased Prussian support for the allied fronts in Italy and Germany the following year.

Inevitably there were difficulties and jealousies to be overcome before Marlborough's assurances about the £250,000 loan and the augmentation of troops could be executed. After more than twenty years' service with the Habsburgs it might have been supposed that Eugen would have been inured to procrastination. But on December 2, 1705, we find him writing impatiently to Marlborough from Italy. His letter contains an excellent account of his basic views on the importance of the Italian front:

'I received your Highness's letter of the 20th from Vienna, and I hope that you are recovered from your indisposition, and that

[1] Coxe, op. cit., I, pp. 356–7.

this will find you at The Hague. His Imperial Majesty has, through Count Wratislaw, communicated to me what passed during your continuance at Vienna, and has ordered me to send this courier to your Highness with my sentiments on the war in Italy. All Europe knows its great importance, as well from the diversion it occasions to the French as from the prodigious expenses it requires, without reckoning the 12,000 men which they have already lost in that country, since the commencement of hostilities. It is evident France maintains 112 battalions and 118 squadrons in the territory between Piedmont and Lombardy, without including the Spanish troops, and those that are stationed in Provence, Dauphiné, and the neighbouring provinces.'

Then comes a most revealing passage:

'It is an axiom that no breach can be made in the Spanish Monarchy except through Italy. This fact is evident from the efforts of the King of France to support this war, and his comparative indifference in other quarters; for this army has never been diminished; but on the contrary, this moment is increasing with considerable reinforcements. . . . France will never offer any reasonable conditions as long as she is in possession of Italy.'[1]

This shows the extent to which Eugen was thinking of the Italian theatre as an end in itself and not merely as a jumping-off ground for an attack on the south of France, as has often been suggested.[2] It was almost an obsession with him that the Maritime Powers persistently underestimated the importance of the Italian front. He was sure that a victory there would thoroughly undermine the spirit of the enemy. So long as things remained undecided there, no possibility could exist of the French coming to terms, while for the Allies to lose in Italy would mean the crumbling of the Empire and the loss of the whole eastern front against France. For this, outside urgent help was needed. As Eugen admitted to Marlborough, rather than face the likelihood of defeat in Italy, he would recommend Joseph to withdraw all his troops and reach an accommodation with the French.

[1] W. Coxe, op. cit., I, pp. 363–4.

[2] Archdeacon Coxe was so blinkered about this that he translated the sentence in Eugen's letter, *Outre cela on ne ferait jamais brêche à la monarchie d'Espagne que par l'Italie*, as follows. 'It is an axiom that no breach can be made in France except through Italy.' See Dr Herman Wendt, *Der Italienische Kriegsschauplatz in Europäischen Konflikten*, 1936.

'. . . in my opinion His Imperial Majesty is incapable of alone supporting this war any longer as he has done hitherto, by exhausting his territories of men and money . . .

' . . . should the maritime powers not act in concert with His Imperial Majesty, I must advise the Emperor not to lose a moment in withdrawing his troops before they are quite ruined, and in recommending His Royal Highness to make the best accommodation in his power. I candidly allow that this advice seems extraordinary, but on considering the state of affairs, it appears the only means not to lose the whole. As to myself, I trust that on many occasions I have proved my zeal for the service of my master; yet I must declare that no consideration shall induce me to make another campaign like the last, in which I wanted everything. . . . I therefore repeat my opinion, that as the only means of supporting this war, the maritime powers must grant a loan of £250,000 on some secure funds, and reinforce this army with 10,000 men, His Imperial Majesty binding himself to recruit his infantry, and remount his cavalry.'[1]

The Duke had sufficient poise and knew Eugen well enough by this time to discount his flurry of expression whilst heeding the substance of his advice. He stuck to the task of carrying out the promises he had made in Vienna. Extra troops were duly hired and the £250,000 loan eventually secured. The money finally reached Eugen via a financial house in Venice which had received it from Frankfurt, thereby satisfactorily circumventing the Imperial court.

Eugen was impatient to visit Vienna. He wanted to meet the new Emperor, Joseph, a blue-eyed, handsome high-spirited epicurean, in boisterous contrast to his ascetic, hesitant father from whom he had inherited neither the exaggerated lip, nor the sense of public duty. It was essential to engage Joseph's interest in the Italian theatre. Eugen was inquisitive too to find out what changes had been taking place behind as well as on the throne. Prince von Salm was the Emperor's chief adviser. A Fleming with an imperfect knowledge of German, he had become the leader of the party in Vienna which hated the Austrian aristocracy and all non-Germans, a force which stood for Imperial rather than Habsburg interests. He had been Joseph's confidant and mentor before the latter became Emperor. He was hostile to Eugen. It was not long before Eugen became the centre of an anti-Salm faction which included Wratislaw.

[1] W. Coxe, op. cit., I, pp. 363–4.

In the talks which Eugen had with the Emperor after arriving in Vienna at the beginning of 1706 he was unconcealedly despondent about the chances of redeeming the allied position in Italy. Unless the Sea Powers could be persuaded to co-operate off the coast he recommended the Emperor to withdraw completely from Italy. However, such a policy would have required more positive action than the Imperial machine could accomplish even under the new Emperor, who was not disposed to exhaust all his energies on the grind of duty. Joseph appealed to Eugen like a brother to save the family honour in Italy. Eugen, therefore, against his own will and in the lowest of spirits, set out from Vienna in early April for the Italian front. However, before he was able to reach his army Vendôme gave it a severe beating at Calcinato. 10,000 men were captured or deserted. But the loss was incomparably greater than that. Marlborough had hitherto been planning to march to Italy. He had even had the necessary hand-mills for grinding corn issued to the troops. But with the fiasco of Calcinato and the defeat which the Margrave of Baden, in command of the Imperial forces in Germany, had suffered on the Rhine, his dream of another epic march across Europe and an Italian Blenheim fought with Eugen must have faded. Nevertheless he was deeply conscious of the need to send urgent relief to Italy. He therefore divested himself of troops in favour of Eugen and reconciled his soul to conducting a minor campaign in the Low Countries with inferior strength.

Pending the arrival of Marlborough's generous support, Eugen decided to pull his troops out of Italy into the Alps. Vendôme and the French Government were absolutely confident that they would never return, and that Eugen, being a realist, would recognize that the most he could hope to do would be to defend the Tyrol. But Eugen, true to character, had drawn courage and inspiration from the calamity. His arrival at the front after the rout of Calcinato had magically invigorated the disintegrating army. 'I succeeded so well,' he wrote apropos of the effect of his arrival on the morrow of the battle, 'that the same day the greater part of the army was reassembled in a matter of hours.'[1] The conduct of the defeated Imperial commander, Graf Reventlau, was much criticized, though Eugen himself rejected the proposal for a court-martial saying: 'It could only have one result, to show that not everyone can command an army.'[2]

What did it take in those days to exercise such a command? Many

[1] Letter to Graf Daun, April 22, 1706, *Feldzüge*, I Ser., VIII, Suppt. p. 86.
[2] Eugen to the Emperor, May 29, 1706, A. Arneth, op. cit., I, p. 361.

of the soldiers of the Imperial army were pressed unwillingly into service or were hirelings, or outcasts; anything but the cream of youth yearning to risk all for the sake of king and country. Nor was there any of the apparatus of propaganda such as modern commanders have to support them. A traveller who visited Vienna during the War of the Spanish Succession was struck more than anything else by the absence of any attempt on the part of the authorities to encourage the will of the people to fight by explaining and publicizing the reasons for the war.[1] Thanks to the incomparable staff-work behind the front, the Imperial troops were invariably underfed and underpaid. As for the battles themselves, they may not have lasted so long, but they were scarcely less grim than those of modern times, with no anaesthetics to treat the wounds, suddenly made more numerous and frightful than hitherto by the new dominance of offence over defence.

Something indeed not far short of a revolution had recently been taking place in the art of infantry warfare. Mention has already been made of the substitution throughout Europe of the flintlock for the matchlock which greatly increased the fire-power of the musketeer.[2] There was another no less important, if slower development, the replacement of the pike by the ring bayonet. It is surprising how long it took to think of fitting a ring round the muzzle of a musket so that firing need not be obstructed. For long the Imperial forces relied on a Swedish invention, the *Schweinsfeder*, or boar spear, a short form of pike (the normal pike was between fourteen and eighteen feet long) which was either stuck in the ground in front of the soldier, or joined up with other spears to form defence barriers, known as *chevaux de frise*, behind which the infantry fired. However, they were awkward to handle and needed special carts for their transport. At one time a bayonet plugged into the musket's muzzle was tried, but the impediment was obvious. The advantages of the ring bayonet were instantaneously apparent. By the early years of the eighteenth century both sides had been armed with various types of it, and this together with the flintlock greatly enhanced the importance of the infantry soldier and the goriness of battles. The proportion of casualties to total forces engaged leapt dramatically in the War of the Spanish Succession compared with earlier wars. This obviously imposed increased responsibilities on the commanders. Not only were the stakes higher, there was also an additional problem of

[1] C. Freschot, *Mémoires de la Cour de Vienne*, 1705, p. 205.
[2] See Chapter IV, p. 44.

morale. It evidently called for great qualities of leadership to get men to face the new risks, and Eugen clearly cast something of a spell over his troops to induce them to fight so heroically. Yet he had many serious handicaps: without common ties of tongue, blood or background with the majority of his soldiers, he also lacked the physical attributes which helped to make Marlborough such a compelling personality. In his simple brown coat with brass buttons he looked more like a Capuchin monk than a soldier. His only affectation and indulgence was to take repeated pinches of Spanish snuff which he carried loose in his pocket. But his negative bearing was offset by the extraordinarily powerful current of selfless enthusiasm which he generated. In the *History of Henry Esmond*, Thackeray has written that Eugen's officers described how in the hour of battle he 'became possessed with a sort of warlike fury; his eyes lighted up; he rushed hither and thither, raging; he shrieked curses and encouragement, yelling and harking his bloody war-dogs on, and himself always at the first of the hunt'. Thackeray contrasts Eugen's furious personal hatred of the French King with 'the calm hostility of our great English general, who was no more moved by the game of war than that of billiards, and pushed forward his squadrons and drove his red battalions hither as calmly as he would combine a stroke or make a cannon with the balls . . .' Thackeray's account is vivid, but in drawing the contrast between Eugen and Marlborough in black and white he misses an important shade of Eugen's character, his ability to be alternately calm and fiery in extreme degree—a rare combination of qualities which more than anything else evoked Marlborough's admiration.

It is always hard to analyse or understand what it was exactly in a person of a bygone age that gave him a magnetic influence over his contemporaries. With so many obvious disadvantages, it is particularly difficult to understand the alchemy of Eugen's charm. But there is no disputing its effect, infectious over tens of thousands of men, making him an army in himself against the French. As to how he got on with his fellow officers there is little evidence on which to draw. The Imperial officers of those times either took great care to see that their private journals never reached the light of day, or, much more likely, they never wrote them; and there are no comtemporary letters which might help to fill the personal gap. But we know a little of how Eugeń got on with his only conceivable rival, Guido Starhemberg.[1] A most capable and courageous officer, Guido Starhem-

[1] See p. 42.

berg did not, of course, suffer from Eugen's handicap of an alien language and background. Eugen and he were almost exact contemporaries and they came to hate each other. How the hostility started is conjectural. For some years they corresponded amicably together, but this suddenly ceased in 1703. Appearances however were maintained and, at any rate until the end of the war against Louis, no damage was done to the Imperial service. On the contrary, their rivalry seemed to serve as a spur to both.

Now, with the unfolding of the 1706 Italian campaign, we come to one of the most dramatic episodes in Eugen's life. There were many times when by force of his personality and decision he appears to have reversed an otherwise inevitable train of events, but there was no other occasion when the change from despair to triumph was so complete as during the amazing Turin adventure; and no other campaign in which he personally made a more decisive contribution. This resulted as much from his control of the preliminaries as from his mastery of the ultimate clash of arms. Like boxers who parry and thrust warily through many rounds knowing full well that one heavy blow by either side at the right time and place may be decisive, the armies of early eighteenth-century Europe sidled round each other often for months, weaving and probing until they had manoeuvred themselves into what they hoped would be the determining position for the few hours of actual battle. Eugen was a professional at such manoeuvre.

Seen from the vantage point of Versailles the French plan for Italy that summer must have looked sublimely simple. Two powerful armies were on foot there. One, under Vendôme, was to keep Eugen cooped up in the Alps, whither he had withdrawn after the French victory at Calcinato. The other, under the Marquis de la Feuillade, was to attack and take Turin. Eugen was over two hundred miles away, and Louis XIV believed, not without good reason, that the capture of Turin, which was defended by a small Imperial force of 7,000 under Graf Daun, would be an easy matter and that the way would then lie open for the French conquest of the whole of Italy. With an army of 40,000, La Feuillade began to lay siege to the city on May 14, 1706, and started to build lines of circumvallation and contravallation shortly afterwards.[1] Meanwhile, however, the Duke of Savoy had escaped from the city with a small force of cavalry and was harassing the French from outside. By this means he succeeded admirably in deflecting the enemy from their main objective of

[1] See footnote, Chapter III, p. 32.

pursuing the siege, a digression helped by the incompetence of La Feuillade, whom Saint-Simon described as having a 'soul of mud'.

During May and June Eugen lay up in the foothills of the Alps awaiting the money and reinforcements promised by Marlborough and biding his time until the moment should come to try to break out and dash to the relief of Turin. On the other side of the river Adige, Vendôme was confidently sealing him in; between Lake Garda and the river and then south-east down the Adige from Verona he constructed impenetrable earthworks and palissades. But then at the end of May, while the two commanders crouched opposite each other as if preparing to spring, an event occurred which was to have profound repercussions on the plans of both of them. On May 23 Marlborough defeated Villeroi at Ramillies. Louis XIV thereupon decided that Vendôme must be transferred from the Italian front to take command in Flanders. The decisiveness of the victory also had the effect of disposing the Republic of Venice to the allied side, which encouraged Eugen to think in terms of infringing their neutrality and marching through their territory in the opposite direction from Turin, thereby throwing the French off the scent. Unlike Vendôme's troops, whose depredations since Calcinato had made them exceedingly unpopular with the Venetians, the Imperial forces had been models of discipline. At the end of June Eugen could assure the Emperor, 'I have been so insistent on the strictest discipline that there have been no excesses; orchards have been quite untouched, harvests gathered without loss or hindrance, whilst where the French have been there has been wholesale spoilation.'[1]

In this propitious atmosphere Eugen decided that he could traverse Venetian territory with impunity and that the best way to go to the relief of Turin was to march right round the French army which was busy defending the upper Adige. The French pinned everything on holding this part of the river. 'The army must sooner perish than abandon this river,' Vendôme wrote to Louis XIV on July 1.[2] He was convinced that there was no other way Eugen could get out of his Alpine strait-jacket and that he would be bound sometime to try to advance across the river. Needless to say Eugen helped to persuade him that this was his intention by ingenious feints and ruses. Indeed he did intend striking across the Adige, but not in the upper reaches

---

[1] A. Arneth, op. cit., I, p. 480.

[2] *Mémoires Militaires relatifs à la Succession d'Espagne sous Louis XIV*, par le Lieutenant Général de Vault, revus et publiés par le Général Pelet, 1835, VI, p. 642.

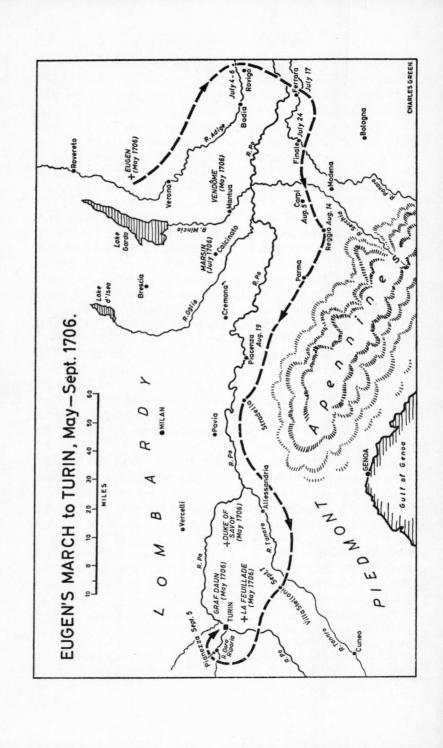

EUGEN'S MARCH to TURIN, May—Sept. 1706.

MILES

LOMBARDY

PIEDMONT

Apennines

Lake Garda

Lake d'Iseo

Gulf of Genoa

Rovereto

Verona

Brescia

MILAN

Vercelli

Pavia

Cremona

Mantua

Calcinato

Badia

Rovigo

Ferrara

Bologna

Modena

Reggio Aug. 14

Carpi Aug. 5

Finale July 24

Parma

Piacenza Aug. 19

Stradella

Allessandria

Turin

Cuneo

GENOA

R. Adige

R. Mincio

R. Oglio

R. Po

R. Panaro

R. Secchia

R. Tanaro

R. Dora Riparia

+ EUGEN (May 1706)

VENDÔME (May 1706)

MARSIN (July 1706)

+ DUKE OF SAVOY (May 1706)

GRAF DAUN (May 1706)

+ LA FEUILLADE (May 1706)

Villaseltonia Sept. 1

Pianezza Sept. 5

July 4-6

July 17

CHARLES GREEN

of the river, nor anywhere near where the French troops were entrenched. His plan, which he started to implement at the end of June without waiting for the arrival of reinforcements, was to march south-east through Venetian territory and to cross the Adige as far east as Rovigo. He was over the river with about thirty thousand men by the end of the first week in July. Astonished at his unmolested progress, he made for the Po with the intention of crossing it and of then marching westwards and turning the whole line of French defences. Even when Eugen was already approaching the banks of the Po Vendôme was still sublimely unaware of the danger. 'You can be sure,' he reported to Versailles on July 10, 'that Prince Eugene will not be able to disturb the seige of Turin. We have too many positions in which to stop him, for his ever dreaming of bringing relief.'[1] But he soon had to take account of Eugen's astonishing advance. Forced to retreat he explained this obviously as a with-drawal to prepared positions. At this point he was mercifully called away north. The Italian front was left under the command of the Duke of Orleans and Marshall Marsin, who withdrew over the Oglio and then again farther west in a vain effort to avoid being outflanked by Eugen. The Prince sped on westwards towards Turin keeping south of the Po. Although the long march was virtually unopposed by the enemy, his troops suffered appallingly from the heat and the difficulties of finding food and water. To escape the unrelenting sun they moved as much as possible by moonlight. It was a feat on the same heroic scale as Marlborough's march to the Danube two years before. By the beginning of September they had succeeded in joining up with the Duke of Savoy at Villa Stelloni about twenty miles south of Turin.

The French commanders, the Duke of Orleans, Marsin and La Feuillade, now hurriedly conferred. Their joint army, which was now assembled before Turin, amounted to some sixty thousand men, as against a total allied force under Eugen and the Duke of Savoy of about thirty thousand. At the end of August La Feuillade had made an unsuccessful and expensive effort to storm the Turin citadel, but otherwise French policy was one of inactivity. This was to prove disastrous. They should clearly have sallied out into open country and attacked instead of merely pursuing the siege and waiting upon the enemy; and this was indeed what the Duke of Orleans who was nominally in supreme command recommended. With overwhelming French numerical superiority it looked to him as though they would

[1] *Mémoires Militaires*, op. cit., VI, p. 200.

be almost bound to win if they took the offensive. But Marsin demurred. If we are to assess correctly the forces at work which ultimately decided the fate of Turin and hence of Italy in these August and September days of 1706, we must take account of the frayed state of Marsin's nerves, brought about by the awful prospect of confronting Eugen. He was too frightened to move. As he confided in a letter to Michel de Chamillard, the French Minister of War, he had been convinced from the moment he received orders to go to Italy that he would be killed there. 'Death,' he confessed, '. . . thrusts itself upon me at every moment and possesses me night and day.'[1] His fear communicated itself to the other generals. They joined with him in persuading Orleans to drop any idea of taking the initiative. As if hypnotized, therefore, these three senior French commanders and their enormous army, which had fought only one battle that year, and this a victorious one, cowered in their lines while Eugen was at liberty to reconnoitre and then to manoeuvre for position. He applied himself jauntily to both activities. A little way from the centre of Turin the Superga hill rises two thousand feet above sea level and commands a fine view of the city. On September 2 Eugen, accompanied by the Duke of Savoy, rode with great deliberation to the top of the hill whence he peered quizically into the enemy's lines. He was astonished at what he saw. The French were in transparent disorder. They had not even completed the lines of circumvallation to the north-west of the city. Viewing this happy scene he turned to the Duke of Savoy and said, '*Il me semble que ces gens là sont à demi battus.*' He promised that there would be no difficulty or delay in beating them. Intoxicated by Eugen's confidence Victor Amadeus vowed then and there that if they won the battle and relieved Turin he would put up a church in commemoration. The Basilica of the Superga stands witness to this day that they both kept their word.

Eugen's plan, which he proceeded forthwith to implement, was to march right round the city from the Villa Stelloni and to attack the enemy between the rivers Dora Riparia and Stura where their entrenchments were weakest. He gave notice of his intentions to Graf Daun so that he could be ready for a sortie from the beleaguered fortress when the time was ripe. By the evening of September 6 Eugen, with his thirty thousand men, was in battle position.

At dawn the next day the Allies advanced. In the tough ding-dong fight which went on all morning Eugen retained the initiative, and at

[1] *Mémoires Militaires*, op. cit., VI, p. 277.

one crucial moment he succeeded in turning on the enemy their own guns which had fallen into his hands. Half of his army were Austrians. They were ably supported by various German contingents including cavalry under the brilliant commander Baron Kriechbaum, and infantry entrusted to the French Marquis de Langallerie, who had defected to the allied side for personal reasons and who was regarded by his compatriots not altogether surprisingly as *enivré de lui-même*. There were also Prussian infantry under Leopold of Anhalt-Dessau, whom Eugen nicknamed 'the bull-dog'. As usual the skill Eugen displayed in conducting the battle consisted of a combination of restraint and dash. He also managed to appear both coolly detached from the vicissitudes of the fighting and deeply involved personally in the most savage engagements. At one moment when giving his commands a page and a servant were killed at his side. At another he had his horse shot under him. He fell heavily to the ground and this produced consternation among his men until he got quickly to his feet and shouted cheerfully that he was unhurt. By midday Marsin was mortally wounded, his army broken and the road into Turin wide open. Eugen's casualties had been heavy, as heavy as those of the French—about 3,000 killed and wounded; but he had captured 6,000 prisoners and 3,000 horses. What the final reckoning amounted to was this, that as a result of months of handy manoeuvre and a few hours of fighting the French army had been smashed, and with it Louis XIV's day-dreams in Italy.

Panic-stricken, the French, instead of marching east into Lombardy where they would have found reinforcements and could have remained masters of the Milanese, fled west towards France. When Eugen heard of the French decision he is said to have exclaimed, 'Italy is ours and its conquest will not be costly.' This was not mere bombast. Turin was the end of effective French resistance in Italy. It also marked the beginning of Austrian, instead of Spanish, hegemony in Italy, which was to last for the next 150 years.

Eugen was impatient to thank Marlborough for the help he had provided in money, and even more important, in the large number of troops he had drummed up from Germany. On the night of the victory he wrote to Marlborough from the Turin battle-field:

'Your Highness will not, I am sure, be displeased to hear by the Baron de Hohendorff of the signal advantage which the arms of His Imperial Majesty and his allies have gained over the enemy. You have had so great a share in it by the succours you have

procured, that you must permit me to thank you again. Marshal
Marsin is taken prisoner and mortally wounded. The troops have
greatly signalized themselves. In a few days I will send you a
correct account; and in the meantime refer you to that which you
will hear from the bearer of this letter, who is well-informed, has
seen everything, and is competent to give an accurate relation.
Your Highness will excuse the shortness of this letter, as I have
not a moment of time.'[1]

Coxe points out that Eugen modestly omits to mention, in excuse
for the abruptness of this letter, the pain of a dangerous wound in
the head, which he received during the attack on the French lines.

Having acknowledged the importance of Marlborough's 'succours'
we must not omit to do justice to Eugen's personal triumph. Perhaps
he could not have done it without this help, but who else could have
succeeded, even with it? A more boastful man than Eugen might
well have used Wellington's words of almost exactly a hundred years
later: 'By God, I don't think it would have been done if I had not
been here.'

The consequences of the victory to Austrian history were as far-
reaching as those of Blenheim to British history. It is indisputable
that the Austrian Government, as such, deserved little credit for
Turin. Ever since the passing of those halcyon early months of the
war when they had stood alone against Louis XIV, they had increasingly given the Allies the impression of being a Jesuit-ridden,
bankrupt, incorrigibly incompetent court, more concerned with the
particular interests of the Habsburgs than the common struggle
against the French. This understandable exasperation towards
Vienna was reaching its high point at the time of Turin; in retrospect
it only emphasizes how much the Allies owed to Eugen personally.
The Emperor thanked him by giving him a diamond-studded sword
and offering him the Governorship of Milan.

Marlborough's praise of Eugen at Turin was unstinted. 'It is
impossible,' he wrote to Sarah, 'for me to express the joy it has given
me; for I not only esteem, but I really love that Prince.'[2] To Heinsius
he enlarged upon his friend's victory: 'I am assured that the French
take more to heart their misfortune in Italy than they did that of
Ramillies.'[3] Nowhere was the enthusiasm for Eugen after the victory

[1] W. Coxe, op. cit., I, p. 459.
[2] W. Coxe, op. cit., I, p. 460.
[3] G. G. Vreede, *Correspondance Diplomatique et Militaire*, 1850, p. 131.

of Turin greater than in England, where, so it is recorded in token of his hold upon the people, a girl bequeathed him two hundred pounds on her death-bed with the expiring regret that she could not have made it two hundred thousand,[1] and a gardener[2] left him in his will a hundred pounds.

Strident though the British Government were in their structures upon the selfishness of Austrian policy during all these years, posterity cannot overlook the great benefit which accrued to British commercial interests from the expulsion of the enemy from Italy (and incidentally also from the Spanish Netherlands) and the opening of trade there to British merchants.[3]

[1] Granger to Eugen, October 20, 1706, A. Arneth, op. cit., I, p. 482.
[2] E. Mauvillon, op. cit., III, p. 42.
[3] The principalities and republics of Italy, though small each of them in population, made up together at this time a total population of 13 million people, a larger population than any unitary state in Europe except France. See G. N. Clark, *The Seventeenth Century.*

CHAPTER X

THE DISASTER OF TOULON, 1707

AFTER THE *annus mirabilis* of Ramillies and Turin and the successes the Allies had had in Spain the same year it looked as though 'in all probability one year's war more would give ease to all Christendom for many years', as Marlborough reported to Godolphin in October 1706.[1] But in fact within a few months it appeared as if the speed of their advance had merely loosened the none-too-secure latches of the Alliance. 1707 was to prove disastrous for the Allies on all fronts —in Spain, on the Rhine and on the Riviera—and to be a particularly bad year for Eugen.

The outset was gratifying enough to him. After the death on January 4, 1707, of the Margrave Louis of Baden, Eugen replaced him as Imperial Field-Marshal. In April he took up his Governorship of Milan, a most lucrative post which he had originally had to decline for political reasons. This honour was timely since he had just been balked of a glittering opportunity to become King of Poland. The Czar Peter had wanted him to have the crown and had proposed this to the Emperor, but Joseph was afraid to back him. Eugen's inner feelings about the idea are difficult to fathom. According to von Arneth he preferred to remain with the Imperial army than become King of Poland. However, in a letter to Joseph he implied that he would have liked to accept and had hesitated only because of the Emperor's opposition. 'In his more than twenty years' service,' he explained to Joseph, 'he had never let vain personal ambition interfere with his duty. He must therefore beseech the Emperor to have regard to nothing but the Imperial interest'[2]—a statement, we

[1] W. Coxe, op. cit., III, p. 98.
[2] Eugen to the Emperor, May 29, 1707, A. Arneth, op. cit., I, p. 486.

must assume from the development of Eugen's character, to have been no less heartfelt for seeming sanctimonious. The Imperial interest certainly ordained refusal. King Charles XII of Sweden was insisting on Stanislaus Leszcyinski as king of Poland, and Joseph was understandably reluctant to risk war in support of Eugen's candidacy.

In focusing attention all these years upon Eugen's and Marlborough's struggles against Louis XIV, the eye must not ignore completely the meteoric rise of King Charles XII in the east. Having defeated Peter of Russia and Augustus of Saxony-Poland, the Swedish King, Spartan in appearance, effulgent in effect, had set up camp in Saxony in the autumn of 1706. It was feared that he might attack the Emperor in the interests of the Silesian Protestants. He had a host of grievances against Joseph, the most malign arising from the alleged maltreatment of Protestants in the Empire, particularly in Silesia. Suddenly the danger point of the allied war shifted east, and all fears centred upon Altranstädt near Leipzig where Charles had established his headquarters. Thither Marlborough proceeded the following April. It was not the first nor the least distinguished of his many strenuous journeys on behalf of the Alliance. He stressed to Charles XII how opposed were the King's interests to those of the anti-Protestant Louis XIV and how pressing was the final settlement of his account with the Czar. In protracted correspondence with Vienna he then persuaded Joseph to make concessions in Silesia. Charles thereupon struck camp in Saxony and marched off with high hopes of dethroning Peter—soon to be dashed in total defeat upon the Russian battlefield of Poltava. Eugen was not on the throne of Poland, but neither was Charles XII in the Hofburg.

The negotiations with the French which the Emperor entrusted to Eugen after Turin provided his only success that year and revealed, incidentally, unexpected deposits of diplomatic talent. Hitherto Marlborough had outshone him in diplomacy and in the general day-to-day management of the Alliance. He was to continue to do so, but from now on Eugen's part was considerable. By nature too intolerant and thrustful for this trade, he had nevertheless by now acquired the reputation, inestimable in a negotiator—*pace* Sir Henry Wotton—of complete honesty and reliability. Thanks largely to his presence in Italy, Louis accepted Joseph's terms for the withdrawal of all French troops from the country. Louis XIV was convinced that Eugen would ensure fair execution. The treaty providing for French evacuation of Italy was signed in Milan on March 13, 1707. It was a moment of triumph for the Empire, in arms against the

French since the opening days of the war. Sir Winston Churchill, however, is highly critical of the Treaty of Milan which he condemns as a separate local peace, damaging to the Alliance as a whole—an act of 'folly and ingratitude of the basest kind'. He argues, in support of this harsh judgment, that the twenty thousand French troops in Italy would inevitably have been made prisoner within a few months instead of being allowed, as they were by the treaty, to rejoin Louis XIV's main armies. In almost the same breath, however, he reproaches the Empire with having 'no army of its own worthy of the name in Italy', and admits that it was about to be forced against its will into participating in an ambitious invasion of the south of France. These very circumstances surely make out a case for the Emperor's 'folly and ingratitude'. They explain why he seized the favourable opportunity following Turin to secure the removal from the Italian theatre of the residue of the well-trained French army which would have been nothing less than a thicket in the Imperial flesh during the proposed advance into France. In such a light the decision does not seem too dishonourable.

The plan for the invasion of southern France forms the main event in Eugen's life in 1707. It was Marlborough's brainchild. He believed that the only way to bring down Louis was to tackle him at both ends; himself from the north, and Eugen, supported by the allied fleet, from the south. But he was not optimistic about his chances of penetrating very far beyond the fortresses of Lille, Mons and Tournai. The Dutch were promising to be particularly difficult again, and Louis had concentrated a large army against him under Vendôme. All hopes at the start then were on Eugen's attack. The objective must be the capture of Toulon. This would ensure allied control of the Mediterranean, enable the amphibious power of England to be brought to bear against France, and force the French army to scurry out of Spain in defence of the homeland. For long Marlborough had wanted to be able to ring down the curtain on the extravagant Spanish theatre.

But the Empire was more interested in sending an expedition to conquer Naples than in a joint attack on France. Ever since the rising there in 1701 against Philip of Anjou, Vienna had been convinced that Naples could easily be plucked for the Habsburgs. Joseph was impatient to support his partisans. He had got wind of overtures which Louis XIV had been making to England and Holland to renounce Spain and the Indies, together with the Netherlands, in return for the cession of Naples and Sicily to the Duke of Anjou.

The Dutch Government, he knew, were strongly in favour of this plan. No delay could therefore be afforded by Vienna in frustrating it. Eugen had been against the diversion of troops to Naples in 1701 when the Imperial position in northern Italy was so precarious. But he was all for the expedition now.

The Duke of Savoy was anxious to prevent Austrian occupation of Naples. He was becoming apprehensive of Vienna's growing ambitions to dominate all Italy. It was the old story for Savoy; the inexpediency of engagement. Victor Amadeus pined for a return to the good old see-saw days when he had been able to hold the balance of power between the Houses of Austria and Bourbon.

The Maritime Powers also were strongly opposed. The Dutch had their special reasons, as we have seen. But apart from these both England and Holland believed that Naples could safely be left to fall by itself. They were convinced that as a matter of urgency the Allies must concentrate all their forces against France. In April, they had been savagely defeated at Almanza in Spain. In May, Marshal Villars had surprised the German watch on the Rhine and overrun the Lines of Stollhofen.

The Imperial Government insisted, however, on mopping up Naples. This must be first priority for Vienna whatever might be happening elsewhere. However much London might be frowning officially, the Earl of Peterborough had been giving the Emperor and Eugen plenty of encouragement for the Naples expedition. Dismissed from command of the allied forces in Spain and recalled by the Queen to explain himself, Peterborough had chosen a devious route home, calling in at various capitals en route, including Turin and Vienna, to volunteer advice contrary on all points to that of the British Government. What in any case had Austria gained out of the war so far? England seemed to be climbing to greatness on her shoulders while talking all the time about the selfishness of others. To London, indeed, the Austrian attitude appeared starkly uncooperative. In June, Godolphin was complaining: 'Vienna has not one thought that is not directly opposite to the interest of the Allies.'[1]

Marlborough, held in Dutch fetters and confronted by able French army, saw the only salvation in the rapid execution of his Toulon *idée fixe*. Eventually, after much wrangling, an agreement was reached: Vienna would continue with their Naples side-show, but she would also take part in the attack on Toulon with Eugen leading the land forces, though under the supreme command of the

[1] G. M. Trevelyan, op. cit., II, p. 288.

Duke of Savoy. All this took time to arrange. The Duke of Savoy also insisted on a much larger supply of powder and shot than was originally provided for, which further held up the start of the Toulon advance.

This delay before the Allies began to march has frequently been invoked as the prime cause of the ultimate failure of the expedition, and English historians have not been sparing in their use of it as a stick with which to beat the Empire. But the facts scarcely support them. For so long as Eugen remained at Turin the French were in a quandary. They knew that some attack was coming, but they did not know where. They could not deplete themselves in Dauphiné, where most of their troops under Marshal de Tessé lay, for fear of an attack from due east over the Alps. Yet they only had a garrison of a few thousand in Toulon should Eugen mean to strike south along the coast. Not until the middle or end of June did they receive secret intelligence of allied plans. Meanwhile on June 30 Eugen started to move south.

From the time the Allies passed Borgo, where the road divided, one running well into Dauphiné, the other south to Menton, the race was on. Savoy and Eugen had about 35,000 men under them. Tessé could call immediately on about the same number, but in addition, since the French victories in April and May at Almanza and the Lines of Stollhofen, he could draw on further reinforcements from Spain and Germany—if there was time. Both sides had a difficult march in the heat, though Tessé if anything had the longer journey to Toulon. There is a contemporary French account of the siege which makes it plain how convinced Tessé and his officers were that everything depended on which army succeeded on reaching Toulon in strength first.[1]

In the second week of July Eugen's army met up with the allied naval forces who were under Admiral Sir Cloudesley Shovell. They had maintained quite a good pace and all seemed to be going well. By July 12, after a successful small combined operation against the French, they were over the river Var just west of Nice, about seventy miles east of Toulon. The next day all the allied generals went aboard the Admiral's flagship where Eugen and Shovell set to work on plans for the next stage. Hitherto Eugen had been sceptical about the wisdom of the whole expedition. A land animal with no belief in the sea, he could not perceive how this amphibious adventure could

[1] J. Donneau de Visé, *The History of the Siege of Toulon*, Translated into English, 1708.

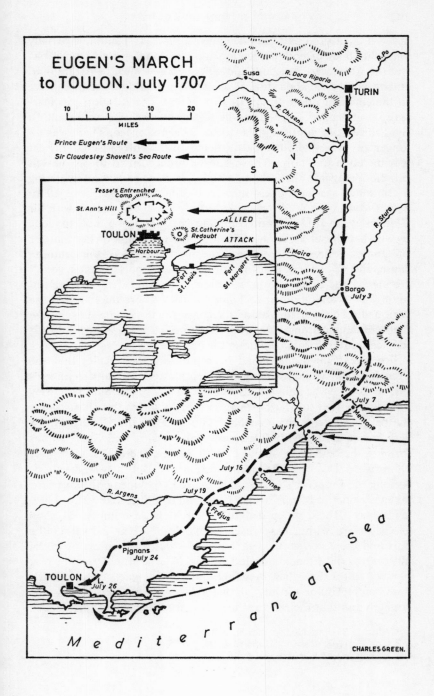

EUGEN'S MARCH
to TOULON. July 1707

10   0   10   20
MILES

Prince Eugen's Route
Sir Cloudesley Shovell's Sea Route

SAVOY

Susa
R. Dora Riparia
TURIN
R. Chisone
R. Po
R. Po
R. Stura
R. Maira
Borgo
July 3
July 7
Mentone
July 11
Nice
July 16
Cannes
July 19
Fréjus
R. Argens
Pignans
July 24
TOULON
July 26
R. Var

Tesse's Entrenched Camp
St. Ann's Hill
TOULON
Harbour
St. Catherine's Redoubt
Fort St. Louis
Fort St. Margaret
ALLIED
ATTACK

Mediterranean Sea

CHARLES GREEN.

succeed against so naturally defended a place as Toulon, especially
when his lines of communication were so long and so vulnerable.
But the Allies were insistent, and unity he knew must be paramount.
In any event once aboard the *Association* he could not be insensitive
to the ebullient optimism of Sir Cloudesley. The Admiral was fearlessly confident of success, and he was persuasive. On an instant all
the Prince's old doubts appear to have been silenced. There was no
longer any worry about the expediency of the enterprise as such; it
was merely a question of how, and he proceeded to throw himself
full-bloodedly into the task, an entirely new one to him, of planning
a combined sea-land operation. In this first flush he hastened to
assure Marlborough of the success of his initial discussions with Sir
Cloudesley, and of his restored confidence: 'You will be able to judge
by our having set aside all difficulties, the eagerness of my zeal for
the august desires of the Queen and for the good of the common
cause, and will believe that the army is united upon the same goal.'[1]
He signed the letter, 'Your affectionate cousin.' The plan agreed
upon was to march direct to Toulon and to ignore the risk that the
various French garrisons along the coast might at some stage harass
their communications. The army therefore set out again on July 15;
the fleet moved in parallel along the coast.

For weeks the English had been assuring their Allies that the
French people would revolt against their masters and rally to Eugen's
side as soon as he showed his colours in Provence. Sir Cloudesley
Shovell reported to Marlborough in mid-June that 'by all disconrse
the people are ripe for a revolt'.[2] However, as the allied army—a
very mixed body, with Prussians, Hanoverians and Saxe-Gothas
forming the backbone—moved on to Toulon there was no sign of
an uprising. This was the first disillusionment. But there were others.
Among the Emperor's troops were many Frenchmen and Bavarians
taken prisoner at Blenheim and Turin and then forced or cajoled into
his service. These proceeded to desert in large numbers as soon
as they were within easy reach of Toulon.[3] Their arrival in the
port and the accounts they gave of the scarcity of provisions in the
allied army did French morale a power of good. Finally, and worst
blow of all for the Allies, they found when they reached the enemy's
lines before Toulon on July 26, that Tessé was already there in some
strength and that the race was lost. It had taken them a fortnight to

---

[1] Winston S. Churchill, op. cit., II, p. 251.
[2] June 13, 1707. *Murray's Dispatches*, III, p. 485.
[3] J. Donneau de Visé, op. cit., p. 46.

cover the seventy miles from the Var; the heat had been appalling, the going hard. The French who had marched much better and who by the end of July had brought as many as 30,000 reinforcements to Toulon with many others on the way, set to work, with an enthusiasm unmatched on the other side, to strengthen and man the defences. The mood of the place turned from fear to one of detached curiosity as to how the combined assault was going to be launched.

When Eugen had a chance to see the town's defences at first hand he was most discouraged. They were far more formidable than he had expected. All his old hesitations revived, and the English Admiral's optimism did nothing to remove them. It was all very well for the Admiral to urge him on to storm the town, but he knew nothing of land warfare, and anyway the amount of help that his ships could give was perforce strictly limited. Nor did he have any problems of supply or lines of communication. 'I have not abandoned all hope,' Eugen wrote to the Emperor at the end of July, 'but I think it my duty to report frankly how things stand.' He did not conceal the pressure he was under from Sir Cloudesley Shovell whose bluff character can be perceived between the lines of the dry official report: 'briefly but firmly the Admiral explained that England and Holland were irretrievably committed to attacking Toulon, and that he had issued orders accordingly'. Eugen then goes on to lay bare to the Emperor his inhibitions about taking too strong a stand on this issue against the wishes of the Sea Powers. If he did so, 'they would point to the detachment of our soldiers sent to Naples and to the fact that if these troops were still here we would have enough to ensure our communications'.[1]

So against his better judgment and for reasons not strictly relevant he continued to acquiesce in the Toulon enterprise.

Marlborough, to whom Eugen also disclosed his doubts, was confident that the mood of irresolution would pass. 'You must not be too much alarmed at his expression,' he wrote to Godolphin on July 27, reporting Eugen's attitude. 'For it is his way to think everything difficult, till he comes to put it into execution, but then he acts with so much vigour that he makes amends for all his despondency. Though he writes in this manner to me, I am sure to the officers of the army his discourse is the contrary.'[2]

John Chetwynd, who had succeeded Hill as British Minister in Turin, was writing disconsolately to Marlborough on July 29

[1] *Feldzüge*, IX, Suppl. p. 178.
[2] W. Coxe, op. cit., II, p. 114.

that 'Prince Eugene . . . has little hopes of our succeeding here'.

Marlborough remained undaunted. He had staked everything on Eugen's success. 'I have been uneasy in my head,' he wrote again to Godolphin on August 4, 'ever since I left off the Spa waters; but if the siege of Toulon goes prosperously, I shall be cured of all diseases, except old age.'[1]

How uncomfortable Eugen felt, despite appearances, emerges in his letter to Wratislaw of August 4:

'The Duke of Savoy, with his usual policy, seeing the great difficulties, not to say impossibilities, of this operation, throws it entirely on me, in order not to disgust England and Holland, who press him extremely, without listening to any reason. He does it with the more cunning, because he praises me on my capacity, and says I can do what I will. He answers them on everything that they must address themselves to me, that he is much inclined to this operation, that he knows the consequence of it, but that he can do nothing, which I do not deem proper.

'They are all enraged with me, and think that I wish not to risk the troops. I answer clearly that I am accustomed to act according to the rules and reasons of war, everyone knowing that I readily hazard when I have the least appearance of succeeding; and that I shall not, from complaisance for England, and for a little envoy[2] who is here, advise a thing if I see it impossible; but that if, in spite of all, the Allies and the Duke will have it so, the troops of the Emperor will not abandon them, and that I will omit nothing to succeed.

'This is the state in which we are. By the journal and my relation you will see the detail. It is the most difficult operation I have seen in my life. We are working at the batteries; we will see the effect of them before we decide on a bombardment or a siege—at least, that is my sentiment.

'I do not doubt that strong detachments will arrive on all sides, the enemy having repassed the Rhine into Germany, being retired into quarters of refreshment in Spain, and the armies of Flanders inactive.'[3]

This letter reveals his dilemma. He must either press on with an action in which he did not believe or abandon his allies already in

[1] W. Coxe, op. cit., p. 121.
[2] The John Chetwynd mentioned above.
[3] W. Coxe, op. cit., II, pp. 146–7.

the line. The latter alternative was really unthinkable. The next day he wrote to the Emperor: 'In spite of the representations I have made to the Admiral, he absolutely insists upon carrying on with the attack. . . . If they wish to proceed despite all the difficulties which they see with their own eyes, the troops of Your Imperial Majesty will certainly not separate from them.'[1] He then added a personal postscript about the appalling lack of everything necessary for a successful campaign, despite the assurance beforehand that all would be well. Indeed in one respect he received more consideration from the enemy than from his own side. Such was the strength of the Generals' International across the tides of war that, according to a contemporary French account:

'. . . four Loads of Ice were sent daily to Valette, for the Generals of the Enemy. Men of Sense, and such who have made constant observation of what has been at all times practicised among great Men, who have had the Command of Armies, and even by ordinary Generals, will not be surprised at these Transactions, since there are abundances of Examples of Civility, which have pass'd between Generals, and Presents made to each other, at the same time as they are most eager in pursuing all measures to come to an Engagement.'[2]

Though initially on July 30 he succeeded in ousting the French from Fort Saint Catherine, the skirmishing and fighting for the outworks of Toulon soon confirmed Eugen's misgivings. They also appear to have had a disturbing effect on the normally serene Sir Cloudesley Shovell. 'I am extremely sorry,' he wrote to King Charles III of Spain, 'not to be able to give you as favourable a report on our enterprise as I had hoped. We have been outside Toulon now for eighteen days, but at the moment there seems little prospect of success. Owing to the large number of cannons all round the city, to the powerful garrison within, and to the numerous earthworks encircling the place, Toulon has been turned into a very strong fortress under the enterprising command of Marshal Tessé. Moreover the number of enemy forces has risen daily until they are by now nearly equal to our own. The success of our undertaking is therefore very doubtful.'[3] But he was already under irrevocable instructions to press home the attack,

---

[1] *Feldzüge*, I Ser., IX, Suppt. p. 179.
[2] J. Donneau de Visé, op. cit., p. 64.
[3] O. Klopp, op. cit., XII, p. 338.

and there were no means of communicating home his change of heart. Eugen appears to have discerned Shovell's sudden disillusionment. He also understood completely that responsibility for sticking to the undertaking at this late stage rested not with the Admiral but with the Admiralty. On August 14 he wrote to the Emperor in desperate vein: 'Although the Admiralty do not understand land warfare, they adhere obstinately to their original point of view without listening to any contradictory arguments. They insist on staking everything on the siege of Toulon although the impossibility of succeeding is as clear as daylight to them. The positions we have taken from the enemy are such that we could scarcely hold them if he attacked with his present strength. I must repeat once again that this siege of Toulon is quite impracticable.'[1]

Defeatist or realistic? At any rate on the very night Eugen wrote this dispatch, the French were able to drive his men from the heights of St Catherine which they had taken only a fortnight before. Since the beginning of August the French lines had begun to receive the much-feared refreshments from Spain and Germany, whilst the Allies on the contrary had been suffering severe losses by disease and desertion. As epitomized by their disappointing attack on Fort St Louis, affairs at sea had gone as badly for the Allies as those on shore. It became obvious to everyone that Toulon could not be taken. The decision to retreat was thereupon quickly reached. Eugen reported the situation to Marlborough in a letter of August 20: 'The siege of Toulon is every day more and more impossible, on account of the enemy's force and situation and the strength of their artillery.'[2] Whilst the allied fleet bombarded the dockyard and silenced the French batteries, the sick and wounded and part of the artillery were embarked in a faultless display of sea-land co-operation. On August 22 Eugen's army started to withdraw along the coast. By the end of the month they were out of French territory. It was a masterly retrenchment. Nothing became the Allies at Toulon like the leaving it.

The admission of failure was accompanied by the inevitable recriminations. In a letter to the Emperor, Eugen let himself go on the 'English, whose nature is that once they have got anything into their heads they stick to it'. That 'popinjay Chetwynd' was once again singled out for special mention: 'a young man without experience in military questions', whose suggestions had been 'sheer nonsense'. Eugen admitted no blame. Indeed he suggested that, 'he

---

[1] *Feldzüge*, I Ser., IX, Suppt. p. 182.
[2] W. Coxe, op. cit., II, p. 142.

His Grace John, Duke of Marlborough, Marquis of Blanford, Earl of Marlborough. ron Churchill, of Sandridge and Baron Churchill of Aymouth; Captain General of all Her Majesty's ces; Master General of the Ordnance; One of y Lords of Her Majestys most Honourable Privy Council, Knight of the most Noble Order of the Garter. Her Majestys Ambassador Extraordinary, and nipotentiary to the States General of the United Provinces and General of the Confederate Armies.

ller S.R.Imp. & Angl. Eques Aur. pinx. 1705   I. Smith fec.   Sold by I. Smith at y Lyon & Crown in Russel street Covent Garden

10. Portrait of Marlborough by Kneller: engraving dated 1705

11 Fuoen at van Somer's picture gallery in Amsterdam: drawing by P. van den Berge who holds the

might well be justified in throwing the blame on the English themselves because they were not prepared to seize the enemy's booms
at the very first, although I represented the urgent need to do so, and
offered to deal with this end myself, and to embark troops to force
the other end with the assistance of the fleet'.[1] This opinion, which
Eugen expressly asked the Emperor to keep to himself, so as not to
cause bad blood—unless the English took the initiative in making
criticisms—was apparently shared by the French. Reflecting the
judgment of Versailles, Madame de Maintenon wrote to the Duke of
Savoy on September 2: 'Reckless though it was, the operation
against Toulon would have succeeded if Prince Eugen's proposals
had been carried out.'[2]

As a result of the expedition Eugen was on the worst of terms with
the Duke of Savoy. They could never be expected to serve together
again. The Prince and the Imperial court regarded the Duke as the
arch-culprit of Toulon. He had been responsible for the agreement
concluded with England in May for the supply of equipment for the
siege; and quite inadequate it had proved. But more sinister than that;
Vienna had come to suspect the Duke's good faith. Just at the time
when the English had decided to place absolute trust in him, the
Austrians had begun to doubt whether the Duke really wanted the
Toulon expedition to succeed. When it was all over, Wratislaw wrote
to Marlborough chiding the English Government for having proved
wrong about the Toulon expedition and for having been hoodwinked
by the Duke, whose only aim was to increase his own power in
Italy.

'The retreat of our army from Toulon justifies the court of
Vienna, and proves it to have been more correct in its predictions
than that of England, which was so urgent for the invasion of
Provence, an enterprise shown by experience to have been impracticable. I have long entreated your Highness that such approbation
and facility should not have been given in England to the projects
of the Duke of Savoy. . . . The Duke of Savoy will never act against
France, except under new and advantageous conditions. . . . Far
from placing the same confidence in him as we have lately done,
we ought to place our confidence in each other, and mutually
communicate what insinuations may be made on his part.'[3]

[1] Eugen to the Emperor, 20.8.1707, *Feldzüge*, I Ser., IX, pp. 185–6.
[2] *Lettres de Madame de Maintenon*, V, p. 101.
[3] W. Coxe, op. cit., II, p. 150.

Marlborough's support for the Duke of Savoy may not have been altogether disinterested. It is reported that Victor Amadeus made him a rich present. This consisted of a set of paintings 'of nude figures in diverse lude and lascivious postures, but the parts that might offend one's delicacy were covered over'.[1] The pictures, which were painted on leather after the fashion of the leather hangings in vogue in the Middle Ages, were said to have been works of Titian but though Sir Winston Churchill repeats the story uncritically, the best opinion is that they were certainly not by Titian and were probably by Alessandro Varotari.[2] The Duke of Savoy certainly knew the way to Marlborough's heart. A natural double-game player, he may really have intended all along to thwart the Toulon expedition. He may have calculated that Toulon in English hands would have spelt English domination of the Mediterranean, and that this would have been no better for Savoy than French domination. The English were so enthusiastic about the Toulon adventure that he was prepared to simulate support knowing that he could assert just enough drag to thwart the whole enterprise. There has been much conjecture on these lines about Savoy's ulterior motives, but little hard evidence.[3]

In their post-mortem the English were naturally bitterly critical of the Empire: of Vienna's self-indulgence over Naples, and of Eugen's failure to show his usual mettle. Toulon was difficult, they admitted, but not more so than many of the expeditions Eugen had undertaken previously with such aplomb. As regards numbers, when he had first set out for Toulon he had had a force of 35,000 men (of whom 25,000 were auxiliaries in the pay of the Maritime Powers) whilst the garrison of Toulon scarcely exceeded 8,000. It was only his own delay that had enabled the French to swell their ranks. In short, the Empire had been unwilling, Eugen irresolute.

But such judgments of history are seldom final. Only four years after Toulon, when the Tories had suddenly dissembled their way into power in England, they sought by all means to blacken the war record of the displaced Whigs. There was no question of 'my country right or wrong'. Party was above, or rather synonymous with, patriotism. In this subjective spirit, the conduct of the war in Spain came under oblique scrutiny, and the Tories succeeded in finding that Galway's shortcomings there had been the principal cause of the

---

[1] G. de Lamberty, *Mémoires pour servir à l'histoire du XVIII siècle*, 1735, IV, p. 598.

[2] Waagen, *Treasures of Art in Great Britain*, 1854, III, p. 132.

[3] G. de Lamberty, op. cit., IV, p. 569, repeated by Winston S. Churchill, op. cit., II, p. 249.

failure of the Toulon expedition. They even carried a vote to this effect in the House of Lords. But the verdict has not rested there. Posterity has not been able to exonerate Eugen completely for the Toulon débâcle. Indeed, some historians persist in laying most of the guilt at his door, while many regard it as the blackest mark in the Prince's career: a military blot such as Marlborough never had on his escutcheon.[1] Yet he was not in supreme command of the expedition. This was the responsibility of the Duke of Savoy whose good faith may have been questionable as we have seen. However, if Eugen is to be blamed, the true cause for censure is, surely, not that he defaulted militarily at Toulon, but that he did not hold out for good against undertaking an action in which he did not believe. Loyalty to the Alliance was the true cause of his undoing, and the fact that he had been wise before the event and had accurately predicted what eventually came to pass only added to the bitterness.

Although the Toulon expedition failed in its main objective, it did produce a number of secondary benefits: the French were forced to scuttle their fleet and were never able again in the time of Louis XIV to dispute British control of the Mediterranean; they also had to hurry troops from Germany to the south of France, thereby limiting their inundations of Germany; and likewise their withdrawals from Spain saved Lord Galway and King Charles III from immediate eviction from the Peninsula. To Vienna, if not to London or The Hague, it was also a considerable consolation that the Imperial forces under Graf Daun were able to occupy Naples without interference from the French.

Before the end of the year Eugen adopted an idea of the Duke of Savoy's for the capture of Susa, a town in Savoy on the French frontier forty miles west of Turin which the French had been allowed to garrison under the Treaty of Milan. It was a potential sally-port for a renewed enemy advance into Italy. Immediately on getting his men back from Toulon, Eugen therefore made a dash for Susa. By the end of September he had succeeded in forcing the town to surrender, and within a few days the citadel had asked for terms. The ghost of Toulon had been laid.

---

[1] Thus J. H. Owen, *War at Sea Under Queen Anne, 1702–1708*, 1938, p. 161: 'The external failure of the expedition owed much to Eugen . . .' He blames him particularly for procrastination at the start.

CHAPTER XI

OUDENARDE AND A
TRIUMPHANT YEAR FOR EUGEN

IN 1707 FORTUNE had once more favoured the centre against the circumference, as it invariably seemed to do in the odd years of the war. Louis had been victorious in Spain, on the Rhine and at Toulon. For the Allies the problem now was not only how to come to grips with the central stronghold of France, but how to protect all of their own exposed perimeter. At no point was there cause for greater anxiety in the winter 1707–8 than in Spain. King Charles III, so recently the proud possessor of Madrid, had been driven into a small segment of Catalonia, where he was in imminent danger of eviction. In this moment of crisis he implored his brother, the Emperor, to send Prince Eugen to take over command of his forces, very few of whom were in fact from the Empire. For this move he found the warmest support in The Hague and London, where Eugen's reputation had never been higher, despite Toulon.

The Pensionary Heinsius stated bluntly that Spain would be lost unless Eugen went there.[1] Already in September Godolphin had written to Marlborough that Prince Eugen's going to Spain 'will be a very popular thing in England, and very much contribute to obtain the necessary subsidies in Parliament'.[2]

The Tory Party and many Whigs were devotees of the Spanish war, notwithstanding all the setbacks there. 'No peace without Spain', a cry which resulted from the terms upon which the Allies had induced Portugal to enter the war, had become ever more strident. Urged on by the ubiquitous Peterborough, they pressed for the transfer of

[1] A. Arneth, op. cit., II, p. 459.
[2] W. Coxe, op. cit., II, p. 152.

troops from the Netherlands to the Peninsula to avenge the defeat of Almanza; whilst General James Stanhope, King Charles III's mouth-piece, laid siege to the English Government with a secret plan for Marlborough and Eugen to enter Spain simultaneously from different sides.[1] 'Such strategy found no foothold with Marlborough', as Sir Winston Churchill expresses it. He was strongly opposed to shifting the main allied effort from the Netherlands to the Spanish side-show. But in compliance with the general will, he was prepared to express support for Eugen's going there. He had replied to Godolphin's letter as follows:

'As to your desire of Prince Eugen's going to Spain, I think he can serve nowhere else; for I dare say he will not serve under the Elector of Hanover, nor can he serve with the Duke of Savoy.'[2]

To Wratislaw the Duke was even more emphatic, writing to him at the end of November:

'One sees that the last resource of the King (Charles III) is in the presence of Prince Eugen at the head of the army next year. . . . The Queen is so convinced of this necessity that she has written in her own hand to the Emperor; and I must say that I share her opinion that nothing but the reputation of the Prince can restore the situation there. I therefore implore you to do everything possible to see that he proceeds to Spain as soon as possible.'[3]

The Queen's appeal to the Emperor to dispatch Eugen to Spain echoed the mounting cry in Britain to switch the war from Flanders to the Peninsula. In mid-December Marlborough was under such heavy fire from the Spanish lobby in the House of Lords that he felt obliged to spike their guns by declaring publicly: 'It is to be hoped that Prince Eugen may be induced to take the Command in Spain.'[4]

All this sounds genuine enough, but in Sir Winston Churchill's unabashed submission it was merely part of Marlborough's deception plan. 'He was accustomed,' Sir Winston writes, 'by the conditions under which he fought to be continually deceiving friends for their good and foes for their bane.'[5] He wanted Eugen with him next season

[1] A. Arneth, op. cit., II, p. 460.
[2] W. Coxe, op. cit., p. 149.
[3] A. Arneth, op. cit., II, p. 459.
[4] W. Coxe, op. cit., II, p. 184.
[5] Winston S. Churchill, op. cit., II, p. 303.

in the north. But he was quite happy to pay lip-service to the Spanish
project which everyone else in England favoured, because he knew it
would never come off. After all, he was nursing a letter he had received
from Eugen in Italy, dated August 31, 1707, which indicated that the
Prince was thinking, like him, in terms of Germany or the Netherlands
for 1708, but not Spain:

> '. . . should it be resolved to remain here (i.e. Italy) on the defensive,
> we ought to have a body which may be withdrawn to form a second
> army on the Moselle, with some detachments from our other
> armies and to act in Germany or Flanders, according as circum-
> stances require. . . . In this case the army in Spain must be put in a
> condition to want no succours, and to support itself.'[1]

Marlborough also knew that Eugen would never agree to serve in
Spain without an effective army, and that this would not be forthcoming. He himself would be able to stop any diversions from the
north, and the Emperor was not in a position to make many
troops available. Wratislaw had told him frankly in September that
'the Emperor is incapable of sending his troops into Spain, and
defraying the expenses of the war'.[2] Marlborough, surely enough, had
his devious way. The idea of sending Eugen to Spain came to nought.
The reason given by Joseph for refusing was that there were not enough
troops in Spain to make a worthy command for Prince Eugen. The
English ministers—as also the Dutch and King Charles III—were
furious. Marlborough joined them outwardly in explosions of indignation, presumably deceiving them once again for their own good.
But, as Sir Winston Churchill remarks sardonically, 'inwardly, we
may suppose, he was able to bear the disappointment with his
customary composure'.[3]

Although he had not been present in Vienna to influence the
decision, Eugen himself must have been delighted with it. He would
certainly not have had an adequate army in Spain. No less important,
his position in Vienna was beginning to improve following the decline in influence of Prince von Salm, hitherto the Emperor's chief
adviser and latterly the most powerful man at court. At such a time
Eugen could not have relished the thought of being sent so far away as
Spain, whence return in winter would have been difficult.

[1] W. Coxe, op. cit., II, p. 207.
[2] W. Coxe, op. cit., II, p. 151.
[3] Winston S. Churchill, op. cit., II, p. 306.

The dangers threatening the Monarchy from all sides—from Louis XIV, the Czar, and the Sultan—were indeed hardly more menacing than the troubles within. Rákóczy had become more uncompromising than ever, and Hungary and Transylvania, far from contributing anything to the Imperial budget, were proving themselves an ever-increasing drain. At the end of 1707 Joseph's overall financial situation was too hopeless to be serious. On top of all this, Vienna was rent by intrigue and strife as distracting as anything Marlborough had to contend with in Whitehall. The pursuit of any consistent war policy by the Emperor or Eugen was to prove quite impossible until Joseph finally summoned up courage in 1709 and dismissed the domineering and temperamental von Salm.

Not wishing to displease the Allies, Joseph was ready with counter-proposals. In place of Eugen he would order Graf Guido Starhemberg to Spain. Starhemberg was well thought of by the English, particularly by Marlborough, who thus had no difficulty in making the best of a good job. Joseph also promised to make fresh efforts to increase the Imperial contribution to the war. For this purpose Eugen was sent off on a round of visits to the different courts of the Empire, and thence to The Hague for a tripartite Conference with England and the Dutch Republic on the arrangements for the next campaign.

Meanwhile, two events favourable to the House of Austria had occurred in England. Firstly, with the dismissal of their leader Harley, the Tories had been excluded from all the principal departments of state. Secondly, the French court had made an abortive attempt to send the Pretender to Scotland which had rekindled public wrath in Britain against France. In this propitious atmosphere Eugen and Marlborough met at The Hague on April 12. At last the two knights who had been hopping about at different ends of the board for so long were able to join together for a concerted attack on the opposing king. Sir Winston Churchill describes the fresh quality immediately given to the conduct of the war by their meeting:

'. . . once Eugen had joined Marlborough their perfect comradeship and pre-eminence established a higher unity of command than had ever been seen in the war. "The Princes", as they came to be called in the confederacy, settled everything between themselves. Neither ever allowed a whisper of disagreement to circulate. They were apparently immune from any kind of jealousy of each other, were proof against every form of mischief-making or intrigue, and in the field at any rate were in practice absolute. The councils of war were frequent, and many opinions were heard. But once "the Princes" had finally spoken all bowed to their judgment.'[1]

Together with Heinsius, whom they admitted to their counsels, they proceeded to work out the strategy for the ensuing campaign. Both sides, the French and the Allies, were impatient for a major show-down which they hoped would be final. And both had decided to make it in Flanders, though the triumvirate at The Hague hoped to conceal their objective by devising an elaborate deception plan. Eugen was to concentrate upon the Moselle and give the impression of preparing for a joint attack with the Elector of Hanover through Lorraine. But in reality he was suddenly to break away from the Moselle and join Marlborough for a massive assault in Flanders. One of the difficulties of this scheme was that it involved hoodwinking the Elector of Hanover almost as fraudulently as Louis XIV. The Elector, the heir to the British throne, was the Imperial Commander-in-Chief on the Rhine. Like the Margrave of Baden four years before, he did not at all relish the prospect of yielding the limelight to Prince Eugen. When the Prince and Marlborough came to visit him in Hanover after The Hague meeting, he showed himself—not without justice, as it proved—both envious and suspicious. Eugen and Marlborough did not think fit to acquaint him with their secret plan—for which, incidentally, he never forgave the Duke. But they managed to persuade him to remain on the defensive, agreeing, as conscience-money, to transfer to him five thousand troops, badly needed in the Netherlands.

The next two-and-a-half months were spent by Eugen in recruit-ment. It was not until the end of June that he had succeeded in getting an adequate army together. He had agreed with Marlborough to stand on the Moselle with 45,000 men until midsummer, when he would begin marching to the Netherlands to link up with Marlborough's 80,000. But delays in enlistment prevented him keeping to his time-table. The weeks of enforced waiting were full of anxiety for Marl-borough. The Dutch Republic and the Low Countries were showing impatience with each other and the war. Under the Duke of Burgundy and Vendôme, the French were hurriedly building up an army of 110,000 men around Mons, the biggest force seen in western Europe for centuries; and they had profited by the enemy's delay to penetrate their design. Marlborough got little support from the British Govern-ment in his apprehension: they had wasted energy in abusing their Allies in Vienna; they had pooh-poohed the French danger in

[1] Winston S. Churchill, op. cit., II, p. 331.

Flanders; and they had pestered Marlborough to return to England. Godolphin had written to the Duke in April:

'. . . I cannot see much ground to apprehend the French preparations there (Flanders), or anywhere, since their disappointment in Scotland, which seems to have very much disordered all their measures.

'I entirely dislike all Prince Eugen's projects, even if they should succeed; for considering how the court of Vienna used us as soon as they were masters in Italy, it would surely be very unadvised to put it into their power to do the same again, by making them masters again upon the Rhine and Moselle, and neglecting the opportunity of our own advantages nearer home, of which our people will be much more sensible.'[1]

Marlborough spent the waiting weeks in reviewing his troops, and imploring the Prince to hurry, even to the point of beginning his northward march before the arrival of the troops promised from the Palatinate. He expounded his precarious position to the British Government in none too resilient terms:

'. . . as God is above, so I trust in him, or else our prospect is very dreadful.

'The enclosed is what came to me by express from Count Rechteren (in command in Eugen's absence). You will see by it how uncertain all measures taken with the Germans are; for the army on the Moselle was to be formed, at farthest, by the 27th May, and by this letter we must not expect it till the beginning of July. Patience is a virtue absolutely necessary, when one is obliged to keep measures with such people.'[2]

Eugen was hurrying all he could. But he would not be bullied by Marlborough into a precipitous start before the arrival of the Palatines. Eventually, when he began his 150-mile march from Coblenz on June 28, 1708, he had only 15,000 troops with him (less than half the number originally hoped for) and of these the Palatines constituted two-thirds.

The news that reached him from the Netherlands as he moved north was so bad that he plunged on ahead of his troops with an escort of Hussars. On reaching Brussels on July 6, he learnt that Bruges and

---

[1] W. Coxe, op. cit., II, p. 213.
[2] W. Coxe, op. cit., II, p. 242.

Ghent—the key to all the waterways of Flanders and to the route to England—had both been taken by the French. Marlborough was crestfallen as a result of these setbacks. Brigadier Grumbkow, the Prussian commissary at the British Headquarters, wrote to Frederick I:

> 'The blow which the enemy dealt us did not merely destroy all our plans, but was sufficient to do irreparable harm to the reputation and previous good fortune of My Lord Duke, and he felt this misfortune so keenly that I believed he would succumb to this grief early the day before yesterday, as he was so seized by it that he was afraid of being suffocated.'[1]

In this mood Marlborough was even more delighted than usual to receive Eugen at Assche, a few miles north-west of Brussels. He tenderly embraced him, saying, 'I am not without hopes of congratulating your Highness on a great victory; for my troops will be animated by the presence of so distinguished a commander.'[2]

Eugen was shocked to find Marlborough so downhearted. According to Arneth's account, based on Grumbkow's eyewitness, the Prince was ' . . . astounded to see such despondency over so relatively a minor misfortune in a general like Marlborough. They were closeted together for several hours, and Eugen succeeded in convincing the Duke that his situation was nothing like so bad as he thought. Once again, Marlborough was sustained by the greater robustness of the Prince. Eugen's serene confidence that Louis XIV would soon be mastered, provided only that no moment was lost in bringing his army to battle, restored the Duke's fighting spirit. "With God's help," Eugen said, "and the readiness to lay down one's life, full satisfaction will be achieved!" '[3]

Though physically much tougher than Eugen, Marlborough was obviously at this moment much the more worried commander. The Prussian cavalry general, Natzmer, affirms the metabolic effect of Eugen's arrival: ' . . . all Flanders was being lost, and there was deep depression in the army. My lord Duke was inconsolable over these sad happenings. . . . But our affairs improved through God's support and Prince Eugen's aid, whose timely arrival raised the spirits of the army again and consoled us.'[4]

All the more staggering is the influence of Eugen's personality

---

[1] Winston S. Churchill, op. cit., II, p. 349.
[2] W. Coxe, op. cit., II, p. 250.
[3] A. Arneth, op. cit., II, p. 19.
[4] *Des General-Feldmarshalls Dubislav G. von Natzmer Leben und Kriegsthaten*, 1838, p. 286.

when his physical handicaps are borne in mind. Here he was, the hero of the Empire, now for the first time poised for battle in the north. 'But to begin with,' von Noorden has described it, 'he had to live down the disappointing impression given by his stunted frame, his slouch, and the pockmarked cheeks which sagged in his pale face. Although thirteen years younger than Marlborough, he was called "the old Italian Prince".'[1] However, so entrancing was his appeal that he not only 'brought a draught of new life to a hard-pressed man', as Sir Winston Churchill describes it, but lifted the morale of the whole Allied army. In Arneth's words: 'Just as Marlborough let himself be led by Eugen, so also did the army—a heterogeneous band of men drawn from many different countries, which nevertheless looked and acted like a single, compact force, in striking contrast to the French army, at the mercy of every word and whim of the King's.'[2]

Eugen and Marlborough learnt that Oudenarde was the next object of French attack. They determined to defend it since possession of it was essential for control of the Scheldt. While preparations for the battle were going forward, Eugen hurried back to Brussels to visit his mother whom he had not seen for twenty years. According to the memoirs of Field-Marshal the Count of Mérode-Westerloo,[3] who claims to write with authority on such events in Brussels at this time, Eugen was cool towards his mother during his short stay. The Countess was much upset by this. Many attributed her death three months later to this grief. Saint-Simon says that she died 'unlamented even by her own son'.[4] Eugen received the news of his mother's death in a message from the Archbishop of Malines. He took it extremely calmly, replying to the Archbishop that he dwelt little upon his sorrow, which he said was much alleviated by the news of how his mother had died in the full rites of the Catholic Church. The Count of Mérode-Westerloo complains that, though he knew all about it, Eugen omitted to thank him even in the simplest terms for having stayed like a son at the Countess's side during her last hours. From now on, his only near surviving relative was his sister, Louise Philiberte.[5] But he does not appear to have shown any interest in her. His family feelings had

[1] Carl von Noorden, *Europäische Geschichte im achtzehnten Jahrhundert*, 1870–82, III, p. 44.

[2] A. Arneth, op. cit., II, p. 20.

[3] *Mémoires du Feld Maréchal Comte De Mérode-Westerloo*, 1840, II, pp. 15–16.

[4] *Mémoires du Duc de Saint-Simon*, op. cit.. VI, p. 148.

[5] See Chapter IV, p. 50.

GENERAL MAP
OF THE NETHERLANDS

10 0 10 20 30 40
MILES

⌐⌐⌐⌐ The Lines of Brabant

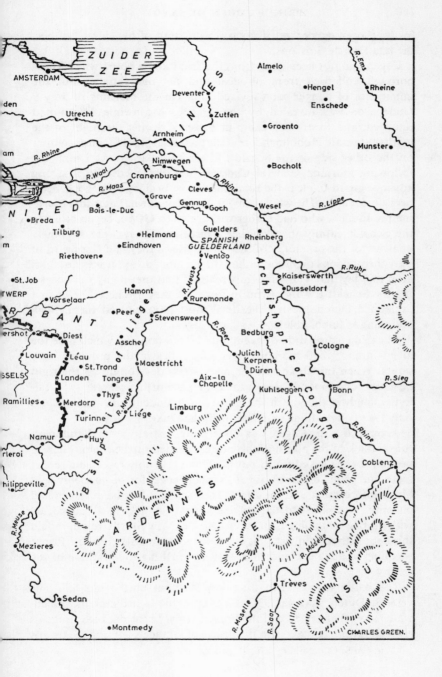

for long been concentrated upon the children of his eldest brother, the late Duc de Soissons.

Eugen had not been gone from the front a few hours when Marlborough collapsed from physical and nervous fatigue. But the imminence of danger soon revived him. On the morning of July 9 Oudenarde was invested by the French. Meanwhile Eugen had returned, and from their camp at Lessines during the night of the tenth the two allied commanders made their final plans for an encounter on the other side of the Scheldt, fifteen miles away. At 1 a.m. the following morning General Cadogan was detached with a strong advance guard to clear the road and throw bridges over the Scheldt near Oudenarde. The whole army followed at dawn. Later that morning the French, who had earlier withdrawn to Gavre, began crossing the Scheldt calmly in a southerly direction. They were sublimely unaware of the proximity of the Allies, whom they had last heard of only the previous night more than fifteen miles away. It was not until after midday that Vendôme fully realized that the enemy were crossing the Scheldt towards them in force. 'If they are here,' he at first exclaimed incredulously, 'the devil must have carried them. Such marching is impossible!'[1]

The main action did not begin until after 4 p.m., by which time the allied infantry had marched over fifty miles in the previous sixty hours. When the Duke saw the main stress developing on the right he gave the command there to Eugen. Henceforth, nearly sixty battalions, including all the British troops, fought under the Prince, whereas only twenty battalions remained with the Duke.

Around 6 p.m. Eugen was under severe strain from Vendôme's third attack of the afternoon. He direly needed further help. There is no sign that he asked for it, but the Duke probably received a report from one of his officers trained in intelligence, for he suddenly sent him reinforcements. At the crisis of the battle of Blenheim Eugen had instantly responded to the Duke's appeal for help and had parted with his one remaining Cuirassier Brigade. Now Marlborough repaid this debt without request. Thanks to his increased strength the Prince was able to advance, and succeeded in breaking the first line of the enemy.

The battle raged on in ding-dong fashion until night fell. The veteran Dutch Marshal, Overkirk, executed a brilliant movement which almost encircled half the French army. In the darkness Eugen's right came into contact with the Prince of Orange's left and the troops

[1] Winston S. Churchill, *op. cit.*, II, p. 360.

started firing upon each other in confusion. About 9 p.m., when there was no light left but fire, orders were given to the allied troops to halt as they stood lest further self-slaughter be inflicted. Bickering with Burgundy to the last, as he had done all day, Vendôme gave orders to the French to retreat. Through the obscurity some thousands discerned a gap in the allied lines and slipped away. Others staggered about, colliding with the armed ring of the Allies. In the tumult Eugen contrived a device for ensnaring stragglers: he ordered his drummers to beat the French retreat and then sent some of his Huguenot officers forward in the dark calling out the names of various French regiments. Many of the enemy fell into the trap and were taken prisoner without resistance. Rain now began to fall and the victorious troops sank into the blood-soaked mud to doze as best they could upon their arms, while Marlborough and Eugen remained on horseback keeping guard throughout the night.

The profit and loss account of the battle was gratifyingly favourable to the Allies. They had suffered about half the 6,000 enemy casualties and taken 9,000 prisoners. The French, so aggressive-looking only a few hours before, with their far-from-forlorn hopes of ousting the Allies from the Netherlands, had been flung back suddenly on to the defensive. In a high-spirited despatch to the Emperor Eugen regretted only that 'there had not been a few more hours of daylight left in which to eliminate the enemy entirely'.[1]

In describing the victory to Sarah, Marlborough singled out for special joy the fact that 'the English . . . suffered less than any of the other troops—none of our English horses having been engaged'.[2] This comment of the Duke's has fired Arneth's wrath. 'How characteristic it is,' he writes, 'that what really pleases the Duke is the relative immunity from casualties of the English troops compared with their allies.'[3] Oudenarde is often regarded in England as essentially a national victory—again much to the annoyance of Arneth and continental opinion. Yet on Marlborough's own admission, Dutch and German troops bore the brunt of the fighting. British soldiers comprised only a little over 10 per cent of the total allied force. They lost only 173 officers and men, killed and wounded, or less than 6 per cent of all the allied casualties. Moreover Eugen, rather than the Duke, commanded the main action, albeit under Marlborough's overall direction as Commander-in-Chief. The Duke was big enough to

---

[1] A. Arneth, op. cit., II, p. 25.
[2] W. Coxe, op. cit., II, p. 265.
[3] A. Arneth, op. cit., II, p. 25.

recognize Eugen's part and to rise above all efforts to breed jealousy between them. 'I dare say,' he wrote at the end of July to one of the agents in charge of disbursements at Blenheim, 'Prince Eugen and I shall never differ about our share of laurels.'[1]

Among the prisoners taken by the Allies at Oudenarde was a French nobleman, Lieutenant-General the Marquis de Biron. He was shown much respect and hospitality in the confederate camp, where everyone was eager for inside news from France which he readily related. Eugen invited him to dine. Saint-Simon records how the Prince spoke to him of the bravery of the troops which had been fighting against him, especially the Swiss. He said that he thought the Colonelcy of the Swiss was one of the finest military posts in France. 'My father held it,' he said with emotion, 'and on his death we hoped that my brother would acquire it. But the king preferred to make one of his natural sons colonel than to pay us this honour. He is the master and no one can gainsay him. However it is impossible not to feel rather pleased sometimes when one is in the position to make him regret his contempt.'[2]

Biron also described the atmosphere of the allied camp and the greater popularity of Eugen compared with Marlborough. 'He was struck by an almost royal magnificence at Prince Eugen's quarters and a shameful parsimony at those of the Duke of Marlborough, who ate the more often at the tables of others; a perfect understanding between the two in the conduct of affairs, of which the details fell much more on Eugen; a profound respect of all the generals for these two commanders but a tacit preference on the whole for Prince Eugen, without the Duke of Marlborough being at all jealous.'[3] Sir Winston Churchill has taken this bait of gossip hook, line and sinker. He expostulates that of course Marlborough could have matched the Prince's popularity if he had dispensed a lavish hospitality in accordance with the custom of those days. But, like most of the great masters of war, Caesar, Frederick and Napoleon, he preferred to live simply in the field. This defence has much appeal, particularly to the modern mind, fervent for austerity amongst high officers at war. Nevertheless, the fact remains that Marlborough was notoriously stingy—a trait which lost him much sympathy, compared with Eugen, amongst his fellow officers.

Eugen, though most open-handed and hospitable, and a lover of

[1] W. Coxe, op. cit., II, p. 270.
[2] *Mémoires du Duc de Saint-Simon*, op. cit., VI, p. 64.
[3] Ibid.

the baroque in entertainment as in architecture, was nevertheless hostile to all manner of vain military display. He attached no importance to great parades which he summed up as *rodomontades*. All the paraphernalia of beautiful uniforms and parade-ground pageantry were to him nothing more than charades. An officer was reputedly once brought before him for punishment because his horse had danced out of line during a march-past. 'Your horse,' Eugen decreed with great solemnity, 'shall be placed under arrest for three weeks. You, however, will become my A.D.C. You will start today.' The appointment proved a great success.[1]

In the after-glow of Oudenarde Marlborough tried to engage Eugen's support for a daring scheme to side-track the frontier fortresses of the Netherlands and invade France from the sea, west of Abbeville. This was to be followed up by a march on Paris which would bring the war to a rapid conclusion. Eugen thought the whole idea impracticable. He was all for going for the French throat as quickly as possible, but he was afraid that the French army under Vendôme, Burgundy and Berwick would fall upon the backs of the Allies as they reached out to grasp Paris, and that they would be easily cut off from all lines of support or retreat. Eugen believed that the first necessity was to establish a *place d'armes* and magazine from which an attack on Paris could subsequently be mounted, and he considered Lille ideally suited for this purpose. It was the capital of French Flanders and the second city of France—the repository at once of power, luxury and culture; the home, Napoleon once said, of the true boulevards of France.

Sir Winston Churchill is critical of Eugen's attitude. The rejection of the Duke's bold plan was, in his opinion, one of the cardinal mistakes of the war. The Dutch would undoubtedly have been amenable had Eugen supported Marlborough and Sir Winston is confident that the venture would have triumphed and the war could have been over in 1708. This is highly speculative. Eugen was never lacking in boldness and we must assume that he had good grounds for doubting the feasibility of Marlborough's plan. Toulon had been a bitter experience for him and had strengthened his inherent distrust of the sea. But whatever the other uncertainties one thing is daylight clear in all this—the relationship revealed between the two Princes at this tense moment. The Duke, far from just issuing orders to Eugen and expecting him to execute them unquestioningly, is shown as submissive to the Prince's opinion, even when this is diametrically

[1] Egon Caesar Conte Corti, op. cit., p. 62.

opposed to his and concerning a matter of the utmost strategic importance. In a short letter to Sarah written at this time he makes three complimentary references to the Prince whom he consults 'daily, not only how to end this campaign, but also the war'.[1] The episode also demonstrates, as Arneth is happy to observe, how Marlborough, instead of maintaining at all times that steadiness which all his English biographers, including the most critical, attribute to him, could, at one moment, as just before Oudenarde, sink into despair, and at the next, as immediately after the battle, surge on a wave of optimism; whereas the French-Italian Eugen, reputedly so mercurial, remained on an even keel throughout, and displayed, at all times, particularly in contrast to the Duke, a most equable temperament. Could it be that modern generalizations about national proclivities are sometimes inapplicable to an earlier age? That British phlegm, like British fidelity, is a recent and largely British discovery? There is good contemporary evidence, at any rate, to suggest that at the beginning of the eighteenth century the English were not renowned for their imperturbability. Writing to Marlborough a few days after Oudenarde, Godolphin said : 'It is the temper of our nation, confirmed by daily experience, that we are at the top of the house in prosperity; and in misfortune, indeed upon the least alarm, we are ready to sink into the earth.'[2]

Eugen's strategic views found general acceptance among the allied generals. After a superbly co-ordinated march, the investment of Lille began on August 13, 1708—Blenheim day—under the Prince's command. Again the French underestimated Eugen's audacity. They could not believe that he would dare besiege Vauban's masterpiece, the town and citadel of Lille, defended by 15,000 men under the command of Marshal Boufflers. Vendôme added to his other misjudgments of the year by declaring publicly that : 'so wise a commander as Prince Eugen would not venture upon such an enterprise'.[3]

At the outset of the siege a large number of the women of Lille asked for permission from the Allies to leave the city before the bombardment. Eugen agreed, but, smartly combining business with chivalry, ensured that the officers sent to receive them should profit from the opportunity to study the approaches to the beleagured city. Whilst Eugen's heavy batteries started to shatter the masonry and earthworks around Lille, the French, withdrawing from Ghent and

[1] W. Coxe, op. cit., II, p. 274.
[2] W. Coxe, op. cit., II, p. 270.
[3] Winston S. Churchill, op. cit., II, p. 425.

Bruges, began to amass in an outer ring, until their strength out-numbered the sandwiched Allies by two to one. But, in the event they flinched from forcing a general battle, much to Eugen's and Marl-borough's regret. The siege continued.

It went so slowly that it gave Marlborough the spleen, as he admitted to Godolphin. To Eugen it imparted bravura. On the evening of September 20 he was taking part in a major assault on the enemy defences. He rushed into the fire to rally his men who were reeling back under the French blows. He was struck by a musket-ball and badly concussed. As usual, he made light of the wound and showed indignation at the fuss being made around him: 'What's all the palaver about?' he exclaimed, 'As you can see, nothing's happened.' He started bandaging himself up and it was only with great difficulty that he was prevailed upon to retire. The following morning Marl-borough, who had heard in the night of Eugen's wound, came to visit him. He found him preparing to mount and to resume his duty. The Duke pressed him to return to his quarters until he was fully recovered, which the Prince only agreed to do on the understanding that Marl-borough took over the conduct of the siege himself. ·

The Prince had another narrow escape. One morning when, appar-ently well out of harm's way, he was dealing peacefully with some correspondence that had recently arrived at his headquarters. The incident is well described by the contemporary historian, Rousset, who served with the allied armies:

'One of the letters came from The Hague, and the Commissary imagined the other came from the same high place, but could not be positive of it. His Highness, opening one of them, found nothing therein but a dirty greasy paper, and not knowing what might be the consequence thereof, threw it carelessly on the ground, without the least sign of surprise. Hereupon, the Prince's Adjutant took it up, and smelt it; immediately after which he was taken with a great gid-diness, and taken so ill, that he was persuaded to take an antidote, and happy was it for him, that he did so: for the poison it contained was so exquisite, that the paper being only tied about a dog's neck, for an experiment, he died within twenty-four hours, notwithstand-ing he had a counter-poison given him. Hereupon, General Dopff, with some others, who were about His Highness, appeared highly surprised at this execrable piece of villainy, and expressed their concern for the hazard the Prince had run; upon which, His Highness said to them, without any emotion: "You need not wonder at it, Gentlemen, I have several times before now received letters of this nature." '[1]

Marlborough found the double burden of pursuing the siege and covering it almost beyond endurance. 'Ever since that he (Prince Eugen) was wounded,' he wrote to Godolphin on September 27, 'I have been obliged to be every day at the siege which, with the vexation of it going so ill, I am almost dead.'[2] It certainly was going badly and the Duke wrote to Godolphin again on September 24:

'You will have seen by my last letter, the unhappy circumstances we are in by the very ill conduct of our engineers and others. Upon the wounding of Prince Eugen, I thought it absolutely necessary to inform myself of everything of the siege; for, before, I did not meddle in any thing but the covering of it. Upon examination, I find they did not deal well with the Prince, for when I told him that there did not remain powder and ball for above four days, he was very much surprised. I own to you that I fear we have something more in our misfortune than ignorance.'[3]

Meanwhile on the other side of the lines there was the same heightening of tension. Even at Versailles they paused momentarily from pleasure. According to Saint-Simon the card tables were deserted for the churches, fasting was preferred to supper parties, and for once prayer became more popular than malicious gossip.

By the beginning of October, Eugen was completely fit again. Thanks to a brilliant action by Generals Webb and Cadogan at Wynendael a new convoy had just arrived. But Vendôme answered this by opening the dykes and flooding the country—a calamity which revived the Duke's earlier doubts about the wisdom of the whole enterprise. There were many people in the allied camp at this time who advised the lifting of the siege. But the Prince was unwavering. He admitted that there were difficulties, yet never doubted the outcome. He was ready to sacrifice himself and, as he declared, his reputation which would cost him a good deal more. This confidence soon communicated itself to others. Scepticism was wrung out of the allied camp and everyone felt their powers of endurance stiffened. If the

---

[1] Dumont and Rousset, *Memoirs of the Lives of Prince Eugene and the Duke of Marlborough*, 1742, II, p. 366.
[2] W. Coxe, op. cit., II, p. 314.
[3] W. Coxe, op. cit., II, p. 320.

Prince could be both dogged and brave—so would they. Their stay-ing-power was eventually rewarded, though only at the cost of heavy casualties. On October 22, Marshal Boufflers beat a parley. Hostages were exchanged and conferences held for the surrender of Lille, other than the citadel itself. As Arneth puts it, 'Eugen treated the garrison with the generosity which their brave defence so justly merited'.[1] He congratulated Boufflers in the most flattering manner and left it to him to fix his own conditions of surrender. 'Whatever you think right, I will agree to,' he offered. The French were per-mitted to evacuate their sick and wounded and to withdraw 4,000 able-bodied soldiers into the citadel to continue the fight, while Eugen sent presents of wine and fresh provisions for the Marshal's table. The bonhomie between rival commanders was such that Vendôme wrote to Eugen, addressing him as 'my cousin', to ask him to forward to Boufflers correspondence from the French King. The Prince also allowed the severely wounded Marquis de Surville to be taken from the citadel to Douai for treatment, a gesture which moved Louis XIV to send him a personal message of thanks.

Despite the almost chronic ill-health and depression which con-tinued to afflict Marlborough as it had done throughout the year, he and Eugen succeeded in driving the French from the Scheldt. As the Duke wrote to Godolphin on November 28: '. . . Prince Eugene and myself shall have that inward satisfaction of knowing that we have struggled with more difficulties, and have been blessed with more suc-cess, than ever was known before in one campaign.'[2] On December 9 the citadel of Lille capitulated after prolonged fighting in which Eugen had again exposed himself and had had his equerry killed at his side. Before finally laying down arms in January 1709 for the remainder of the winter, Marlborough and Eugen achieved a further remarkable triumph in forcing the surrender of Ghent and Bruges.

So ended, in Arneth's words, 'this extraordinary campaign, certainly one of the most renowned that has ever been fought'. It had gone on an unprecedented time, always at full pressure. 'He who has not seen this had seen nothing', was how Eugen summed it up.[3] The Allies had been constantly outnumbered. At Oudenarde they had had to surprise and beat an army posted in a highly favourable position; at Lille to besiege a place believed to be impregnable when

[1] A. Arneth, op. cit., II, p. 39.
[2] W. Coxe, op. cit., II, p. 335.
[3] Johann Mathias von der Schulenburg, *Leben und Denkwürdigkeiten*, 1834, I, p. 368.

they themselves were surrounded by a force twice the size; and at Ghent and Bruges to win back in the depth of winter two heavily defended forces. All of these successes had been attained against the generalship of Vendôme, Burgundy and Berwick, considerable commanders each one of them, but seemingly impotent against the united Marlborough and Eugen.

So uncompetitive was the relationship between Marlborough and Eugen that it may seem egregious now to try to draw comparisons between them. But the British legend, which has been fostered down the years and which represents 1708 as Marlborough's year and Oudenarde as Marlborough's battle, enjoins the striking of a new balance. Even Sir Winston Churchill, usually so fairminded in acknowledging the Prince's contribution to the partnership, abides in this instance by the habitual lore. Thus it was 'Marlborough's grand campaign . . . England had been raised by Marlborough's victories to the summit of the world . . . One man and three battles had transformed all. . . . In Marlborough the ramshackle coalition had found . . . its organic unity.'[1]

Sir Winston admits that Eugen, 'the noble Prince', had not only served and aided but inspired; however, he insists that his rôle throughout had only been secondary. There is no doubt that in one sense it had: the Duke was unquestionably the Commander-in-Chief of the grand circus. But equally, much of the most dazzling performance in the ring, particularly at Oudenarde and Lille, had been that of Eugen. Moreover, throughout the year he had shown himself more resilient than Marlborough, firmer in health, nerve and decision—and with none of the Englishman's hankering after personal gain.[2] Hitherto in his career, Eugen had shown unmatched verve and courage. But in 1708 his outstanding quality had been tenacity, a readiness to stick it out and infuse all about him with confidence when bad times looked as though they would never end.

Vendôme had paid him an indirect tribute in the wrangles he had had with the other French generals about the best strategy to pursue

[1] Winston S. Churchill, op. cit., II, pp. 470–471–485.
[2] In the thick of the campaign, on the night when the capitulation terms of Lille were finally agreed, Marlborough, who had already been in correspondence with him across the lines, wrote to his nephew, the Duke of Berwick, suggesting that France should ask for an armistice. He promised his support on the understanding that he would receive in return a douceur of two million livres. This unsavoury episode is recorded frankly by Sir Winston Churchill. It raises the doubt how far Marlborough's much trumpeted claim to serve the Alliance and nothing but the Alliance was genuine if he could include a private bribe in a transaction of such importance to all the 26 allied states.

before Oudenarde. He had wanted to take the initiative and attack, but was over-ruled. 'Mark my words,' he is said to have warned Burgundy and the other more cautious French commanders, 'I make this prophecy and you will see how soon it is fulfilled that if Prince Eugen is able to perceive that we are anxious to avoid battle, he will surely conduct himself so as to make a battle unavoidable.'[1]

'If Eugen had not come north to the Netherlands,' Wratislaw wrote to the Emperor, 'everything would have gone sour. Marlborough and the Dutch Deputies had fallen out. The army was apprehensive. The battle of Oudenarde might well not have taken place and in the ensuing uncertainty all that could have been hoped for would have been a bad peace.'[2]

If Wratislaw is considered too partisan, then refer to the verdict of the States-General of the Netherlands, which resolved that: 'After God, thanks for the successes achieved must go to the intelligence, efficiency and boldness of Prince Eugen.'[3]

In Holland a medal was struck representing the city of Oudenarde, and beneath it the French cavalry retreating before Prince Eugen, with this inscription:

Vandomus, in Flandria, sicut in Italia,
Victus, victorem agnoscit Eugenium.[4]

England, only yesterday a tender and divided plant, buffeted by every breeze from France, had grown up within a few years into a strong, independent nation, rooted upon a national church and Parliament, and branching out over newly-mastered seas to wealthy lands beyond. Historical truth, if not national gratitude, insists that some of the credit for this transition should go to Eugen.

[1] Egon, Caesar Conti Corti, op. cit., p. 61.
[2] A. Arneth, op. cit., II, p. 46.
[3] A. Arneth, op. cit., II, p. 466.
[4] The Duke of Vendôme being overcome in Flanders, as well as in Italy, acknowledges Prince Eugen to be his conqueror.

CHAPTER XII

1709–1710: PEACE NEGOTIATIONS
AND MALPLAQUET

MARLBOROUGH AND Eugen agreed to play box and cox in the Netherlands throughout the winter 1708–9. It was arranged that the Prince would leave first and remain away until the end of February. The Dutch were far too nervous to allow both to be absent at once, and there were indeed good reasons why at least one of them should remain on guard: firstly, there was always a possibility of a surprise French attack, to retake Lille for instance; secondly, there was a pressing need to prepare for the next campaign which both commanders expected to be the last and biggest; and thirdly, and most important of all, though this necessity consorted ill with the other two, there were peace discussions with the French which, having rippled on for long beneath the surface, suddenly bubbled up into the open early in 1709.

The French, already exhausted by war, were suddenly struck by a new and natural calamity. The great frost which gripped Europe from December 1708 to March 1709, freezing all the rivers, killing the cattle, and congealing the seed corn in the ground, faced France with certain famine. At last, so it looked to the Allies, the Grand Monarch must be on his knees ready to sue for peace. Certainly he had sunk low. By May he was showing willingness to accept far-reaching conditions.[1] But the Allies were guilty of crass misjudgment in supposing that he had reached such depths as would compel him to clutch at their

---

[1] Nothing less than the following: the cessation of the entire Spanish monarchy to the House of Austria, and the acknowledgment of Charles as King of Spain and the Indies; the recognition of Queen Anne, and the Protestant succession, in England; the demolition of Dunkirk; the expulsion of the Pretender from France; the cession to England of Newfoundland; and the delivery to the Dutch of their long-sought barrier fortresses.

preposterous terms. Now it was their turn to be exorbitant. They insisted on a guarantee from France that Spain would be evacuated by Philip and surrendered to Charles. This, Louis could not agree to. Prepared though he was to recognize the Habsburg claim to Spain, he nevertheless refused to commit himself to a written undertaking which might make him liable to drag his grandson by force from the Spanish throne and expel him from the Peninsula. In 1703, at the time of the Portuguese Treaty,[1] when the substitution of Charles for Philip first became one of the allied war aims, Louis could with a mere word have rid his grandson of the crown. But in the intervening years the Spanish people had developed a strong attachment to Philip, and Philip to Spain. This fact the Allies refused to recognize, particularly the English Whigs who, coming to power in November 1708, re-echoed the cry, 'No Peace without Spain'.

'There is no doubt,' in Sir Winston Churchill's view, 'that responsibility for the loss of the peace in 1708 lies largely upon England.' Marlborough himself was not blameless. He knew that London was being unwise. But he also knew that his own influence at home with Queen and Cabinet had contracted. To stand up to his own side—always the most difficult posture in any international negotiation—was now a task beyond his powers. Eugen, who represented the Emperor in the tentative peace talks, was anxious to keep them going. According to the evidence recorded at the time by a British officer, Colonel Cranstoun: 'It is certain the Imperial ministers and Prince Eugene were not for breaking upon that point (Article XXXVII; the guarantee).'[2]

In a letter to the Emperor written in mid-June 1709, Eugen lamented the collapse of the negotiations and expressed concern at what the next campaign might bring forth: 'True the army is no smaller than last year and is in excellent condition. We should therefore be able to hope for a successful outcome to the season. But since nothing on earth is so variable as luck in arms the Emperor should bear in mind how much is now at stake. There can be no doubt that the next battle will be the biggest and bloodiest that has yet been fought.'[3]

[1] See Chapter VII (p. 83).
[2] Winston S. Churchill, op. cit., II, p. 554.
[3] A. Arneth, op. cit., II, p. 69. Only two months later, Marlborough expressed the same view on the fickleness of war. After Charles XII had been dramatically defeated at Poltava—a battle which reduced Sweden to her former small-power status, and opened the breach to Russian greatness—the Duke observed: 'Constant success for ten years; two hours' mismanagement.'
One of Napoleon's favourite sayings summed up Eugen's and Marlborough's views: *Du sublime au ridicule il n'y a qu'un pas.*

His forebodings were quickly and cruelly fulfilled. At the opening of the 1709 campaign, Marlborough wanted to besiege Ypres, but Eugen favoured Tournai. The Duke deferred once more to the Prince's views. After a two-month copy-book siege, in which Eugen commanded the covering army while his colleague attacked, the citadel of Tournai, another of Vauban's labyrinthine masterpieces, fell to the Allies. A letter from Peter Wentworth to his brother Lord Raby (later the Earl of Stafford),[1] then British Ambassador in Berlin, gives an idea of coffee-house opinion in London at this juncture of the war. It also conjures up the magic of Eugen's name: 'At our coffee-houses we are very angry that the news talks of our besieging Tournai, for their opinion is that we ought not to amuse ourselves in taking towns, but march directly to Paris. When they are told that an army can't march without having such a train of provisions with them as will subsist an army that is to burn and destroy all before them, they give no answer to this but—"How did Prince Eugene march his army over the mountains without such a train or money, and his march to the relief of Turin was in like manner; 'tis but to employ him and the business is done." '[2]

Then on September 11, the anniversary of the Battle of Zenta, came Malplaquet, the toughest and bloodiest battle of the whole Spanish Succession war. The French fought with unaccustomed frenzy. The promise of bread had lured famished men to the colours. Allied greed had at last given them primordial cause to fight. The war had been suddenly converted from a royal adventure for dynastic expansion into a national struggle for survival; and the new French commander, Marshal Villars, well knew how to exploit the emergent passions of his army.

In all his long years of war Eugen never confronted a more redoubtable opponent than Villars. He had known him in the old days in Austria when Villars had been the French representative there.[3] He perceived in him a unique combination of attractive and repellent qualities. Handsome, conceited, courageous and inordinately vain, he had acquired a reputation alike for luck and management, both of which virtues had served him well in his recent successful command on the Rhine. It was obvious why Louis XIV had clutched at him now in place of the deflated Vendôme. With Marshal Boufflers

---

[1] See footnote on p. 188.
[2] Peter Wentworth to Lord Raby, June 21, 1709, *The Wentworth Papers, 1705–1739*, ed. James J. Cartwright, 1889, p. 90.
[3] See Chapter VII, p. 76.

appointed to support Villars, the French at last had a formidable team against Eugen and Marlborough. They were determined to prevent the Allies taking Mons, their next objective after the heartening capture of Tournai.

At an early stage in the battle of Malplaquet Eugen demonstrated his taste and capacity for combining the responsibilities of General-in-Chief with the hazards of close personal combat. It was a performance witnessed by many prominent visitors who had come to see the battle and learn something of the military art at first hand; the most important of these was the twenty-one-year-old Prussian Crown Prince, Frederick William. Eugen was in command of the right wing which consisted mostly of Imperial troops, with a few Danish soldiers and Dutch cavalry. The first imperative was to master a wood, the wood of Sart, whose approaches were barricaded and whose interior was strongly fortified. Schulenburg, in command directly under the Prince on the extreme right, was forced back in his first attempt to penetrate the wood. A brave and resourceful officer, he succeeded in reforming his troops, and was on the point of returning to the attack when Eugen, sensing the danger to the whole Allied line, placed himself at the head of the Saxons and led them forward into battle. He carried the first line of entrenchments, then the second and third. But the French, cleverly exploiting the density of the forest, mustered within and resisted strongly. The action wavered long and the fighting was bitter on both sides. Exposing himself to the point almost of foolhardiness, Eugen was wounded with a musket-shot behind the ear. Those about him begged him to have the wound dressed, but he waved them aside, saying, 'there will be time enough for that at night'. Simultaneously he spurred on his horse to a place where he saw his presence necessary, and continued giving orders with as much tranquility and presence of mind as if nothing had happened to him.[1] At last, after several hours, the Allies succeeded in mastering the wood.

The battle on the allied left wing under Marlborough started later than that on the right, but it soon became, as it remained, just as intense. Never throughout the Spanish Succession War did the Dutch troops, who were under the intrepid Prince of Orange, give a better account of themselves than at Malplaquet. They were at times opposed to forces twice their number. Fortunately, just as the situation looked highly dangerous for them and for the English and Germans alongside, news of Eugen's success in the wood of Sart reached Villars and compelled him to withdraw. As the fighting raged on into the

[1] Dumont and Rousset, op. cit., I, p. 105.

afternoon Eugen forced Villars into a serious error of tactics. Closing
up his battalions, he suddenly charged the French line so vigorously
that Villars decided he must concentrate everything possible against
him if he was to escape annihilation. The effect of this was to weaken
gravely his communications with his right wing. Boufflers was almost
isolated. It may be that Villars took the risk relying on his capacity
to retrieve the situation once he had overcome the Imperialist attack.
If so, he took too much upon himself. Certainly he succeeded in forcing
the enemy back at the point of the bayonet, but as he turned his horse
quickly to repair contact with Boufflers, a bullet struck him on the
knee and he had to be carried from the field. No one else had the skill or
authority to restore the communications immediately, and Eugen,
perceiving the weakness in the enemy position and the faltering morale
consequent upon Villars' removal, rallied his flagging troops and
attacked the French left wing. The results were devastating.

At the other end of the line, attack and counter-attack had been
succeeding each other indeterminately. Eventually, however, the
Prince of Orange re-formed his men and assaulted the entrenchments which covered the approaches to Malplaquet. His courage
and endurance were triumphantly vindicated and the enemy
withdrew.

By 3 o'clock Boufflers began a general retreat and Marlborough and
Eugen were left masters of the field. But at what sacrifice! It is true
that a few weeks later they had no difficulty in capturing Mons—to
save which Villars had offered battle at Malplaquet. But the cost of
Malplaquet was enormous. It was Marlborough's and Eugen's last
combined battle. It was the only one in which they had had numerical
superiority. Yet it was also the only one in which their casualties had
exceeded the enemy's. They had lost 24,000 in killed and wounded
against France's 12–15,000.[1]

The British losses were just under 2,000; the Dutch the enormous
figure of 8,000, a third of the allied total—thanks partly to the impetu-
ousness of the Prince of Orange. Much truth was there in Villars'
boast that 'the enemy would have been annihilated by such another
victory', or in Boufflers' consoling remark to Louis XIV that 'never
was misfortune attended with more glory'.

Malplaquet was grist to the mill of Marlborough's gathering
enemies at home. True, the Whigs were still in power, were still true

[1] Not until a century later, at Borodino, was this slaughter surpassed. At
Waterloo Wellington lost 22,469, out of a total of 69,686—not much more than
half the size of Marlborough's and Eugen's army at Malplaquet which numbered
about 110,000.

to the war, and still crying—'No Peace without Spain'. With their majorities in both Houses of Parliament they voted thanks to the Duke and generous supplies for the continuation of the war. But as Klopp acutely observes, if this was the supreme it was also 'the last pinnacle of Marlborough's career'.[1] The Tories discerned in the growing war-weariness of the country and the 'butcher's bill' of Malplaquet, as they described it, a hell-sent opportunity of raising the dust of national indignation and riding back to power on the whirlwind cry of peace. Although British casualties at Malplaquet had in fact been only about 8 per cent of the allied total, the propaganda of the Tories under their leader, Robert Harley, was quite capable of making amends for this. Marlborough was accused of prolonging the war for his own profit. His incautious request to be made Captain-General for life was turned against him. It was alleged to have laid bare his Cromwellian soul. The Queen, as tired as anyone of the war and more so than most of the Whigs, and smarting from her quarrel with the brimstone Sarah, was lending herself to the plans being made in the winter 1709–10 for the Duke's immolation. It soon became apparent to the world, including the French who took much heart from it, that Marlborough was being prepared for sacrifice by royal fire on the altar of English party politics.

Just when Marlborough's influence in England had begun to disintegrate, Eugen's in Vienna was consolidating. Though the Monarchy had owed so much to him in the past few years he had never occupied such a towering position at home as had Marlborough in the noonday of his power. Intrigue against him had been incessant and often effective. Only recently the Emperor had been cajoled into depriving him of the Governorship of Milan, a post which he had been given in 1707 after his triumph at Turin the previous year.[2] So strenuous had been his other preoccupations since then that his enemies had had little difficulty in reminding the Emperor of his limited attention to the affairs of Milan. The leader of the hostile battery had been the Emperor's first Minister, Prince von Salm.[3] This diseased and vindictive old man had been moved not merely by personal animosity towards Eugen but by his desire to see the Duke of Modena, the husband of his niece, made Governor of Milan. In this underground operation he had had the powerful support of the Empress Amalie, sister-in-law to the Duke of Modena.

[1] O. Klopp, op. cit., XIII, p. 370.
[2] See Chapter X (p. 137).
[3] See Chapter IX (p. 125).

Eugen's friends at court, particularly Wratislaw, impressed on the Emperor the injustice of divesting him of the Governorship of Milan without adequate compensation. King Charles came forward with the proposal to make him Governor of the liberated Spanish Netherlands. He had thrice offered this post to Marlborough, but the Duke had refused each time in deference to strong and envious Dutch opposition. Now there seemed to be a chance of granting Eugen his long-overdue reward. But after much shilly-shallying the preferment was thwarted. Arneth states that this was because of Vienna's reluctance to offend and anger Marlborough, whom he describes as known to be still covetous of the appointment. But there is no corroboration for this. On the contrary, Marlborough is believed not only to have rejected the post quite categorically but to have suggested in writing that it be given to Eugen. What is more, Arneth himself published the textual evidence for this, two chapters before his other unfounded explanation.[1] The real obstruction was probably caused by the intersecting restraints of friends and enemies: the former not wishing to be bereft for long of his presence in Vienna; the latter objecting to his being honoured anywhere abroad, whether in Milan or Brussels.

However, von Salm's chances of doing Eugen ill were soon curtailed. The Emperor removed him from the position of *Obersthofmeister*, or First Minister. Eugen's ally, Trautson, was appointed in his place. Joseph also reorganized his Cabinet, creating, in addition to the normal large *Conferenzrat*, an inner group limited to Trautson, Eugen, Seilern, Sinzendorff and Wratislaw.

The Emperor wanted to do more for Eugen. He was sensitive to the unfair way the Prince had been successively balked, first of the Polish throne, then of the Governorship of Milan, and finally of the Governorship of the Netherlands. On December 17, 1709, therefore, he issued a decree ordering the Royal Hungarian treasury to make over to Eugen a property valued at 300,000 florins from amongst those which had reverted to the national Exchequer. Nothing came of it, however, whether because no suitable estate was available or because Eugen was not interested. Instead, the Emperor gave Eugen an equivalent sum of money. It should be recognized, however, that this was not all that generous or exceptional, since many others in the Habsburg Monarchy, much less deserving than Eugen, were seeking and obtaining grants in what Arneth describes as the veritable scramble for loot which now began.[2]

[1] A. Arneth, op. cit., II, p. 467.
[2] For a variety of reasons the Duke of Modena never actually took up the

Back in Vienna that winter 1709–10 after the blood-letting of Malplaquet, Eugen took part in prolonged discussions in the inner cabinet. There were all the old perennials to attend to. Hungary, blooming for a change, with the rebels on the verge of complete defeat; Spain blighted again, with Charles III crying balefully for help: and the Imperial Exchequer, like a neglected rose, withering once more upon the stalk. But there were also new stirrings; problems more of diplomacy than of war. Eugen had been coming to the conclusion that Austria's alliance with the Dutch Republic and England was insufficient. The Sea Powers were not altogether reliable as friends. The Barrier Treaty which England and Holland had signed in October 1709 stripped Charles III of half his inheritance in the Spanish Netherlands in favour of the Dutch. This, together with a promise to share with the Dutch the right to trade with South America, had been England's bribe to Holland to keep her in the war without having to incur additional cost themselves in men or money.[1] England's persistent meanness over land forces ever since the Alliance had first been formed was another reason for Eugen's decision to reconnoitre elsewhere for allies. The idea which had begun to form in his mind was for an alliance with Russia, a form of reinsurance which had been unthinkable earlier beneath the forbidding frown of Charles XII of Sweden. Peter's victory over Charles at Poltava in June 1709 had encouraged the rulers of Hanover, Denmark and Saxony to re-enter the Northern war as Russia's allies against Charles, while Prussia cast eyes on Swedish territory. For Austria, the rehabilitation of her alliance with Prussia was a more urgent and practical necessity than closer relations with Russia. This alliance had been frayed by mutual fears and jealousies. Austria, for her part, was resentful of King Frederick I's assumption of leadership of the German Protestants. She was afraid that Prussia was on the point of negotiating a separate peace. As Eugen observed to Heinsius: 'It is clear that the King of Prussia is behaving most extraordinarily, and if he had as much tenacity as he has ambition he could cause us great embarrassment.'[2]

---

appointment of Governor of Milan. Eugen therefore continued to hold the office until 1715–16; the day-to-day administration was delegated to a commissioner.

[1] For a detailed account of the fears which the English Government had felt ever since the autumn of 1705 that the Dutch would encourage French overtures for peace, see Douglas Coombs, *The Conduct of the Dutch*, 1958.

[2] A. Arneth, op. cit., II, p. 473.

In Prussia itself there were many people also who were troubled over the direction of the King's policy. There were loud entreaties for Eugen to hasten to Berlin, in Grumbkow's words, 'to save us from the abyss into which we will otherwise throw ourselves'.[1] He therefore decided to return to the Netherlands via Berlin. He arrived there in April 1710. His visit was a diplomatic triumph. He succeeded in binding Prussia tightly to the Grand Alliance once more.

Then on he hastened to join in the peace negotiations with the French which had just been resumed at Gertruydenburg. Here, in Sir Winston Churchill's words, 'diplomatists and plenipotentiaries, surrounded by a host of agents and busybodies, official and unofficial, manoeuvred sedately around the clauses of the peace treaty, incapable as were the armies of reaching a decision'. The allied bargaining position, based as it now was upon the ashen foothold of Malplaquet and of the simultaneous failures in Spain and Franche Comté, was a good deal groggier than it had been after Oudenarde. Furthermore, the pyre was beginning to mount beneath Marlborough, since the Tories, the peace party, were now only one leap away from power in England. All of which encouraged Louis XIV to try to hold out. Yet the Allies did not see fit to abate their demands by one iota. Eugen, who had been eager for concessions to end the war the previous year, was now first among the intransigents. He displayed here a lack of judgment which was to prove uncomfortably consequential. He appears to have overestimated the malaise of France and to have underestimated the difficulty of delivering the coup de grâce upon the battlefield. He was impatient to continue diplomacy by other means. He had his way, and fighting began again in April before the Gertruydenburg negotiations had finally broken down.

The year 1710 was a dull campaign of sieges, each as stereotyped as a quadrille. The main highlight of the year in Eugen's career was the gleam cast upon his indispensability, both to the Emperor and to Marlborough.

There had been much talk in Vienna of moving him from the Netherlands to the Rhine, from where it was believed the best chance lay of penetrating into France. But from the Netherlands there had been contradictory pressure upon the Emperor to bring all his troops there from the Rhine. A compromise was accordingly suggested by which Eugen was to resume his post in the Netherlands and then, when the campaign was under way, to dash off to the Rhine and, when once everything was under control there, return to the Netherlands.

[1] A. Arneth, op. cit., II, p. 473.

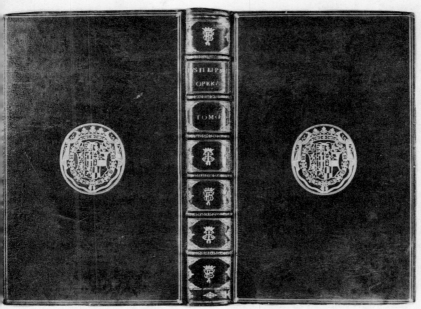

12. A binding for Eugen, with his coat of arms on the covers, and devices of entwined E's, the arms of Savoy, and the Golden Fleece on the spine

13. Eugene in conference in the Upper Belvedere

14. Entrance hall of the Upper Belvedere, with view of the garden and city of Vienna

15. The Picture Room in the Upper Belvedere:
Eugen's Dutch and Flemish cabinet pictures

But Eugen objected strongly to this, saying that he could not be expected 'to chase around Europe like a postillion'.

As for Marlborough's dependence on him, we know from a letter to Sarah how low his spirits had plummetted under the weight of worry about the next campaign. On April 14, 1710, he wrote: 'I am so discouraged by everything I see that I have never, during this war, gone into the field with so heavy a heart as I do this time.'[1]

It was thanks largely to Eugen that his spirits recovered. No sooner were they together again than the old united drive was exerted between the allied shafts. But somehow they were unable to find a way of piercing Villars' *Ne Plus Ultra* lines defending France. They succeeded in taking the fortress towns of Douai, Béthune, St Venant and Aire during the year. But these were plodding captures in an oblique pawn game, achieved not without loss of men, morale and tempo. Despite their superiority in numbers and equipment, the two commanders showed uncommon reluctance to launch a major offensive against the hobbling Villars, who still had his knee in an iron frame after his wound at Malplaquet.

The honours of the year undoubtedly went to Villars. The two Princes had been united as ever, but they had lost the initiative. France, in spite of them, was still inviolate, and the French army vigorous. Meanwhile, in England, in contrast to the dreary continuando of the war, the tempo of Tory intrigue had been stepped up. By the autumn of 1710 a new government under Robert Harley (later 1st Earl of Oxford) and Henry St John (later 1st Viscount Bolingbroke), backed by a majority in the House of Commons, was to assume power and initiate a separate policy of peace, regardless of allies—an event of greater and more malign influence upon the common cause than anything that had happened on the battlefield in the ten years of war, and one which should have made Eugen rue the short-sighted insouciance he had shown over the recent breakdown in the Gertruydenburg negotiations.

[1] W. Coxe, op. cit., III, p. 39.

CHAPTER XIII

BRITAIN CHANGES GOVERNMENT
AND NEGOTIATES
FURTIVELY FOR PEACE

THE FORTUNES of Eugen and England now became fatefully entwined. It is the climax of the Prince's career and one of the great headlands of British history, a time of glorious failure for Eugen and of inglorious success for England, the one ineluctably contingent upon the other. It was Eugen's fate to be first and foremost amongst those thrown overboard when England, violating every tenet of international good faith, embarked towards the end of 1710 upon a secret course in pursuit of her own national interests and in total disregard of all her allies. Not least at Eugen's expense did England at this time so justly earn the title of Perfidious Albion. The setbacks which he suffered in the years 1711–13—the break-up of his partnership with Marlborough, the disruption of the Grand Alliance, and his consequent military defeat for the first time against France—these reverses, the worst of his life, were the bitter fruits of British policy. England, which owed so much to Eugen for his decade-long leadership against the common enemy, repaid the debt, not in the customary political currency of ingratitude, but in the simpler, baser coinage of betrayal.

Already in the middle of the slow 1710 campaign, Eugen had sensed the acute danger of a change of government in Whitehall. Upon his prompting the Emperor wrote to Queen Anne in his own hand, and his representative, Graf Johann Wenzel Gallas, made representations to Her Majesty in person in support of the existing régime. But the Queen responded by dismissing her First Minister, Godolphin. This was a decisive step. In Klopp's view 'the fearful carnage of Malplaquet was ... less important to the development of the peoples of

Europe than the bloodless change of the Ministry in England. . . .'[1]
The French, of course, were delighted. Eugen quickly seized upon
the implications. To Marlborough he was all equable encouragement, but to the Imperial representative at The Hague he unfurled
his feelings:

'I am afraid that we must expect things to go from bad to worse
in England so long as a woman is in charge. She lets herself be led
by many wrong-headed people. . . . I have spoken about it to the
Duke of Marlborough and implored him not to despair but to wait
and see what the next campaign brings forth.'[2]

Eugen believed that the most useful thing for him to do was to
try to keep up Marlborough's spirits and prevent him resigning. If
need be he was prepared to hurry over to England on the Duke's
behalf. Marlborough reported this to Godolphin: 'Prince Eugene
is so desirious of doing good, that whatever I should think for
my service, he would undertake, even to making of a journey to
England.'[3]

Eugen's instinct was as good as his intention. With his immense
prestige he might possibly have succeeded in fortifying the ranks
behind Marlborough, had he gone to England at this stage. Delay in
going was to prove fatal.

In an effort to hinder the Duke's resignation, Eugen also announced
that he would not serve under anyone else in Flanders. In fact, the new
English Government, which were now supported by a Tory majority
in the House of Commons following the general election in October,
had decided that for the time being their interests would best be
served by keeping Marlborough at his post. He was the only person
who could be expected to keep the allied leaders sweet and the French
army in check until such time as they had accomplished the infamous
deed they had decided upon, a secret and separate peace with
Versailles.

In Vienna that winter 1710–11 Eugen found even more than the
customary righteous indignation over the state of the war, though
perhaps it was more justified than usual. London was the focus of
anxiety. At the beginning of January 1711, the Duchess of Marlborough was dismissed from her post at court. We may be sure that

[1] O. Klopp, op. cit., XIII, p. 440.
[2] A. Arneth, op. cit., II, 477.
[3] W. Coxe, op. cit., III, p. 128.

the responsive Eugen, whose entire life-course had been determined by his mother's fall at Versailles, was sensitive to the effect on Marlborough of Sarah's royal disgrace. Gallas, always a penetrating observer, reported that the Duke was likely to be left in command 'merely out of fear of public opinion . . .' but with no real power. The pressure and maltreatment might, however, be such that he would be forced to resign, 'or else die of anger and disappointment'. He had suffered so much that 'he no longer looks like himself'.[1] Added to this, the smell of the clandestine peace talks, which had been going on between London and Versailles since October 1710, was already beginning to reach the Austrian capital. At Eugen's instigation, stiffening orders were sent to Gallas remonstrating against any possible change of policy and emphasizing the indispensability of Marlborough for the continued prosecution of the war.

Meanwhile there were other cares awaiting the attention of Eugen and the Vienna cabinet. Cock-a-hoop over events in London, the French threatened a mid-winter attack in Bavaria and actually carried one out in Spain confusing Starhemberg and capturing Stanhope.

At last, after eight years of war, the Hungarian insurgents were ready for peace. After successive defeats in the field in the three years 1708–10 the country had been afflicted by an appalling outbreak of the plague. This killed off nearly half a million people, or almost a sixth of the entire population. On January 30, 1711, Pálffy, Rákóczi and Károlyi met for talks at Szatmar. Pálffy agreed to an armistice while negotiations were proceeding. Eugen, always intolerant of the *kurucz* (literally crusader; i.e. anti-Habsburg) spirit amongst the Hungarians, was annoyed at this concession. 'Graf Pálffy should be reprimanded,' he said, 'it is not right that the rebels should be given such hopes or treated so well.'[2] However, before the balance of his none too favourable Hungarian account can be struck one further event should be reported to his credit. After the Hungarian war had finally been brought to an end by the Treaty of Szatmar on April 30, 1711, the Austrian Government tried to wriggle out of paying Károlyi the sum of money which they had promised at the cease-fire. Eugen insisted on the Imperial War Council keeping to their commitment. 'What is promised must be adhered to,' he said, 'otherwise all faith and confidence are destroyed.'[3] The Treaty of Szatmar gave little

[1] O. Klopp, op. cit., XIV, p. 27.
[2] A. Arneth, op. cit., II, p. 157.
[3] A. Arneth, op. cit., II, p. 175.

immediate satisfaction to the Hungarians, but their fanatical resistance did have one lasting reward. Vienna could never again discount the possibility of another violent revolt if they carried oppression too far.

From further east, the Russians, now frightened of the Turks, were pressing for an open alliance with the Emperor. But Eugen, who earlier had toyed with the idea of a Russian alliance, was nervous that it would provoke the Turks into making fresh incursions into Hungary. After describing erratic courses for so long, the Habsburg, Ottoman and Russian empires were now rotating in fixed orbits, their paths held equidistant by the balanced forces of fear and attraction. The Turkish ellipse was just about to reach its closest point to Vienna. At the beginning of February 1711, the Sultan's plenipotentiary, Seifullah Aga, set out from Constantinople, arriving in the Habsburg capital two months later. After he had driven round the town in oriental splendour he was received by Eugen in his winter palace in Himmelpfortgasse seated upon a throne and surrounded by the political and military leaders of the Empire. In the course of the next fortnight there were many conferences between them. There was much formality and politeness. East and West met each other on Eugen's baroque stage in a clash of ritual and showmanship. Yet when the pageant had all faded nothing of substance remained. The Turks had been out to secure the renewal of the Treaty of Carlowitz. But Eugen, supported by the other Imperial advisers, had been unreceptive. They had no wish to get any closer to the Sultan than to the Tsar.

Had it not been for the Turk, Eugen would have left Vienna sooner to return to Flanders. Marlborough had arrived back at The Hague on March 4. He had been sorely tempted to resign and had been restrained only by loyalty to the Whigs at home and his friends abroad, particularly Eugen. According to Sarah, the exhortations of the Prince had the greatest effect in inducing her husband to retain his command.[1] Nor were Harley and St John yet ready to jettison him. Knowing well how best to touch him to the quick they promised to pay the money necessary for the resumption of work upon Blenheim Palace. But despite this and the Government's solemn affirmations for the common cause with which he was packed off to allied headquarters, he felt deeply uneasy. He knew that peace talks between England and France were going on behind his back. He was a stool-pigeon. He had but a shadow of his former authority. More than ever he needed Eugen's support. '*Au nom de Dieu, mon Prince,*' he

[1] W. Coxe, op. cit., III, p. 178.

wrote to him on March 9, '*hâtez votre voyage autant qu'il est possible*.'[1]
In frequent subsequent letters from The Hague he begged him to
hasten his journey.

Eugen was delayed by a most unexpected and fateful event: the
death from smallpox on April 17 of the Emperor Joseph. The Prince
had already left Vienna on his way back to the front when he heard
the news. It was a grave misfortune, both for him personally and, as
he soon realized, for the whole allied cause. To Marlborough he
wrote: 'Your Highness knows what a blow it is for the affairs of
Europe, but it is even worse for those who have always had such a
strong attachment to him personally.'[2]

Instead of proceeding directly to the Netherlands, Eugen complied
with fresh instructions he received from home telling him to take over
supreme command on the Rhine. Vienna was afraid that France might
seize upon the moment of flux following Joseph's death to launch
another offensive against Germany. They were also worried that
Louis XIV might try to advance the Bavarian claim to the Imperial
crown by interfering in the Diet's election of Joseph's brother Charles
as Emperor. But all remained quiet—at any rate for the time being.
Eugen considered that he could be of more immediate use elsewhere.
He therefore handed over command at Bruchsal to the Duke of
Württemberg and made off for the Netherlands, canvassing various
German Princes en route to support Charles's election at Frankfurt.

He did not reach Marlborough's camp until May 23. They were to
be together for only three weeks. For by early June the nervousness
in Vienna over the possibility of a French attack eastwards had reached
a high pitch. News had been received of the despatch of French
troops from the Netherlands to the Rhine. Eugen was hastily
ordered to march off to the Rhine with 20,000 men. On June 14 the two
commanders parted. They were never to be together again in the field.
The impact of Eugen's withdrawal on the strength and morale of the
allied army was enormous. The Dutch were dismayed. They insisted
on the transfer of troops from the line to strengthen their frontier
garrisons. The Field Deputy Goslinga expressed his country's concern
over the departure of a commander 'whose genius for war', in his
opinion, was 'greatly superior to that of the Duke'.[3] Opening his
career of assiduous attention to the interests of the Duke of Marlborough, Henry St John, who had become Secretary of State in

---

[1] *Murray Dispatches*, op. cit., V, p. 266.
[2] A. Arneth, op. cit., II, p. 481.
[3] Winston S. Churchill, op. cit., II, p. 839.

Harley's new ministry, joined in the pillage and took five British battalions away in a vain attempt to capture Quebec. Marlborough was finally left with a force sadly depleted in spirit, and inferior in number to that of Villars. But notwithstanding this he fought a brilliant campaign. In an operation which he regarded as his masterpiece he succeeded in completely out-manoeuvring Villars. From the side-lines in Germany, where the rains and inundations detained him in his camp, Eugen watched Marlborough's progress eagerly. In August he wrote: 'You are fully convinced, I trust, that no person takes a greater interest in your concerns than myself.'[1] The Duke sensed that Eugen was feeling out of it. He also wanted his advice. He therefore sent him details of his plans for the siege of Bouchain and asked for his comments. Eugen responded by giving him his views positively but deferentially upon all manner of things from the Duke's health to his entrenchments. Although unable throughout the rest of the season to do anything directly to compass Louis XIV's defeat, Eugen did succeed in his limited purpose of deterring the French from undertaking an attack upon Bavaria or interfering with the Imperial election.

After Joseph's death in April, the Vienna Cabinet had appointed his mother, the Empress Eleonora, as Regent. They had also sent messages to Spain imploring Joseph's brother and heir, Charles, to return as soon as possible and secure possession of the Imperial crown. But Charles had been commendably reluctant to abandon the Catalans at the lowest ebb in their fortunes. They alone of the Spaniards had consistently supported him. He therefore waited five months before sailing from Barcelona, and left his wife behind as a pledge of loyalty. When he finally arrived back on October 12, he was elected Emperor by the Imperial Diet the same day.

Eugen, who had done much to drum up support for his election, joined him soon afterwards at Innsbruck. The most urgent matter for their attention was the policy of the English Government. Gallas had just been given a brief and perfunctory account of the 'Preliminary Articles of Peace' which had been signed between the French and English on October 8, 1711. The Imperial Government were incensed at this news. They considered that the English had been guilty of outrageous double-dealing at the expense of their friends; the manner and substance of their *fait accompli* were a flagrant violation of the letter and spirit of the Alliance. Under the terms of the proposed peace, the Bourbon King, Philip V, was to

[1] W. Coxe, op. cit., III, p. 230.

retain the crown of Spain and Spanish America. This struck at the very root of what had become the principal Austrian war aim: the establishment of the Archduke Charles on the Spanish throne. Unfortunately for Vienna, the death of the Emperor Joseph provided the English with a convenient pretext for their change of policy. Originally so they would argue, they had backed Charles for the Spanish inheritance in the belief that Joseph would have an heir and that there was no chance of Charles acquiring the Empire of Austria as well as that of Spain. But now that Joseph had died childless everything was changed. They could not be a party to the revival of the overweight Empire of Charles V. England must therefore accept Philip in Spain, whilst compensating Charles elsewhere. This line of reasoning was, in fact, nothing more than a highly plausible cover for a policy which London had already decided upon for less honourable motives—namely peace for private gain. Britain had secured as a *quid pro quo* from France immense strategic and commercial advantages including the Asiento, or monopoly of the slave trade with Latin America. In reality the broad outlines of the 'Preliminary Articles' had been agreed upon before Joseph's death by Henry St John, the new Secretary of State, and by Godolphin's successor as First Minister, Robert Harley; they had worked them out with Louis XIV's Foreign Minister, Torcy. So privily were the negotiations initially conducted on the English side that Harley kept the other members of his government in ignorance of them. Indeed, on the very day the news of Joseph's death reached London, Gallas was given a promise that the cabinet would back Charles for Emperor as well as continuing to support him for the Spanish throne.[1] If this assurance was not the fruit of Cabinet ignorance then it must be judged one of the first flowers of Harley's infamous double diplomacy.

Ever since England had begun fighting Louis XIV in 1702 there had been a lack of certainty about her war aims. This was due to something more than a national shyness of policy definitions. It came really from the complexity of her motives. She had ostensibly joined the Grand Alliance in the first place to prevent the crowns of France and Spain from being united; but this was merely a dynastic reflection of the more profound aim of stopping the French from dominating Europe; and this object in turn, though derived in the first instance from military fear of the French army, had come in the course of time to be based more and more on commercial con-

[1] O. Klopp, op. cit., XIV, p. 92. Winston S. Churchill, op. cit., IV, p. 803.

siderations. With the French army no longer the overwhelming strength it had been a decade before, the time was now ripe for England to reassess her economic advantage; and this seemed to lie in making peace with France in disregard of the Austrians and at the expense of the Dutch. At least that was how the Tories appear to have reasoned.

The Dutch naturally were furious with England over the 'Preliminary Articles of Peace'. The Barrier Treaty, which the former English Ministry had signed in 1709, and which gave Holland specific fortresses and considerable commercial rights, was now a scrap of paper. The 'Preliminary Articles' made no provision whatever for the Dutch Republic's economic needs, and the barrier in the Netherlands was only mentioned in the most general terms. Yet the Dutch had only agreed two years previously to turn a deaf ear to Louis' siren song of peace on the strength of the Barrier Treaty's promises. In one respect only could the Dutch feel that they had been less shabbily treated than the Austrians; the gist of Harley's deal had been first communicated to them in April 1711, whereas it had not been given to the Austrians or any of the other Allies until six months later.

As they discussed the problem together at Innsbruck Eugen and Charles must have derived some comfort from the strength and unity of the opposition which had immediately declared itself to the English Government. The furtive selfishness of British policy had rallied opponents at home and abroad. However easy the Tory leaders might find it to overlook the objections of the Dutch Republic and Austria, they must surely be disturbed by the hostility of the heir to the British throne, the Elector of Hanover. He had condemned the 'Preliminary Articles' as a flagrant betrayal of the allied cause. They must also be embarrassed by the outspoken criticism of Marlborough. Most heartening of all to the Imperial leaders confabulating in the Tyrol was the combined frenzy of the English Whigs who, though outnumbered in the House of Commons, still had a majority in the Lords.

The Emperor was kept well informed of events and opinions in England by the pro-Whig Gallas who had early smelt treachery in the air and was zealous in reporting it. He had no illusions about the brilliant St John: 'Neither his rank, his credit, capacity or steadiness make one believe him;'[1] and: 'The Ministers and the dominant party are enemies rather than friends of the Alliance.'[2] But unfortunately for Gallas, St John had bribed his way into the secrets of the Ambas-

[1] O. Klopp, op. cit., XIV, p. 116.
[2] Ibid.

sador's cypher and was able to read these agreeable comments. What
worried him most, however, was not the personal disparagement but
the plan which Gallas was revealed to be working on for the despatch
to London of a leading personality from Austria to try to thwart the
Tory peace policy. Eugen was the obvious person to come. This
must be stopped at all costs, for what damage might the Prince not
do if, in the present state of crisis in London, he were able to consort
with the Whigs and the friends of Marlborough? It was urgently
necessary therefore to crush Gallas. Accordingly, on October 26,
1711, the Master of Ceremonies informed him that, owing to the
displeasure his conduct had caused her, the Queen had forbidden
him the Court!

Meanwhile the idea of sending Eugen to England had slowly
taken root in Charles' mind. He must restore his relations with
Queen Anne. If England were to have her way and peace talks with
the French were to take place it must be on some other basis than the
hated 'Preliminaries'. Charles had been impressed by the Prince's
performance in the long ministerial conferences which he had been
holding in Innsbruck. 'Prince Eugen argues well and to the point,' he
wrote; 'Sinzendorff prattles terribly.'[1] When he left Innsbruck in
December to be crowned Emperor at Frankfurt, he therefore commissioned Eugen to proceed to England.

By the time he reached The Hague in mid-December en route for
London Eugen learnt that the Dutch had yielded to English pressure
and had agreed to send representatives to Utrecht for peace negotiations. This was a blow; and it was obvious that the Dutch were overawed even to the point of fearing to show him hospitality. With the
English, Eugen immediately ran into difficulties. Their representative,
Strafford,[2] made such heavy weather about discussing the next campaign that the Prince was deeply suspicious. To the Dutch Deputies
he said that he had much he wished to say about the forthcoming
operations but he was hesitant to do so in front of Strafford, 'because
he couldn't be sure if he was speaking before an Englishman or a
Frenchman'.[3] Strafford's main concern was to try to stop Eugen
continuing his journey to England. He received a stream of instructions to this effect from St John. 'Your Excellency is to discourage
as much as possible, this Prince from coming over. It is high time to

[1] A. Arneth, op. cit., II, p. 190.
[2] Thomas Wentworth, Baron Raby and third Earl of Strafford, 1672-1739.
Soldier and diplomat; one of the negotiators of the Treaty of Utrecht.
[3] A. Arneth, op. cit., II, p. 195.

put a stop to this foreign influence on British councils; and we must either emancipate ourselves now, or be for ever slaves.'[1] Quite a tribute to Eugen's influence.

[1] *Letters and Correspondence of Henry St John, Lord Viscount Bolingbroke*, ed. Gilbert Parke, 1798, II, p. 52.

CHAPTER XIV

EUGEN'S VISIT TO LONDON,
JANUARY–MARCH 1712

THE STORY of Eugen's visit to London is a prodigy of governmental inhospitality. In their efforts to prevent him from coming the English ministers first tried to frighten him. They claimed that the public were so clamorous for peace that they might demonstrate against him. St John, the Secretary of State, assured the Austrian representative manfully that everything possible would be done to hold the hostile mob in check so that the Prince would not suffer injury, but such was the strength of public feeling that nothing could be guaranteed.

These methods of intimidation of course had the opposite of the intended effect on Eugen. In fact, he drew heart from them. As Arneth puts it, 'If anything could have been certain of filling Prince Eugen with hopes for the visit, it was the anxious efforts made by the English ministers to prevent his coming.'[1] He was also encouraged by a letter from Marlborough:

'The reports you have been given of the attitude of the English people to you are an insult to us; in truth everyone is dying to see you, and I am quite certain that you will be received everywhere with the respect and applause due to Your Excellency personally and to the services you have rendered Europe.'[2]

To crown their obtuseness Harley and St John suggested that, rather than face the London mob, Eugen should discuss everything

[1] A. Arneth, op. cit., II, p. 196.
[2] *Murray's Dispatches*, op. cit., V, p. 573.

in the Netherlands with Strafford,[1] who, they kindly assured him, was fully briefed on their views.

First the terrors of the crowd, then the offer of Strafford . . . Eugen was more determined than ever to get to England. But the English Government were equally ready with impediments. They decided to cancel the agreement they had already given to Eugen's request for a yacht and a frigate for the crossing. Unfortunately for them, before this counter-order arrived Eugen had set sail for Harwich on January 7, 1712. He was accompanied by his twenty-year-old nephew, the Chevalier of Savoy, the youngest son of his deceased eldest brother, the Duc de Soissons.[2]

He sailed in ignorance of the Government's latest stroke, the dismissal of Marlborough from all his offices. This was the culmination of the frenzied struggle which had been going on in London ever since the news had become public in October of the Tory Government's secret deal with France. For long it was touch and go whether the Government would survive. But at the crucial moment, the Queen's First Minister, Robert Harley, and the Secretary of State, Henry St John, discharged their deadliest weapon, the poisonous ink-sack of Dean Swift. In *The Conduct of the Allies*, published at the end of November 1711, Swift reviled the Allies for having broken all their engagements and accused them of leaving it to England to do most of the fighting, whilst hogging all the honours and prizes themselves. It was one of the most pernicious and effective pamphlets ever written: an address to the atavistic emotions of the British, an inspiration to their insularity and self-satisfaction, a pot-denigrating-the-kettle tract which appealed all the more effectively to the nation's spleen by appearing to speak to their head. According to one estimate it sold 11,000 copies in one month, a staggering figure for those days.[3] More than anything else it finally tilted the scales of opinion in favour of the Government. But the Whigs still had some fight left in them. They passed a motion in the House of Lords in December declaring as unsafe and dishonourable, both for England and Europe, any peace which ceded Spain and the Indies to the Bourbons. Marlborough spoke strongly in support. This brought forth the double-barrelled counter-fire of the Government: the Duke was sacked and twelve new Tory Peers were created, sufficient to ensure a majority in the Lords as well as Commons. These twin disasters to the Whig cause

[1] See footnote on p. 188.
[2] See Chapter IV, p. 49.
[3] Douglas Coombs, op. cit., p. 280.

were announced to the world in the *Gazette* on New Year's Day 1712. By the time Eugen set foot in England on January 16 the battle for an honourable, concerted peace which he had been sent there to wage had virtually been lost. Indeed the evident firmness of his intention to come may well have accelerated the Government's decision to jettison Marlborough.

The weather for the crossing was vile and at one moment he was in danger of being taken by a French privateer. Eugen tossed about for nine days before he reached the English coast, an appalling but fitting prelude to what was to come. He had originally intended to land at Harwich, but on learning of the large crowds thronging the road to London to give him a triumphal welcome, he decided to sail on discreetly round to the Thames. For he certainly did not want to embarrass the Government. The first person to come aboard to greet him as he sailed up the river was one of Marlborough's officers. From him he heard all the latest depressing news. The Government also sent an emissary to receive him. This was John Drummond, a Scottish merchant who had been Harley's agent in the United Provinces, where Eugen had known him. Drummond questioned him on his intentions and suggested the need for caution in his relations with the fallen Marlborough, a warning which Eugen treated with the contempt it deserved. He said that it was a mistake to suppose that he had come to England for the purpose of trying to upset the Ministry. His aim was to restore harmony between the two countries. But he could not forsake his friend in his hour of need. 'I had to tell Drummond,' Eugen reported to the Emperor, 'that since it was known all over the world what a firm and intimate friendship I had fostered with the Duke of Marlborough, now finding him in misfortune, I could not do otherwise than uphold my friendship with him, lest the world should say, and I leave it as an evil echo after me, that I deserted and abandoned a friend in his hour of sorrow and stress when fortune had forsaken him.'[1]

He thought of landing at Greenwich, but again the crowd was black. It was the same at the Tower, which he reached in darkness at 6 p.m. on January 16, 1712, so he came on up with the tide to Whitehall Steps, where he set foot for the first time in England. There was no one there. He took the first cab he saw and drove to Leicester House where the outcast Gallas had formerly lived. The first Englishman to welcome him in London was Marlborough, who called late the same evening. They were together an hour. Shortly

[1] *Feldzüge*, II Ser., V. App. 14.

after arriving at Leicester House, Eugen sent his General-Adjutant, von Hohendorff,[1] to Harley and St John to announce his arrival and ask for an interview. At midnight St John let him know that he would call the following morning. He was there to time, and the two men conversed for a quarter of an hour—in French, which St John spoke exquisitely, Eugen having little English. St John took possession of the Prince's special credentials and left, promising to seek an audience for him with the Queen. This was granted the following day, at 6 p.m. Without any panoply, the two men drove to St James's Palace in St John's coach. After appropriate expressions of respect Eugen handed Her Majesty a letter in the Emperor's own hand with the request that she read it to ascertain the reason for his visit. The Queen gave it only the most perfunctory glance before delivering herself of the response learnt by heart from her ministers in advance, namely that any business which Eugen might wish to discuss should properly be taken up with her representative in Holland. Respectfully but firmly, the Prince suggested that the Queen could not be referring to the first aim of his mission, the restoration of close relations between her Majesty and the Emperor. Anne, however, was not to be drawn into giving him any encouragement. She had been well drilled beforehand by Harley and St John. She fell back upon ill-health, that inexhaustible stock-in-trade of all international negotiations, despised though it may be for lesser dealings between individuals. 'I am sorry that the state of my health does not permit me to speak with your Highness as often as I wish,' she said, adding, with a gesture towards her ministers, 'I have ordered these two gentlemen to receive your proposals whenever you think proper.'[2] As Eugen observed in the report he sent the Emperor on the interview, Anne was visibly embarrassed by the uncongenial rôle which she was forced to play.

Eugen's main worry in his first few weeks was how he was ever going to get down to business. He had to receive so many ceremonial calls and such incessant public acclaim that the time flew by without his being able to bite upon his agenda. Having failed to prevent his coming, the Tories now did their best to see that he was submerged in social life—but of a trivial kind; the City of London was prevented from giving a banquet in his honour and none of the ministers enter-

---

[1] Georg Wilhelm Hohendorff, 1670–1719. Born in Prussia, he became a distinguished soldier and diplomat of the Monarchy. He was also an eminent scholar and connoisseur of the arts—a warrior aesthete after Eugen's own heart.

[2] W. Coxe, op. cit., III, p. 288.

tained him. To two of the leading City merchants who called upon him
Eugen succeeded, however, in expressing his gratitude for the loan
which London had made him during the war. 'The raising of the
siege of Turin, and the successes that followed,' he told them, 'were
next to God mainly owing to the seasonable supply of money I
received from England.'[1] As Boyer reports in his *Annals*, the spleen
and malice of the Tory Party showed their ugly heads a few days
after the Prince's arrival in the newspaper, the *Post Boy*, which
published a rude piece about Eugen's mother—an affront which he
'overlooked with his usual magnanimity'. The Tories also tried to
turn him to their own account in their campaign against Marlborough,
proclaiming him as much the greater general of the two and by far
the finer character. The Whigs were not to be out-done in exploitation. They hailed him as the Duke's loyal friend bent now upon
preventing the forced liquidation of the allied partnership. Despite
the obvious difficulties, Eugen succeeded in remaining outwardly
aloof from this tug-of-war over his body.

Everyone in England seemed eager to see him. Setting the pace,
Addison brought Sir Roger de Coverley all the way from Worcester-
shire to London to 'stand in some convenient place where he might
have full sight of that extraordinary man, whose presence does so
much honour to the British nation'. Bishop Burnet, an eye-witness,
writes that the 'Prince's character was so justly high, that all people
for some weeks pressed about the places, where he was to be seen,
to look on him'. The Bishop—admittedly a fanatical Whig—also
gives an enthusiastic account of the impression Eugen made on
him:

'I had the honour to be admitted, at several times, to much
discourse with him: his character is so universally known, that I
will say nothing of him, but from what appeared to myself. He has
a most unaffected modesty, and does scarcely bear the acknow-
ledgments that all the world pay him. He descends to an easy
equality with those with whom he converses: and seems to assume
nothing to himself, while he reasons with others. . . .'[2]

From a contemporary diary we get a sharp glimpse of Eugen's
appearance: 'I was at Prince Eugene's Levée at Leicester house. He

[1] A. Boyer, *The History of the Reign of Queen Anne digested into Annals*, X,
pp. 377–8.
[2] Bishop Burnet, *History of His Own Time*, 1838, p. 879.

is not so little as I have heard him represented to be, of a swarthy complexion, and something very brisk about the eyes.'[1]

Wherever Eugen went he was met with enthusiastic crowds; those that cried out for peace were always most respectful and enthusiastic. According to Lady Strafford, writing from St James's Square, 'the mob are so fond of Prince Eugen that his coach can hardly go about'.[2] Shortly afterwards another eye-witness described him as being 'in some danger of being killed with good cheer, having been allow'd but one day to dine at home'.[3] A few days later it was reported that: 'Prince Eugene has been every day entertain'd at some great man's. Lord Portland has given him one day a dinner, musick and a dancing; everything was mighty fine there. The Duke of Buckingham treated him a Saturday, and if he did not outdo Lord Portland within doors he did without, for he had a whole regiment of the militia all in buff, to stand to their armes for the Prince's coming and going from his house.'[4] The multitude not merely thronged round his coach and the entrance to Leicester House, but penetrated to his living-room where they hung about all day gaping in admiration. Those who had business to do could scarcely get near him for the throng. There was much firing of guns in St James's Park and at the Tower. In the cities of London and Westminster, so Boyer records, 'there were ringing of bells, bonfires, illuminations and all other public demonstrations of joy'.[5] There was not one hostile incident.

Not until he had been in London four days did he have the chance of a serious talk with Harley. And it was highly unsatisfactory. As soon as he started asking about the war or the peace negotiations, Harley changed the subject, assuring him with transparent dis-ingenuousness that no commitments had yet been entered into. He could get no nearer reality with St John, who in fact sent the French Secretary of State, Torcy, a secret message on January 23 assuring him that Eugen's 'stay will not last long, and that his proposals will not have the effect which the Imperial court hope for'.[6]

After a week of frustration, Eugen decided to submit his views in

[1] H. Isham Longden, *The Diaries (Home and Foreign) of Sir Justinian Isham, 1703–1736.* Transactions of the Royal Historical Society, 1907, I, p. 198.

[2] Lady Strafford to the Earl of Strafford, January 19, 1712, *The Wentworth Papers*, op. cit., p. 244.

[3] Lord Berkeley of Stratton to the Earl of Strafford, February 6, 1712, *The Wentworth Papers*, op. cit., p. 258.

[4] Peter Wentworth to his brother, the Earl of Strafford, February 10, 1712, *The Wentworth Papers*, op. cit., p. 260.

[5] A. Boyer, op. cit., X, p. 344.

[6] *Letters of Bolingbroke*, op. cit., p. 156.

writing. His memorandum of January 24 was answered by a long silence. Eventually St John replied orally: the request for Gallas to be allowed to take leave of the Queen in normal fashion, rather than be dismissed the court as he had been without farewell ceremony, was flatly refused; the suggestion for a new basis other than the 'Preliminaries' for the peace negotiations was met with evasive criticisms; finally, Eugen's proposal to discuss the next campaign, and his offer on behalf of the Emperor to double the Imperial forces in the field and bear a large share of the cost of the Spanish operations, were countered with nothing but abuse of the Austrian contribution to the war, particularly in Spain, coupled with self-praise of England's part. The Government's attitude on the first two points was so negative that Eugen decided to pursue them no further, but to concentrate on the third and most urgent matter, the prosecution of the war. The problem of Spain cried out for early attention. The Imperial troops there had not been paid for months despite the English Government's obligation to do so. Notwithstanding this, Guido Starhemberg had succeeded in relieving Cardona and it only needed the combined follow-up of the Allies to transform the situation there.

Both in person and in a second memorandum Eugen repudiated the complacent English assumption that they had borne the whole brunt of the fighting with little help from Austria. At the outset of the war in Spain, so he reminded the ministers, the Sea Powers had asked the Emperor for nothing more than the person of the Archduke Charles. Now Vienna was coming forward with the offer to provide three-quarters of the total allied force in the Peninsula. As for the past, the Empire had had to fight frequently on several fronts. They had so denuded themselves of troops that at times the security of Vienna was in jeopardy. Nevertheless now they were offering to put over one hundred thousand men into the field against France. The Dutch had had over one hundred and twenty thousand in the field in Flanders in the previous campaign, the English about seventy thousand, of whom two-thirds were foreigners.[1] Looking at these figures it is impossible not to admire the effrontery with which the English, in extenuation of the abject betrayal of the Dutch Republic and Austria, were to claim that they alone had lived up to the needs of the Grand Alliance. Compared with their allies, the English had scarcely felt the war in terms of either military service or sacrifice. Their wealth had enabled them to hire the men. They had hired a great many from the princes of the Empire who had been readier to earn money in

[1] The exact number was 48,817 foreigners, 21,965 British subjects.

this way than to make the direct contribution they might have done to the Imperial army. But it ill became the English to blame the Emperor for not having provided these soldiers when they themselves had already taken them on as mercenaries, thus relieving themselves of the necessity to find Englishmen for the line.

Eugen had experienced enough by now to be quite convinced that the English ministers had already reached a firm secret agreement with the French. But it was difficult to persuade the new Emperor that things had gone so far as that. Indeed Charles was eager for Eugen to stay on in London despite the unfavourable reception he had had from the Government, and was reluctant to believe that he would not soon be able to send Gallas back. Moreover Eugen observed, not without some hope, that the serene progress of England's treachery was running into certain difficulties. Starhemberg's success in Spain was the first of them. It had produced a wave of allied optimism about the war there—the last thing the Tory Government wanted. Secondly, the English representatives at Utrecht, where peace talks had begun at the end of January, had met trouble both from the Allies who thought they were yielding too much, and from the French who were proving unexpectedly exacting. Finally, the deaths early in 1712 of the eldest grandson and great-grandson of Louis XIV had aroused old fears that Philip of Anjou might become King of France as well as of Spain. All these difficulties forced the Tory ministers to prevaricate in their dealings with Eugen. Both he and the Emperor nourished a slight hope that the English Government would not after all be able to survive.

While he was awaiting an answer to further Notes which he addressed to the British Government about the war in Spain, Eugen suffered a personal disaster; his nephew, the young Chevalier of Savoy, who had been serving as his A.D.C., died suddenly of smallpox. From her listening post in St James's Square, Lady Strafford reported that nothing else was being talked about but the nephew's death. She added that 'most people say he had more distempers than one, and they say he never went to bed sober since he came, and he was a great admirer of ladies'.[1] Lady Strafford, a vivid witness of Eugen's London visit, should not be ignored. But neither should we overlook her strenuous efforts to make her evidence as entertaining as possible. Thus she wrote on one occasion to her husband, '. . . you are very fond of folly. I am glad of it believing you will grow fonder than ever

[1] Lady Strafford to the Earl of Strafford, March 7, 1712, *The Wentworth Papers*, op. cit., p. 270.

of me since folly has your affection. I have taken it into my head that
Prince Eugen has been some time or other wounded in the ——, for
I never saw anybody sit down so stiff.'[1] Clearly we should not under-
estimate this gift of fantasy in assessing Lady Strafford's comments
on the death of Eugen's nephew. Her final observation on the tragic
event was: 'They say Prince Eugen is not much troubled for him.'
Now the Chevalier of Savoy may well have liked the bottle and loved
the ladies. But it seems most unlikely that he was quite unlamented
by his uncle. At the time of his death he was closer to Eugen than
any other relation, and it would have been inherently improbable
that he would have been brought to London as confidential aide unless the Prince had had some feelings for him.

At any rate it was in the disturbed atmosphere of his nephew's
death that Eugen at last received an answer from the British Government to his insistent entreaties. What they said can in no way have
consoled him. They made it clear that the support he had been asking
for in the Spanish theatre must depend upon a vote in the House of
Commons—a constitutional excuse invoked by the British Government not for the first or last time as a pretext for inaction. Indeed
this reference to the House of Commons was but one example of the
intense use made throughout the crisis by Harley and St John
of public opinion as a means of support for what they had already
decided upon. They were not, needless to say, governed by the
clamour of the mob. But they were astute enough to perceive the use
that could be made of it. Playing upon the war-weariness of the population and the latent xenophobia of the English, they saw to it that mass
feeling was whipped up and exploited. As a modern historian has
observed of this episode. 'Diplomacy resting upon an appeal
to public opinion is a technique usually associated with nineteenth-
century statesmen and twentieth-century demagogues, but it had been
unmistakably foreshadowed in the campaign against the Allies.'[2]

It was at this time too, after he had been in London many weeks,
that Eugen started to experience the full deviousness of Harley's
tactics. Recognizing the Prince's power on the Continent, and aware
of his none-too-secure position at home, Harley could not afford to
make an outright enemy of him or to let him leave the country
offended as well as empty-handed. Knowing that he had nothing of
substance to offer him, he decided to try to smooth him over with

---

[1] Lady Strafford to the Earl of Strafford, January 19, 1712, *The Wentworth
Papers*, op. cit., p. 243.
[2] Douglas Coombs, op. cit., p. 384.

flattery and to give the impression that the two of them were joined in some great conspiracy—a naïve English technique sometimes construed as subtlety.

First of all he got in touch with Hohendorff, and suggested with a great air of mystery that he should serve as intermediary between the Government and the Prince, a totally unnecessary rôle since Eugen was eager for direct discussions with Ministers. Hohendorff said so frankly, and a meeting was eventually arranged between the two principals. Without beating about the bush Eugen referred to his strong suspicion that some agreement existed already between England and France. Harley denied it categorically. The only admission he was prepared to make was that the English Government no longer believed in excluding Philip and the House of Bourbon from the Spanish throne, to which Eugen rejoined bluntly that in that event he might as well leave London immediately. Not wanting to break off on that note, Harley fixed another meeting and arranged for Eugen to be admitted surreptitiously to his house through a secret door. Once again it was utterly fruitless. Harley was not going to be diverted from his long-laid plan of dishonour to the Alliance by Eugen's frank persistence. Eugen was not going to be satisfied by Harley's confidential evasiveness. Once more he decided to put his views in writing. Parliament had at last voted money for the Spanish war, but the Government had only asked for a third of the sum which Eugen had been urging as the minimum. The House of Commons had been treated to a travesty of the truth in the account the Government had given of the origins and obligations of the Spanish war. For years English ministers had been declaring unequivocally that no peace would be concluded which did not transfer Spain to the House of Austria. The English Government had indeed been the first to make this stipulation. With their trade interests in the West Indies and their new treaty with Portugal, the English Government had insisted nearly ten years previously on extending the terms of the Grand Alliance to provide for the exclusion of the House of Bourbon from Spain and its overseas territories. It was England who had forced the Emperor to assert the Habsburg right to Spain. English ministers had made it clear that they did not expect Austria to incur any additional obligations in troops or money. All that they had to do was to send the Emperor's son, the Archduke Charles, to the Peninsula to maintain his claim to the throne of Spain. The Sea Powers would make themselves responsible for the necessary troops and supplies. Queen Anne, to whose care the Emperor thereupon entrusted his son, promised Charles 'to do all that is in my power towards the maintenance and good fortune of Your Government'.

Yet now English ministers were not merely going back on all that their predecessors had been saying for so many years. They were also trying to shift the blame for their impending betrayal on to Austria by accusing her of having defaulted on her obligations. In the Queen's address to the House of Commons it was stated that 'although the Spanish undertaking was begun at the express and urgent request of the Imperial court . . . yet neither the present nor the previous Emperor has supported any troops there at his own expense except 2,000 men last year'.

As the French Secretary of State, Torcy, has observed wryly in his memoirs, 'A person of such quick penetration as Prince Eugene had no need of great experience in affairs to perceive that his stay in London was very disagreeable to the Queen, and still more so to her ministers.'[1] The Queen and her ministers did their best to hasten his departure by embarrassing him. A yacht was put at his disposal and he was reminded frequently and with great ceremony that everything was ready aboard for him to sail just whenever he pleased to embark. But Eugen was not to be pushed out quite so easily as that. He was determined to stay on until he was convinced beyond any shadow of doubt that no change of heart or government was possible. He was prepared to endure all his hosts' hints in the process. Vexed by such resilience, the English ministers thereupon decided to resort to tougher tactics. Their aim was to discredit Eugen once and for all publicly and privately. They also hoped to blacken Marlborough and to stampede the public into accepting the idea of a separate peace. For this strategem the English Government gave currency to the fabrications of a double agent, named Plunket. This man claimed that a coup was being planned to set fire to London, seize the Queen, assassinate Harley and his chief ministers, and place the Elector of Hanover immediately on the throne. The ring-leaders of this plot were alleged to be none other than Eugen and Marlborough, helped by a number of leading Whigs. It so happened at this time that a gang of ruffians known as Mohocks had been raiding the city at night, committing robbery and assault; and it was claimed that these thugs were identified with the pretended conspiracy of Eugen and Marlborough.

There is no doubt that many people believed these calumnies.

[1] *Memoirs of the Marquis of Torcy*, translated from the French, 1757, II, p. 270.

Jonathan Swift reported them as if they were gospel. In a book published posthumously he described Eugen as not without a 'natural tincture of that cruelty sometimes charged upon the Italians; and being nursed in arms, hath so far extinguished all the pity and remorse that he will at any time sacrifice a thousand mens' lives to a caprice of glory or revenge'.[1] He then proceeded to give an account of the treasons and assassinations which Marlborough and Eugen were said to have plotted after having arranged for the City of London to be softened up by the Mohocks.

A very different book was published in London in the year of Eugen's visit. A typical contemporary satire, its main message for us now is to show how intense was the interest aroused by the Prince's arrival in London. The book was called:

PRINCE EUGENE
NOT THE
MAN
YOU TOOK HIM FOR:
or, A
MERRY TALE
OF A
MODERN HEROE.[2]

Eugen's mother appears under the name of Hecate and foretells as follows the 'mischief that should be done to France, by her offspring, in revenge of the disgrace offered to her:

The Time shall come, when France shall feel
Great woes and great calamity;
My Brat shall make that Crown to reel,
In revenge of what it did to me.'

A piece of doggerel was published from Pater-Noster Row at the same time, a poem eulogizing the Prince:

Such is the Man, whom Germany has lent
To bridle France, and curb the Continent:
To whom kind heaven Valour and Prudence gave,
Cool, but not Dull, and without rashness Brave.

---

[1] Jonathan Swift, *The History of the Four Last Years of the Queen*, 1951 edition, p. 26.
[2] Printed and sold by J. Baker, 1712.

Go, Dauntless Prince, and stem the Gallick Rage,
Act in one Year the business of an Age.

Tho' no new Instance in the World appears
Of Pylian Age, and Patriarchal Years;
Yet if our Time by Action numbered be,
H' has liv'd Three Hundred, who has fought like Thee.[1]

By the middle of March, Eugen saw that there was no point in prolonging his mission any further. As he set sail for Holland on the 17th he must have realized that the visit had been the failure which he had very much feared it was going to be. However, it had not been totally without balm for him personally. In the long intervals of waiting for the English ministers to be ready to talk business he had been able to escape the throng of admirers and enjoy himself poking about among the antique book shops of London. This is said to have been the starting-point of his great library; and he was no doubt accompanied in his searches by Hohendorff, a passionate bibliophile.[2] It must also have been some consolation to him to be able to look back upon the extremely warm treatment he had received personally from so many people. Apart from Ministers the only exception has been the Queen, but her coolness towards him had probably been due to his outspoken loyalty to the now hated Marlborough. Even Anne had tried to make amends for her initial unfriendliness by honouring him later with the present of a sword, richly set with diamonds.

Although throughout his visit Eugen had been scrupulously correct in his dealings with Government and Opposition, he had not tried to hide his feelings of contempt for the defamers of Marlborough, and had omitted no opportunity to praise him. At a dinner which was given for him, Harley said in a speech of welcome: 'I consider this day as the happiest of my life, since I have the honour to see in my house the greatest captain of the age.'

Alluding to the dismissal and absence of his friend, the Prince replied laconically: 'If it be so, I owe it to your Lordship.'[3]

---

[1] *A Poem on Prince Eugene*, A pamphlet printed for J. Baker in Pater-Noster Row, London, 1712.

[2] G. A. Bogeng, *Die Grossen Bibliophilen*, 1922, I, pp. 352–3. See Chapter XIX.

[3] W. Coxe, op. cit., III, p. 288.

CHAPTER XV

ENGLAND'S TREACHERY
AND EUGEN'S DEFEAT

DEFEAT AND humiliation, frequent and unequivocal, darken the next period in Eugen's life. The underlying causes of the setbacks he suffered in the field must be examined to see how far he personally was to blame; and we must consider what effects the disasters had on his character and career.

There is no doubt that Eugen's military reverses in the campaigns of 1712–13 were more severe than anything inflicted on any other allied commander throughout the war. More questionable is whether his part in the débâcle can fairly be judged—as it has been judged by Sir Winston Churchill amongst others—to have cast a cloud over his whole military record and to have justified the drawing of unfavourable comparisons between him and Marlborough. Indeed the conclusion suggested by a reading of the full record of the time is that, though Eugen certainly had a bad patch and made mistakes, the root cause of his downfall was England's abject betrayal of the Allies in the field. Against this sore thumb which sticks up in England's record, Eugen's serenity in trouble shines out magnanimously. Despite betrayal he did not become bitter. Despite the disastrous campaigns, he was able to hold the confidence of his Government and to enter into delicate and protracted peace negotiations with Marshal Villars with no loss of self-confidence, remaining firm and flexible until the terms of a treaty were eventually agreed at Rastadt on March 7, 1714.

After the fiasco of the London visit, Eugen succeeded in convincing the Emperor that no good was to be expected of the English as allies either in the field or conference room. He was therefore

ordered to Holland to make plans with the Dutch for an attack due
south into France. The Emperor had told him that 'the best and
surest peace will be that which you secure in the field, sword in hand'.
He had another aim: to stiffen the Dutch in the peace talks at Utrecht.
These were still in the doldrums caused by the extravagance of the
French demands, and by the fear of a union of the French and Spanish
crowns which had been revived by the series of sudden deaths in the
French royal family.[1] Not even St John, it seemed, could favour
making peace without some guarantee against this danger, so while
he continued his underground talks with the French, it was agreed, as
spring advanced, that the English should join the armies of the Allies
already assembling for the next campaign. On April 9 the Duke of
Ormonde, who had been appointed to succeed Marlborough in
command of all British and British-paid forces, reached The Hague.
He had only just been made a General of Cavalry and had never
commanded an army in the field. The Dutch and the Imperialists
naturally expected that he would serve under Eugen as Supreme
Commander of the whole allied force. But the English would have
none of this. They insisted on Ormonde having an independent
position. They insisted, if need be, on dividing the allied army
rather than accept a non-British Commander-in-Chief. Eugen
had no alternative but to acquiesce and to put the best face on it. He
was determined to overcome all personal feelings and to enter into
the best relations possible with Ormonde, who had indeed arrived in
Holland with assurances from the Queen of her determination to
prosecute the war with all vigour. He had also made much personal
parade of his custom to act only in accordance with his honour as a
soldier and as an Englishman. It is true that at the end of April
St John sent him disparaging instructions about Eugen and insisted
on the need for caution; but this did not alter his demeanour which
remained robust and debonair.

There were other grounds for the optimism which Eugen felt as he
joined his forces with Ormonde's in the middle of May 1712. Following Marlborough's brilliant campaigns of the year before, the French
had been bereft of their two outer lines of fortresses protecting the
country on the vulnerable northern frontier: the complexes of Lille-
Tournai-Mons and Aire-Béthune-Douai-Bouchain. Eugen's headquarters were at Tournai. The allied army had overwhelming superiority in infantry and artillery. Finally, in preparation for attack,
enormous barges full of supplies and ammunition had been sent up

[1] See Chapter XIV, p. 197.

the rivers Scheldt and Scarpe. Eugen was convinced that there was a better chance of beating the French now than at any time since the beginning of the war, a view which Louis XIV and Villars, the French Commander-in-Chief, shared with him. Only one successful battle was needed to open the way to Paris. Villars had his quarters at Cambrai; his armies held the line from there to Arras in the east and Landrecies in the west.

Yet as plans were going forward favourably for a final breakthrough into France St John was maturing in his mind his masterstroke of treachery. Without having obtained from the French the necessary assurance against the union of the two crowns or a settlement of the Dutch barrier, and just at the moment when a little more military pressure was all that was needed to secure French compliance, he decided precipitately on his own initiative to pull the British forces out of the allied lines. Convinced that this was the only way to win over the French and that the Dutch would soon follow suit and withdraw, he sent Ormonde the notorious Restraining Orders on May 10, 1712. These instructed him to avoid participation in any siege or battle, and to keep the command secret from the Allies. But it was the postscript that was the most egregious part of the whole document and eventually to be the main exhibit in St John's impeachment. With an air of innocence this read:

'P.S. I had almost forgot to tell Your Grace that communication was given of this order to the Court of France.'

Torcy, the French negotiator in London, to whom news of the order was given, asked St John's advice on what Villars should do if Eugen refused to knuckle under and persisted in taking the offensive. He received the immediate reply that 'There would be nothing to do but fall on him and cut him to pieces, him and his army'.[1]

St John added how anxious he was both that Villars should be kept fully informed of England's attitude and that Eugen and the Dutch should be left in complete ignorance. At least it cannot be said that there was anything half-hearted about St John's betrayal. He had ordered the desertion of the allied lines on the eve of battle; he had enjoined the concealment of this decision from Eugen; and finally he had arranged for the disclosure of it to be made to the enemy, so that the Prince and his troops who had stood in line with the Allies for eleven years could the more easily be taken

[1] G. M. Trevelyan, op. cit., III, p. 218.

by surprise and despatched. As Eugen was later to point out to Ormonde the Restraining Orders involved a breach of the very letter of the Grand Alliance which forbade any of the Allies from concluding a peace or armistice without the agreement of the other parties. Not without prescience he said that the person who had issued these orders 'would thereafter be in constant fear of losing his head on the scaffold'. There can be no more full-blooded condemnation of St John's compound treachery than Sir Winston Churchill's judgment : 'Nothing in the history of civilized peoples has surpassed this black treachery.'[1]

But happily the treason did not go entirely according to plan. Eugen possessed a good secret source from which he got wind of the Restraining Orders. Collateral evidence was provided by the suspicious way Ormonde prevaricated whenever Eugen tried to pin him down to plans for operations. Eventually the Duke broke down under Eugen's cross-examination and confessed.

Even then, however, he did not reveal all. He admitted the instruction but did not disclose that Villars had been informed. Not that Eugen had any illusions by now. He noticed how Villars, despite his bad strategic position, seemed quite unafraid of attack by Ormonde. Without any more beating about the bush he accused the Duke of connivance with the enemy.

'A commander as vigilant as Villars,' he said, 'would not have left his army unprotected in so weak a place unless he could have been sure that he would not have been attacked.'[2] Ormonde made no attempt to give a convincing answer.

If Eugen now had to abandon the idea of a full-scale attack, he must at least proceed with the mopping up of further fortresses. At the beginning of June, therefore, he began the investment of the fortress of Quesnoy. Quick action, so he hoped, would commit the troops in British pay—mostly Prussians, Hessians, Saxons, Hanoverians and Danes—to carrying on the war. Of the total allied army of about one hundred and twenty thousand men, British troops amounted to twelve thousand; those in British or part-British pay, fifty thousand. At first Ormonde hedged by allowing some of these dependents to take part in the siege of Quesnoy. It was only after violent protests from Villars that he gave orders at the end of June for them to prepare to withdraw from the line. But defection was not to prove quite so contagious as he had hoped. General Von Bülow

[1] Winston S. Churchill, op. cit., II, p. 945.
[2] *Villars D'Après sa Correspondance*, op. cit., II, p. 13.

of Hanover to whom he addressed himself first, thinking that the link with the British crown would make him the most amenable, refused bluntly to obey the Duke's command, saying that nothing in the world would induce him to behave so dishonourably. It was the same with most of the other commanders, regardless of their financial dependence on London. Prince Leopold of Anhalt, acting on explicit orders from the King of Prussia; Prince Karl Rudolph of Württemberg, who commanded the Danish troops; General Bielke of Saxony; and the Crown Prince of Hesse-Cassel—all were determined to stick by Eugen.

All this, of course, infuriated St John. In a letter to Harley, he vilified Eugen as 'a beggarly German General' who had caused the troops in British pay to desert. He assured him, however, that 'the Queen and all who serve her are determined to resent this insult offered to the British nation by our mercenaries'.[1] This abusive tone was, needless to say, the outcome of fear rather than of confidence, for St John and Harley were suffering momentarily from the awful prospect that the Austrians and the Dutch might succeed in carrying on the war successfully without England and thereby frustrate all their nefarious designs. According to contemporary pamphlets, the English Ministry, rather than see this happen, were actually prepared to use force on France's side against Eugen.[2]

Indignation towards the British swept through the allied lines as news of the Restraining Orders spread. The Dutch seriously thought at one moment of disarming the 12,000 British troops—which in Eugen's view could have been accomplished with little resistance. He believed that disillusion in the ranks of the redcoats had gone so far that the Elector of Hanover or his son could have swung the British army over to their side had they but presented themselves at the crucial moment of separation. To be sure, such was the consternation amongst the English soldiers that when, in mid-July, Ormonde finally marched them off from the allied camp, 'terrible scenes were witnessed of men breaking their muskets, tearing their hair and pouring out blasphemies and curses against the Queen and the Ministry who could subject them to that ordeal'.[3]

Meanwhile at the beginning of July Eugen had succeeded in forcing the surrender of Quesnoy. The Emperor went into rhapsodies over it and sent Eugen a long manuscript letter, as revealing about

---

[1] *Letters of Bolingbroke*, op. cit., II, pp. 422–3.
[2] Douglas Coombs, op. cit., p. 337.
[3] Winston S. Churchill, op. cit., II, p. 955.

the intrigues prevalent at court, as it was redolent of gratitude towards the Prince:

'There are people who try to ingratiate themselves by denigrating others. But I am confident that should any such person approach you they would not be able to arouse in you the least doubt about my absolute trust in you—which you should already be fully aware of, but which I could impress on you all the more if we could meet in person, since one can say so much more that way than by letter.'[1]

The departure of the British did not immediately deprive the Allies of their predominance in numbers and equipment. But bare computation did not do justice to its disruptive effect. The Dutch insistence on having Deputies attached to the commander in the field had been inhibiting enough to the combined leadership of Marlborough and Eugen. It was to become infinitely more hampering now Eugen was alone. Apart from the loss of the Duke's personal influence, the withdrawal of England from the war made Eugen much more dependent on the Dutch, and there was no way of concealing it. There is a story of how one of the Deputies, who had been in the forefront of obstruction, came across the Prince one day sunk deep in thought and asked him why he was so preoccupied.

'I am only wondering,' Eugen replied, 'if Alexander the Great could have achieved his victories and conquests quite so gracefully and quickly if he had been obliged, before carrying out his plans, to obtain the consent of the Dutch Deputies.'[2]

While Eugen, convinced of the need to maintain momentum, besieged Landrecies, Villars re-deployed for a counter-attack. He decided to make a bid for Denain on the Scheldt, in order to destroy the large magazine at Marchiennes, on the Scarfe, hoping thereby to force the lifting of the siege of Landrecies. Making Eugen think that he was going for Landrecies direct, and profiting by Ormonde's sudden withdrawal of all the pontoons which had been lent to the Dutch, Villars succeeded in defeating the Dutch army under the Duke of Albemarle at Denain on July 24. So completely was Eugen wrong-footed that he and his army were able to play no part in the battle, being still several hours away when Villars attacked. Allied casualties at Denain were extremely severe. Thanks to withdrawal of the pontoons several of Albemarle's battalions were unable to retreat

[1] A. Arneth, op. cit., II, p. 239.
[2] Egon Caesar Conte Corti, op. cit., p. 77.

across the Scheldt and were forced into the river and drowned; of his total force only a quarter escaped death or capture. Strategically, the loss of Denain meant the break-up of the strong allied position between the Scarfe at Douai and the Scheldt to the south-east. Finally, in terms of morale, the effect of the battle was traumatic. The full appalling impact of Denain on the Allies was summed up by Napoleon's verdict, given a century later, that it 'saved France'.

However, Eugen refused to be rattled, or to join in the general hue and cry for a scapegoat. In the Dutch Republic there was savage criticism of the Duke of Albemarle, which he refused to countenance though it might have been in his own immediate interest to do so. Many months later when these recriminations had still shown no sign of abating Eugen wrote to Heinsius in human and generous terms:

'It is with astonishment and grief that I hear of the injustice to which the Duke of Albemarle is exposed and of the unworthy stricture made against him on account of the action at Denain. I know of course how prone people are to judge only by results and how readily they criticize those who are unlucky. But what surprises me is that these calumnies are accepted by sturdy and reliable people, which can only be the result of the strenuous efforts of the Duke's enemies. It would be a dereliction of my duty as an honourable man if I did not speak out on a matter which I have witnessed at first hand. The Duke did on this occasion all that a bold, intelligent and watchful general could do; and if the troops had given a proper account of themselves, the action would have had a different outcome. But when after the first attack the troops took to their heels, there was nothing that could hold them and no general in the world could have done anything about it.'[1]

Keeping up the pressure after Denain, Villars succeeded, precisely as he had hoped, in forcing the lifting of the siege of Landrecies and the surrender of Marchiennes. Sensing the cautious influence of the Dutch, he became even more intrepid. On September 8, after only a month's siege, he took the fortress of Douai which had cost the Allies 15,000 men to capture two years before. Eugen could do nothing to stop the landslide. By now he was outnumbered; and the Dutch were refusing to fight. 'It is unbelievably difficult,' he wrote, letting off steam as usual in a private letter, 'to restrain oneself when you have to deal with such people.'

[1] A. Arneth, op. cit., II, p. 256.

The dismal procession of defeat was rounded off for Eugen by the loss in the late autumn of Quesnoy, only two months after its capture, and the surrender of Bouchain after only eight days' resistance. In the space of three months he had lost a third of his army and five key fortresses; in one summer the whole forward allied position built up so laboriously over the years as a spring-board for a final assault on France had been precipitously abandoned.

How far was Eugen responsible for this débâcle? It must be acknowledged that he did commit an appalling error of judgment when he went too far forward too soon after the capture of Quesnoy and then allowed himself to be hoodwinked by Villars before Denain. Obviously the interventions of the Dutch Field Deputies were a contributory cause of the disaster. Eugen clearly thought them decisive. When he came to sum up the 1712 campaign and the prospects for the next one he said that you have to make up your mind whether you are pursuing peace or war:

'If we act with decision there is no doubt that we can strike terror into the hearts of the French and their new friends. The poor result of this campaign is not attributable to Denain, but to the spirit of irresolution which prevailed in Holland and predominates amongst their Field Deputies and Generals. If it had not been for that, the places would not have been taken. What must be done before the end of this campaign is to decide whether it is war or peace we are engaged upon. Otherwise the enemy will force us to his will step by step, and apart from impressing on us an unworthy peace, will be able to boast that he had led us by the nose.'[1]

It is indisputable too that the acute shortage of funds in the Imperial Treasury once again stultified Eugen's efforts in the field. As soon as the first military setback occurred, bickering broke out amongst the Allies about costs. Initially, under Eugen's pressure, the Emperor had agreed, following Ormonde's apostasy, to meet some of the former English subsidies. But by the autumn there were not even funds enough for the Emperor's own troops. To his entreaties Eugen received the answer that Imperial troops elsewhere had not been paid for a long time; why should those in the Netherlands get preference? Eugen's comment on this was characteristically scathing; 'It is really like saying: "Well, if troops are to perish in one theatre therefore, they might as well perish elsewhere." '[2]

But none of these events—Eugen's misjudgment, Dutch obstruc-

[1] Oct. 3, 1712, A. Arneth, op. cit., II, p. 500.
[2] A. Arneth, op. cit., II, p. 267.

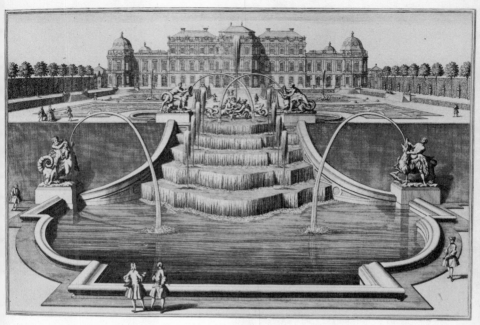

16. The Grand Cascade in the Belvedere garden

17. The Lower Belvedere: the garden front

18. Eugen's menagerie in the Belvedere

19. Some of Eugen's rare animals and plants, including species from Africa, India and America

tionism, or the lack of funds—would have had the grave consequences it did, had it not been for England's defection. This was the prime cause of the sudden turn in allied fortune, and from it all else irrevocably flowed.

CHAPTER XVI

A DISASTROUS CAMPAIGN;
THEN PEACE WITH FRANCE

IN THE winter of 1712–13 two interrelated events occurred which depressed yet lower Eugen's spirits and his hopes for the Monarchy. Firstly, Wratislaw[1] died. Besides being Eugen's closest friend and supporter in Vienna, he had for long sided with Eugen in urging the Emperor to make peace. Then, partly no doubt as a result of the removal of this pressure, Charles flatly refused to agree to what were in fact not unreasonable peace terms.

The English, obviously with French connivance, put forward proposals under which Spain and the Indies would remain Philip's, and in return the Emperor was to get the Spanish Netherlands and the Spanish possessions in Italy except Sicily (to go to Savoy) and Sardinia (to go to the Elector of Bavaria). Spurred on, however, by his Spanish courtiers, the Emperor refused to renounce Spain. If need be he was ready to continue the war alone against France. When, therefore, the rest of the Allies made peace with the French at Utrecht in April 1713 and offered the Emperor till June 1 to sign, he held out. It was partly obduracy—his refusal to abandon the Peninsula and to antagonize all his closest supporters. But he probably had an inner faith that if Eugen were sent to take command of the Imperial forces he might yet achieve a miracle and defeat the French single-handed. After all had not the Empire stood alone twelve years before when the auspices were just as unfavourable? Paradoxically, though Spain was the ultimate objective, it was decided to give up the fighting there. For strategic reasons the Imperial forces had to be concentrated on the Rhine and withdrawn from all other fronts.

[1] See Chapter VIII, p. 92.

To achieve this the Emperor agreed with the French and English upon a Treaty of neutrality for Spain, Italy and the Netherlands which was also signed in Utrecht in the spring of 1713. The withdrawal from Spain was not without its personal effect on Eugen. It meant that the Empress Elizabeth and her advisers, who had been governing Catalonia since the Emperor's departure in September 1711, now moved to Vienna and added their weight to the already considerable Spanish junta there. Foremost among these were Count Rocca Stella, known as Charles' 'nighthawk', from his persistent attendance on the Emperor after dark, and the lawyer, Ramon de Vilana Perlas, ennobled by Charles as the Marquis Rialp.

The Emperor's concentration on the Rhine was not so formidable as it sounded. The Imperial Army there had spent much of its time recently in dispiriting frontier duties, and its condition was bad. When Eugen took over command at the end of May 1713 he was confronted not only with this problem of morale, but with the marked reluctance of many of the Princes to continue contributing either troops or money. The Landgrave of Hesse-Cassel, the Prince of Saxe-Coburg Gotha and the Elector of the Palatinate all seemed less than enthusiastic about a further campaign intended merely to satisfy the Emperor's whim.

Yet the frontier Eugen had to defend on the Rhine was long, and he had to protect territory west of the river around Landau as well. He appointed General Vaubonne to hold the Upper Rhine and what were known as the Lines of Ettlingen. These lines stretched from Ettlingen to the Rhine and then southwards to the Swiss frontier. Eugen decided himself to watch the middle Rhine. Meanwhile Villars, in command of a strong French force, started to advance towards Rastadt. Eugen, thinking he was going to attack the lines of Ettlingen, moved forces south from Philippsburg. This was precisely what Villars wanted. He suddenly changed direction and succeeded in severing Eugen's communications between the Rhine and Landau, which he then besieged. By the end of June he had taken the important bridge across the Rhine at Mannheim.

Despite the precariousness of Eugen's position, many of the Princes continued to withhold support and to make particular difficulties over money. Predictably, of course, the Imperial Exchequer had defaulted on its financial promises to them, and the deadlock was only resolved by Eugen pledging his personal credit. Reinforcements, he realized, must be obtained at all costs. If his army were defeated on the Rhine nothing stood between the French and the heart of the Empire.

Landau and the territory west of the Rhine would have to be forfeited rather than risk the penetration of the bastion on the right bank. As the lesser of two evils therefore Landau was surrendered on August 19.

Not content with a plan for capturing further fortresses, the audacious Villars decided to go for the Lines of Ettlingen at the southern end of the Black Forest, to try to penetrate to the valley of the Danube via Freiburg and then to advance upon Vienna, repeating the threat of 1704. He all but succeeded. At first he was able to keep Eugen guessing about his intentions and to make him spread out his forces so as to be ready to defend fortresses all the way from Mainz in the north to as far south as the Swiss frontier. After many feints he crossed the Rhine at Strasburg, pierced Vaubonne's incompetently defended lines and laid siege to Freiburg. The city was defended by the skilful and courageous von Harsch, who received orders from Eugen to hold out 'to the last extremity'. Unable to go south to help him for fear of leaving the Lines of Ettlingen exposed, Eugen eventually, after a prolonged and cruel siege, ordered von Harsch to make the best terms he could. Freiburg capitulated on November 17 and von Harsch was able to march off with seventeen battalions to join Vaubonne at Rottweil. By his resolute resistance he had delayed Villars sufficiently to prevent him carrying out his threatened thrust down the Danube.

It had been another disastrous campaign for Eugen personally. He had failed once again to see through Villars' stratagems or to match his rapid footwork. But as Turenne has said, 'he who has made few mistakes has made little war', and Eugen had been at war for thirteen successive years. There was never the slightest chance that the Empire, bankrupt and exhausted as it now was, could alone bring France finally to her knees when the combined Alliance had already failed to do so. Vienna, of course, should never have undertaken the campaign, and Eugen was now more convinced than ever of the need to make peace before disaster spread further. Yet such an extension of the catastrophe seemed precisely what the Spaniards at Vienna appeared bent upon bringing about. In a mood of violent frustration they were goading the Emperor to restart the war in Italy so as to prevent the Duke of Savoy from taking Sicily, as provided for under the Treaty of Utrecht. Alone of the secret cabinet Eugen stood out against this.[1] His influence eventually prevailed, and he was authorized

[1] The secret cabinet consisted, since Wratislaw's death, of Eugen, Trautson, Seilern, Starhemberg and Sinzendorff. When he was in Vienna Eugen presided, otherwise Trautson.

to enter into peace talks with Villars in Rastadt at the end of November.

The two men had known each other on and off in peace and war since 1687, when they had fought side by side against the Turks. Their friendship dated from Villars' appointment as French diplomatic representative in Vienna.[1] It was the fusion of opposites, a reconciliation of contrasting characters and opposing interests; the self-controlled aesthetic aristocrat and the exuberant pleasure-loving upstart; unlike-minded members of a close military fraternity joined together by the bond of war. In Villars' memoirs we have a happy picture of the two marshals dining and playing cards together every evening for the next few months. No sooner were the formal greetings over than they applied themselves, in good military fashion, to the important task of drawing up plans for their mutual hospitality and entertainment; they agreed to dine alternately in each other's mess accompanied by a few close advisers (their total retinue included a hundred infantrymen and a hundred horses each) and to play cards every evening afterwards. To begin with they played piquet. Just as many years before in Vienna Villars had won considerable sums off Eugen, so now at the outset in Rastadt everything went the Frenchman's way. But the luck soon turned. Villars began to show distress, so Eugen, realizing no doubt the bigger stakes at issue, agreed to switch to the more modest game of brelan.

At the outset of the negotiations, which were to drag on for many months, Eugen asserted a degree of personal ascendancy over Villars which he was to maintain throughout the conference. The Marshal was not experienced in such matters, and he was also less sure of his position at home. Though Eugen had found him invariably resolute in the field, he detected in him now in negotiation a sense of insecurity and a tendency towards 'long-winded, confused and variable speeches'. Villars seemed to believe that only by obtaining a settlement at Radstadt could he safeguard his standing at Versailles. As Eugen described it to Sinzendorff:

'Villars is apprehensive, ignorant about previous negotiations, and very anxious for a treaty. As I see it, if it depended upon him alone, he would concede everything here so long as he could enhance his credit at court.'[2]

This personal involvement played to some extent into Eugen's

[1] See Chapter VII, p. 76.
[2] A. Arneth, op. cit., II, p. 511.

hands. He had only to threaten to throw the switches and make ready to return home, as he did several times, for Villars to bring increased pressure to bear on Versailles. He explained this leverage to Vienna:

'. . . he is afraid that if I should leave here he will be recalled and someone else sent to conclude the treaty.'[1]

Not that he wanted Villars recalled. He believed that he had more influence on Versailles than anyone else was likely to have, and the main difficulty, so it emerged as the talks proceeded, came from the extremists at the French court—just as his own most obstinate problems were caused by the intransigent Spaniards in Vienna.

At one moment at the end of December when the negotiations were stumbling, Eugen said to Villars:

'Monsieur le Maréchal, you wish me to judge you by myself, and I beseech you to judge me by yourself. It is generally believed that we both wish the war to go on; yet I can assure you that peace will never be made if it is left to others than us to negotiate. We behave as men of honour and have none of the wiles usually thought necessary in negotiations. For my part I have always thought, and I think you do likewise, that there is no greater finesse than to have none of it.'[2]

This was the note that Eugen sought to establish from the outset of the talks: that he and the Frenchman were birds of a feather and could settle everything satisfactorily if only they were left to themselves. 'I am sure,' he confided to Villars at the beginning of January, 'that if our masters had not sincerely wanted peace, they would not have let themselves be represented by people like us who are not born to plead.'[3] The trouble was that their masters began to be suspicious of the close relationship. Louis XIV, in particular, was afraid that the bonhomie between the two generals would lead Villars to accept unnecessarily hard terms. He was needlessly suspicious. In fact, though they were always personally friendly and maintained the civilities, the negotiators did not mince their words in argument. Villars wrote later that anyone overhearing them would scarcely have believed that they would be able to stick together for two days. Most

[1] A. Arneth, op. cit., II, p. 320.
[2] *Mémoires du Maréchal de Villars*, 1891, IV, p. 18.
[3] Ibid., p. 19.

likely it would have been Villars they would have overheard, for he was the more turbulent and readier for scenes and showdowns.

Eugen's handling of one of the most intractable points in the negotiation shows his readiness to sublimate personal feelings to interests of state. The French were pressing for the transfer to the Princess des Ursins of a Principality in the Netherlands. The Princess, known irreverently as the Abigail Hill of the Spanish court, was the confidante of King Philip's wife. Eugen reacted against the proposal with instinctive intolerance, and he was not afraid of showing a certain priggishness in his reply to Villars:

> 'If the King of Spain asked for territory for a prime minister or for a general to whom he had obligations as great as he has towards you, the Emperor would not be surprised, but to ask for it for this woman—you will please forgive me if I am unable to conceal my astonishment.'[1]

However, the French pressed the claim, and Eugen was prepared to swallow his objections when he realized that it was only by satisfying the Spanish court in this way that there was any hope of securing the privileges which Charles wanted for the Catalans. But the Emperor would not hear of it. Without any question of a *quid pro quo*, he insisted upon an amnesty for all Spaniards who had fought for him and for guarantees of self-government for the Catalans. These must be unequivocal and explicit. He was right: it was a matter of honour that should have touched the whole Alliance. The Spaniards had been encouraged to revolt against Philip by the Allies, particularly by England, and Charles was now trying to prevent them being cast upon the mercy of a vengeful court in Spain. He was only doing what England should already have insisted upon at Utrecht had they not been in such single-minded and dishonourable haste for a peace treaty. But Villars explained to Eugen that Louis could not make himself responsible for what happened in Spain, any more than he, Villars, could persuade the King to do what he thought was right in order to secure a fair settlement.

'My reproaches to Villars over the attitude of the French Government would have been much more severe,' Eugen wrote to the Emperor, 'if he had not generally agreed with my views and had he not complained with even greater bitterness than I over his own court.'[2]

[1] *Mémoires du Maréchal de Villars*, op. cit., IV, p. 5.
[2] A. Arneth, op. cit., II, p. 336.

After prolonged but amicable negotiations the two men agreed on terms to recommend to their Governments. Louis refused to accept them. Villars, under the spell of Eugen's powerful personality, could not bring himself to communicate the news in person. He was driven to employing an intermediary.

French intransigence across the whole board of negotiations was such that Eugen decided in February to deliver an ultimatum and to walk out of the talks. This manoeuvre had the desired effect. Versailles came forward with more reasonable proposals and after three weeks' absence Eugen returned to reach final agreement with Villars on a treaty which they signed on March 7, 1714. By the Treaty of Rastadt France retained Strasburg and Landau but gave up all fortresses on the right bank of the Rhine. The Empire acquired the former Spanish Netherlands, Milan, Naples, and Sardinia as well as fortresses and harbours on the coast of Tuscany. The Electors of Cologne and Bavaria were reinstated in their territories.

To anyone who looks at the Treaties of Utrecht and Rastadt together one thing sticks out like a sore thumb. A war which had lasted fourteen years, caused appalling human suffering and devastated a large part of Europe was concluded on terms which still left a Bourbon on the throne of Spain and which the Allies might well have secured at the outset of hostilities. Furthermore, the Allied gains were inferior to those that might have been obtained on a number of occasions during the war. England, there is no denying, had done well. They had greatly increased their colonial and commercial power, whilst securing a permanent footing in the Mediterranean by the acquisition of Minorca and Gibraltar. They had even succeeded in providing a counterweight to the Habsburgs in Italy by supporting the claim of Victor Amadeus of Savoy to Sicily. The Dutch had done less well and had suffered more in proportion. But they had achieved some security against French ambitions by the barrier of towns they were allowed to garrison in the former Spanish Netherlands, now transferred to Austria. In addition to the Netherlands, the Emperor had obtained one great advantage. He had checked French expansion south over the Alps and had established the House of Habsburg in Italy.

Had Eugen fought personally in Spain he might not have countenanced the betrayal of the Catalans, one of the blackest spots of the whole peace settlement, but it is difficult to perceive under what conditions he or anyone else could have induced the French to yield on this. Standing back with the perspective of history, we can see now

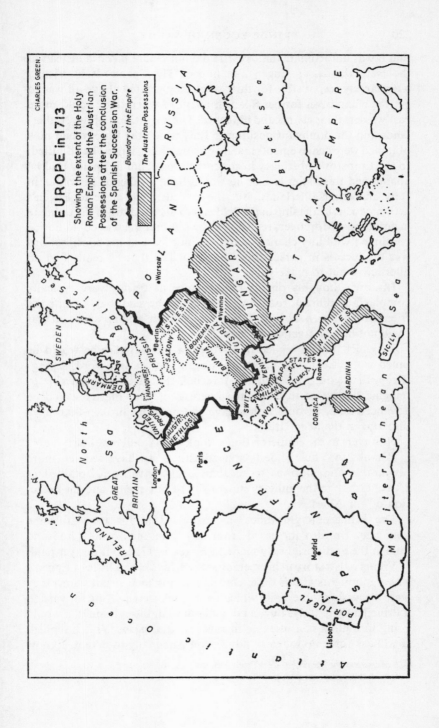

CHARLES GREEN.

EUROPE in 1713

Showing the extent of the Holy
Roman Empire and the Austrian
Possessions after the conclusion
of the Spanish Succession War.

━━━ Boundary of the Empire
▨ The Austrian Possessions

that it was unfortunate that Austria did not secure Bavaria instead of the Netherlands, as Eugen had hoped. The Spaniards in Vienna were largely responsible for this; what they wanted above all was to get their hands on former Spanish territory where they could more easily assert their claims and influence. The acquisition of the Netherlands and the dominant position in Italy which the Empire had now obtained were achievements that owed something, it must be admitted, to the Emperor's obstinacy in sticking to his claim to Spain. Had he abandoned this claim earlier he would have weakened his rights in Italy and the Netherlands. But they owed much more to Eugen's actions: to his leadership in the field and to his handling of the ultimate negotiations. Moreover, realizing as he did that the war could not be continued with any chance of success, not least of his contributions was his success in persuading Charles at last that he really had no alternative but to make peace.

His own thoughts on his performance at Rastadt are typically complex and difficult to fathom. To Villars he said that, despite the friendship between them, he felt badly let down 'and I assure you that I will not be well treated in Vienna'.

To which Villars replied by saying that he was sure he would be much worse treated at Versailles. Eugen had the last word, saying: 'I repeat to you, Monsieur le Maréchal, that if I had been able to imagine the extent to which the interests of your master would be advanced here, I would rather have had my arms broken than have undertaken the negotiation.'[1]

However, to the Emperor Eugen took a very different line: 'Thanks to Your Majesty's steadfastness we have secured more favourable and glorious terms than could have been obtained at Utrecht, despite the military superiority of our enemy and the defection of our Allies.'[2]

The Emperor's gratitude was expressed in his usual fulsome language. He also increased from 300 thousand to 400 thousand gulden the grant originally made to Eugen in 1712, but not yet paid.

Villars tells a story in his memoirs which lays bare a little of Eugen's private thoughts at this time. One day during their negotiations they were discussing some claim which the French were putting forward to a Principality in Italy. Eugen pointed out that, though small, it would bring in quite a considerable income. 'If that is so,' Villars replied, 'I will ask for it no longer. I advise you personally to take it. I know

[1] *Mémoires du Maréchal de Villars*, op. cit., IV, p. 30.
[2] A. Arneth, op. cit., II, p. 342.

that you who have won Italy for the Empire could have something much bigger. But I am not aware that you have any place of retirement. Neither your palaces in Vienna nor your island in the Danube serve for this. Although it is clear that your services to the House of Austria will always give you the dominant position at the Emperor's court, it is only wise to have somewhere to retire to, and I seem to recall your telling me that there have been times when you have thought of retiring.'

Eugen replied:

'I am not surprised that a man with a family should think in that way. But, as for me, I assure you that if I retire it will be a matter of indifference to me whether I have an income of a million or 12,000 livres.'[1]

After their months of intimate disputation at Rastadt, Eugen and Villars remained on the best of terms. Following the official signing of the Peace Treaty on behalf of the Holy Roman Empire at Baden in the autumn, Eugen sent Villars some Imperial Tokay. The Marshal thanked him profusely saying that he had 'drunk his health in it in the company of some beautiful women'. At Villars' request Eugen sent him a portrait of himself which was hung in the Marshal's private apartment in Versailles. 'Everybody flocks to see it,' Villars wrote to him on January 4, 1715, 'and I can assure you that there is a steady stream of visitors.'[2]

They remained in frequent correspondence over the next few years, settling various problems arising out of the peace treaty, and discussing outstanding international issues. By this means they contributed not a little to removing some of the traditional rivalry between Versailles and Vienna and to bringing about an *entente* between the two monarchies. Their efforts were commemorated in a medal struck in France showing the two 'thunderbolts of battle', who, having disturbed Europe for so long with the din of war, now had the glory of giving it peace: *Olim duo fulmina belli, nunc instrumenta quietis.*

It is something of a tribute to Eugen's capacity for personal relations that he had succeeded in being the closest of friends with both Marlborough and Villars, the outstanding military commanders on either side in the Spanish Succession War, and that these friendships rendered a service to the Habsburg Monarchy which endured for a generation.

[1] *Mémoires du Maréchal de Villars*, op. cit., IV, pp. 16–17.
[2] *Villars D'Après Sa Correspondance*, op. cit., II, p. 127.

CHAPTER XVII

TRIUMPH OVER THE TURKS

THE TURKS saw to it that Eugen, now over fifty, was still not to find
the peace he wanted. Trusting to Austrian neutrality they believed
the moment had come to try to recapture some of the European territories they had lost to Venice by the Peace of Carlowitz in 1699.[1] The
threat which this presented to the Monarchy had convinced
Eugen at Rastadt of the urgent need to make peace with France.

In the early summer of 1715 we see Eugen in his palace in Vienna, a
diminutive, wiry, ageing yet alert figure, dressed in red silk embroidered with gold, seated on a red plush gilded chair beneath a heavily-
decorated baldachin, surrounded by the principal officers of state,
peering out from beneath a wide-brimmed hat to receive with elaborate ceremony the special representative of the Sultan—a scene very
similar to that of four years before when, with his own blend of public
show and personal modesty, he had received Seifullah Aga, the
previous envoy of the Porte, at a time of acute tension between
Vienna and the Porte.[2] The Turks were hoping now to get a firm
assurance of neutrality from the Emperor in the war they had launched
against Venice a few months before, but they might as well have
stayed at home. Austria at first offered to act as intermediary
for peace, but the Turks ignored this. Eugen began to have suspicions. Any attempt by the Porte to regain its former strength in
Europe must, he realized, be an unacceptable threat to the Monarchy.
When, therefore, Ottoman troops had brought off some staggering
successes against Venice, capturing all their fortresses in the Morea,
Eugen in April 1716 succeeded, with the strong backing of the Church,

[1] See Chapter IV, p. 47.
[2] See Chapter XIII, p. 183.

in persuading the Emperor to conclude a defensive alliance with the Republic. Choosing to regard this as a breach of the Treaty of Carlowitz, the Porte declared war upon Austria. The Grand Vizier, Damad Ali-Pascha, wrote to Eugen in terms at once blunt and inapposite, 'there is no doubt that the blood which is going to flow on both sides will fall like a curse upon you, your children and your children's children until the last judgment.'[1] To his own officers whom he summoned to make war upon the Empire, he gave this message: 'Attack the infidels without mercy . . . Be neither elated nor downhearted, and you will triumph.'[2]

By August 1716 the attack on the infidels seemed to be directed at the Austrian fortress of Peterwardein.[3] Eugen had been sent there by the Emperor with a force of 60,000 men, but his position looked grim. The numerical strength of the Ottomans was over twice his. Besides, one result of the Grand Vizier's triumphs in the Morea was that he had acquired a formidable reputation as army leader which his notorious addiction to astrology and his inordinate pride had in no way impaired. Faced with such a commander and such numbers, many senior officers in Eugen's camp implored him to avoid risking open battle. They urged him to let the Turks exhaust themselves in a war of attrition against the Peterwardein fortress. But such tactics, besides being foreign to his nature—less cautious than ever when confronted with the Turks—would, he was sure, be bad for morale. The troops were eager for a fight and had just shown their battle-worthiness in a spirited action under Graf Pálffy. Though Eugen had not fought the Turks for many years he knew their strengths and weaknesses. Many were still armed with antiquated weapons, even bows and arrows. They were difficult to resist in headlong assault, but they could be disconcerted by unorthodox tactics, and were apt to lose formation if forced to retreat. As for the Grand Vizier, his very bravado no doubt betrayed to Eugen a lack of self-confidence. Allowing for all this, therefore, Eugen decided upon an immediate offensive.

Without going into the details of the battle of Peterwardein which was fought on August 5, 1716, it may be useful to single out those features of Eugen's tactics which made his presence on the field unique and decisive. Firstly, he extracted every ounce of advantage from the lie of the land, letting the flanks of his main army rest one on the Danube and the other on the fortifications of Peterwardein, and

[1] J. De Hammer, op. cit., XIII, p. 301.
[2] Ibid., pp. 299–300.
[3] See Map at end for Eugen's campaigns against the Turks.

utilizing a double line of entrenchments which had been constructed twenty years before. Then he took up a commanding position whence he could watch the progress of the whole battle. At 7 a.m. he ordered Prince Alexander of Württemberg to attack on the left with six battalions of infantry. This went well, but the Turks began to counter-attack against the Imperial centre which had tried to advance under the shelter of Württemberg's left thrust. With their tails up at this initial success, the janissaries looked at one moment as though they would put the Imperialists to rout. There was an air of crisis in the allied camp. But Eugen calmly ordered Württemberg to wheel to his right and attack the exposed Turkish centre in flank. The Imperial centre he reinforced for a counter-offensive. The resulting flank and frontal attack on the janissaries was too much for them; while on the left the cuirassiers and hussars of the Austrians and Hungarians swept the spáhis from the field in one tremendous charge.

During all this time the Grand Vizier had remained immobile before his tent beneath the sacred standard of the Prophet. But when he saw the spáhis in retreat, the janissaries reeling, and the whole army on the point of flight, he plunged despairingly into the mêlée to be mortally wounded by an Austrian bullet.

After five hours of cool and remorseless control Eugen had won the battle. The Turks had lost 6,000 killed, twice the Imperial casualties. By midday the entire Turkish camp had fallen into Imperial hands with all its fabulous booty: harness and saddlery encrusted with precious stones and metals, richly decorated Turkish and Persian carpets and fabrics, beautiful horses and camels which the Imperial soldiers looked upon with wonderment like children suddenly possessed of a circus. 'It is very certain,' a contemporary historian wrote, 'that if those spoils had been sold to their full value, and the money had been distributed amongst the soldiers, they would have had enough to have lived upon comfortably for the rest of their lives.'[1] Eugen himself retained the Grand Vizier's tent, a sumptuous affair of many apartments decorated in gold with silk embroidery, so enormous as to require 500 men to pitch it. We get an idea of the wonderland of a Turkish camp from a contemporary account which, after describing the many-coloured tents with their pointed roofs and multifarious standards, said that it resembled 'a gigantic flower-bed full of every kind of blossom'.[2]

---

[1] Dumont and Rousset, op. cit., I, p. 116.
[2] M. de la Colonie, *The Chronicles of an Old Campaigner, 1692–1717*. Translated from the French, 1904, p. 417.

There was great excitement throughout Christendom over the defeat of the Infidel at Peterwardein. In Vienna the streets were packed. In Rome the Pope ordered all the bells to be rung and the streets illuminated. To Eugen he sent a biretta and sword in recognition of his outstanding military services to Christendom and the Catholic Church. The biretta, violet in colour and trimmed with ermine, decorated with the figure of a dove and embroidered in pearls to symbolize the Holy Spirit, and the sword, encrusted with jewels and held in a magnificent sheath, the length of the Prince himself, were presented to him by a Papal Envoy at a special ceremony. It was just the kind of grandiose occasion Eugen hated most. He could only endure it by thinking of the absurdity of his own overladen figure, and the amusement he would have in describing it to the Emperor. Charles certainly entered into the spirit of Eugen's description and replied saying how much he would like to have been there and to have shared the joke with him.

Already the Emperor had written to him in a tone of almost abject gratitude for his performance at Peterwardein, imploring him at the same time not to go on exposing himself to so much danger.[1] He had also sent him his portrait describing it three times in one letter as 'my shameful face' and explaining that it was a token of the love, esteem and confidence he continued to have for him despite their separation. In the arch tone he had come to adopt in his dealings with Eugen, Charles added the threat that he would withdraw the portrait, and with it his friendship, if the Prince persisted in risking his life.

Perhaps what pleased Eugen more than any other tribute was the congratulation he received from Marshal Villars. In the most fulsome language the Frenchman assured him that he frequently drank his health. If this were a signal that the Tokay the Prince had given him was running out Eugen gave no indication of taking the hint.

Before the year was out Eugen captured the fortress of Temesvár,

[1] The flavour of the Emperor's language is conveyed in the following extract from his manuscript letter to Eugen of August 8, written in his favourite mixture of German and French: 'in all diesen hab ich eins, worin gar nicht mit ihnen zufrieden bin, dass ist die Geringhaltung undt wenige Achtung auf dero Person, wie auch schon vernomen auch in dieser action geschehen. E.L. gedenken, das ihnen allein ich mein Armée undt also landt undt leut anvertraut, dass ich in sie allein in allen mein grest undt innig wahre Confidenz gesezt undt beständig seze, ich will nichts sagen von mein particolar lib gegen dero Person, also hofte ich, dass als dis E.L. dero von mir so estimirte Person besser in Acht nemen werdten, undt werdt dis vor ein Zeichen der Lieb E.L. gegen mich nemen. Bitt also pour amour de moy, changes vous en cela at ayez plus de soins de votre personne si vous aimes ma personne et mes interets.' A. Arneth, op. cit., III, pp. 512–13.

which the Turks had nicknamed the Gazi (victorious) fortress—a necessary prelude to the siege of Belgrade. Again there was ecstasy in Vienna. The fortress had been in Turkish hands for 164 years; its recovery marked the restoration of Imperial rule throughout the Bánát. Such was the consternation in Constantinople that the authorities did not for some time dare announce the loss. The only insight into Eugen's character afforded by the battle is the way he handled the defeated garrison and the inhabitants of Temesvár. They were provided with transport and money to get away and orders were given that all hardship should be reduced to a minimum. So smoothly did the exodus go that it was reported that the infidels were able to withdraw with as much 'liberty and tranquility as if they had been in Constantinople'.[1] Contrary to normal practice, age had made him more concerned about other people's security, and less about his own. When the Turkish general begged that the Hungarians who had served under the Turkish flag should be allowed to leave unmolested, Eugen gave orders in Italian which he affected to use in his more debonair moments; *la Canaglia puó andare dove vuole*.[2]

The freeing of the Bánát paved the way for an important experiment by Eugen in colonization. On Eugen's initiative engineers, doctors and, craftsmen were brought from Austria and Germany. Temesvár was reconstructed as the capital of the region, and later on a large cathedral was built there by Emmanuel Fischer von Erlach. The town earned the name of Klein-Wien. Kossuth complained over one hundred years later that 'our towns are largely German—so German that there is hardly a sign of Magyar influence in them'. Eugen was partly to blame for this.

The colonization of the countryside of the Bánát was even more far-reaching. The area had become sadly depopulated—the result of war and occupation. At Eugen's instigation Imperial officials in Germany, particularly in Regensburg, Ulm, Frankfurt and Cologne, organized the immigration to Hungary of thousands of peasants and craftsmen, disillusioned and impoverished as a result of the long war with France, and eager to start a new life elsewhere. Though it is estimated that 20,000 emigrated to America from the Palatinate, many chose the uncertainties of Hungary rather than face the rigours of an Atlantic crossing and a new continent. Moreover, the immigration commissioners made attractive offers: free journeys for all the family; grants of land; free fuel, tools and seed corn; and six years'

[1] Dumont and Rousset, op. cit., I, p. 119.
[2] A. Arneth, op. cit., II, p. 406.

exemption from taxation (ten for craftsmen). In the great rush of volunteers many serfs fled by night from masters unwilling to let them go. In resettling the Bánát Eugen's aims—which were largely achieved—were fourfold; to force loyalty on Hungary by diluting the Magyars; to seal Hungary off from the Balkans; to extend German culture eastwards; and to make the country the granary of the Monarchy.

The campaign of 1716 had been enough for the Turks. In the following winter they asked for an armistice, but the Empire refused to agree to the conditions stipulated. Eugen's view, which the Emperor accepted, was that in any case another round of defeat was necessary to put an end once and for all to the expansionist dreams of the Turks. England thought otherwise, seeing herself again in the rôle of mediator between Vienna and the Porte, as she had been at Carlowitz. To Eugen it seemed that the mainspring of England's policy was not the high-flown wish for peace which they trumpeted, but the desire to maintain the balance of power in Europe, so essential to their interests. If their advice were accepted and peace were made hurriedly now, the Turks would only make war again in a few years' time when the Empire, and indeed Western Christendom, would be an easy prey. So the war continued for another campaign, during which Eugen captured Belgrade, a triumph which, perhaps, bears the hall-mark of his genius more vividly than any other battle.

Situated in the triangle formed by the confluence of the rivers Danube and Save, Belgrade was held by a garrison of 30,000 men, including the élite of the janissaries, under the command of the redoubtable Mustapha Pasha. But this was but a fraction of the force that Eugen had to confront before the city could be taken. As he was constructing his siege lines on the base of the triangle enclosing Belgrade, the main Turkish army, bigger, according to the rumours reaching Belgrade, than any army hitherto assembled, and certainly numbering over 200,000, started marching towards him from Adrianople under the command of Khálil Pasha. It had been one of Eugen's objectives, in besieging Belgrade, to entice the main Turkish army away from its base and then to force it to join battle at a logistical disadvantage. But any hope of defeating the Belgrade garrison quickly before the arrival of Khálil's army was dispelled by various disruptive sorties made by Mustapha Pasha, and by a terrible cyclone on July 13 which wrecked Eugen's bridges over the Save and Danube and sank many of his supply ships. He had to face the fact that before he could take Belgrade he would be sandwiched between enemy forces totalling nearly five times his own, and he would first have to dispose of Khálil's army with a strength which, under the ravages of dysentery, had now shrunk to only 50,000.

By August 1 Eugen was completely invested. The news spread throughout Europe that he and his army were doomed men. There was much criticism of his foolhardiness, and few believed he could extricate himself. Never before, his rivals alleged not without *Schadenfreude*, had a besieging army allowed itself to become so hopelessly besieged. But Eugen remained calm. Followed by a retinue of Princes from the royal houses of Europe sent to learn the art of war under him, he methodically carried out every day an inspection of his own and the enemy's lines. The patience he displayed towards his pupils was remarkable. Whenever he stopped to make some detailed examination, the visitors would push themselves forward to see what had attracted his attention, regardless of the obstruction they were causing to his view. But he did not remonstrate. He said nothing. He just waited until they had satisfied their curiosity before continuing his own investigation. It had become clear to Eugen by the middle of August that the Turks had given up the idea of an attack. They had presumably decided that it would not be necessary. With their enormous numerical superiority and better position they had only to sap their way into the Imperial trenches, construct a network of mines, blow up the entire camp and victory would be theirs. They would then merely have to follow up the explosion with a dash forward by their massive forces. This, Eugen realized, must be their plan. Victory must seem to them inevitable. And indeed, as the weeks of summer went by, bringing unprecedented heat and mounting illness in the Habsburg lines, and as the Turkish artillery intensified its attacks, the cannon-balls ricocheting off the baked earth, shattering everything as if in a skittle-alley, Eugen came to the conclusion that he could not hang on much longer and that he had no alternative but to strike out himself though the odds were heavily against him. 'Either I will take Belgrade, or the Turks will take me,'[1] he is said to have declared defiantly.

Having made up his mind, he assembled his leading generals on August 15, 1717, and explained to them the details of his plan to attack Khálil's army the following day. The officers were to give their orders quietly and patiently so as not to disconcert the men. No one, whether officer or man, was to depart by a hairsbreadth from his appointed rôle, except under explicit orders; and there was to be no looting, on

[1] Corti, op. cit., p. 87.

penalty of death. The cavalry were only to shoot in the last resort, but the infantry which were mixed everywhere with the cavalry were to maintain a constant fire, since experience had shown that the Turks were more easily alarmed by steady pressure than by sudden bombardment.

In the early hours of August 16, the Imperial army started their advance. It was a brilliantly clear night and they had little chance of proceeding far unnoticed. However, Eugen soon had his first stroke of luck. A mist suddenly arose at about 3 a.m. concealing his men from the Turkish sentries. But the cloud soon became so thick that his soldiers had difficulty in finding their way. The first line of the cavalry on the right wing under Count Pálffy lost their bearings and rode into some new trenches that the Turks were in process of digging. The alarm was given, whereupon the whole Ottoman force was quickly under arms. The spáhis fell upon the Imperial cavalry and inflicted severe damage.

The mist performed another service for the Ottomans, though it also allowed Eugen to demonstrate his supreme skill in a crisis. Profiting by the murk, a powerful Turkish division penetrated the Imperial lines and severed one flank. Had they been under more determined leadership they could easily have annihilated Eugen's right wing, but the opportunity was missed and as the fog lifted Eugen galloped at full speed to bring up cavalry and his second line of infantry. It was a split-second decision executed instantly and the gap was successfully closed. He was now determined to seize the initiative and engage the enemy in the centre. He therefore ordered the Imperial infantry, supported by cavalry on either flank, to advance to the attack with colours flying and drums beating. Despite the murderous bombardment from the main Turkish battery they held their fire until they were within close range and then lowered their bayonets and charged. The effect was shattering. Not even the janissaries could withstand them, and in a few minutes the battery fell and the whole enemy line was reeling. It was virtually the end of the battle. The time was barely 9 a.m.

Eugen was as cautious in this moment of triumph as he had been daring when everything looked black. The Turkish camp with all its fabulous treasure lay temptingly open to the Imperial troops. Yet Eugen commanded them to halt. Not until the Turks were well out of sight would he let his men enter the enemy lines. Experience had taught him the dangers of the plundering hour. 'For,' he explained, 'I feared the Turkish army less than their conquered camp.' With his soldiers lost in the euphoria of looting they would have been an easy prey to a surprise Turkish counter-attack.

No sooner had Khálil's army been defeated than Belgrade itself treated for surrender. On August 18, Mustapha Pasha marched out with all honours of war. Four days later the Imperial army took possession of the fortress with its flotilla, its six hundred guns, and enormous stores of arms.

Ottoman casualties had been appalling. They had suffered a total of 20,000 killed and wounded. Nor had the casualties of the Imperial army been slight; they had amounted to 1,500 dead and 3,500 wounded, including Eugen himself. When the Emperor heard of Eugen's wound he wrote to him, as he had done after Peterwardein the year before, reproaching him for having exposed himself to such danger: 'If you had not survived, the greatest victory of all time would have been a tragedy and meant an irreplaceable loss.'[1] Eugen's part in the battle might not have become quite the legend it is were it not for the famous song written about it which begins, *Prinz Eugenius Der Edle Ritter*. Nobody knows who wrote the words or music, and it refers mysteriously to 'Prince Ludwig' falling in the battle, though no prince of that name was on the field. However, such inaccuracies of detail are no handicap in folk-lore, and the *Edle Ritter* song, chanted by generations of Imperial soldiers as they have gone into battle, has taken a place in the continental song-book not very inferior to that held by *Malbrook s'en va t'en guerre*.

There was great excitement in England over the victory of Belgrade. In a poem printed and published in Warwick Lane the plea was made, apparently without irony, that:

> *Perhaps e'en Addison himself may deign,*
> *To write a second War, a new Campaign;*
> *To sing the Brother Chief, and make Eugene*
> *In equal Lustre with great Marlboro' shine.*[2]

In the peace conference which took place in the summer of 1718 at Passarowitz, Eugen preferred to stay in the wings, leaving the day-to-day negotiations to others. He kept firm control of the proceedings, however, and on one occasion, to make the Turks more amenable, he started moving troops in such a way as to suggest that war might be resumed. The Turks quickly came to heel. By the Treaty signed at

---

[1] *Feldzüge*, II Ser., VIII, p. 185.
[2] *Belgrade, a Poem*, Printed for J. Roberts, 1717.

Passarowitz on July 21, 1718, the Porte was finally excluded from Hungary, and the Emperor was left in possession of Temesvár, the Bánát, Belgrade, part of Bosnia, Serbia, and Wallachia.

It was the end of the Turkish threat to western Europe. Two brief campaigns had succeeded in dispersing for ever the menace that had hung over Christendom for a century and a half. Eugen's capture of Belgrade despite grave numerical inferiority had shattered the Ottoman reputation for siege-warfare, hitherto second only to that of the French. It was an unqualified triumph for the Empire, and for Eugen personally.

CHAPTER XVIII

EUGEN IN PEACE

IF INGRATITUDE towards their leaders is the mark of strong peoples, the Austrians, judging by their attitude to Eugen, were cast in a Herculean mould. The years immediately following his greatest triumph at Belgrade were those of his smallest influence in Vienna.

Given his forthrightness of tongue and scant respect for status, it is surprising that he had lasted until now so relatively unscathed in Vienna. So long as there was an external threat to the Monarchy from France and Turkey his services were needed of course, and he was more or less immune from internal intrigue. But when, as now, the security of Austria seemed assured, his enemies at last felt emboldened to combine against him, and the Emperor, whose attitude towards him had become increasingly ambivalent, thought it safe, and indeed desirable, to cut him down.

He remained nominally in charge of many offices. He was still Chairman of the Secret Conference of Ministers. He was also Governor-General of the Netherlands. He had been appointed to this post following the conclusion of the Barrier Treaty of November 15, 1715, which regulated the terms on which the former Spanish Netherlands were handed over to the Emperor. Finally, he was President of the Imperial War Council. In this capacity he was preoccupied with, though he did not participate directly in, the war with Spain. Instigated by Alberoni, Philip of Spain was trying to recover by force from Austria the former Spanish territories in Italy given to the Emperor under the Treaty of Utrecht. This war, which continued until 1720, involved the dispatch of Habsburg troops to Sicily and eventually led Victor Amadeus of Savoy (a momentary ally of Spain's) to cede Sicily to the Emperor in return for Sardinia.

The Imperial Forces in Italy included a detachment under the Comte de Bonneval, a professional renegade who keeps cropping up in Eugen's life, now foe, now friend, and then foe again; not a central figure in history, but a gad-fly who epitomized more completely than any of his contemporaries the spirit of insouciant apatriotism which prevailed among the leading families of Europe. Born at Limoges in 1675, the son of a landowner, Bonneval first joined the French navy at the age of eleven. Dismissed the service as a result of a duel, he was admitted to the army and served against Eugen in Italy in the War of the Spanish Succession. Financial unscrupulousness led to a row with the French Minister of War which in turn impelled Bonneval to desert to the Imperial lines and to offer his services to the former enemy. He served under Eugen with great distinction and bravery, both against the French and the Turks. He was severely wounded at the Battle of Peterwardein. His quarrelsomeness and overbearing character led to rows with his superiors during the war against Spain in Italy 1719-20. A few years later his seditious behaviour in the Netherlands caused him to be arrested. Eugen, though frequently forced to reprimand him officially, had remained on close personal terms with him, attracted by his ebullient and eccentric character and by the French background they had in common. Though the charges of sedition levelled against him were incontrovertible, Eugen favoured leniency. Nevertheless Bonneval was given a prison sentence. After his release a year later he made his way first to Venice then to Turkey where he devoted the remaining twenty years of his life to working for the Ottomans against the Empire. He served them well, introducing long-needed military reforms in the 1730's, and founding a school of Bombardiers. He died in 1747.

Eugen was also closely concerned with the diplomatic negotiations which resulted in the resumption of the former alliance with England.[1] Despite England's recent disloyalty to the common cause and his own painful experiences at their hands, he had no intention of sacrificing what he believed to be the Habsburg interest for the sake of personal revenge. He recognized that the Monarchy needed the

[1] Bilateral Treaty of Westminster signed in May 1715. Austria, Britain and France formed an alliance in August 1718, called the Quadruple Alliance because the Dutch Republic was expected to sign, which they never did. See Ragnhild M. Hatton, *Diplomatic Relations Between Great Britain and the Dutch Republic, 1714–1721*, 1950.

support of a strong fleet to protect its territories in Italy against a Spanish invasion, and that England alone could provide it.

Eugen's position was clearly strong on paper, at any rate for war and diplomacy. But the reality of power lay elsewhere, particularly in domestic affairs. For the day-to-day running of the Empire he was virtually in eclipse during the years immediately following the Spanish Succession and Turkish wars. Control was in the hands of his enemies. First amongst these was the clique of old families whom he had both disturbed in their privileges and offended in their persons. The Schönborns were typical of these. 'In their eyes,' Eugen said, 'the interests of the Schönborns transcend all others.'

Then there were various individuals whom Eugen had antagonized for one reason or another. Amongst these, and not the least prominent, was General Graf Guido Starhemberg, originally a friend in war, but now an enemy.[1] Into this category also fell Eugen's cousin, Victor Amadeus of Savoy, who perceived in Eugen the main obstruction to the schemes he nourished for aggrandisement in Italy through the marriage of his eldest son to one of Joseph I's daughters.

Finally there was the Spanish *camarilla* whose influence over the Emperor had become great and who were jealous of Eugen and in fundamental disagreement with him on basic issues of policy. These 'Spaniards' sought to bring about a coalition of all the anti-Eugen forces in Vienna to reduce, and if possible, extinguish, the Prince's influence and power at the court. For a time they were almost completely successful.

Charles VI does not stand forth in history either in a particularly honourable or in a particularly ignoble light. For one thing, however, the beacon of renown shines upon him—the dogged persistence with which he tried to secure, through acknowledgment of the Pragmatic Sanction, the succession of his daughter, Maria Theresa, to the undivided inheritance of the House of Austria. It is somewhat surprising, therefore, to see what opposite qualities, what fickleness and pusillanimity, he invariably showed in his dealings with Eugen. So long as he needed him in war he remained fiercely devoted to him and refused to countenance the machinations of his enemies. He was fulsome in his expressions of affection, admiration and gratitude. But when the blast of war had ceased to blow in his ears he dropped all his devotion and allowed himself to fall completely under the spell of the Spanish junta. This was partly a

[1] See Chapter IX, p. 128.

reflection of his innate preference for sycophants, the result in turn of vacillations of character and early misfortunes. He distrusted anyone who could possibly be a rival, whether by reason of birth or status or reputation. He was more than half afraid of anyone who might question his absolute authority, for he never felt strong enough to distinguish disagreement from insubordination. As a corollary, he liked under-dogs, elaborate deference and punctilio. This made him adore the Spaniards. They genuflected and served him on their knees. Compared with these spaniels Eugen must have appeared a disrespectful terrier.

There was another reason for the Emperor's coolness. By temperament Charles was attracted to innovation. Anyone who could promise him an easy way to promote industry and trade was sure of an enthusiastic welcome. It can be imagined that in this era of the Mississippi Company and the South Sea Bubble, mountebanks were not wanting in Austria. Eugen was just as sceptical as Charles was credulous of panaceas. He made no effort to temper himself to the wind of fashion. 'If anyone starts to represent himself as a man of ideas,' he wrote on one occasion, 'it is sufficient for me to lose any good opinion I may have had of him'.[1] It is not difficult to perceive that in the relationship between the Emperor and Eugen it was as if the laws of dynamics had been temporarily suspended: there was friction without contact.

Of all Charles' entourage his favourite was Graf Johann von Althan, who, though Moravian by birth, belonged most emphatically to the Spanish set. He had endeared himself to the Emperor in Spain by denigrating his uncle and patron, Prince Lichtenstein, the Grand Master of Charles' household. Althan's wife, a beautiful Spaniard, was the Emperor's mistress. But this does not seem to have produced any complications, perhaps because royal blood dispelled the shame of cuckoldry, perhaps because the Emperor seemed to show as much affection for Althan as for his wife.

One of the accusations that Althan and his friends brought against Eugen was that he was indiscreet in his private life. Some time previously he had become close friends with the Gräfin Eleonore Batthyany, the widow of a Hungarian officer. He was to be seen playing piquet with her every evening. Rumours were put about that he had fallen so completely under her influence as to discuss confidential matters of state with her. It was even said that the

[1] Eugen to Giulio Visconti, August 30, 1727, A. Arneth, op. cit., III, p. 515.

Gräfin, far from being incorruptible, was the paid mouthpiece of the country's enemies. St Saphorin, the British Ambassador, reported to London on the deleterious influence which these stories were having on Eugen's reputation, particularly with the Emperor:

'Eugen's credit diminishes from day to day because the Emperor has been convinced that his views on any subject have been put into his head by the Gräfin Batthyany or by her referendaries; and on this assumption the Emperor is always saying that he is prepared to defer to Eugen's opinion provided he can be satisfied that it is his own judgment that is involved; he does not feel disposed to adopt the views of the Gräfin Batthyany.'[1]

Althan decided to play on the Emperor's pathological fears of rivalry. He put it about that Eugen was becoming too powerful and was overshadowing the Monarchy. All the old bitter feelings against the Prince dating from Rastadt and the betrayal of the Catalans were re-kindled amongst the Spaniards; and it was not long before the anti-Eugen cauldron in Vienna had reached the critical temperature required by Victor Amadeus of Savoy for what he believed would be a fatal explosion. Convinced that he would never get anywhere with his designs for expansion in Italy so long as Eugen remained predominant at Vienna, he was determined to do everything he could to destroy him. Not being present in person, he had to operate through intermediaries. As chief saboteurs he chose the Abbé Prosper Tedeschi, a Florentine, and the Imperial Chamberlain, the Graf von Nimptsch, a brother-in-law of Graf Althan. They were to devise whatever plot they thought best to bring about Eugen's downfall.

They found in the Emperor, if not an accomplice, at any rate a ready listener. Charles implored Nimptsch to keep him informed secretly of all the Prince's alleged machinations and arranged for him to have private access to the palace by day and night.

It was in keeping with the spirit of the times that the plot against Eugen was unearthed by a betrayal from the other side. Nimptsch's valet began to be suspicious of his master's comings and goings at all hours of the night in different disguises; of the surreptitious arrivals of unknown men who would be closeted with him for hours in secret confabulation; and of the frequent prolonged meetings with Tedeschi. Convinced that some dangerous plot was afoot but

[1] St Saphorin. May 7, 1719, A. Arneth, op. cit., III, p. 516.

uncertain of its exact nature, the valet decided he must tell someone about it, someone in authority who was also above the level of petty Court intrigue. Eugen was the obvious person, and to him he went and recounted his suspicions.

Having obtained documentary evidence from the valet Eugen sent him abroad for his own safety. He then summoned a group of friends and told them of his intention to go straight to the Emperor and demand an immediate investigation and trial. With their unanimous support he thereupon sought an interview with Charles at which he asked for an immediate formal enquiry into the plot. Unless this took place and unless those found guilty were condemned and punished he would resign all his posts. The Emperor was in a difficult position. The accused were his friends and he had lent a ready ear to their whisperings. To allow the enquiry to go forward would be to admit a *prima facie* case of their guilt. However, the threatened alternative of Eugen's resignation, with all the scandal and chaos that would result, was even worse. Charles therefore agreed to establish a high-level commission of investigation.

Eugen refused to hold meetings of the Secret Conference or Imperial War Council until the whole matter was cleared up. Nobody else dared call meetings in his absence. The public business of the Empire thereupon came to a standstill, notwithstanding the continuation of war in Italy.

The commission found both Tedeschi and Nimptsch guilty. Severe sentences were passed and carried out. Tedeschi was put in the pillory in the midst of Vienna for two hours. Thirty stripes were given him on the bare back from a rod wielded by the Public Prosecutor. He was then banished from Austria. Nimptsch was imprisoned for two years, deprived of all offices and exiled from all places where the Court might sit.

Naturally Althan was grievously put out by his brother-in-law's sentence. He decided to punish the Emperor in the way he thought most painful—by depriving him of his company. Indeed not until Althan's death in 1722 was Charles entirely liberated from his Zvengali spell; and it was not until the dominating Archbishop of Valencia died shortly afterwards that he was able to shake himself free from the influence of the whole Spanish set.

With the decline of the Spaniards, Eugen inevitably became more powerful again. By December 1724, we find the Emperor writing to him once more in the old war-time terms. He asks tenderly after his health, implores him to look after himself and tells him how much he looks forward to seeing him and to embracing him so as to show *'combien je vous aime'*.[1] When Eugen was ill again a few years later Charles wrote to him with passionate sympathy. Three times in the same letter he said how keenly he wanted to embrace him—'but I will deprive myself of this solace for a short time until Your Excellency has recovered from your indisposition, which I hope will be within a matter of days, particularly if Your Excellency takes more care'.[2] Till the end of Eugen's life, the Emperor's solicitude continued to be expressed in the same affectionate, if somewhat medical key.

What of Eugen's other relationships? What in particular of the controversial subject of his relations with women about which there is such a tantalizing lack of first-hand material? Mention has already been made of the scurrilous statement by the Duchess of Orleans about Eugen's immorality as a boy.[3] She saw nothing of him after he left France at the age of twenty in 1683; yet she continued to be convinced of his homosexuality. In 1710 she wrote: 'He does not get on well with women, a couple of pretty page boys would seem to be more his line.'[4]

This also seems to have been the view of Lady Mary Wortley Montagu who visited Vienna in 1717. She gave the following description of Eugen in a letter: '. . . I am as unwilling to speak of him at Vienna as I should be to talk of Hercules in the Court of Omphale if I had seen him there. I don't know what comfort other people find in considering the weakness of great men (because it brings them nearer to their level) but 'tis always a mortification to me to observe that there is no perfection in humanity.'[5]

How far this represents Lady Mary's own observation or whether it merely repeats the gossip of the town, is impossible to say. She was a notoriously unsqueamish woman, and the impression she seeks to convey of having had to steel herself and overcome great inhibitions to mention his alleged immorality in a private letter to her sister casts considerable doubt upon the substance of what she says.

As we have seen, when Eugen was in London in 1712 he was pursued socially. But he does not appear to have responded to female attentions as much as was hoped. 'The ladies here don't admire

[1] The Emperor to Eugen, 27.12.1724, A. Arneth, op. cit., III, p. 519.

[2] The Emperor to Eugen, 18.9.1729, A. Arneth, op. cit., III, p. 57.

[3] See Chapter I, p. 9.

[4] Max Braubach, op. cit., p. 112.

[5] Letter to the Countess of Mar, January 16, 1717, *The Letters and Works of Lady Mary Wortley Montagu*, ed. Lord Wharncliffe, 1893, I, p. 269.

Prince Eugene', Lady Strafford wrote, 'for he seems to take very little notice of them.'[1] There may be a touch of sour grapes about this as about several other references by hostesses to Eugen's alleged lack of interest.

We also have to take account of the much quoted dictum about Eugen, that he was a 'Mars without Venus'. This again is mud in the sling of those who charge him with being abnormal or at least with misogyny. But it does not seem really to warrant a very serious interpretation being put upon it; it was really nothing more than a colourful way of saying that he never married.

Finally, supporters of the homosexual theory adduce as evidence to back their case the strong influence which Eugen's mother exercised over him in his early years. They infer that he suffered from an Oedipus Complex which explains his whole public and private life. Helpful though it would be to find so simple a key to such a complex being, the theory is implausible. Though he was much under Olympia's influence as a boy, he appears to have been disillusioned early in life by her behaviour and to have severed all relationship with her. Moreover, far from renouncing the society of other women, Eugen, as will be shown, came to depend heavily on their company—a fact sufficiently well established at the time to support the charges of indiscretion and insecurity levelled against him by his enemies.

That women played an important part in his life is confirmed by many contemporary writers. Villars' message to Eugen after the Treaty of Rastadt, that he had drunk his health in the company of some beautiful women, does not suggest that Villars had derived the impression from their long evening talks together during the Treaty negotiations, that Eugen was altogether uninterested in the opposite sex. In his memoirs of the Imperial court, the French diplomat the Comte du Luc wrote of Eugen on September 1, 1715:

'He spends his time with various women who have formed a small court. The Countess Batthyany has more hold over him than any of the others. She is not in her first youth but has a lively personality.'[2]

Legend abounds as to the exact nature of Eugen's relationship with the Gräfin Batthyany. One of Eugen's recent biographers has claimed that he was the father of the Gräfin's two sons. This seems inherently improbable since the boys were both born before 1700—

[1] *The Wentworth Papers*, op. cit., p. 244.
[2] Max Braubach, op. cit., p. 114.

that is before the time when Eugen is believed to have first become acquainted with her. But we have disappointingly little hard evidence to go upon. There is not a line in her hand any more than in his own on the subject. She was born in 1672, the daughter of an Imperial Minister, Strattmann, of bourgeois German origin. She married a Hungarian aristocrat who died in 1703. It is not known precisely when her friendship with Eugen began. But his acquisition after the Battle of Zenta of property in Hungary made them neighbours. All that is certain is that in the years immediately following the War of the Spanish Sucecssion they were known to be close friends, and that she became the centre of the world of poets, writers, painters and collectors whom Eugen gathered around him. From 1715 she begins to be mentioned regularly in diplomatic correspondence as Eugen's Egeria, and within a few years she is referred to as his constant companion and his mistress.

Sharp featured and with dark hair, she was not altogether unlike Eugen's mother in appearance. By all accounts she was vivacious and attractive. She was also ambitious. Apart from the general criticism by Graf Althan and his set that she was untrustworthy and venal, a number of specific accusations were made against her. It was said for instance that she had such power over Eugen as to make him appoint her nominees to desirable posts in the public service. It was also suggested that on one occasion, in the 1715 negotiations which led to the Barrier Treaty, she had induced him to promote Dutch rather than Austrian interests. Finally it was believed that she persuaded Eugen to give more attention than he would otherwise have done to Hungary's affairs. A story is told in support of this. After the Peace of Passarowitz in 1718 the Prince, who was then serving in Hungary, received secret orders to stay there with his army because the Emperor intended bringing the country more directly under Vienna's control. Eugen is said to have confided this information to the Gräfin who, having been married to a Hungarian aristocrat, remained a zealous Hungarian patriot. On receiving Eugen's news, she hastened to the Gräfin Althan. When, that evening, Charles called on his mistress, he was received by both ladies dressed in mourning and weeping. They implored him not to carry out his proposed policy in Hungary—or at least to see Eugen before doing so. Charles thereupon summoned Eugen to Vienna. Gräfin Batthyany hurried off in her travelling carriage to fetch him back. On his return Eugen saw the Emperor and dissuaded him from carrying out his original intentions.

Amongst the governments of Europe the conviction became established that the Gräfin Batthyany was the most influential person at the Imperial court. Ambitious as she was, she no doubt encouraged people to think that she dominated him and that she was the main link between Eugen and the outside world. But a number of observers thought that her real influence was probably less than she liked to convey. Though she was his constant companion there is absolutely no evidence that she was his mistress, and the relationship may well have been a platonic one, the intense but chaste friendship of two like-minded members of a small intellectual coterie. She no doubt succeeded in hoodwinking a good many of her contemporaries about their connection and about her power over Eugen, which in policy, as distinct from appointments, was probably small. Lady Mary Wortley Montagu has attested to the peculiar position of women, particularly middle-aged ones, in the Austrian capital, and there is no reason to suppose that the Gräfin Batthyany was any exception. Casting her eye upon the Vienna scene in the autumn of 1716, Lady Mary has recorded the following impression of the *moeurs* prevalent there:

'. . . I can assure you that wrinkles, or a small stoop in the shoulders, nay, grey hair itself, is no objection to the making new conquests. . . . A woman, till five-and-thirty, is only looked upon as a raw girl, and can possibly make no noise in the world till about forty . . . 'tis a considerable comfort to me to know there is upon earth such a paradise for old women . . . and then that perplexing word reputation has quite another meaning here than what you give it in London; and getting a lover is so far from losing, that 'tis properly getting reputation, ladies being much more respected in regard to the rank of their lovers, than that of their husbands. . . .

'. . . A man makes but an ill figure that is not in some commerce of this nature; and a woman looks out for a lover as soon as she's married, as part of her equipage without which she could not be genteel.

'Thus you see . . . gallantry and good-breeding are as different, in different climates, as morality and religion.'[1]

The inflamed opposition to Eugen which kept erupting in peace-

[1] Letter to Lady Rich, September 20, 1716. *The Letters and Works of Lady Mary Wortley Montagu*, op. cit., I, pp. 244–6.

time Austria owed something to a particular irritation which
he caused beneath the ruling surface. He never succeeded in winning
a body of devoted adherents among the other leaders of the
Monarchy. He never tried to do so. He did not try to bind a group
of highly-placed persons to himself by taking them into his confidence, seeking their advice, bestowing occasional favours on them
and generating in them a vested interest in his power. His way of
working was to gather around him a small coterie of junior officials
and advisers—many of them low of birth as well as of rank—to
discuss things with them and to govern through them pragmatically,
guided by nothing more subtle than the star of public good. These
private secretaries were also required to meet a humdrum need, to
make up for Eugen's deficiency in the German language. Of all the
official minutes, reports and letters he left behind, there is not one
in German in his own hand. French, of course, was his first tongue,
and the only one he mastered. He was also at home in Italian. He
had little Latin or Spanish and no English. Beneath French and
Italian documents he wrote his name in the appropriate language.
German papers he signed with a curious ungrammatical mixture of
the three: *Eugenio von Savoy.*

This *Sekretärsherrschaft* was naturally much resented by the
elderly aristocrats and more senior officers. They saw the Monarchy
being run by a group of inexperienced usurpers, minions of a
foreign Prince, who—and the thought came easily to them—were
no doubt bent on feathering their own nests rather than serving the
public interest—synonymous in their eyes with the interest of the
ruling families. There is no evidence, it should be recorded, that any
of Eugen's secretaries—who included Johann Michael Langetl,
Wilhelm Brockhausen, and Ignaz Koch—served their master or the
Habsburgs in any but the most honourable and disinterested way.

There were other reasons for his lack of a close personal following
in civilian life. Eugen did not have the gift of persuasion. He did not
think it necessary, and certainly did not know how, to cajole or
convince in order to get his way. As a soldier he gave orders and
expected them to be carried out. But the Monarchy could not be
run in peace time through a one-way current and Eugen's short-
coming in this respect was a hindrance to good government. Though
he had something of the aloofness and vision of a statesman, he never
learnt the give and take of politics. Nor did he believe in any unique
gospel or philosophy of government. He stood clearly for certain
principles of behaviour and administration. But he did not have, and

20. Eugen at the battle of Belgrade, 1717; engraving after a contemporary picture by van Huchtenburgh

21. Schlosshof, Eugen's favourite country palace, reconstructed for Eugen by J. L. von Hildebrandt

22. Façade of Eugen's Winter Palace in Vienna to the design of J. B. Fischer von Erlach

Äußerliches Ansehen des Pallasts, welchen Ih. Dürchl
Printz Eugenius von Savoien, Käis. Maytt. General Lieutenant,
Zu Wien in der Himelport-gaßen erbauet; Samt dem Einzüge des Ao:
1711 d. q. Apr. von Groß-Vez, ir abgeschicken, und daselbst zur Audientz geführten Aga.

Façade du Palais, que So. Alt. Mnor. le Prince Euga
de Savoie Lieutenant General de Sa Ma: Imp. a fait bâtir à Vienne d
la rue dite Himmelporten, avec l'entrée de le Aga ou eye du Grand Vezir, qu
y mena à l'audience l'an. 1711 le 9 Avril.

indeed distrusted, anything in the nature of a political dogma. He was not indeed an evangelist. He had people about him who admired and loved him as a person. But he did not have disciples.

It would be wrong, however, to give the impression that he was unsociable. It was merely that he was not gregarious, and if he had to see people, he preferred them to be people of his own choosing, irrespective of rank or status, such as scientists, philosophers and artists. It is striking that all his closest friends were non-Austrians: the philosopher Leibniz, the writer Jean Baptiste Rousseau, the collector Pierre Jean Mariette and the connoisseur Cardinal Alessandro Albani, the Berenson of his day.[1] This was not merely his natural sympathy as a foreigner for outsiders. It was also because the Maecenas side of his character had to be satisfied and this could only be done from abroad since Austria, Bohemia and Hungary were so deficient at this time in eminent men in the sciences and fine arts. Apart from the architects Fischer von Erlach and Hildebrandt, both of whom were Italian-trained, there is not a great name to be found between the Thirty Years War and the time of Charles VI and Maria Theresa. 'I don't find that learned men abound here,' Lady Mary Wortley Montagu observed, 'there is indeed a prodigious number of alchemists at Vienna; the philosopher's stone is the great object of zeal and science.'[2] It is outside the scope of this work to examine what the causes were of this desert in the heart of the Habsburg Monarchy, but there is no denying the aridity of climate produced by the external menace of the Turks and the internal oppression of the Jesuits.

Leibniz, inventor (simultaneously with Newton) of the calculus, progenitor of the idea of calculating machines, lawyer, historian, statesman, philosopher and scientist, was perhaps the last universal genius of the modern world. It is known from correspondence that Eugen read and much admired Leibniz's *La Théodicée*, published in 1710, and that he asked him to write a condensed statement of the main principles of his philosophy. This Leibniz did and sent it to him. There is doubt whether the document produced was the *Principles of Nature and of Grace* or the *Monadology*. The former, which consists of only eighteen paragraphs, was a very brief summary of Leibniz's views; the latter, which comprised ninety para-

[1] See Chapter XIX.
[2] Letter to unknown addressee, *The Letters and Works of Lady Mary Wortley Montagu*, op. cit., I, p. 266.

graphs, is a complete account of the philosopher's 'system'.[1] At any rate, whichever of the two documents it was, Eugen was delighted with it and kept it like a jewel in a case, so that Bonneval wrote to Leibniz: 'He keeps your writing as the priests at Naples keep the blood of St Januarius; he lets me kiss it and immediately shuts it up again in its casket.'[2]

Eugen's friendship with Leibniz lasted only four years, from 1712 until the philosopher's death in 1716. But it was characterized by the intensity typical of the two men, each attracted by the versatility of the other. Besides supporting him as a philosopher, Eugen encouraged Leibniz's attempt to found an Academy of Learning in Vienna. But lack of funds prevented the scheme being realized— until 150 years later.

With Jean Baptiste Rousseau[3] Eugen's friendship was longer but less sublime. Rousseau's epigrams and satires had made him many enemies in France, and as a result of a libel action he was banished from the country in 1712. However, before judgment was given he fled to Switzerland where he was befriended by the French Ambassador, the Comte du Luc, who took him with him to the Congress of Baden. There the ambassador introduced him to Eugen. In 1715 when the ambassador was posted to Vienna, he brought Rousseau along with him. It says something for the independence of diplomats in those days that an ambassador could befriend a banished countryman and latch him to his entourage without fear of reproach from home. Rousseau was enchanted to find himself at the Vienna court where he was immediately lionized and where, as he said, 'everyone speaks our language'.[4] Eugen took him up enthusiastically. 'I made acquaintance yesterday with the famous poet Rousseau,' Lady Mary Wortley Montagu wrote on January 2, 1717, 'who lives here under the peculiar protection of Prince Eugene by whose liberality he subsists.'[5] Rousseau was lyrical about the

[1] Herbert Wildon Carr, *The Monadology of Leibniz*, 1930, pp. 3–4.

[2] Leibniz, *The Monadology*, ed. Robert Latta, 1898, pp. 215–16. See also W. Suchier, *Prinz Eugen als Bibliophile*, 1928, p. 27.

[3] Jean Baptiste Rousseau, 1671–1741, described thus by a recent biographer: 'Once thought of as the great French lyric poet, the Pindar, the Horace of French poetry, he sank into oblivion in the middle of the nineteenth century and has remained there since.' Henry A. Grubbs, *Jean Baptiste Rousseau, His Life and Works*, 1941, Preface. He still seems to remain there despite Mr Grubbs' efforts at salvage.

[4] Letter from J. B. Rousseau to M. Boutet, July 15, 1715, *Lettres de Rousseau*, 1750, I, p. 77.

[5] Letter to unknown addressee, *The Letters and Works of Lady Mary Wortley Montagu*, op. cit., I, pp. 265–6.

Prince: 'Never have I seen in one man such greatness combined with such simplicity.'[1] On another occasion he wrote: 'He is well versed in all branches of learning, but it is difficult to perceive where his personal preference lies. He has the most perfect judgment. In manner he is exceedingly simple. He is a soldier-philosopher, indifferent about his own honour and reputation who describes his own faults with the same frankness as if he was speaking of someone else.' Rousseau also describes how 'he was reserved on first acquaintance but extremely forthcoming when you get to know him. He is far readier to admire virtues in others than to perceive them in himself.'[2] An inscription by Rousseau to a portrait of Eugen contained one of his more penetrating comments:

> *Ce fut en apprenant à se vaincre soi-même;*
> *Qu'il apprit à dompter ses plus fiers enemis.*[3]

Rousseau wrote two odes to Eugen full of such treacly sentiments as: 'Greater than his victories in battle are those over the hearts of men.'[4] Lady Mary Wortley Montagu deplored the fact that, 'he passes here for a free-thinker, and what is still worse in my esteem, for a man whose heart does not feel the encomiums he gives to virtue and honour in his poems'.[5] There were plenty of such encomiums and he wrote a particularly effusive one on the occasion of the Gräfin Batthyany's birthday. When, in 1715, there was great indignation in Vienna at the Turkish threat to Venice he appointed himself the mouthpiece of the prevailing belligerency and produced an *Ode aux Princes chrétiens sur l'armament des Turcs contre la république de Venise.*[6] As has been truly said of him, *faute d'idée, il allait faire une ode.*

Eugen was exceptionally generous to Rousseau. He gave him valuable presents and found him a post he wanted in the Netherlands. After Rousseau had left Vienna to take up this appointment they kept in touch by correspondence. Eugen sought his advice about

---

[1] Letter from J. B. Rousseau to M. Boutet, *Lettres de Rousseau,* op. cit., I, p. 79.
[2] Letter from J. B. Rousseau to M. Brossette, June 30, 1716, *Lettres de Rousseau,* op. cit., II, pp. 98–9.
[3] A. Arneth, op. cit., III, p. 520.
[4] *Oeuvres de Jean Baptiste Rousseau,* 1820, pp. 177–88 and 262–70.
[5] Letter to unknown addressee, *The Letters and Works of Lady Mary Wortley Montagu,* op. cit., I, p. 266.
[6] This poem contained a line which even Sainte-Beuve is said to have admired: *Leurs ossements blanchis dans les champs d'Ascalon. . . .* See Henry A. Grubbs, op. cit., p. 129.

French literature. He asked him to send him any recent French plays from Paris. He also requested a copy of Voltaire's *Henriade*, which had just been published. When he later received and read this he explained to Rousseau that he did not think much of it and asked him to indicate those passages he liked best and those least. His dislike of the *Henriade* may have been partly due to its religious scepticism. He hated fanaticism whether in politics or religion. He was a believer and read the scriptures regularly; indeed his arrival on the first rung of political power had probably owed something to the intervention of the Jesuit, Bischoff, who was confessor to the Emperor Leopold at the beginning of the century.[1] But, in spite of this, in all his long years of war against the Turks he never saw himself as a crusader engaged in some mission for Christianity. He was opposed to Papal intervention in temporal affairs. Moreover as Governor-General of the Netherlands he did everything he could to uphold the rights of the Jansenists against Papal oppression.

About Rousseau's own poetry Eugen was uncritically enthusiastic. He tried to discourage him from turning to history or biography. 'However determined one is to keep within the strict bounds of truth,' he wrote to him, 'there are always distinguished people, and indeed whole nations, who will be offended no matter how objectively and dispassionately you describe them.'[2]

Eugen's geese were apt to be swans. Not surprisingly there were many shocks and disillusionments. Rousseau's sycophancy towards Eugen should have served as a warning to him. But though not usually taken in by flatterers, he seems to have been a dupe for recreants. Rousseau had not been in the Netherlands long before he started an intrigue to remove Eugen from his post of Governor-General. When Eugen heard about this his reaction was typical; sorrow rather than anger, silence rather than recrimination. All he is ever known to have said on the subject was: 'I never thought that Rousseau would become involved in that sort of intrigue.'[3] It was much the same disenchantment as Frederick the Great experienced over Voltaire, but Eugen took it more philosophically.

It must be admitted that there was something anomalous about Eugen's long absentee tenure of the Governor-Generalship of the Austrian Netherlands. Initially, after his appointment in 1716, he was prevented from proceeding to his post by the Turkish War.

[1] See Chapter VII, p. 78.
[2] A. Arneth, op. cit., III, p. 521.
[3] A. Arneth, op. cit., III, p. 522.

Then such were the intrigues against him in Vienna that he did not
feel it safe to leave the capital. He was often on the point of going
and on one occasion had even dispatched his luggage. But in fact
he never visited his domain. Perhaps it was as well. He would have
been ill-equipped by temperament either to listen patiently to all the
grievances and petitions of the Belgians, or to resist them. 'The
conqueror of France and the Turks,' as the historian of modern
Belgium has described him in this context, '. . . was not of the metal
from which political instruments are made.'[1] Had he gone to the
Netherlands he might well have provoked a dangerous incident
such was the discontent of the population. Or, perhaps more likely,
and even worse for the Emperor, he might have taken the side of the
oppressed citizens.

The Austrian Netherlands had been subjected to grave disabilities
by the Barrier Treaty of 1715, in particular the gross expense and
inconvenience of supporting an enormous Dutch army garrisoning
the barrier fortresses. Some slight alleviation was obtained from the
States-General of the United Provinces in December 1718, thanks
to the tenacity of Eugen's deputy, the Marquis de Prié, who had
been sent to Brussels in the Prince's place in November 1716. But
the situation remained vexatious and humiliating. De Prié, an
Italian who had been employed as a diplomat by the Duke of Savoy
before he transferred to the Austrian service, had owed his success
in life to divining and meeting the wishes of his superiors, but this
was scarcely the quality he now needed for the direct responsibility
of government. Nor was he disinterested. To the Flemings he soon
acquired the nickname *Pillé*. He proved himself quite incapable
of fulfilling the country's overriding need, which, after years of
divided rule, was for the re-unification of the country.

In a way it suited Eugen's character to administer from afar. His
impatience and impulsiveness were less manifest by post than in
person. He plied de Prié with a constant flow of detailed instructions.
In view of his scarcely liberal attitude towards Hungary, it is interesting to see Eugen declare *à propos* of the running of the Austrian
Netherlands: 'A Government must safeguard the rights of the
individual and must be prepared to reward people according to
their service.' However, nothing could make the Barrier Treaty
popular with the inhabitants. There were outbreaks of disorder in
Antwerp and Brussels. De Prié complained of the bitter criticism on
all sides. Eugen adopted a paternal line: 'If you do what you have

[1] H. Pirenne, *Histoire de Belgique*, 1926, V, p. 176.

to do, you are immune from the consequence of the criticism to which everyone is exposed.'[1] The back-biting, instigated by Bonneval and continued by a compeer in apostasy, the Marquis de Mérode-Westerloo, eventually led Eugen in November 1724 to resign his Governor-Generalship. De Prié was recalled shortly afterwards.

During his tenure of the Governor-Generalship Eugen took a stand on one vital local issue which showed his readiness to make forfeits at the periphery, however unpopular this made him personally, for the sake of what he conceived to be the overriding Habsburg interest. The merchants of Antwerp, Brussels, Ghent and Bruges, restricted at home by the conditions of the peace settlement, were anxiously seeking outlets overseas and chances to import and trade profitably. They were encouraged by many promoters and seamen, including several Scots and Irishmen, who were eager to form an Ostend Trading Company for trade with the East. They applied to the Emperor for permission. He was sympathetic, but Eugen was not. There were two reasons for Eugen's opposition. Firstly, with the lessons of the Mississippi crash and South Sea Bubble recently in mind, he distrusted the British financiers behind the Ostend venture. Secondly, and most important, he knew that the formation of such a company would inevitably invoke the wrath of the Maritime Powers. Already in 1719 St Saphorin, the British representative in Vienna delivered a formal protest to the Austrian government about alleged interlopers in the trade of China for which the English East India Company claimed a monopoly.[2] However, by a coincidence, just at the time when pressure from Belgium was at its strongest Eugen's influence in Vienna was at its nadir. The 'Spaniards', in the ascendant at this crucial moment, exhorted the Emperor to follow his own inclinations and to grant a charter. This he did. The announcement of the granting of his authority to the establishment of the Ostend Trading Company was given to the world in December 1722.[3]

The Company met with instantaneous success. The China trade proved particularly profitable. Silk, tea, coffee, chintz, and paper were imported. There was a marvellous expansion in the wealth of Ostend. But, as Eugen had foreseen, the English and Dutch were immediately aroused to fury, and indeed some of them began

[1] A. Arneth, op. cit., III, p. 530.
[2] Huisman, *La Compagnie d'Ostende*, 1902, p. 121.
[3] Gerald B. Hertz, *England and the Ostend Company*, the English Historical Review, 1907, p. 255 et seq.

straight away to take the law into their own hands. In London there were fierce protests in Parliament. The pamphleteers fulminated. As the East India Company started to feel the pinch of competition there was an injured outcry in the City of London against the threat to 'the liberties of England' and 'the Protestant religion'.

'We are the greatest country in the world,' Defoe declared. 'Our climate is the most agreeable to live in; our Englishmen are the stoutest and best in the world.'[1] For that reason apparently they would insist on maintaining their trade monopoly with the East even though it meant depriving their neighbours the Belgians of the opportunity of economic recovery from the war.

English and Dutch pressure on the Emperor to suspend the company became intense. Eugen, who by now had regained his former influence, succeeded before long in persuading him to terminate the charter, at first provisionally in 1727, and then completely in 1731. Eugen was not indifferent to the needs of the Belgians, but he had been moved all along by the conviction that so long as the company continued to exist it would run the Monarchy into bitter conflict and perhaps war with Holland and England. In a manner that perhaps did more credit to his head than his heart, he believed that the Emperor should be prepared to sacrifice the Belgians for the wider interest of Austria, and he had the courage to say so insistently.

[1] D. Defoe, *The Compleat English Tradesman*, 1726, p. 369.

CHAPTER XIX

THE PATRON OF THE ARTS

THE VICTOR of Blenheim and Belgrade was also the creator of the Belvedere in Vienna and one of the greatest collectors in European history.

As soon as the rewards of his victories gave him the resources, Eugen became, on the grandest scale, builder, patron of artists, creator of gardens and collector of pictures, sculpture, prints, books and manuscripts. A keen, well-informed patronage of the arts was typical of the early eighteenth-century nobility. But Eugen's vast activity points to something more. It is as though he who never became husband or parent found compensation in the glory of building, in the paternalism inherent in patronage of artists and in the passion of collecting. To these he devoted himself with the same seriousness that he gave to the battlefield.

Eugen's greatest contribution to baroque art was the building of his three splendid palaces in Vienna—the Stadtpalais and the Upper and Lower Belvedere. Towards the close of the seventeenth century, in the mood of confidence which followed the success of the Austrian arms against the Turks, the Emperor and the aristocracy had begun erecting the stone and stucco palaces for which Vienna is famous. It was in 1693 and 1694,[1] when Eugen was hardly past his thirtieth year, that he began to buy the ground plots both for a palace in the centre of Vienna and for a garden palace in the country just outside the walls. The town palace or Stadtpalais was, like similar Viennese palaces, a combination of official residence and home. The architect whom Eugen employed was Austria's greatest, Johann Bernhard

[1] See Chapter III, pp. 37–38.

Fischer von Erlach. It has been suggested[1] that Eugen chose an Austrian-born architect because he wished to identify himself completely with his adoptive country. But this national sentiment does not accord with the international outlook of European patrons and the free migration of foreign artists to Vienna in the baroque period; still less with the background of an aristocrat of Savoyard–Italian origin who had been born and bred in Paris. The choice of Fischer von Erlach is more likely to have been made because he was surveyor of the Imperial buildings and prominent as designer of the Emperor's great new garden palace of Schönbrunn.[2] Eugen was, in fact, employing the most eminent local architect of the day.

The site of the Stadtpalais was close to the Imperial palace of the Hofburg. But, as elsewhere, the demand for a grand design was hampered by the mediaeval lay-out of the city. The cramped impression Vienna gave was described by Lady Mary Wortley Montagu during a visit there in 1716:

'The streets are very close, and so narrow, one cannot observe the fine fronts of the palaces, though many of them very well deserve observation, being truly magnificent, all built of fine white stone, and excessive high, the town being so much too little for the number of the people that desire to live in it, the builders seem to have projected to repair that misfortune by clapping one town on the top of another, most of the houses being of five, and some of them of six storeys. . . .'[3]

The Stadtpalais is a masterpiece of architectural dexterity. Built in the Himmelpfortgasse, a street no wider than a lane, Fischer[4] designed the façade so as to be viewed obliquely. Great flat Ionic pilasters rise from the *piano nobile*; the windows are crowned with the emblems of battle—warriors' helmets and standards; over the three doorways are balconies resting on voluted consoles and garlanded with putti and vases. Above the main windows are gigantic crests; and thirteen statues of gods, now lost, crowned the attic. The façade thus combined severity in the architecture with richness in the decoration. Inside, the chief feature is the famous staircase,

[1] B. Grimschitz, *Das Belvedere in Wien*, 1946, p. 6.
[2] He had been appointed in 1689 to teach architecture to the eleven-year-old heir apparent. H. Sedlmayr, *J. B. Fischer von Erlach*, 1956, p. 6.
[3] Letter to the Countess of Mar, September 8, 1716, *Letters and Works of Lady Mary Wortley Montagu*, op. cit., I, pp. 235–6.
[4] The palace was later extended by Johann Lucas von Hildebrandt.

miraculously contrived in a restricted space, which coils powerfully up past bowed colossi before dividing into two branches. The great achievement of the staircase is the impression one gets of light long before reaching the top—a typical baroque effect, paralleled by the symbolism of the decoration: the lower part of the staircase is dominated by a statue of Hercules; above, in the ceiling, are depicted the sun-god Apollo, the fall of Icarus, and Fame.

We must now take account of a surprising turn in Eugen's architectural life—even before his first palace is completed. He suddenly ceases to employ Fischer and begins to commission Johann Lucas von Hildebrandt. Why he switched his patronage is uncertain. It may have been less a deliberate falling out with Fischer than a chance falling in with Hildebrandt, who had served under him as a field architect in the Imperial Army in Piedmont during the campaigns there in 1695–6. Born in Genoa and trained as an architect in Rome, Hildebrandt was a versatile character, not unlike his contemporary Vanbrugh. Eugen first engaged him to design the interior, and then later to extend the façade of the *Stadtpalais*. He also gave him detailed instructions for the building of a country palace at Ráckeve on the island of Csepel on the Danube. This work, which started in 1701 and took twenty years to complete, resulted in a three-winged, single-storey building. A two-tiered central hall was crowned by a magnificent octgonal cupola. It was an island pavilion in the baroque style the originality and charm of which are still discernible today despite two centuries of dilapidation. The great cupola was destroyed by fire in 1819, the grand hall was turned into a granary in the last century and the trees in the courtyard were allowed to grow up and smother the building. Yet conversion might surely have been less merciful than neglect. Ráckeve remains an enchanting place: the Danube flows by on one side; on the other a water meadow, peopled with ducks and geese, merges into the village green; and between them the disintegrating roof-tops and statues of the palace can just be seen amidst the overgrown vegetation.[1]

Meanwhile, in Vienna, Eugen and Hildebrandt proceeded to plan and build the grandiose complex of the two Belvedere palaces, which have been virtually unaltered to this day.[2] The Lower Belvedere, completed in 1716, is a single-story building of which the main

[1] At the time of writing, February 1963, the Hungarian Government were engaged upon an ambitious scheme for renovating the palace.

[2] For a detailed account of the Lower and Upper Belvedere see B. Grimschitz, *Johann Lucas von Hildebrandt*, 1959, and *Das Belvedere in Wien*, 1946.

architectural features are the broken line of the roof, the pavilions either end and in the centre the grand entrance hall, walled with marble and rising to a height of two stories. It was designed to lead, without the punctilio of steps, straight into the garden. In 1717, the year of Belgrade, Eugen commissioned the Elector of Bavaria's gardener, Dominique Girard, to come to Vienna to help him with the laying out of the palace garden and fountains.[1] Eugen's aim was to create something both classical and new. The idea was simple: palace and garden were to be one, and the whole was to be formal without being portentous, and gay without being frivolous. The lawns, fountains, avenues and statues were to merge imperceptibly into the palace.

To this garden he brought rare plants and trees from all over the world. He even won the botanists' crown—he had a new species of myrtle named after him. He also indulged a new passion, one that was not in the usual catalogue of patronage, but which may have responded to an unrequited *Wanderlust*; he started to collect wild animals. With characteristic thoroughness he succeeded in building up one of the biggest zoos of his time, a menagerie of fifty species of mammals. His fantasy soared further. He set about gathering strange birds—much as his mother had done at their home in France many years previously. His favourite bird was an eagle which he fed himself by hand every day when he was at the Belvedere. Scarcely a ship from the East could put into a European port without Eugen enquiring whether it had brought some rare bird that he could purchase for his aviary. The Imperial Consul-General in Cadiz was given standing instructions to keep a special lookout for ships from the Canaries.

The Upper Belvedere, built by Hildebrandt between 1719 and 1724, is a much more grandiose palace than the lower one. It consists of a series of pavilions with cupolas. From the garden side you enter a loggia of three arches beneath a curved pediment. Inside is the caryatid hall, with four columns of giants—the work of Mattielli. The palace is richly decorated throughout with frescoes and ceiling paintings and with baroque furniture, ornaments, chandeliers and mirrors.

After Eugen's death the Upper Belvedere passed into the possession

---

[1] There is evidence that the waterworks were begun a year or two earlier. Thus Graf von Schönborn wrote in 1715: 'A beginning is to be made in early November with Prince Eugen's famous water *das famose Wasser des printz Eugeny* costing about 20 m. florins.'

of the Habsburgs, becoming the backcloth to many of the ups and downs in the family's fortunes. From there, for instance, the Arch-duke Franz Ferdinand set out for Serajevo in 1914. Later, when it became the property of the State, it was used for conferences—much as Lancaster House is used in London; there, for instance, the Aus-trian State Treaty was signed in 1955. Both it and the Lower Palace are now galleries of Austrian painting and sculpture. In the high central hall of the Lower Belvedere stands the enormous white marble statue of Eugen by Balthasar Permoser. Symbolizing alike his fame and modesty, it represents him transported by cherubs, trampling the enemy underfoot and with one hand trying to muffle the mouth of the horn by which Fame seeks to spread his renown throughout the world.[1]

Today the Belvedere is no longer in the country. Vienna has grown up on all sides, yet this only adds to its beauty; it makes all the more dramatic the transformation of view which occurs when you turn off from the busy thoroughfare of the Rennweg and pass through the unimposing entrance to gaze suddenly upon the ex-quisitely proportioned garden leading up to the baroque grandeur of the upper palace; a change of scene scarcely less climacteric than that which occurs when you pass through the ceremonial archway at Woodstock and catch sight of the palace and park at Blenheim. The two palaces most closely identified with Eugen's and Marlborough's names, dissimilar though they are in size and style, are alike in their sudden impact and in their evocation of their respective masters.

Yet even the Winter Palace in Vienna, the Belvedere Palaces and the island pavilion in Hungary were insufficient apparently to satisfy Eugen's appetite for building. As compensation for his loss of the Governor-Generalship of the Netherlands at the end of 1724, the Emperor gave him an estate and two villages in the Marchfeld in Lower Austria. They were 'to provide an enjoyable place for outings and relaxation'.[2] Charles went on to explain with characteristic tact

---

[1] The statue was executed by Permoser in Dresden between 1719–21. There are insights into the ways of eighteenth century patronage in the letters between Eugen and a friend in Dresden which deal with Permoser's work on the statue. (See H. Beschorner, *Permoser's Apotheosen Prinz Eugen's und Augusts des Starken*, in Neues Archiv für Sächsische Geschichte und Altertumskunde, XXXIII, 1912, pp. 301–31.) The face of Eugen was done from a portrait. When the statue arrived in Vienna Eugen's Private Secretary, Ignaz Koch, reported that it was 'not entirely to the taste of His Highness'. This evidence scarcely sup-ports Mr Francis Haskell's statement (*Patrons and Painters*, 1963, p. 201) that Eugen 'himself designed' the Apotheosis.

[2] A. Arneth, op. cit., III, p. 80.

how important this was since the prolongation of his life was a matter of close interest both to himself and the State.

Eugen was already in possession of a property in the Marchfeld, Schlosshof, which he soon extended by the purchase of the adjoining Schloss, Engelhartstetten. The fertile plain of the Marchfeld lying between the left bank of the Danube and the right bank of the March was Eugen's favourite haunt outside Vienna. He could reach it much more quickly—either by road or water—than his property in Hungary. He loved the vast triangle of luxuriant vegetation in the elbow of the two rivers. He loved the billowing trees, the shimmering fields of corn, the wide horizons and the associations: here was the last outpost of the Romans against the Germanic Marcomanni and Quadi. Here Marcus Aurelius died in 180. Here, a millennium later, Rudolph defeated Ottocar of Bohemia, with the result that Vienna became the seat of the Habsburgs. With Hildebrandt's help Eugen reconstructed Schlosshof, making it luxurious inside and strong as a fortress outside to provide for its security in 'caso di necessità', as the architect described it. The park surrounding the place was extensive and became a favourite hunting place—not that Eugen much approved of the excessive time devoted to the sport in his day.

How beautiful the baroque Palace of Schlosshof must have been, with its stone steps and parapets leading in a horseshoe to the gardens and cascades beside the river, can be seen today in Bernardo Bellotto's paintings, done between 1758-1760, which hang in the Kunsthistorisches Museum in Vienna. In 1755 Maria Theresa bought Schlosshof. Later a new floor was added, hardly helping the proportions, but vandalism did not entirely triumph until the end of the nineteenth century when the original palace and gardens were completely reconstructed to serve the needs of an artillery school.

Apart from enabling him to indulge his architectural ambitions such palaces came to serve the essential purpose of housing his vast collections. In Paris Eugen was known as 'curieux des belles choses';[1] in Italy he had the reputation of a Maecenas—a 'generous protector and supreme lover of the fine arts and especially those of

[1] P. J. Mariette, *Abecedario*, ed. P. de Chennevières and A. de Montaiglon, 1853–4, II, p. 260.

our native land'.[1] The list of artists who worked for Eugen is long: there were Italians, among them Giuseppe Maria Crespi and Francesco Solimena; but there were also Dutch, Flemish, German and Austrian painters.[2] He sat several times for his portrait, including once to Godfrey Kneller during his visit to London. Austria's finest medallists cast a series of his portraits in commemoration of his victories; and two artists were long employed by him in depicting the scenes of his battles.[3]

Eugen took a close personal interest in the main Italian painters whom he employed. He bestowed many honours and favours on Crespi, and in 1716, in return for the gift of a *Nativity*[4] at Christmastime sent Crespi profuse thanks, one hundred scudi and an honorific certificate declaring him to be one of his household.[5]

He treated Solimena with the formality and respect due to an old and highly successful painter of international fame. But with a third Italian painter, Marcantonio Chiarini, his relations were less formal. He often visited the painter when he was at work on the scaffolding in the Stadtpalais in 1697, and treated him generously for his work in the Lower Belvedere, carried out in two visits to Vienna in 1709-14 and from 1715 onwards. Like Crespi, Chiarini was honoured with the title of member of Eugen's household; and in his honorific diploma his son Guido, a musician, was similarly mentioned.[6]

Eugen the collector of pictures—as distinct from patron of living artists—appears in a Dutch drawing of the early eighteenth century which shows him looking at pictures in an Amsterdam dealer's shop. This is significant because there is little doubt that most of Eugen's large collection of pictures was acquired by purchase. Nothing is known to have come to him by inheritance, and only two pictures

---

[1] G. P. Cavazzoni Zanotti, *Storia dell' Accademia Clementina di Bologna*, 1739, I, p. 275.

[2] See Appendix B for an account of some of the artists who worked for Eugen and of his collection. See also T. von Frimmel, *Geschichte der Wiener Gemäldesammlungen*, 1899, p. 16.

[3] One of them was Jan van Huchtenburgh whose pictures are in Turin. See Appendix C on The Sale of Eugen's Pictures.

[4] Presumably the picture now in the Turin Gallery.

[5] Zanotti, loc. cit., L. Crespi in *G. Bottari, Raccolta di Lettere*, 1759, III, pp. 316–17.

[6] Zanotti, op. cit., II, pp. 272–8.

as gifts. The total number of his pictures at his death was probably about four hundred. But this includes two hundred and three at his country residence at Schlosshof,[1] few of which are likely to have been important.[2] Eugen's picture collection has not survived as a whole. At his death it was inherited, like all his possessions, by his niece, Princess Anna Victoria of Savoy.[3] She at once decided to sell everything, and has thus aroused the anguished scorn of every Austrian to this day. But, though she was determined to get rid of the pictures as profitably as possible, she agreed in the end to dispose of them at less than the maximum price in order to keep them together. They were bought by Charles Emanuel III, King of Sardinia and the head of the House of Savoy.[4]

As a result of this sale an important part of Eugen's collection can be seen today in the Turin Gallery. Many of the pictures which the King bought have disappeared. Some, including a version of Titian's Venus and Adonis, may have perished when Charles Emanuel ordered a fire of thirty-eight pictures containing nude figures which his confessor had persuaded him were indecent. Yet ninety-one pictures can still be identified in Turin as Eugen's.[5] In addition, four important pictures once in Turin are in public galleries in France, Belgium and the United States. In Vienna itself, in the Kunsthistorisches Museum there are the two Crespis, one Solimena and battle pictures by Parrocel, which must all have been acquired by the Emperor. In Eugen's Vienna palaces there are many ceiling paintings and a few other pictures still *in situ*. Finally, we have the details of the lost Turin pictures which are listed in the catalogue which Princess Anna Victoria produced in 1737. Though its attributions cannot be relied on, it at least shows the subjects of the pictures and who were claimed to be the painters.

We are thus in a fairly good position to judge the character and quality of Eugen's collection. The finest of the earlier Italian pictures

[1] T. von Frimmel, op. cit., pp. 31–2.
[2] See Appendix B.
[3] See Chapter XXI, p. 290.
[4] A. Vesme, *Sull' acquisto fatto da Carlo Emmanuele III Re di Sardegna della quadreria del Principe Eugenio di Savoia: ricerche documentate*, in Miscellanea di Storia Italiana, 1887, XXV, pp. 161–256. For further details of the negotiations leading up to the sale see Appendix C.
[5] The figure of ninety-one is based on Vesme, op. cit., and the further researches of T. von Frimmel, *Die Gallerie des Prinzen Eugen von Savoyen*, in Berichte und Mittheilungen des Alterthums-Vereines zu Wien, 1890, pp. 31–40. Vesme's excellent *Catalogo della Regia Pinacoteca di Torino*, 1909, also notes the pictures which came from Eugen's collection. Unfortunately there is no more modern full catalogue for the Galleria Sabauda (as it is now called) in Turin.

were probably Poussin's *St Margaret* (Turin);[1] a Benedetto Castiglione landscape (now lost);[2] and Guido Reni's St John Baptist (Turin), a late work of the master showing the Baptist as a beautiful young man. Whatever the truth of the theory that Eugen was homosexual,[3] works such as this and the Greek bronze of 'The Praying Boy'[4] show that he was not unappreciative of the young male form. There were also good Albanis, now in Brussels (*Adam and Eve*) and Turin (*Salmacis and Ermafrodito*); other works by Guido or his school; and an authentic Salviati now in Turin. Among contemporary Italian pictures the Crespis and Solimenas stand out. But the pictures ascribed to the great names of Titian, Raphael, Correggio, Guercino and Holbein were in fact school works, or copies, or the work of lesser painters.[5] There was far greater strength in Eugen's Dutch and Flemish pictures. They outnumbered the Italian works by three to one; and included many original works and some masterpieces.

The collection thus contained many paintings of high quality but only a few masterpieces of the first rank, certainly fewer than he and his contemporaries supposed. Notable features are Eugen's concentration on the seventeenth century, and within that century some preference for the Bolognese school and an extreme devotion to Dutch and Flemish painting. It is evident that he either possessed great knowledge himself of the painting of the Low Countries or was well advised by active agents. Certainly no commander in modern times except Wellington has owned, let alone collected, a comparable gallery.

If the quality of Eugen's pictures was uneven, his famous library and his large collection of prints are beyond censure. Their cost and luxury are mentioned with astonishment in contemporary accounts; but it is the quality, rarity and condition of their contents which entitle Eugen to a place in the first rank of book and print collectors.

His library of fifteen thousand printed books and two hundred

[1] Published as an original by Roberto Longhi (Bull. de la Societé Poussin, 1948, p. 5ff.) and exhibited at the Poussin exhibition in Paris in 1960 (no. 58).

[2] See F. Haskell, *Patrons and Painters*, 1963, p. 341, where there is also evidence of another 'Poussin' in Eugen's collection.

[3] See Chapter XVIII.

[4] See p. 263.

[5] See Appendix B.

and thirty-seven illuminated and other manuscripts[1] was purchased by the Emperor and is now preserved as a single collection in the Austrian National Library in Vienna, in the place of honour in a splendid baroque setting beneath Fischer von Erlach's cupola. Eugen was a bibliophile. Already in 1716 Jean Baptiste Rousseau was able to write: 'The Prince's library is very extensive and consists of exceptionally fine books beautifully bound. But what is most remarkable is that there is scarcely a book in it which the Prince has not read or at least looked through. It is difficult to believe that a man who almost alone carries such a public burden for all Europe, who is Field-Marshal and the Emperor's Prime Minister, can find the time to read almost as much as someone who has nothing else to do.'[2] Rousseau was a sycophant and not a completely reliable witness, but he seems, on the basis of other evidence, to have been recording the truth in this respect. Shortly afterwards, when Eugen's enemies were doing their best to destroy him, he confided to St Saphorin, the British representative: 'Come what may I can live quite happily on an income of ten thousand gulden, and I have such a supply of excellent books that I can never be bored.'[3]

The collecting of this library was the work of some twenty-five years. In England in 1712, as we have seen, Eugen could not withstand the 'irresistible temptations' (as Gibbon called them) of London's bookshops.[4] He also had an international network of agents working to execute his commissions for books in The Hague, Paris, London, Brussels, Milan, Rome and Bologna. Eugen himself was in the habit of writing to authors for copies of their new works; and even war did not interrupt the pursuit of books. Thus we find him on June 1, 1717, at the height of preparations for the capture of Belgrade, writing to Jean Baptiste Dubos for a copy of his work on painting and poetry.[5]

Since Eugen was the great nephew of the founder of the Bibliothèque Mazarine in Paris, and in his youth had read a good deal and been thought fit to become an abbé, it is hardly necessary to look for persons who may have 'influenced' him into becoming a biblio-

---

[1] A. Arneth, op. cit., III, p. 523, and W. Suchier, op. cit., p. 27. In 1730 the total of printed books had reached 14,000 (J. G. Keysler, *Neueste Reisen*, 1751, p. 1224 quoted by Suchier, p. 17).

[2] Letter from J. B. Rousseau to M. Brossette, June 30, 1716, *Lettres de Rousseau*, op. cit., pp. 98–9.

[3] W. Suchier, op. cit., p. 14.

[4] See Chapter XIV, p. 202.

[5] A. Arneth, op. cit., III, p. 71.

phile. Undoubtedly he took advice from many, including his friend Domenico Passionei, bibliophile, connoisseur and Papal Nuncio in Vienna.[1] The Sardinian envoy in 1737 went so far as to say that Eugen's library had been 'chosen with great care by the Nuncio Passionei and by other capable persons'.[2] But this does less than justice to a quarter of a century's sustained collecting and to the decisive direction needed for the formation of a great library.

The library was housed in three rooms in the Stadtpalais. The largest room contained books of all classes, uniformly bound in morocco, mostly in red, with gilt lettering and embellishments on the spine, and with the arms of Savoy impressed in gilt on both covers of every volume. 'And so (a contemporary description runs) a particularly fine appearance is made by the boxwood bookshelves, every row of them being mounted with green cloth because of the dust.'[3] The lower shelves contained Eugen's great collection of engraved portraits and other prints. As Eugen was specially interested in plants and animals, there were many fine botanical and zoological books, drawings and engravings.[4]

The next room was furnished like the previous one, but was also painted by the German artist Heinitz with allegorical figures, books and instruments symbolic of Philosophy, Geography, Mathematics and Medicine. Over one of the doors a youth sat turning the pages of a book. This room was devoted to books on ancient and modern history. It also contained a celebrated and costly 'atlas'—really a survey of the world—perhaps the finest in existence at that time.[5] Another special collection, carefully assembled over the years from many separate engravings, recorded festivals and celebrations, a

[1] Passionei (1682–1761) was Nuncio in Vienna from 1730, and was made a cardinal in 1738. He became Prefect of the Vatican Library.

[2] Canale to d'Ormea, August 17, 1737, Vesme, op. cit., p. 180.

[3] Quoted by W. Suchier, op. cit., pp. 20 ff.

[4] Two of the finest engraved books were obtained in Paris by Pierre-Jean Mariette (according to A. Arneth, op. cit., III, p. 523): the *Recueil d'Oyseaux les plus Rares tirez de la menagerie Royalle du Parc de Versailles*, with coloured engravings by the King's painter Nicolas Robert (5 vols., 1676); and *Recueil de plantes cultivées dans le jardin royal à Paris*, done to the order of Colbert (10 vols., 1680). Eugen paid 1,200 livres for them in 1728.

[5] This was the *Atlas Major seu Geographia Blauiana*, an enlargement of the well-known atlas in eleven volumes published in 1662 by the Amsterdam geographer Johannes Blaeu. Eugen's unique edition was expanded to fifty folios by the addition of five hundred and seventy-one hand-coloured drawings and engravings by Dutch artists of various cities, palaces and countries. The artists included Domeer, Esselens, Moucheron, Saftleven, Schellinks and Zeeman. Eugen bought the Atlas in 1732 from the bookseller Moetjens of The Hague for 6,000 gulden (A. Arneth, op. cit., III, p. 523).

'Recueil de Fêtes et Pompes' in many volumes which reminds us that Eugen was collecting at the height of the scenic and festive age of the baroque. From this room a narrow passage hung with plans of buildings led to a third room containing what would now probably be considered the rarest, most valuable and most interesting sections of the library: incunabula, illuminated manuscripts and a collection of books on the Index. The illuminated manuscripts included works of Greek, Persian, Turkish, French, Flemish, Dutch and Italian origin and ranged from a Greek New Testament of the twelfth century to Greek manuscripts illuminated at Bucharest and in Wallachia about the year 1700; and the collection was particularly rich in later mediaeval French and Flemish works.[1]

The library was not without English associations. It contained, to name a few of its first editions of famous English books: Brian Walton's *Polyglot Bible* (London, 1657), Colin Campbell's *Vitruvius Britannicus* (London, 1715), and Hobbes' *Leviathan* (London, 1651). It seems likely that Lady Mary Wortley Montagu did not know the library's full resources when she wrote her feline account of her visit in 1717. 'Prince Eugene was so polite as to shew me his library yesterday; we found him attended by Rousseau and his favourite Count Bonneval . . . the library, though not very ample, is well chosen; but as the Prince will admit into it no editions but what are beautiful and pleasing to the eye, and as there are nevertheless numbers of excellent books that are but indifferently printed, this finnikin and foppish taste makes many disagreeable chasms in this collection. The books are pompously bound in Turkey leather, and two of the most famous bookbinders of Paris were expressly sent for to do this work. Bonneval pleasantly told me that there were several

[1] Three manuscripts, perhaps, are of outstanding interest, different in character but of equal importance, the one for French painting, the second as a unique historical source, and the third for Eugen's own life. One is the manuscript illuminated in France in the third quarter of the fifteenth century for Duke René of Anjou to illustrate his own romance, the *Livre du Cuer d'Amours Espris*. Possibly acquired by Eugen from Prince Charles of Lorraine (E. Trenkler, *Das Livre du cuer d'amours espris des Herzogs René von Anjou*, 1946, p. 15). Its sixteen half-page miniatures depicting the hero's courtly and pathetic adventures belong to the finest achievements of French book painting. Of no artistic but of unique historical value is the Peutinger Table (so-called after the German antiquary Peutinger who once owned it), the copy (made in Germany in the thirteenth century) of a fourth-century road map of the Roman Empire, which Eugen acquired in 1715. Again we find him consulting the French expert Dubos about the purchase of this work, on the very eve of battle against the Turks. Above all Eugen treasured Leibniz's manuscript which the philosopher had given him, and which he kept locked up in a case and showed gingerly to visitors. See Chapter XVIII, p. 244.

quartos on the art of war, that were bound with the skins of spahis and janissaries; and this jest, which was indeed elegant, raised a smile of pleasure on the grave countenance of the famous warrior.'[1]

There is a detail which illustrates Eugen's constant preoccupation with his library, as it also reminds us of the limited nature of war then compared with today. His confidant, von Hohendorff, who had accompanied him to London in 1712 and no doubt nosed about the bookshops there with him, was in Paris in 1713, and on Eugen's instructions he commissioned a bookbinder, Etienne Boyet, whose father was bookbinder to Louis XIV, to go to Vienna on a large salary and look after the Prince's library. Boyet left Paris while the war was still on, took up the post and remained in Vienna for over twenty years.

Like the library, Eugen's very large collection of prints and drawings was purchased in 1737 by the Emperor and has also passed into the Austrian national collections.[2] The prints number two hundred and seventeen portfolios of portraits and two hundred and ninety of engravings of other sorts.[3] The great quantity of portraits shows a predilection of Eugen's carried out on a princely scale. Indeed, the whole collection struck contemporaries as one of the wonders of his library. The traveller Johann Georg Keysler writes of the great portfolios of portraits, bound in red morocco with gilt backs and titles, and grouped according to the various countries: 'Portraits of famous military heroes, potentates, ladies, scholars etc. . . . Their number increases daily, and there are in fact already 48 volumes for France, 61 for Germany, 10 for the United Netherlands, 9 for the Spanish Netherlands, 2 for Lorraine, 13 for Great Britain, and in particular 13 for religious orders.'[4] Leporello's catalogue of Don Giovanni's conquests does not show a keener appetite. For the painter Huchtenburgh the print collection was one of the strongest proofs of Eugen's connoisseurship: '*Il fait même une Collection d'Estampes, si nombreuse et si bien choisie qu'elle passe avec raison pour une des plus riches de l'Europe.*'[5]

The contents and quality of these collections of prints and drawings

---

[1] *Letters and Works of Lady Mary Wortley Montagu*, op. cit., I, p. 266.

[2] The prints are in the Austrian National Library and the drawings in the Albertina in Vienna.

[3] A. Arneth, op. cit., III, p. 523, apparently describing the collection as it was in his day.

[4] J. G. Keysler, op. cit., p. 1224.

[5] Huchtenburgh's preface to J. Dumont's *Batailles gagnées par le sérénissime Prince Eugène*, 1725.

cannot be studied in detail here.[1] But there is evidence of the same rigorous search for quality which was characteristic of Eugen as a book collector, and of a determination to make his print collection as complete as possible. In the year 1717 a young man who was already an expert came from Paris to Vienna and worked on Eugen's collection. Pierre-Jean Mariette (1694-1774) is perhaps the first of all French connoisseurs and collectors of prints and drawings.[2] Looking back on his work in Vienna, he wrote: 'Of Principe Eugenio's rich collection of prints I have a full knowledge, more than anyone, because I put it in order and I made the catalogue of it.'[3]

Mariette stayed nearly two years in Vienna. Eugen's collection must already have been large. Some part in its creation had probably been played by Pierre Mariette, father of Pierre-Jean and well known as an engraver and print seller of Paris. For in the years before 1717, Pierre-Jean relates, 'my father was in correspondence with M le Prince Eugène'. The house of Mariette in Paris may thus have been a principal supplier of engravings to the French-born Eugen. It is certain that there was some business relationship; for the elder Mariette was the agent in one of Eugen's most spectacular purchases: the antique Greek bronze statue of the so-called *Praying Boy* now in Berlin (a work of the fourth century B.C. related to the school of Lysippus). Pierre-Jean Mariette recalls how his father acted as intermediary in the sale of the statue, which was at Vaux-le-Vicomte in the possession of the Marquis de Belle Isle, whose father Fouquet had acquired it in Italy on Le Brun's advice. Negotiations with Eugen at first came to nothing, 'because it did not suit the Prince's finances which were committed to more urgent expenses'.[4] (This was presumably at the time of heavy expenditure on the Belvedere.) But in 1717 the older Mariette secured it for Eugen. It remained in one of his palaces in Vienna until his death, and subsequently was

[1] No account of these collections has yet been published. The only contemporary reference to the drawings appears to be that in *Des grossen Feldherrns Eugenii . . . Heldenthaten*, Theil 6, Nürnberg, 1739, cf. W. Suchier, op. cit., p. 21.

[2] '*Le plus illustre des amateurs français*' was the opinion of J. Dumesnil (*Histoire des plus célèbres amateurs français et de leurs relations avec les artistes*, 1856, I, p. 7). The first volume of this work is devoted entirely to Mariette and is the only valuable account of him. When over seventy, Mariette learned English with the object of translating and commenting on Walpole's *Anecdotes of Painting*.

[3] Mariette to Cavaliere Gaburri, January 28, 1732, in G. Bottari, *Raccolta di Lettere*, ed. S. Ticozzi, 1822, II, p. 330.

[4] P. J. Mariette, op. cit., II, p. 260.

acquired by Frederick the Great who placed it on the terrace at Sans-Souci.

In Pierre-Jean Mariette Eugen was in contact with the foremost expert of the century; and he in turn benefited from intimacy with his patron's collections. Eugen was highly satisfied with the young man's work in his library, as he told correspondents, and in 1718 when Mariette formed the project of an Italian tour Eugen willingly helped him with letters of introduction. Several times in later years Mariette appears as Eugen's agent, executing a commission of trust in Paris, supervising an order for French furnishings of gilt bronze, supplying books, and above all seeking out and advising on prints. Thus on July 27, 1724, we find Eugen writing to him with the request *'de continuer les soins à me rendre la collection de portraits la plus complette qu'il sera possible'.*[1] The surviving documents in which Eugen and Mariette refer to each other breathe the spirit of friendship and respect. The patron was even able to help the expert, and Mariette was proud to write of Eugen's generosity in giving him one of two sets of engravings by Stefano della Bella which the Prince had succeeded in obtaining from the Grand Duke of Tuscany 'after many entreaties'.[2] The relations between the military genius who was a collector and the great connoisseur who served him are among the most creditable in the history of art.

If Mariette was the principal, he was certainly not the only connoisseur upon whom Eugen depended. Friends, relatives, Austrian representatives abroad and professional art dealers all contributed to the growing collections in the Vienna palaces. The names of many of these agents are no doubt lost. It can only be conjectured, for instance, that in the purchase of his many illuminated manuscripts of Greek origin, some of which date from Eugen's own time, he was assisted by von Hohendorff, who was familiar with the Greek lands and language. Like other collectors in the eighteenth century Eugen looked especially to Italy as the great reservoir of antique and modern works of art. Three of the earliest statues excavated at Herculaneum reached him as a gift from the pioneer archaeologist Prince Elbeuf. Eugen placed them in the Belvedere where they must have been seen by a connoisseur who seems to have been—at least in Eugen's later years—his principal agent for works of art from Italy. Alessandro Albani (1692-1779) is famous

[1] A. Arneth, op. cit., III, p. 522.
[2] Mariette to Cavaliere Gaburri, November 11, 1731, G. Bottari, op. cit., II, p. 300.

as the cardinal who was the patron of Winckelmann and creator of the neo-classical Villa Albani in Rome with its collection of antiques. Early in his career (1720) he came as papal envoy to Vienna. His friendship with Eugen must have begun at this time and it continued after his return to Italy. Though not yet thirty when he came to Vienna, his knowledge of art had so impressed Eugen that he was soon instructing an agent in Rome that nothing should be sent to Vienna unless it had passed Albani's scrutiny.

Such, in outline, were Eugen's activities as builder, patron and collector. In some departments, notably in pictures, others have surpassed him in quality, but taking his buildings, gardens and collections of all sorts together it is hard to think of any private citizen in Europe who surrounded himself with more splended works of art. In the words of Francis Haskell, the learned historian of patronage in the age of the Baroque, Eugen was 'the most grandiose and influential private patron in Europe'.[1]

[1] F. Haskell, op. cit., p. 201.

CHAPTER XX

EUGEN AS DIPLOMAT
AND STATESMAN

FROM AS early as 1703, when he first became President of the Imperial War Council, Eugen had been concerned with the high-level diplomatic activity inseparable from war. The working out of the Blenheim campaign with Wratislaw and Marlborough was an early example of these interlocking rôles. But inevitably in his early years, when he was in command of armies in the field for much of the year, the military side of his life predominated, though he did find the opportunity to clash on various foreign issues with Prince von Salm during the latter's term of power under Joseph I.[1] It was not really until 1712 that he started to play a leading part as a diplomat; and, as so often happened in his life, England provided the occasion. The English Government's threat to betray the Grand Alliance and walk out of the war induced the Emperor Charles, in one of the first acts of his reign, to send Eugen to London.[2] Unsuccessful though the mission was, it gave him both valuable experience and the chance, which he seized, to show his diplomatic talents to the Emperor. Then, after Wratislaw's death at the end of the year, when Eugen no longer felt he had a kindred spirit on foreign affairs at Court, he realized that he would have to exert himself more directly in Vienna if the Spanish courtiers were not to become too powerful, and if their spokesman, the opportunist Hofkanzler Sinzendorff, was to be kept in check. Eugen's increasing intervention in foreign policy was prompted, at this stage, not so much by a wish

[1] See Chapter IX, p. 125.
[2] See Chapter XIV.

to make some positive personal contribution, as by his desire to counter the Spanish *camarilla*. How quickly he succeeded in establishing his authority in diplomacy was shown by the wide discretion given him to negotiate the peace treaty of Rastadt at the end of the Spanish Succession War.

He was largely instrumental in getting the Emperor to go to war with the Turks in 1716. Nevertheless it was not till after the last Turkish campaign the following year that his status as President of the Imperial War Council and Chairman of the Secret Conference gave him the dominating position on paper in foreign affairs. Thereafter there was a period of eclipse while the Spanish set were in the ascendant, but after their decline in the mid-1720's his influence became paramount in practice as well as in theory. From then on, for a decade, his was the predominant voice in Habsburg diplomacy at a time when, in the absence of any general war, and with communications still primitive, the business of diplomacy was a venerable profession requiring almost artistic skill and wielding enormous power.

His methods were unorthodox. He conducted his diplomacy by means of a voluminous personal correspondence with the Emperor's representatives in the various capitals. Much of it was kept secret from the other Austrian ministers; most of his own letters were drafted in Germany by his secretary, from 1725 on the invaluable Ignaz Koch. The reason for using this private channel was not the love of mystery for its own sake but the confidential nature of the correspondence, a great deal of which was about the sensitive business of suborning and paying agents, and about the intelligence they produced. The beginning of the eighteenth century was a golden age of bribery and espionage, and Eugen had no scruples about opening up new seams for the Monarchy in promising foreign courts. Nor was he different from many of the statesmen of his, or for that matter of any other, age, in tending to give more credence to what he learnt through covert than overt channels and to what he paid for, rather than what was given.

Much of his correspondence is concerned with details. Thus we learn from his letter sent in the autumn of 1730 to Seckendorff, the Imperial representative in Berlin, that he would be sending him 2,000 ducats and 688 gulden in two pouches for secret pensions and disbursements to agents; and we are told that for pensions to the Prussian Court Seckendorff estimated a sum of 5,100 ducats and 8,160 gulden for one year, which suggests that the diplomatic bag must have been some burden for the eighteenth-century courier.[1]

What was the mainspring of Eugen's foreign policy during the decade when his influence was supreme? With the failure of France's bid for hegemony, no single power could now hope to dominate the European continent; each sought allies; none trusted the others not to desert. It was a time of protracted Congresses and shifting alliances; but beneath the brittle surface it was apparent that Eugen had a particular theme in addition to the pursuit of peace. His underlying aim was to create a lasting counterweight to the Bourbons, whose hostility to the Emperor he regarded as fundamentally ineradicable. European politics for much of the time were dominated by the triumvirate of Walpole in London, Fleury in Paris and Eugen in Vienna, all interested passionately in preserving peace, each governed less by principle than by expediency. But Eugen was also guided by a less rational faith, not a religious faith, not a belief in any idea of Christian solidarity, but a vision of the destiny of the Habsburg Monarchy, the right and duty of the Monarch to dominate and govern his hereditary possessions. He always stood firmly, if somewhat romantically, for the interests of the House of Habsburg, as distinct from those of the Holy Roman Empire. In agreement with Wratislaw and in opposition first to Salm and then to Schönborn, he believed in backing the House rather than the Empire whenever there was a conflict between the two. He objected to the disjointed nature of the Empire, and resented the insistence of the Princes on their privileges. He was naturally impatient that the Imperial Diet, for all its theoretical responsibilities, had no control over taxation, and that the Princes had even succeeded in maintaining control over the upkeep of fortresses within their territories. The need for greater centralization and administrative efficiency, if Austria was to keep up with the other powers of Europe in the changing scene of the eighteenth century, was much greater than elsewhere yet even more difficult to satisfy. The Habsburg lands were far-flung and poor in communications. Their economies were backward. Their ruling nobility, the owners most them of enormous estates, were profoundly conservative and deeply jealous of their rights and privileges.[2] The position has been summed up by a recent writer: 'If the nobility in eighteenth-century England held power without privileges, and the reverse be true of France, the Austrian nobility at the beginning

---

[1] See Max Braubach, *Die Geheimdiplomatie Des Prinzen Eugen von Savoyen*, 1962.

[2] cf. M. S. Anderson, *Europe in the Eighteenth Century*, op. cit., pp. 97–8.

of the eighteenth century and almost up to the middle of it can be said to have held both: power and privileges, or at any rate, a considerable measure of power and very wide privileges.'[1] The lack of adequate central authority was one of the reasons, Eugen believed, why Vienna was always short of funds, as it was also one of the root causes of the difficulty in maintaining a strong army. He was not, however, a supporter of absolute control at the centre. There must be some allowance for regionalism if the Monarchy was to retain its universalist character. He believed in moderate change, not revolution; although he does not appear to have conceived it his duty to bring this about. He wanted to see a monarchy widespread yet more closely knit. He did not believe in unlimited expansion, but he believed that a greater unity would make possible the creation of a stable central European block which would best serve the Empire and maintain the European balance of power.

Ironically, in an era outstanding for the mutability of international engagements, when treaties were only made to be broken and friendships only formed to be reversed, the Emperor attached fanatical importance to securing the formal recognition by all the states of Europe of the Pragmatic Sanction.[2] This objective is, in fact, almost the only constant discernible in the game of general post played by the leaders of Europe in these years. Eugen did not sympathize with Charles' obsession. His view was that the Emperor should spend less effort in trying to get promises of recognition from abroad—for which he would inevitably have to pay a price—and more on ensuring his daughter a full treasury and adequate army, without which all foreign assurances would be vain—a caution to be justified all too soon after Charles's death when Frederick the Great invaded Silesia, encouraged by Maria Theresa's military and financial weakness.

Eugen could admire the single-mindedness with which Frederick's father, Frederick William I, built up Prussia's strength. He could also see that on grounds of expediency there might be advantage in an alliance between Vienna and Berlin. But it was tantamount, of course, to supping with the devil. He and King Frederick William were antipodean in character and methods. Eugen, unlike Frederick William, did not enjoy, let alone inflict, corporal punishment. He did not make a practice of personal rudeness and intimidation. He

[1] H. G. Schenk, *The European Nobility in the Eighteenth Century*, ed., A. Goodwin, 1953, p. 102.
[2] See Chapter XVIII, p. 234.

had no love of nocturnal orgies, or of excessive drinking or rollicking. He did not share Frederick William's contempt for intellectuals. He had no passion for military giants or outsize horses. Having, unlike Frederick William, seen much of war, he did not share his passion for vast peace-time military spectacles.

'I am quite aware of the drilling of Prussian soldiers,' he wrote on one occasion, 'but there has always seemed to me something artificial about it. It is not surprising that large well-fed bodies which have undergone no strain should make a good show on parade.'[1]

Whether as a deliberate reaction to Prussian drilling or because it corresponded to his own tastes, Eugen, it must be recorded, appears to have overdone his opposition to peace-time training. The lax state into which the Imperial forces subsided during the decade or two following the end of the last Turkish war must be attributed partly to his own pet aversion to the barrack square, except in time of war when he was ardent for drill and firing practice.[2]

Frederick William's regard for Eugen went through various phases. He had served under him in 1709 and much admired him. Subsequently he was poisoned against him by a swindler called Klement, who insinuated to him that Eugen was at the bottom of an Austrian plot to kidnap him. However, when in the mid-1720's Frederick William wanted to improve relations with Vienna, it was through Eugen that he decided to proceed. With characteristic lack of human insight he tried to insinuate his way into the Prince's heart by bribery. The reaction was typically sea-green, though also typically complex. Frederick William offered wild animals for Eugen's menagerie and horses for his stable. Eugen rejected the horses but accepted the valuable elks—rather the opposite of the present practice by which running expenses are permitted as douceurs but not minks. However, in 1728, when relations between the two countries were being put on a more stable footing by the signature of a treaty—involving the recognition of the Pragmatic Sanction and the reciprocal guarantee of frontiers—Eugen's scruples seem to have evaporated. He was able to accept all Frederick William's gifts without demur, and even sent some horses in return.

Eugen believed that the Monarchy should try to ensure the friendship of the Crown Prince well in advance of his accession to the throne. After Frederick's attempt to run away from his father in 1730 it was largely as a result of Eugen's pressure that the Emperor

[1] A. Arneth, op. cit., III, p. 203.
[2] See Chapter XXI, p. 281.

interceded with the King for clemency, to spare his son's life. It was probably only as a result of the Emperor's intervention that Frederick William was restrained from executing his son.

But if, after 1728, when he was virtually in control of Austria's foreign policy, Eugen strove to remove the tension between the Hohenzollerns and Habsburgs and favoured an alliance between Vienna and Berlin to help Austria recapture the leadership of the Empire, he was always fearful of Prussia's expansionist tendencies and dreaded the day when she would have clearly become the second strongest power in the Empire. It was the threat this posed to Habsburg leadership that had stimulated him to say many years earlier that the Emperor should have hanged the person who advised him to sanction Prussia's claim to become a kingdom.[1]

This alliance with Prussia helped to offset Austria's fears about the dangers of too close a relationship between London and Berlin. England was doing everything possible by diplomatic means to bring to an end the Emperor's beloved Ostend Trading Company.[2] There was also the threat of a marriage between Crown Prince Frederick and the daughter of George II and between the Prince of Wales and the daughter of Frederick William—a dynastic coupling which, it was feared in Vienna, could hardly favour the Habsburgs.

Eugen viewed England with the same wary eye that he cast on Prussia. Austria needed both but both should be treated with suspicion. Soon after the close of the Spanish Succession War, Eugen had favoured the resumption of the former alliance with England in order to ensure the support of a strong fleet against a Spanish invasion of Italy.[3] But a decade later, by the end of 1727, Eugen was writing to Seckendorff that England's purpose was to disrupt the Empire and to keep the countries of Europe disunited and envious of each other. They did this so as to be able to dominate the whole of Europe more easily. Their policy of the balance of power, he said, was nothing more than a policy of British predominance.

Not surprisingly, in view of his own experiences, Eugen was never impressed by the high moral tone and would-be objectivity of British pronouncements. It was hard British interests that their statesmen were out to serve, not lofty sentiments. He was always warning the young Austrian representative in London, Graf Kinsky,

[1] See Chapter V, p. 62.
[2] See Chapter XVIII, p. 248.
[3] See Chapter XVIII, p. 233.

against the duplicity of English ministers who said one thing while meaning and doing another. The Minister was to be ever on his guard in dealing with such dangerous characters. He had another piece of advice for him:

'One of the most important rules of conduct in dealing with the English is to avoid showing yourself too forthcoming. The more you show you want their goodwill, the less is the chance of obtaining it. The infallible way to make dealings with them harder than ever is to give the impression that friendship with England is absolutely indispensable for the Emperor.'[1]

However, he believed that the old wartime alliance with England had to be restored in the face of the mounting threat of a Franco-Spanish alliance. His fundamental belief in close relations between Vienna and the Maritime Powers lay at the bottom of his opposition to the idea of the Ostend Trading Company, which he knew would excite their envy.[2] He had no illusions about the immediate objectives of French diplomacy since the end of the Spanish Succession War, which were to sever the traditional links between the Emperor on the one hand and Britain and the Dutch Republic on the other; the ultimate aim, of course, was to isolate and weaken Vienna. But to this customary danger a new twist had been added. France had been antagonized by Austria's alliance with Russia concluded in 1726. This seemed to them to jeopardize French influence in Sweden and Turkey.

It should be observed in passing—a small but significant landfall on the horizon of Eugen's life—that Russia was beginning to emerge for the first time as a power of weight in the European balance. This development and the growth of Prussian power were perhaps the two most powerful currents beneath the choppy surface of European events during the second quarter of the eighteenth century.

Spain was becoming dangerously restive. Vienna had achieved a reconciliation with Madrid by the Treaty of Vienna of 1725. This new relationship prospered for some time, aided by the winning personality of the Imperial representative at Madrid, Graf Königsegg. The ambassador had the qualities unusual amongst higher servants of the Monarchy of not liking the sound of his own voice and of being prepared to listen to others without showing the least sign of

[1] A. Arneth, op. cit., III, p. 279.
[2] See Chapter XVIII, p. 248.

boredom, however tedious and prolonged the subject and disquisition. This made him of course extremely popular amongst his diplomatic colleagues and with foreign ministers and foreign courts. But it did not suffice to produce an enduring *entente* with Spain. Queen Elizabeth Farnese craved above all for the transfer by Austria of the Duchies of Parma and Tuscany to her son Don Carlos. This dominating woman, described by Frederick the Great as having '*la fierté d'un Spartiate, l'opiniâtreté d'un Anglais, la finesse italienne et la vivacité Française*',[1] had achieved complete mastery over the half-witted, over-sexed king. She had resolutely refused to acquiesce in the sacrifices in Italy which the Treaties of Utrecht and Rastadt had involved for Spain. She was determined to get back the Duchies, and she was aggrieved that this had not so far been brought about by the Treaty between Madrid and Vienna. Nor had she secured the hoped-for betrothal of Don Carlos and Maria Theresa. Frustrated and impatient, Spain was therefore ready to switch sides once again. In 1729 they concluded with France and England the Treaty of Seville, under which these two powers were committed to going to war with the Emperor if within six months he did not permit Spanish troops into the Duchies.

It seemed to Eugen that there was only one way of countering this danger: by remaining on close terms with the land power of Prussia bolstered by support from the new ally Russia, whilst restoring the old alliance with England. Indeed, from 1729 on, much of Eugen's secret diplomatic correspondence was devoted to the task of re-establishing the old partnership between the land power of the Monarchy and the sea power of Britain. Likewise, much of Walpole's energies were devoted to trying to reach agreement directly and secretly with the Emperor so as to avoid the possibility of a European war. This became all the more urgent when, after the six months' time limit had elapsed, the French, who were pressing London for an attack on the Austrian Netherlands, got wind of these clandestine dealings with Vienna. It was made no easier by King George II's personal hostility to the Emperor for having refused formally to recognize his right, as Elector of Hanover, to the Duchies of Julich and Cleves.[2]

However, Walpole's and Eugen's patient efforts were finally crowned with success by the signature in Vienna on March 16, 1731, of a treaty between England and Austria. Under this treaty, known

[1] Frederic II, op. cit., p. 17.
[2] See J. H. Plumb, *Sir Robert Walpole*, 1960, II, pp. 233–4.

as the Second Vienna Treaty, Austria acquiesced in the despatch of Spanish troops to Parma and Tuscany. They also agreed to wind up the Ostend Trading Company which had been such a grievance to England, as Eugen had predicted. Finally the Treaty provided for an English guarantee of the Pragmatic Sanction.

The Dutch Republic and Spain were quickly induced to accept the Treaty's terms. It was a triumph for Walpole, who, overcoming George II's inhibitions, had managed to resolve the problem of Austro-Spanish relations which had overawed Europe for a decade. It was a triumph too for Eugen, whose diplomacy at last seemed to have achieved that balance and security for Austria which had been lacking ever since the break-up of the Grand Alliance in the closing stages of the War of the Spanish Succession. Robert Walpole bore witness to the leading part Eugen had played in bringing about the Second Vienna Treaty. In a letter of congratulation sent in June 1731, he wrote:

> 'I would be guilty of a gross injustice if I had delayed an instant in expressing my gratitude to you and in congratulating you on the success of such an important and worthy task. For everyone is aware that Your Excellency played the leading role.'[1]

The outlook for Austria can scarcely ever have seemed more secure, nor that of the Habsburg Monarch more auspicious, than it seemed immediately after the conclusion of the Second Vienna Treaty. Likewise Eugen's reputation, which had never before stood higher, was now grounded in diplomatic as well as military achievement. Had he died then he would have gone down in history not only as one of the greatest soldiers, but as one of the world's most successful statesmen. But with the death of Augustus II of Poland at the beginning of 1733 and the outbreak of war with France over his successor, the security system which he had constructed with such pain collapsed ingloriously. Once again it was England that let him down most heavily. She had derived important benefits from the Second Vienna Treaty; the termination of the Ostend Trading Company was advantageous to London commercially; further, Walpole was relieved to be rid of the immediate threat of a European war arising from Spanish-Austrian differences. But he had given a hostage to fortune by committing England to a guarantee of the Austrian dominions against unprovoked attack. Before long the

[1] A. Arneth, op. cit., III, p. 574.

23. The Upper Belvedere from the Great Forecourt

24. Statue of Eugen executed by Balthasar Permoser in Dresden in 1718–21 from a portrait

Emperor was asking for this promise to be redeemed. The outbreak of the Polish Succession War forced him to seek English support—but with disastrous consequences.

CHAPTER XXI

WAR AGAIN AND DEATH

ON FEBRUARY 1, 1733, King Augustus II of Poland died. The crown was elective; the king was chosen by the Polish nobility, most of whom were under the influence of one or another foreign power. The governments of Europe had been in long and acrimonious discussion about Augustus' successor, so far without agreement. There were two candidates; first Stanislaus Leszczynski, who had worn the crown long ago, before being deposed; he was Louis XV's father-in-law and was strongly supported by France; and second, the Elector of Saxony, the son of Augustus II, who was the choice of the Emperor. Russia and Prussia also backed the Elector. The French forced the pace. With their help Stanislaus was introduced surreptitiously into Poland and then in early September proclaimed King by the Polish Diet. Far from accepting this as a *fait accompli* the adherents of the Elector encouraged him also to enter Poland, which he did with the support of a Russian army. Stanislaus was abandoned by most of his troops and fled the country. This was enough to make France decide that the best riposte was to attack the Habsburgs at their weakest spot, northern Italy. Even since Louis XIV's reign the French had been unable to reconcile themselves to the absence of territory or influence in Italy. Marshal Villars, now eighty years old, was given command of an army and sent across the Alps. At the same time another old veteran of the War of the Spanish Succession, the Duke of Berwick, was despatched with a second army to the Rhine. Europe was at war once again. Once again the Emperor was the first to be assailed. Once again he suffered immediate diplomatic and military reverses.

The diplomatic setback seemed to Charles and Eugen to be less the outcome of Austria's own feebleness than of bad faith on the part of her allies, Prussia, Holland and England. Frederick William was reluctant, at any rate at first, to risk losing any of his giant soldiers unless there was a direct threat to Prussia. The Dutch Republic had made a Treaty of Neutrality with France which precluded her from giving help under the Second Vienna Treaty. England argued that by the terms of the Treaty they were not pledged to act alone; they maintained that Austria in any event had recently behaved so provocatively towards France over their candidate for the Polish Throne that their allies were released from their obligations. Eugen exerted all his influence to try to rally support, arguing that if France's aggression 'did not constitute a *casus foederis* then it was all up with loyalty and trust and there can be no further point in making alliances. How can the already unsteady European balance be sustained any longer if the House of Bourbon, having taken over the Spanish Monarchy, succeeds in acquiring a third Crown in Italy? The Empire has so often made sacrifices for the common good, and will do so again now . . .'[1] Eugen was bitter about England's lâcheté. To Kinsky, he wrote at the end of 1733:

'It was mainly at England's wish that the Emperor undertook to support the candidacy of the Crown Prince of Saxony for the Throne of Poland. Solely out of consideration for England did he agree to allow Spanish troops into Italy and to give up the advantages that would have accrued from the continuation of the Ostend Company. It would be doubly painful therefore if the price of so many concessions by the Emperor was to be the complete absence of, or only nominal, support from his ally. The efforts we are making exceed our powers. We cannot continue them without bringing the Austrian lands to their knees. . . . It is indispensable that the other Powers who have the same interest in saving freedom should make the necessary contribution towards its defence.'[2]

However, Walpole was determined to keep England out of the war. On strictly legal grounds he may have been justified in wriggling out of the obligations of the Second Vienna Treaty, though King

[1] Prince Eugen to Graf Uhlfeld, November 21, 1733, A. Arneth, op. cit., III, p. 392.
[2] Prince Eugen to Graf Kinsky, December 30, 1733, A. Arneth, op. cit., III, p. 392.

George II did not think so, and it is difficult to see how the Emperor can fairly be accused of provocative behaviour when it was Louis XV who had launched Stanislaus into Poland. Walpole may have been serving England's immediate commercial interests, for if England had gone in while the Dutch Republic remained out the latter would have been able to capture much of England's peace-time trade. And he no doubt thought that he was contributing to his own position at home where an election was due to be held the following year and where the idea of involvement in a continental war was unpopular with the constituencies.[1] But in the longer term the disservice done to England's credit as an ally, by what was indubitably a breach of the spirit of the Vienna agreement, revived the reproach of perfidy and left London friendless in Europe.

With no prospect of military or financial support from outside, the Empire's position was appalling.[2] 'The danger to the Monarchy cannot be exaggerated,' Eugen wrote the Emperor in October 1733. 'It has never been so great.' As if to show that he was full of the old mettle he added: 'However, its very gravity makes it all the more important not to lose heart.'[3]

Villars was able to sweep through Italy mopping up several of its fortresses at a most unoctogenarian pace. To the Empire the threat from the French on the Rhine was even more menacing. The Emperor realized that the only hope of salvation was to persuade Eugen to become Commander-in-Chief of the Imperial Army in Germany. The Prince was a tired old man of seventy. His constitution, never good, had deteriorated. He had a serious chest complaint. He was racked with a perpetual cough. He had taken part in thirty-one campaigns. The peace-time desk work in Vienna had been even more exhausting than the battlefield. There is also first hand evidence to show that his memory was failing, that he no longer spoke with the old incisiveness, and that he had become so human with the years that he might well doze off in the afternoon in the middle of a conference. However, despite these handicaps, the Emperor was convinced that Eugen was still head and shoulders above any other

[1] J. H. Plumb, op. cit., II, p. 289.

[2] Throughout the reign of Charles VI his war establishment was never more than 160,000 men; but over half this number were always kept on garrison and security duties. His financial situation was little better now, towards the end of his reign, than it had been at the beginning. His revenue, which amounted to some 30 million Florins (see page 78 for table of comparative values) was quite inadequate to the needs of war. See W. Coxe's *House of Austria*, III.

[3] A. Arneth, op. cit., III, p. 389.

possible Imperial commander. The only person of comparable stature was Guido Starhemberg, but he was four years older than Eugen and half paralysed. So Eugen was appointed Commander-in-Chief and set off in April 1734 to take charge on the Rhine.

Outnumbered by Berwick by five to one, Eugen had to abandon the idea of holding the line of the Rhine. He was forced to withdraw first to Bruchsal and then to Heilbronn. He sent an urgent summons to the contingents of the Empire to hasten their arrival and not to hold back for the selfish defence of their own territory. He told the Emperor frankly that he might be forced to retire still further; it depended entirely on the movements of the enemy. He was in the position, 'of one man fighting five', but he added gamely: 'I will do everything possible in a situation more perilous than any I have known during all my long years of campaigning.'[1] The Emperor assured him of his complete confidence and implored him to look after his health.

Eugen was more at the mercy of the enemy at this moment than at any time in his life. But providence intervened in a most unexpected way. Berwick was a superb commander. However, mixed in with his dashing Stuart and Churchill blood there flowed a stream of caution. Fortunately for Eugen this caution suddenly predominated. Instead of hustling the enemy out of Heilbronn, as he could easily have done, Berwick contented himself with besieging Phillippsburg, which gave Eugen a sorely needed month's respite.

'I confess,' he wrote to the Emperor on May 20, that, despite all my preparations, I do not know how I should have warded off the enemy's attack if he had done what he ought to have done. As little do I understand why, during the last twelve days, he has remained inactive, contenting himself with ravaging the country. He has given me time to refresh my tired troops, to send away my heavy luggage, to draw troops to myself, so that in a few days I shall have thirty thousand available fighting for me.'[2]

The French, besides giving Eugen a valuable breathing space, were also doing themselves much damage by antagonizing the local population astride the Rhine with their looting and excesses. The Emperor stood to gain militarily the longer this went on, but to Eugen the arguments of humanity outweighed those of immediate expediency. The sufferings of the people must be stopped. He decided therefore to address an appeal direct to Berwick 'to put an end to

[1] A. Arneth, op. cit., III, p. 408.
[2] Ibid, III, p. 414.

excesses on a scale hitherto unknown between civilized and Christian nations.

'Not content with burning and plundering every village, including those provided by you with letters of safe conduct, your soldiers are committing excesses unsurpassed in history. They respect neither churches nor holy shrines. Priests are bound and exposed naked at open doors and windows. Women are nailed to trees through their hands and then assaulted. Innocent children are brutally mutilated.'

He concluded with an appeal *ad hominem*: 'There are limits even to the horrors of war. And it seems to me that the laws of humanity should never be overlooked by the armies of such great Monarchs as those we have the honour to serve.'[1] To Berwick's credit the offenders were punished and the looting and hooliganism stopped.

Though he was nominally in command of the covering army Berwick also directed the siege of Philippsburg. Every morning he rode down to the trenches to examine the work of the night before and plan the next night's operations. One morning, as he was making his observations, the guns from the opposing batteries continued to fire, and a ball from one of them carried off his head. We do not know what Eugen's thoughts on this were, but can only surmise that he would not have disagreed with Villars. 'I was always right in saying that Berwick was more fortunate than I,'[2] Villars exclaimed when he heard the news of his colleague's tidy death in action.

Reinforcements from Prussia and Hanover at last began to arrive by the beginning of June. The Prussian troops had committed appalling atrocities on the way, which no doubt confirmed Eugen in his earlier scepticism of the value of constant peacetime drilling and parades. Not that he can have been too pleased with the state of the Emperor's troops as they had shown themselves in action so far in Italy and Germany. It must be reckoned as something of a reflection on Eugen's control over the war machine during all these years that when it came to war in 1734 the army proved itself so ill prepared and inadequate. Resistance to his reforms[3] had been resolute, certainly, and the forces of reaction had been able to have their head during the long period of his fall from grace after the end of the last Turkish war. Then, from 1725 on, he had been heavily involved as virtual Prime Minister of the Monarchy with many other matters of State.

[1] A. Arneth, op. cit., III, p. 413.
[2] G. B. Malleson, op. cit., p. 257.
[3] See Chapter VII, p. 79.

Finally, as he recognized himself, the long interval of peace had had a debilitating effect on officers and men alike. He reported to the Emperor in June 1734: 'The senior officers have the right spirit but lack experience and there are many among them who have either never taken part in a campaign, or, if they have, have served only as subalterns. But this is only the inevitable result of a long period of peace.'[1] To complaints that the Imperial infantry in Italy had shown themselves green in the handling of firearms, he said that intensive training was now necessary, 'for just as I am against too much unnecessary firing in peace-time, so am I convinced that in time of war there must be the maximum practice with arms'.[2] Throughout his life he threw himself with equal zest and energy into both war and peace, but he was not quick to see their interrelation, and he resented the idea that sacrifices might have to be made in time of peace as a precaution against worse sufferings in war. In this respect he was more behind the times than Frederick..

In the third week of June Eugen set out from Heilbronn to go to the relief of Philippsburg whose commander, von Wutgenau, had begun to send out distress signals. It was noticeable, however, that Eugen did not show the old speed in going to the fortress's defence. Nor, when he had approached the enemy's lines, did he show his former eagerness for a fight, though von Wutgenau was warning him that unless the French were quickly attacked they might succeed at any moment in storming the fortress.

Eugen was fully aware of the need for a major victory to make up for the heavy losses the Monarchy had suffered in Italy. He had assured the Emperor before he had set out from Heilbronn that he would do everything possible to bring this about. But he had added in an unaccustomed tone of caution: 'The consequence of a military defeat would be so grave, particularly at this time of crisis for the Empire, that it is impossible to contemplate a battle with the old lightheartedness.'[3]

The same uncertainty, the same unnatural circumspection, was noticeable when at last his army was drawn up in array on the Rhine opposite the French. He was hesitant to take the plunge. The former drive and impulse had gone, and in its place there seemed to hover an indefinable but unmistakeable lack of confidence in himself. It was as if he had begun to doubt his own ability to seize an opportunity

[1] Eugen to the Emperor, June 10, 1734, A. Arneth, op. cit., III, p. 457.
[2] *Ibid*, p. 420.
[3] A. Arneth, op. cit., III, p. 422.

and to be able to carry it through to victory. That he was aware of the limitations which had overcome him, that he knew that he was no longer the man of Cremona, Blenheim, Turin or Malplaquet, was perhaps fortunate. It was his misfortune that it should have been there in the field that he had to witness his own shadow instead of in peaceful retirement. When in old age Marlborough confronted his portrait done in the prime of life, he was so shocked by the change he saw that he turned away with the words, 'That was once a man'.[1] But at any rate he was in the shade at home, instead of being still in the limelight with the weight of an empire persistently on his shoulders.

There were other reasons for hesitation. Nothing but Eugen's army barred the way into Germany. It was heavily outnumbered by the French. It seemed unjustifiable to risk its destruction and thereby open the way into the heart of the Empire for the sake of one fortress, Philippsburg. As the lesser of two evils he must let the fortress fall rather than jeopardize the security of the Empire as a whole. He was convinced of this though the Emperor was maintaining strong pressure on him to attack: 'A sweeping victory is the only human means left,' he wrote to Eugen on June 29, 'to save me, my royal house and the whole of Europe from domination by the House of Bourbon.'[2]

It cannot have helped Eugen at this difficult moment to have been called upon to receive at the front two very important visitors: King Frederick William of Prussia and the Crown Prince Frederick. However Eugen was glad of any opportunity to try to wean the Crown Prince away from his French entourage. The Prince was reported to be very much under the influence of the French Minister in Berlin, the Marquis de Chetardie, and many people went so far as to think that he would appoint him Prime Minister on assuming the crown. 'A great deal depends,' Eugen wrote to the Emperor, 'on winning the Prince who one day can make more friends in the world than his father has, and will do as much good.'[3]

The King sent the Crown Prince on ahead asking Eugen to take him under his wing and teach him all he could of the art of war. But there was a limit to the amount of deference that was to be shown to Frederick: 'He can be treated lightly, but he should not be accorded an Imperial Bodyguard, because he should not be allowed

[1] Winston S. Churchill, op. cit., II, p. 1036.
[2] A. Arneth, op. cit., III, p. 424.
[3] A. Arneth, op. cit., III, p. 432.

to get any higher opinion of his own importance than he already has.'[1]

If only the Crown Prince could have been left alone with Eugen! But within a day or two the tyrannical old man arrived himself, his natural ill-temper aggravated by a bad attack of gout. Indeed it was thought he was dying.

Inspired no doubt by the bad news of his father's health and partly by the stimulus of Eugen's company, Frederick engaged in long military and political discussions with Eugen, who counselled him to study the history of earlier campaigns in great detail and to try to imagine himself in the position of the opposing generals and to decide in his own mind what was the right course at any given moment. By his youth and eagerness to learn the young Prince seems to have had a correspondingly stimulating effect on Eugen who suddenly became much more forthcoming than usual. Though talkative and ready with opinions as a young man, Eugen had become laconic, almost morose in old age. He could rarely be prevailed upon to talk or give his advice on military matters. He would make decisions with the minimum of explanation. This caused personal resentment; it was also a public loss. Indeed the poor quality of the senior officers who grew up under Eugen has been attributed partly to his reluctance to bestow on them in training the benefit of his knowledge and experience. What the reason for this reserve was must remain conjectural, but it is in keeping with his developing tendency towards qualification, a growing doubt in his fitness to judge people and events in quite the same old sweeping and categorical way. It also went with increasing modesty. Many men, particularly those accustomed to command and decorated throughout their lives with success, become more categorical, more self-assured and bigoted with age. But not Eugen. He became less and less absolute, and increasingly tentative in behaviour and judgements. There was nothing didactic, boastful, or censorious about him as an old man, and this strengthening of the human side of his character came of course as grist to the mill of those who in his later years, whether from personal rivalry or instinctive malice, kept grinding out that the former hero was going soft.

Frederick confessed at one moment that his father had kept him in complete ignorance of the terms of the agreement between the two countries relating to the Pragmatic Sanction; but he asked Eugen to assure the Emperor that he would abide by its terms

[1] A. Arneth, op. cit., III, p. 429.

completely when he became King. He also said that he hoped Charles would maintain even closer relations with him than he had with his father.

A note of conspiracy then creeps into the conversation as reported by Eugen to the Emperor. Frederick implored Eugen not to let the Emperor know of this promise he had just made about the Pragmatic Sanction since it would be bound to upset his father. He worked his way even closer into Eugen's confidence. He expressed the hope that if Frederick William recovered the Emperor would exert all his influence over him to stop the continual persecution to which his father subjected him. Finally, he asked for the removal from Berlin of the Imperial ambassador, Seckendorff, who, he complained, was so hostile to him. On hearing of all this, the Emperor asked Eugen to remind the Crown Prince of his constant support for him: how he had written previously to the King in his own hand asking him to spare his life; and how he had frequently helped him with money. He would continue to feel as warmly as always towards him. He would remove Seckendorff.

Frederick was impressed by Eugen's personality. He acknowledged later in life his great debt to the Prince for all that he had taught him. But his admiration was not unqualified. If he picked up a great deal of theory about war from Eugen, he also learnt with his own eyes a lot about the practical weakness of the Imperial forces. Moreover, by the time he succeeded to the throne six years later, the deductions to be drawn for Prussia from this second lesson must have over-ridden any personal gratitude flowing from the first. Knowing Frederick as we do, it is not surprising that within a few years he went back on all the assurances of 1734. Nor, knowing Eugen as we do, is there anything startling in the way he appears to have thought that the Prince would be held for the rest of his life by the bonds he had forged at the age of twenty-two. The loyalties he, Eugen, had embraced as a young man were to dominate him thoughout his life. He had never seriously contemplated for any length of time any departure from the faiths of his early twenties. It was natural, therefore, for him to attach the importance he did to trying to influence and win over the Crown Prince at his most impressionable age, particularly when the Prince, like himself at the same age, was in revolt against his family and background. It was perhaps naïve, though it was also typical, that Eugen should not have made sufficient allowance for Frederick's later cynicism and treachery.

By mid-July Eugen had finally renounced the idea of a full scale attack on the French lines for the relief of Philippsburg. He had hit instead upon an ingenious device which was intended to bring about the same result without a shot being fired. He would try to deflect the over-swollen waters of the Rhine and flush the French out of their lines. The bank of the river was duly cut and the Imperial troops stood by waiting for the water to do their work for them. But no sooner had the stream started to flow obediently towards the French than, as if by divine command of the Lorelei, the level of the Rhine began to fall and the enemy were left high and dry in their entrenchments. We can imagine with what contempt Frederick must have surveyed this agreeable but unsuccessful water game.

Philippsburg fell on July 18, 1734. This was followed by a good deal of marching, counter-marching and skirmishing. Prisoners were taken. There were many skilful ruses and successful feints, but there was little savage fighting and no decisive battle. In retrospect it all reads as if, once water had been discarded, the two sides had decided to see the year out by playing some large-scale land game, a cross between tig and French and English, a game which indeed went on with no great advantage to either side until the whistle blew in October for both teams to go into winter quarters.

Referring generally to the European wars between 1713 and 1739, H. A. L. Fisher has written that it seems, 'as if the element of savage perseverance was wanting to these hostilities'. This was certainly so of 1734 on the Rhine. In Italy, however, the French, joined by the Spaniards and the King of Sardinia, had been quite savage enough. The Empire had suffered great losses of men and territory. The Milanese, Tuscany, Naples and Sicily had all been taken.

Back in Vienna for the winter 1734–5 Eugen took part in critical ministerial meetings. The overall military scene had all the familiar hues: no pay available for officers or men anywhere; little chance of loot, which until then had been the main inducement to keep the soldiers with the colours; no bread for weeks on end for the troops in Italy; the growing risk both of the Bavarians making common cause with France and of the French subsidizing the Turks to attack the Empire in the East; and finally, no prospect of reinforcements for the Empire from elsewhere.

England indeed was very pleased with her neutrality. Walpole said to the Queen proudly at the end of the 1734 campaigning season: 'Madam, there are fifty-thousand men slain in Europe and not one Englishman.'

He could not have confirmed more clearly Eugen's suspicion that England was always prepared to fight in Europe to the last German.

At the beginning of November of 1734, the inner circle of ministers in Vienna were asked to express their view urgently on whether or not the war should be continued. As the matter was of such importance they were requested to give their answers in writing—as soon as possible. It took them three months to comply. With Eugen in the van, there was a strong body of opinion in favour of peace. Proposals for ending the war were also put forward by the Sea Powers. But the Emperor, obstinate as usual and sustained by advice from his Spanish courtiers who were no more disinterested than ever, refused to contemplate giving up Naples and Sicily. The war must go on.

In May 1735 Eugen, nearly seventy-two years of age, went to war for the last time. He was in the worst of health. His cough was now so bad that to save him from speaking the Emperor had refrained from exchanging views with him except in writing. Even more serious, his mental powers had also waned. Guido Starhemburg had been keeping up with him in decline. By now the lower part of his body was completely paralysed, though he was as alert as ever mentally. 'I am growing old from the feet up,' he quipped, 'but I know someone who is deteriorating just as fast from the head down!'[1] But Charles still preferred to rely on Eugen, decrepit as he was, than to turn to anyone else.

The situation Eugen found on reaching his camp was chaotic. His generals were quarrelling with each other. There was no discipline. Desertion was rife. Yet the Emperor was egging him on from Vienna to undertake a major offensive. 'The more critical the situation is on all sides,' the Emperor wrote to him at Bruchsal on May 28, 1735, 'the greater is my confidence that your Excellency will do everything possible to undertake a major operation against the enemy.'[2] Charles' importunity was tempered as usual with appeals to Eugen to look after his health, and as usual the good effect was spoilt by the explanation that his health was indispensable for the Emperor's purposes.

With bad news reaching him from Italy, Eugen was no keener than he had been the previous year to risk an offensive with the Rhine Army 'on which alone the security of the Monarchy depends'. He would take advantage of any favourable opportunity for an

[1] A. Arneth, op. cit., p. 781.
[2] A. Arneth, op. cit., III, p. 464.

attack which might occur if the French Army moved east across the Rhine, or if it took some initiative such as an assault on Mainz which might lend itself to exploitation by the Imperial Forces. Meanwhile some delay would be of assistance since he was awaiting the arrival of a Russian Corps, thirteen thousand strong, whose transit through Bavaria the Elector was threatening to disrupt. These Russians eventually reached him at Heidelberg at the end of August—the first Russian troops ever to be seen in western Europe. Eugen found them 'a beautifully trained and disciplined body of infantry, whose condition was astonishing after so exhausting a march'.[1]

Before they could be used, however, France started putting out peace feelers suggesting that terms should be discussed bilaterally without the intervention of the Sea Powers. Vienna was suspicious. She still nourished the hope that England and the Dutch Republic would eventually come into the war. From the front, Eugen strongly advised the acceptance of terms even though some territorial sacrifice might be called for. The Emperor could not in his view hope to carry on the war alone. He believed that it was illusory to expect the support of the Maritime Powers. Without England there was no alternative for Austria but an accommodation with France, much though the idea of this went against the grain. What mattered most for the Monarchy in the long run was, so Eugen believed, the marriage of the Archduchess Maria Theresa. He thought he saw the way of killing two birds with one stone. He was concerned both about the marriage, and about the continuing danger to the Empire from Bavaria. This danger could be met either by disarming the Elector by force, which was hardly within the Monarchy's capabilities, or by conciliating him by a marriage. But his proposal for marrying Maria Theresa to the Bavarian Crown Prince, though in theory it may have looked very neat to the old soldier sitting in his tent on the Neckar, suffered from a serious practical flaw. Maria Theresa was nineteen years old. The Bavarian Crown Prince was nine. The Monarchy could not wait.

The Emperor accepted Eugen's advice about making peace, but not about the marriage of his daughter. She was to marry Duke Francis of Lorraine, an arrangement tacitly accepted by France in the Peace Treaty, the terms of which were agreed to in Vienna in October-November 1735. By this Treaty France also guaranteed the Pragmatic Sanction. Stanislaus had to renounce the throne of Poland, but as a face-saver he was to be allowed to retain the title

[1] A. Arneth, op. cit., III, p. 471.

of King and was given the Duchies of Lorraine and Bar. On his death these were to revert to France. The transfer to him of Lorraine however, was to wait until Duke Francis could be compensated with the gift of Tuscany. Finally the Emperor was to recover most of the Milanese and the Duchies of Parma and Piacenza. Naples and Sicily were ceded to Don Carlos.

This Treaty cannot be regarded as a disaster for Austria whose military performance had merited worse terms. But for Eugen personally the Polish Succession War had been something of a tragedy. By ordinary standards he had not done badly. With a far inferior force he had checked the advance of the French army into Germany and had only lost one fortress. How much more the ordinary run-of-the-mill Austrian commander was capable of losing in war was to be shown soon after Eugen's death in a series of unparalleled military disasters which befell the Monarchy. But judged by the pattern of Eugen's early life, the years 1734-5 must be regarded as a time of failure diplomatically and militarily. Many years later Frederick the Great drew on the calamity of Eugen's last campaigns to illustrate one of his beloved aphorisms:

'What a humbling reflection for our vanity. That a Condé, an Eugen, or a Marlborough should have to witness the decline of their mental powers before their physical powers. The greatest geniuses end up as imbeciles. Poor humanity, boast of your glory if you dare!'[1]

On his return to Vienna in October 1735 Eugen was unable to carry on any longer with his official duties. The laying down of office only accelerated his decline. He began to have the greatest difficulty in speaking. He was entirely dependent upon his devoted secretary Koch for communication with the outside world. From all accounts he appeared senile. A lady of the court described his condition when he paid a visit to Schlosshof soon after getting back from the front: 'He came, as he had left, feeble in mind and body. He had plenty of company and everyone tried to keep him amused with masques and children's games, more appropriate to the feebleness of his age than to his character.'[2]

It was not as though this second childhood was serene. To his chagrin he was too ill to attend the marriage of Maria Theresa to

[1] Frédéric II, op. cit., p. 12.
[2] Gräfin Fuchs to Field-Marshal Graf Schulenburg, October 29, 1735, Max Braubach, op. cit., p. 427.

Duke Francis of Lorraine which took place on February 12, 1736. And he was in constant pain. Yet he was also racked by conscience. Some old streak of puritanism prevented him from accepting drugs. It was only after the intervention of the Papal Nuncio that his scruples permitted him to take them.

Then suddenly with the spring he seemed to recover. He started seeing people again and going out in the evenings. He enjoyed life once more. On April 20 he gave a lunch party. He refused to sit in an armchair saying he was more used to a stool. As was his old custom, he accompanied each guest to the door when they left. That evening he was with Gräfin Batthyany as usual playing piquet until 9 p.m. It was noted that his breathing was heavy. He was accompanied home by Graf Emmanuel Sylva Tarouca, a Portuguese, who had left his country at the age of twenty and served under Eugen in the last Turkish war. Tarouca was a close friend of Eugen's and belonged to what might be called the Belvedere set. On reaching home Tarouca implored Eugen to take some medicine. But the Prince refused to do so, saying that there would be time enough before morning. Tarouca was the last person to see him alive. Eugen's servant who called him the next morning found him dead, and from the position of his body and the expression on his face he seemed to have died peacefully. He was in his seventy-third year.

The Emperor ordered a state funeral with full honours, 'so that everyone should see that for me the greatness of the deceased would never fade'. But his inner thoughts seem to have been more equivocal, as they were so often when Eugen was concerned. After a long entry in his diary about Eugen's career and the circumstances of his death, Charles added the words: 'Now, see, everything will be better organized'[1]—a postscript he was to rue before many months were up, when the Turks attacked the Empire once again and inflicted heavy losses. 'Has then our lucky star completely disappeared with Eugen?' he asked bitterly. How much Eugen meant to the Monarchy, feeble and broken though he was in his latter years, could not have been assessed more objectively than it was by the British Minister in his report to Walpole two months after the Prince's death, though it might have been expressed more elegantly: 'During the last two years of his life, even the remainder of what he had been kept things in some order, as his very yes or no, during his sounder age, had kept them in the best.'[2]

[1] Max Braubach, op. cit., p. 431.
[2] Mr Robinson to Mr Walpole, June 27, 1736. William Coxe, op. cit., II, p. 193.

Eugen's embalmed body, dressed in regimental uniform, scarlet cloth with black velvet facings, lay in state for three days. For an hour each day, between noon and one p.m., all the bells in Vienna tolled.

As if to symbolize the duality of his life, his heart was sent to Turin and buried alongside his Savoy ancestors. His body was buried in Vienna where the funeral took place on April 26. The long candle-bearing procession took three hours to file by. It was led by inmates of the work-house and from hospitals in Vienna. It included the wounded of Eugen's wars, as well as representatives from all the military, civil and religious orders of the Monarchy. But no relative of the deceased or member of the House of Savoy was present. To a triple salvo fired by detachments of cavalry and infantry posted outside the cathedral his body was lowered into the vault of the Kreuzkapelle of the Stephansdom. It rests there in a simple stone coffin bearing in relief an image of the battle of Belgrade, surmounted by a pyramid inscribed with his name.

In his family relationships Eugen was as unlucky in death as he had been in life. He may not have had the same dynastic urge as Marlborough—his royal birth obviated it—but there seems no doubt that throughout his life he took pleasure in the idea of creating a patrimony. Brought up poor he could never escape the love of property and accumulation; and behind the immediate compulsion to collect pictures and construct palaces was the desire to leave something tangible behind by which his taste as much as his renown would be commemorated. But it was to prove much easier to found an inheritance than to establish an heir. All his brothers and sisters died before him, as did all his nephews. The eldest of the sons of the Duc de Soissons, Emmanuel, upon whom Eugen for long pinned all his hopes for posterity, died last of all, in November 1734. By then, as has been shown, Eugen was fast losing his strength, and was once again preoccupied by war. It may have been partly for this reason, but also because there was no obvious relation left in sight for the succession, that Eugen died intestate.

There were two possible successors: his niece, Princess Anna Victoria of Savoy, the only living daughter of his eldest brother; and his cousin, Victor Amadeus of Carignan, the son of his father's eldest brother, the deaf-mute, Emmanuel Philibert. It was decided that the niece had the closer relationship and that she should therefore inherit everything.[1]

[1] See Chapter IV, p. 50.

There is no evidence to show that there had been much contact between Eugen and his niece, or that he was particularly fond of, or interested in, her. She appears to have followed faithfully in the dissolute tradition of the female members of Eugen's family. When she arrived in Vienna in July 1736 to take over her inheritance she was fifty-two years old, an unattractive spinster with no feelings of respect for her uncle, and no intention of cherishing or safeguarding his property or collections. She appears, on the contrary, to have been interested only in loot. Her purpose was to sell off as quickly as possible for as much money as possible, as large a part of the inheritance as she could realize. She set about her task with energy. Nothing was spared. His medals, his personal trophies such as the sword presented to him by Queen Anne, and the portrait given him by the Emperor Joseph, were all torn from his palaces and sold together with the antique furniture, old masters, scenes of battle fields, and statues.[1] Of the palaces themselves, the Emperor bought the Belvedere with its library. Schlosshof and the Stadtpalais went to Maria Theresa.

The bitterness in Vienna against the Princess as she proceeded unsentimentally with her task found expression in a couplet which was pinned on her door:

> '*Est-il possible que du prince Eugène la gloire*
> *Soit ternie par une si vilaine Victoire.*'[2]

Embellished with her fantastic dot, Princess Victoria then proceeded to buy a husband, the Imperial Quartermaster, Prince Friedrich von Sachsen-Hildburghausen. But the marriage did not prosper. It was not long before she left him behind in Austria and went off first to France and then to Turin, where she eventually died in 1763.

The senile display of his final campaigns and the failure to provide satisfactorily for his inheritance form a sad and unheroic culmination to Eugen's career. But if we stand back from this tragic end and try to view the course of his life as a whole, then we see that his achievements as soldier, statesman and patron are towering landmarks in European history. Service had been the lodestar of his life, art the abiding passion. The epitaph which suits him best, and which expresses his own intense loyalty in the prevailing apatriotism of the

---

[1] See Appendix C on the sale of Eugen's pictures.
[2] Egon Caesar Conte Corti, op. cit., p. 128.

times, is that he, born a Frenchman, the son of an Italian mother and Savoyard father, devoted his life to the service of the House of Habsburg.

APPENDIX A

THE HABSBURG MONARCHY AND
THE HOLY ROMAN EMPIRE

IT WOULD be difficult in a short space to give a full definition of the
division of power and territorial responsibility between the two
institutions, the Habsburg Monarchy and the Holy Roman Empire.
But a resumé of the fundamentals may be useful.

The Habsburg rulers were elected Emperors of the Holy Roman
Empire from 1438 until the dissolution of the Empire in 1806, with
but one break in the eighteenth century during Maria Theresa's
reign. But although the Habsburg Monarchy and the Imperial
Crown were thus for long united in one person, the territories of the
two were not the same. The possessions of the Habsburgs were really
a collection of entailed estates, acquired many of them by good
marriages in accordance with the family tradition:

> *Bella gerunt alii, Tu felix Austria nube;*
> *Nam quae Mars aliis, dat tibi regna Venus.*

Some of these possessions were outside the Empire, e.g. Hungary.
Most of the lands of the Empire were not hereditary possessions of
the Habsburgs. To add to the complications, the Habsburgs never
became Kings of Austria. There was no such thing. They were
merely the Archdukes of Austria.

The Habsburgs exercised more authority over their hereditary
possessions—even Hungary—than in their capacity as elected
Emperors of the Holy Roman Empire of the German nation. The
post-mediaeval structure—if that word may be used without giving
an impression of close articulation—of the Empire was formed at

two Diets in 1495 and 1512. It was then modified by the Treaty of Westphalia in 1648, and adjusted thereafter as practice required. At the 1495 Diet an Imperial High Court (*Reichskammergericht*) was set up to solve disputes within the Empire. In 1512 the Diet organized the Empire into ten circles (*Landfriedenkreise*) for local administrative purposes: Austria, Bavaria, Swabia, Franconia, Upper Rhine, Lower Rhine, Burgundy, Westphalia, Lower Saxony and Upper Saxony. The Reformation and the Thirty Years War shattered any idea that a single religion or ruler would succeed in binding tightly together the three hundred odd lay and ecclesiastical states which constituted the Empire. Moreover, since the Peace of Westphalia, 1648, which recognized the coexistence of Protestant and Catholic countries and the limitations on any Habsburg ambitions for close German unification, the rulers of the separate states of the Empire had absolute control over both internal and external affairs. The Imperial Diet met and talked; but lacked effective power. Indeed the loose confederation which the Empire amounted to came to be held together in practice by little more than respect for the Imperial Crown. The Estates, representing the privileged orders in each principality, had the right to levy and collect taxes. Even in Vienna the Emperor's power was diffused as a result partly of administrative incompetence and overlapping, but also because of inherent conflicts between the interests of the Habsburgs' Court and those of the Empire. The Emperor by the end of the seventeenth century was elected by the nine most important Princes (called Electors), three of whom were ecclesiastics—the Archbishops of Mainz, Cologne and Trier—and six of whom were laymen—the King of Bohemia, the Count Palatine of the Rhine, the Duke of Saxony, the Electors of Bavaria and Hanover, and the Margrave of Brandenburg.

Until the sixteenth century the Habsburgs were an Austrian power owning exclusively Austrian lands, but in 1496 Maxmilian's son Philip was married to Joanna of Spain, the daughter of Ferdinand and Isabella, and their son, Charles V, inherited both the Spanish and Austrian dominions. These included the Duchies of Austria and Styria, the Tyrol, Vorarlberg, Carinthia, Carniola, and Gorizia; the Netherlands, Artois, and Franche Comté; Sardinia, Naples and Sicily; Spain and all the Spanish Colonies in the Indies and America. Charles' brother, Ferdinand, added the Crowns of Bohemia and Hungary to the Habsburg dominions as a result of marriage. After the abdication of Charles V in 1556 the Habsburg Monarchy was divided between the Spanish and Austrian branches of the family.

To the Spanish branch went Spain, the Netherlands, Franche Comté, the Italian and Mediterranean possessions, and the territories in the New World. Austria acquired the remainder.

The last Habsburg King of Spain, Charles II, died in 1700. Henceforth the Crown of Spain was worn by the Bourbons, and the only Habsburg lands were those of the Austrian-Danubian branch of the family.

APPENDIX B

AN ACCOUNT OF SOME OF THE ARTISTS EMPLOYED BY EUGEN AND OF THE PRINCIPAL PICTURES IN HIS COLLECTION

EUGEN WAS renowned among his contemporaries for his patronage of Italian artists; but his range was international. He commissioned pictures from G. M. Crespi and G. A. Boni of Bologna, Vittore Ghislandi of Bergamo, and Francesco Solimena and Giacomo del Po of Naples. Louis Dorigny (French but working in Italy) painted three canvases for the ceilings above the staircase of the *Stadtpalais*, and Marcantonio Chiarini came from Bologna to fresco its gallery and other rooms. In the Belvedere palaces frescoes were painted by Carlo Carlone, Gaetano Fanti, Martino Altomonte and Jonas Drentwett. Statues were made by Giovanni Giuliani, Lorenzo Mattielli and Domenico Parodi and by the Italian-trained Bavarian Balthasar Permoser. Eugen's portrait was painted by van Schuppen, Kupetzky and Kneller, to name only the principal portraitists to whom he sat. A much longer list of Italian, German and Netherlandish artists who worked for him could easily be compiled.[1]

Eugen's dealings with the two main Italian painters whom he employed are fairly well documented. Crespi's first picture of Eugen, usually dated about 1700, is *The Centaur Chiron teaching the young Achilles to draw the Bow*, now in the Kunsthistorisches Museum in Vienna. The unorthodox, genre-like treatment of the classical subject—the Centaur is encouraging the struggling Achilles with a tap of his hoof—displeased some contemporary critics, but not Eugen. This touch of informality in the noble rendering of a heroic theme is just what we might have expected to appeal to his adventurous cast

[1] See T. von Frimmel, *Geschichte der Wiener Gemäldesammlungen*, 1899, I, iii, p. 16.

of mind. 'The Prince,' Crespi's biographer says, 'was very pleased with it, so much so that lo Spagnuolo had the opportunity to work for him for more than five years.'[1] This alone indicates a considerable body of work for Eugen.[2] One other picture by Crespi which was probably painted for him is the *Aeneas and The Sibyl with Charon*, now in Vienna, which is so like the *Centaur and Achilles* in size, subject and treatment that it may be supposed to have been ordered later as a companion piece. These commissions for Eugen were executed when Crespi was comparatively unknown. But the painter's response equalled the patron's discernment, and the two Crespis in Vienna are justly numbered among his masterpieces.

Eugen's first approaches to Crespi were through an Italian connoisseur in Bologna.[3] For the three pictures which he ordered from Francesco Solimena he used the good offices of friends who were successively Austrian Viceroys in Naples, but also corresponded in Italian with the painter at intervals between 1720 and 1730.[4] First, a large picture of the legend of *Cephalus* was commissioned in 1720 for a ceiling in the Upper Belvedere; next a *Resurrection* for the chapel, for which, as the correspondence shows, drawings and a bozzetto were approved by Eugen in 1721.[5] Later, another picture for the chapel, a *Deposition*, was commissioned from Solimena, who finished work on it at some time between the years 1728 and 1731. The first two pictures have remained in their original places in the Belvedere; but the *Deposition* was bought by the Emperor after Eugen's death and is now in the Kunsthistorisches Museum in Vienna.

Eugen's principal pictures, which were in Vienna, numbered about two hundred. They were displayed in two galleries in the Upper Belvedere. The engravings of Salomon Kleiner[6] show us,

[1] Zanotti, op. cit., II, pp. 43–4.

[2] Eugen's diploma given to Crespi for his services was dated 1716 (Luigi Crespi in G. Bottari, Raccolta di lettere, 1759, III, p. 316), so that the early dating of the *Chiron and Achilles* implies a connection of over ten years. A pastoral by Crespi was bought from Eugen's heirs by Zanetti—who called it 'one of the finest things he ever painted'. (Haskell, op. cit., p. 341.) For three Crespis stated to have been executed for Eugen see the *Catalogo* of the Mostra del Settecento Bolognese, Bologna, 1935 (p. 18).

[3] Zanotti, op. cit., p. 43.

[4] See P. A. Orlandi, *L'Abecedario Pittorico*, 1733 (Life of Francesco Solimena), and B. de Dominici, *Vite dei Pittori, Scultori ed Architetti napoletani*, 1846, pp 432–9.

[5] F. Bologna, *Francesco Solimena*, 1959, p. 280.

[6] Salomon Kleiner, *Résidences mémorables de l'incomparable Héros de notre siècle ou Représentation exacte des Edifices et Jardin de son Altesse Sérénissime, Monseigneur le Prince Eugène François*, 1731.

with a degree of detail unique for the period, how the pictures were hung. Kleiner's *Résidences mémorables* contains three engravings of the walls of the picture galleries and a floor plan showing their position. There is also a contemporary description, consistent with Kleiner's illustrations, in J. B. Küchelbecker's *Allerneueste Nachricht vom Römisch Kaiserlichen Hofe*, 1730 (pp. 785–8).

The larger of the two rooms, described by Kleiner as 'Gallerie' and 'Bildersaal', was a long, narrow room which cor⁺ained a total of thirty-two pictures elegantly spaced. One of the end walls had nine pictures symmetrically arranged on it. In the centre was Guido Reni's *Adam and Eve*, flanked on one side by a Cleopatra of the school of Guido Reni, and on the other by Salviati's allegorical figure of Geometry. Below these were two other, smaller pictures: a battle piece by Wouwermans and a landscape not now identifiable. At the left-hand end of the wall were a version of Titian's Venus and Adonis, and below it a Sleeping Venus, in Titian's manner (possibly by Padovanino); in the corresponding positions on the extreme right hung two works of Francesco Albani: *Salmacis Rejected by Ermafrodito* and *Adam and Eve*.

The other gallery in the Upper Belvedere, known as the 'Cabinet' and 'Bilderzimmer', was more intimate. It was situated between the library and Eugen's bedroom and contained a great number of the small Dutch and Flemish paintings of which he was so fond. No less than ninety-nine works can be counted on the three walls at one end of the room in Kleiner's representation of it, among them Dou's famous *Woman with a Dropsy* in its original case. Whereas the pictures in the 'Gallerie' were hung two or at most three deep, here they were arranged in a pattern in columns which were five, six and even seven deep and reached from the wainscot to the coved ceiling. A visitor is shown peering at picture in the bottom row, as well he might since it was impossible to see most of the highest pictures properly. The effect is like highly decorative wall-paper. But it would be a mistake to infer that such arrangements in depth were unique: they were common from the seventeenth to the nineteenth century. Other examples are, for instance, the Archduke Leopold Wilhelm's gallery in the seventeenth century, as it appears in Teniers' paintings, and Sir John Soane's picture room as arranged by himself in the early nineteenth century.

Elsewhere in the great palace, to judge from Kleiner's illustrations, there were no pictures except for overdoors and pictures fixed *in situ* in ceilings or on the walls of the chapel where Solimena's two religious paintings were displayed. The only exception was a version of Titian's picture of *Perseus and Andromeda* which hung flanked by fruit and flower pieces on the largest wall of the Audience Chamber, or as Kleiner calls it the *Parade und Audienz Zimmer*. Indeed, the walls in the Upper Belvedere as we see them in Kleiner's illustrations were covered only with rich stuffs or papers. But in the two galleries the effect was striking. The careful symmetrical arrangement of the pictures was enhanced by heavily foliated gilt frames, some of which can still be seen in Turin. They differed in their ornamental details, but all were carved in the same form and all bore the same elaborate baroque E.

As regards the authenticity and quality of some of the paintings ascribed to great names it should be noted that Eugen's two pictures with Titian designs—the *Venus and Adonis* and *Perseus and Andromeda*—were not by Titian, as the originals in Madrid and the Wallace Collection respectively never belonged to him. The portrait of Erasmus by 'Holbein' (number 50 in the 1737 catalogue), and the 'Guercino' (number 24), which are identifiable in Turin, are not by these painters. The two 'Raphael's (numbers 175 and 178 in the 1737 catalogue) cannot be considered as his (one of them, identifiable in Turin, is given to another painter). Of the two 'Correggios', one (number 28 in the 1737 catalogue) was removed from Turin by Soult and, before its disappearance, was held not to be by this artist.

In the 1737 catalogue 124 pictures are given to Dutch and Flemish painters, as against 39 Italian. A high proportion of Eugen's Dutch and Flemish pictures now in Turin are signed and were catalogued by Vesme (1909) as originals. Eugen owned Rembrandt's *Visitation of the Virgin* (signed and dated 1640), which passed from Turin to the Dukes of Westminster and was purchased by the Detroit Institute of Arts in 1927. It was listed by Hofstede de Groot as formerly in the King of Sardinia's collection (*Verzeichnis der Werke der holländischen Maler*, 1915, VI, number 74) and was number 122 in the 1737 sale catalogue of Eugen's pictures. Gerard Dou's *Woman with a Dropsy*, now in the Louvre, was presented by the Elector Palatine to Prince Eugen at whose death it became the property of the House of Savoy and was placed in the Royal Gallery at Turin. (Smith, *Catalogue Raisonné*, 1829, I, p. 32 f., number 95.) In his collection there was a fine Paulus Potter of *Four Bullocks* and Pieter Saenredam's *Interior of a Synagogue*, both in Turin.

Eugen had a wealth of Dutch seventeenth-century landscapes, battle-pieces, genre scenes and still-lives. A minor painter represented in exceptional strength was the elder Jan Griffier (c. 1645-1718), a Dutchman who worked for several years in London, sixteen of whose landscapes were in Eugen's collection. Among them two views of London and the Thames are perhaps a sign that his abortive visit there in 1712 had not embittered him. These two views and twelve other Griffiers are in Turin. The Flemish pictures were nearly as numerous as the Dutch. They included Van Dyck's equestrian portrait of Prince Tomaso of Savoy-Carignan. (This was given to Eugen by his cousin Count Vittorio Filippi, given by Princess Victoria to the King of Sardinia in 1741, and is now in Turin.) Eighteen of the Flemish pictures were landscapes by Jan ('Velvet') Brueghel, and there were twelve genre scenes by the younger Teniers, as attributed in the 1737 catalogue. Many of these thirty pictures were identified in Turin and the old attributions were retained (some of the pictures being signed) by Vesme in his 1909 catalogue. There were also some few German pictures, and a few by French or Austrian artists. Three pictures each were attributed in 1737 to the Germans Mignon and Rottenhammer, and two to 'Holbein'. Borgognone, painter of two battle-pieces, was born in Franche-Comté and painted in Italy. Eugen did, of course, employ the Italianised Austrian Martino Altomonte for the painting of ceilings.

APPENDIX C

THE SALE OF EUGEN'S PICTURES

ONE OF Princess Anna Victoria's first moves in the disposal of the collection, as early as June, 1737, was to send Huchtenburgh's ten pictures of Eugen's battles to Charles Emanuel III, the King of Sardinia, who was head of the House of Savoy. Despite an accompanying bill, she evidently thought him, as head of the family, a fitting owner for these works, which, however artificial they may seem to us, were of contemporary fame and importance. The rest of Eugen's collection aroused the interest of Count Canale, the King of Sardinia's ambassador at Vienna. 'The Princess' (he reported to Turin in a letter to the Marquis d'Ormea), 'has the most magnificent pictures imaginable. God knows where it all will go; till now she has sold very little at a good price, but she is seeking to sell them all.'[1] In the following month (July, 1737) the ambassador communicated the news that the Princess was having a catalogue of the pictures printed, with prices: 'The purchase of these pictures would be an acquisition worthy of the King.' It is this catalogue which provides our main information about Eugen's pictures. It listed 176 of them, with names of artists and descriptions of the subjects, and probably included nearly all of Eugen's most valuable pictures. The catalogue, which was in French, is lost, but a German translation was published in Meusel's Miscellaneen artistischen Inhalts (Heft XIII, Erfurt, 1782, p. 152). An Italian translation from the German is in Vesme's article. The original was entitled: 'Catalogue des Tableaux trouvés dans l'Hoirie de S.A. Sme le grand Prince Eugène de Savoye. Ceux qui voudront en acheter en gros, ou en détail, pourrons [sic]

[1] A. Vesme, op. cit., XXV, pp. 161–256.

s'addresser au Sr. Vinzelli, Banquier à Vienne en Autriche. Chez Brissant Libraire à Vienne.'

Negotiations were opened with Charles Emmanuel III for the sale of these works; but they broke down on disagreement over financial terms. Then, in 1738, the Princess's marriage to Prince Friedrich of Sachsen-Hildburghausen took place, and presumably put an end to all thoughts of selling the pictures. But in 1740, after the rapid break-up of her marriage, she offered them again to the King. Del Carretto who was acting for D'Ormea in Turin wrote to Canale, July 23, 1740: '*Madame la Princess Victoria vient d'écrire à Monsieur le Marquis d'Ormea que si le Roi étoit en intention d'acheter ses tableaux, ils étoient bien à son service.*'[1]

Canale was thereupon instructed, first to send a copy of the catalogue 'so that the King can be informed more or less on their quality and above all on the subjects which they represent'.[2] Charles Emmanuel was a destroyer of pictures which he thought indecent; but the preponderance of Dutch and Flemish genre and landscape scenes may have reassured him. Later, the King sent instructions to get the pictures at the lowest possible price. The ambassador, pleading that he was no connoisseur, was authorized to take expert advice. His choice fell on Bertoli, director of the Imperial gallery in Vienna and a crony of his, who committed himself to a valuation which he told Canale was hardly more than one-third of what Eugen had given for the pictures; and then, in collusion with Canale, visited the Princess to persuade her that her price was too high. A reward— or bribe—of fifty ducats to Bertoli was authorized by Turin when the deal had been successfully completed.[3] Possible competitors in August III of Poland and General Lukas Pallavicini were outwitted by the ambassador, and after some haggling Charles Emmanuel III became the owner of 176 of Eugen's pictures. They arrived in Turin in August 1741. 'The King (Canale was informed) is very pleased with the said pictures.'[4] The King paid ninety thousand Piedmontese lire for the pictures and their frames, and a further one thousand ducats for Huchtenburgh's battle-pieces.

[1] A. Vesme, op. cit., pp. 202–3.
[2] *Ibid.*
[3] A. Vesme, op. cit., p. 215. For Bertoli's convenient valuations and complicity with Canale see also Canale's letters of August 31, 1737, and August 13, 1740.
[4] A. Vesme, op. cit., p. 221.

SOURCES

AS MENTIONED in the Introduction, no personal archives of Prince Eugen have ever been found. This has created a problem. Did Eugen write anything? If so, what has happened to it? If it was destroyed, why? Alas! There is no satisfactory evidence upon which to base an answer to these tantalizing questions. The mystery has inevitably encouraged rumour and forgery. In 1809, the so-called *Mémoires du Prince Eugène de Savoie* were published in Weimar, only to be shown up as the agreeable forgery of Charles Joseph, Prince de Ligne. In 1811, a collection of letters was published in Tübingen, *Sammlung der hinterlassenen politischen Schriften des Prinzen Eugen von Savoyen*. The editor was Joseph Edler von Sartori, librarian at the Theresianum in Vienna. But again the work was revealed as a complete falsification. Dr Bruno Böhm, Eugen's principal bibliographer, devoted over a hundred pages to exposing Sartori in his *Die Sammlung der hinterlassenen politischen Schriften des Prinzen Eugen von Savoyen, Eine Fälschung des 19. Jahrhunderts,* published in 1900.

We are also under the handicap, to which reference has been made in the text, that there are no private journals or letters by Eugen's contemporaries which throw any light on his personal life. The Habsburg Monarchy may have inspired all manner of devoted service from all kinds of people, but it does not appear to have encouraged the chronicler.

If, however, there is a lack of reliable material on Eugen's private thoughts, there is plenty available on his life as soldier, statesman and art patron. I have given at the foot of each page the sources of all quotations of any length, so there is no need to troop them all out again in a lengthy bibliography. As stated in the Introduction, no full-scale biography has ever been published in the English language, an omission which Winston Churchill deplores in his work on the Duke of Marlborough. One or two scarcely definitive descriptions of his exploits as an army commander were written in English during, or just after, his life. Then a brief account of his military career was produced in the last century by Colonel G. B. Malleson and published in 1888. Another purely service life, by Lieutenant General Sir George Macmunn, was brought out in 1933. There is a third book in English, a translation published in 1934 of Paul Frischauer's biography of the Prince—a work in the Guedalla school.

I have relied heavily on the standard biography by Alfred Arneth. Written in the middle of the last century, this three-volume work has never been surpassed. It suffers from a tendency to exonerate everything Habsburg, and Eugen's warts are apt to be concealed under the general whitewash. Based on all the available first-hand evidence, Arneth's book is a thorough piece of scholarship, which, since no important sources have come to light subsequently, has inevitably made all later biographies appear derivative. It has never been translated into English. Of modern historians, Professor Max Braubach of Bonn, who is at present working on a several-volume biography, is much the most authoritative. I have found his *Geschichte und Abenteuer: Gestalten um Prinz Eugen,* 1950, invaluable for Eugen's personal life, and his *Die Geheimdiplomatie des Prinzen Eugen von Savoyen,* 1962, indispensable for the diplomatic side. Of other recent lives it may also be worth mentioning, Alfons Czibulka, *Prinz Eugen,* 1958.

For the military campaigns the main primary source is the twenty-one volume *Feldzüge des Prinzen Eugen von Savoyen, herausgeben von der Abteilung für Kriegsgeschichte des K.K. Kriegsarchivs Wien,* 1876–92. O. Klopp, *Der Fall des Hauses Stuart,* 1875–88, is also useful. For the Turkish campaigns J. De Hammer, *Histoire de L'Empire Ottoman,* 1838, has been drawn upon, and I have found Count Marsigli, *L'Etat Militaire de L'Empire Ottoman,* 1732, entertaining and instructive. Unequalled on the War of the Spanish Succession in any language is Winston S. Churchill, *Marlborough, His Life and Times.*

No exhaustive study of Eugen's activities as patron of the arts has yet been made. A. Ilg, *Prinz Eugen von Savoyen als Kunstfreund,* 1889, is the best there is; it draws extensively on Arneth's very excellent chapter on the subject. On Eugen's buildings there are the following: H. Sedlmayr, *Johann Bernhard Fischer von Erlach,* 1956;

B. Grimschitz, *Johann Lucas von Hildebrandt*, 1959; and B. Grimschitz, *Das Belvedere in Wien,* 1946. On the pictures, T. von Frimmel, *Geschichte der Wiener Gemäldesammlungen,* 1899, is fundamental. The only study worth mention of Eugen's library is W. Suchier, *Prinz Eugen als Bibliophile,* 1928. A short list of his more notable books and MSS. is given in the 'Verein der Museumsfreunde in Wien's' *Katalog der Prinz Eugen Ausstellung* held in Vienna in 1933. Material for his illuminated manuscripts is in H. J. Hermann's catalogue, *Beschreibendes Verzeichnis der illuminierten Handschriften in Oesterreich,* 1930 et seq. There is a special work on Eugen's Greek manuscripts, A. Weinberger, *Die griechischen Handschriften des Prinzen Eugen von Savoyen,* 1930.

For general histories of Austria which cover this period I recommend, Hugo Hartsch, *Die Geschichte Oesterreichs,* 1951. In English there is probably still nothing to surpass William Coxe, *History of the House of Austria,* 1847.

Finally mention must be made of the extensive bibliography by Böhm, *Bibliographie Zur Geschichte des Prinzen Eugen von Savoyen und seiner Zeit,* 1943.

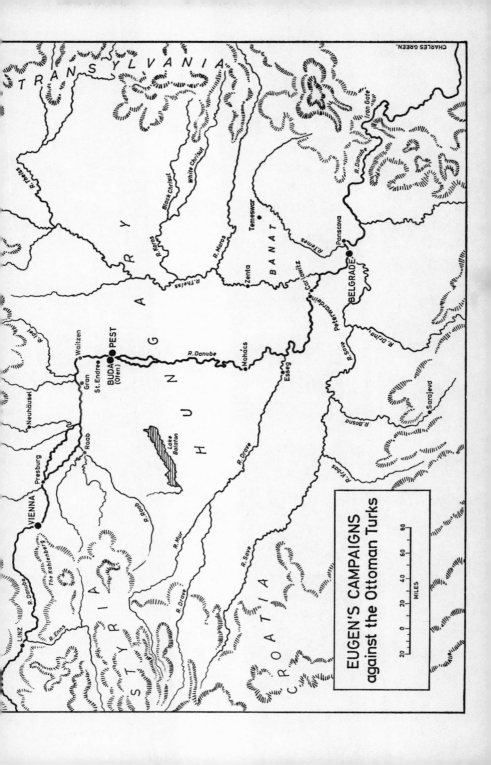

EUGEN'S CAMPAIGNS
against the Ottoman Turks

CHARLES GREEN.

EUGEN'S CAMPAIGNS
in NORTH ITALY

CHARLES GREEN

MILES

10 0 10 20 30 40 50

ADRIATIC SEA

LIGURIAN SEA

Gulf of Genoa

DOLOMITES

LEPONTINE ALPS

SWISS ALPS

ALPS OF SAVOY

FRENCH ALPS

MARITIME ALPS

LIGURIAN ALPS

APPENNINES

VENICE
Rimini
Treviso
R. Piave
Bassano
R. Brenta
Padua
Rovigo
Ravenna
Vicenza
Legnano
R. Adige
Ferrara
R. Po
R. Reno
BOLOGNA
Bolzano
Trento
Rovereto
Rivoli
Verona
Peschiera
Mantua
R. Mincio
Mirandola
Carpi
Modena
R. Panaro
Luzzara
R. Secchia
Lake Garda
R. Oglio
Brescia
Calcinato
Cremona
Parma
R. C.
R. Crostolo
Chiari
Lake d'Iseo
R. Adda
Lodi
Piacenza
R. Trebbia
Bobbio
La Spezia
Leghorn
Lake Como
Lake Lugano
R. Adda
Como
MILAN
Pavia
R. Ticino
R. Po
R. Tidone
GENOA
Acqui
Varese
Lake Maggiore
Novara
Mortara
Vercelli
R. Sessia
Casale
Allessandria
R. Bormida
R. Bormida
Alba
LIGURIAN ALPS
R. Rhone
Gd. St. Bernard Pass
Lit. St. Bernard Pass
Ivrea
R. Dora Baltea
Chivasso
R. Orco
TURIN
R. Po
Carignano
Fossano
R. Tanaro
R. Stura
Cuneo
R. Maira
R. Po
R. Chisone
R. Dora Reparia
Mt. Cenis Pass
Lake Geneva
Nice

INDEX